A Sixteenth-Century
German Reader

A Sixteenth-Century German Reader

EDITED WITH
INTRODUCTIONS AND NOTES BY

W. A. COUPE

Professor of German in the
University of Southampton

OXFORD
AT THE CLARENDON PRESS
1972

Oxford University Press, Ely House, London W. 1

GLASGOW NEW YORK TORONTO MELBOURNE WELLINGTON
CAPE TOWN IBADAN NAIROBI DAR ES SALAAM LUSAKA ADDIS ABABA
DELHI BOMBAY CALCUTTA MADRAS KARACHI LAHORE DACCA
KUALA LUMPUR SINGAPORE HONG KONG TOKYO

PRINTED IN GREAT BRITAIN
AT THE UNIVERSITY PRESS, OXFORD
BY VIVIAN RIDLER
PRINTER TO THE UNIVERSITY

PREFACE

In British university departments of German the teaching of the sixteenth century has traditionally fallen to the lot of medievalists and philologists. The natural consequence of this has been that sixteenth-century texts have tended to be treated not in their own right, but as documents illustrative of the history of the language, or as quarries from which exotic linguistic forms can be extracted. This in turn results in a situation where the impression is often created in the student's mind that the example of so-called *Rückumlaut* in the first line, or the extended athematic verb with an 'n' infix in line seven, or the inorganic final dental in the last paragraph is somehow more important than the fact that this was a text which in its day was read and studied because it seemed to have something important to say or because it interested and amused the reader. I do not, of course, wish to deny the validity of the academic study of historical grammar: in editing these pages I have on occasion been sharply reminded of its value. What I am suggesting is that such study can often become academic in the bad sense, pursued narcissistically as an end in itself divorced from the context which gives it meaning. Ultimately, of course, the emphasis on historical grammar in sixteenth-century German studies is the result of an accidental division of labour consequent on the absence of major writers. The same period in French literary history is, after all, not usually regarded as an apanage of the Middle Ages in university departments of French: Ronsard, Rabelais, and Montaigne demand to be treated in their own right!

The approach in the present anthology is based on the twofold belief that texts must be seen in their historical context and that it is possible to read and understand them without adopting a primarily philological approach. The intention is to present the student with authentic sixteenth-century texts and, by translating difficult phrases and sentences and providing detailed notes and a glossary, to enable him to read and understand them *quickly*, to appreciate their importance in the context of their age, and then to pass on.

Anyone who sets out to compile an anthology learns very early in his editorial career that he will probably satisfy no one—least of all himself. In spite of the generosity of the Press, it was impossible to include everything I would have wished to include—even once I had accepted that many texts could not be printed in full, but must appear in the necessarily unsatisfactory form of excerpts. The arrangement of the anthology was suggested by the material itself. The size of the section devoted to the Reformation reflects the latter's obvious importance, both for its own age and for the subsequent course of German history. The other sections on Moral Satire, Drama, the Lyric, and Narrative Prose will, I hope, in spite of their selective nature, enable the student to gain a fair and balanced picture of the sort of thing that was being written and read by Germans throughout the century as a whole. I have not regarded it as part of my task to 'establish a text', or even to obtain a copy of the first edition where none was readily available. With the exception of the passage from Dürer (p. 44), which exists only in a later manuscript, all the texts reproduced are, however, taken from sixteenth-century editions and have not been subjected to any kind of editorial emendation or modification: it did not seem appropriate to me to attempt to normalize the texts, resolve the abbreviations, or modernize the punctuation—students soon learn that 'kōmen' = 'kommen', 'stim̃en' = 'stimmen', etc., and that a *virgula* can often have the force of a modern full stop and a full stop the force of a modern comma! Misprints, especially difficult abbreviations and misleading punctuation have been explained in the notes.

In conclusion it is my pleasant task to thank the large number of people who have in one way or another helped me with the preparation of this anthology, especially the staffs of the libraries mentioned in the acknowledgements. Since, however, what one learns first stays with one longest, I must record my indebtedness to my teachers, Mr. W. E. Brown and Dr. F. J. Stopp, who—many years ago now—first introduced me to the sixteenth century. My colleagues in Reading, Mr. S. E. Ievers, Professor W. B. Lockwood, Professor F. P. Pickering, and Mr. K. D. White, have frequently and patiently listened to my problems and helped me to solve them. In this connection I must mention especially Mr. P. A. Thurlow, who was instrumental in obtaining photographic copies of a number of texts for me, with whom I have often discussed the meaning of obscure or difficult phrases, and from whom a number of formulations in the notes derive. Mrs. Marga Black, also of Reading, greatly aided the progress of my work by agreeing at very short notice and considerable inconvenience to type a rather difficult manuscript. Finally, I should like to thank my pupils in the Universities of Aberdeen, Exeter, and Reading, whose complaints, mistakes, and suggestions have often opened my eyes to unsuspected difficulties and caused me to look again at many an over-hasty conclusion.

W. A. COUPE

Reading, May 1970

ACKNOWLEDGEMENT

THIS volume could not have been produced without the active co-operation of a number of libraries. The editor would particularly like to record his indebtedness to the following institutions: the University Library, Reading, for the unfailing patience of its staff; the Herzog-August-Bibliothek, Wolffenbüttel, for permission to reprint the Twelve Articles of Memmingen and the extract from *Das Rollwagenbüchlin*; the Germanisches National-Museum, Nürnberg, for permission to reprint the passages from *Flöh Haz* and *Das Lalebuch*; the Staatsbibliothek (Preußischer Kulturbesitz), Berlin, for permission to reprint the scenes from *Vom reichen Manne*; the University Library, Edinburgh, for permission to reprint Hubmaier's pamphlet on the Eucharist; the Deutscher Verein für Kunstwissenschaft and Professor Dr. Hans Rupprich for permission to reprint the extract from Dürer's diary. All the other passages are taken from copies held by the British Museum and are reprinted by courtesy of the Trustees.

CONTENTS

CONTENTS   xi

LINGUISTIC NOTE

COMPARED with the regularity and orderliness of modern standard German or normalized Middle High German, the language of the sixteenth century exhibits a bewildering multiplicity of forms and spellings. Texts abound in local and archaic forms; anacoluthon and ellipsis are common; frequently texts are innocent of all punctuation, or—worse still—are punctuated in such a way as to be highly misleading; spelling is highly idiosyncratic and a word may be spelt in two or three different ways in as many lines. But if the total effect of this state of affairs is to call forth in the modern reader an impression of almost complete chaos, forces were nevertheless at work which in the course of the century were to produce, if not a strictly unified language, at least something which would constitute a basis for such a language.

Tendencies towards unification had been operative in the German dialects long before the sixteenth century. The growth of commerce and the attendant improvement in communications in the later Middle Ages had combined with the development of vernacular-based political administration to produce a number of more or less standardized languages in which business could be conducted: laymen with little or inadequate Latin increasingly replaced their clerical predecessors in governmental service, and Latin never had been the language of commerce. The 'administrative languages' (known in German as *Kanzleisprachen* because they were used in the chanceries of the territorial princes, Mainz, Vienna, Prague, etc.) showed a certain standardization in matters of orthography, vocabulary, and morphology which had been produced by the simple need to communicate effectively. At the same time, however, they were all regionally based, influenced by, and in turn influencing, the local *Verkehrssprache* or commercial language: the language of the chancery of Maximilian I, for example, exhibited regional characteristics similar to those of the commercial language known as *das gemeine Deutsch*, which had currency amongst merchants and business houses throughout

the principal area of Habsburg dynastic influence from Nürnberg to Vienna.

In view of the limited nature of their application, these
commercial and administrative languages were unlikely of
themselves to develop into a unified written language of any
consequence or range; nor did the invention of the printing-
press in the middle of the fifteenth century give an immediate
impetus towards the development of a written standard. The
few books that began to appear in German were intended
primarily for local consumption and, far from unifying the
language, can even be held to have contributed to a positive
diversification by giving permanent literary form to local
linguistic differences. Even with the steady growth of the
printing industry, the tendency for the printer to print in his
own dialect was not eliminated, and at the beginning of the
sixteenth century no less than six 'printers' languages' (*Drucker-
sprachen*) were in use: Austro-Bavarian was used by the printers
of Vienna, Munich, and Ingolstadt, East Central German was
used in Wittenberg and Leipzig, Swabian in Ulm and Augsburg, Alemannic in Strassburg, Basel, and Zürich, West Central
German in Mainz and Frankfurt, and Franconian in Nürnberg
and Bamberg. It is easy to exaggerate the difficulties and
problems resultant on these dialectal divisions and to create
the impression that they constituted insuperable barriers across
which authors could not communicate with the reading public,
whereas in point of fact such a book as Brant's *Narrenschiff*
(1494; p. 92) could enjoy popularity everywhere in High
German areas (a Low German translation appeared in 1519)
in spite of its strongly Alemannic language. Even so, dialectal
variants clearly did not facilitate understanding, and the bigger
printing-houses had an obvious vested interest in the establishment of a written standard which would obviate any sales
resistance of a purely linguistic nature and latterly they played
an important role in spreading a normalized language.

Looking back with historical hindsight, it is obvious that the
question at the beginning of the sixteenth century was not
whether a normalized language would emerge, but what pho-
nological and morphological basis that language would have.
The coincidence of a widespread *Verkehrssprache* in *das gemeine
Deutsch* with the sphere of Habsburg dynastic influence might

in other circumstances have led to the establishment of a norm based on Upper German of an Austro-Bavarian variety. The fact that this development never took place was in large measure a consequence of the Reformation.

With its inherent appeal to the layman and its consequent emphasis on the vernacular, the Reformation inevitably gave a tremendous boost to the publication of books printed in German. Wolfgang Stammler records that 55 new titles appeared in 1516; in 1517 this figure fell to 37, but rose again to 71 in 1518 and to 111 in 1519. In 1520, with the further quickening of religious controversy, a total of 208 was achieved, a figure which held steady at 211 in 1521, but leapt up to 347 in 1522 and to 498 in 1523. Even more significant than this remarkable increase in productivity on the part of the printers is the fact that some third of all the German works published between 1518 and 1523 bear the name of Martin Luther. Not all these works were polemical in nature, of course; throughout his life Luther kept up a steady stream of strictly pastoral writings, but clearly, whether pastoral or not, such a volume of literature and the stimulus it gave to others to read (and themselves to write in support or condemnation of Luther's position) could not fail to exercise a profound effect on the development of the German language.

But the impact of Luther's pamphlets and sermons—phenomenal as it undoubtedly was—pales in comparison with the tremendous influence exerted by his translation of the Bible. As a publishing success his New Testament, which appeared in 1522, was entirely without parallel. In the course of the next two years it was reprinted no less than eighty times (sixteen Wittenberg reprints, sixty-four elsewhere in Germany from Leipzig to Basel). A similar success attended the full Bible which appeared in 1534: one single printer, Hans Lufft of Wittenberg, sold something like 100,000 copies between 1534 and 1584—for those times a truly astronomical figure. The Bible is still a best seller today, of course, but in the sixteenth century it came to enjoy a place in the lives of countless households such as can only be compared to that enjoyed by radio or television in our own day. The practice of reading aloud, or of learning long passages from it by heart, was widespread, so that the language of Luther's translation in a very real sense moulded the vocabulary, speech, and even the thought-patterns of generations of Germans. Nor did this apply merely in Protestant lands. Just as Luther by his polemical writings forced his opponents to write in German instead of the traditional Latin, so too by the excellence of his translation he succeeded to a remarkable extent in imposing his Bible on Catholic Germans as well. Emser's 'orthodox' translation of 1527 is strongly influenced by Luther's New Testament of 1522, and it was in turn on Emser's rendering that Johann Eck based his Upper German Bible of 1537 (cf. p. 34), so that, as Luther sarcastically remarks in the *Sendbrief von Dolmetschen* of 1530, his opponents tended to steal his language and, as 'ungrateful disciples', to propagate his translation under their own name.

Luther enjoyed a number of significant advantages in linguistic matters. His native speech was that of Thuringia, a variety of Central High German, but his childhood was chiefly spent in Mansfeld, where the language was then Low German. In his maturity, in Wittenberg, he witnessed the gradual advance of High German at the expense of the Low German hitherto spoken there. This background naturally gave him an awareness of linguistic problems and a readiness for linguistic compromise, but Luther was also fortunate in that in the 'official' language of Saxony, as represented by the East Central German of the Electoral Chancery at Meissen, he had before him a form of written German which, as well as being close to his own native speech, also occupied a middle position amongst contemporary German dialects and had already achieved wide currency. Although of local origin, the language of the Saxon Chancery was by the early sixteenth century not restricted merely to the Wettin domains in Saxony: since Albrecht of Meissen had become Archbishop of Mainz and Imperial Chancellor in 1480, imperial decrees were commonly printed in Meissnisch and thus ensured ready acceptance for the language. We have Luther's word for it, as represented by a famous passage in the *Table Talk*, that he was well aware of the advantages to be obtained by following the usage of the Saxon Chancery: 'Ich habe keine gewisse, sonderliche eigene sprache im deutschen, sondern gebrauche der gemeinen deutschen sprache, das mich beide, Ober- und Niederlender, verstehen mögen. Ich rede nach der sechsischen cantzlei, welcher nachfolgen alle fürsten

und könige in Deutschland . . . Kaiser Maximilian und chur-
fürst Friderich haben im römischen reiche die deutschen
sprachen also in eine gewisse sprach gezogen.'

Historically, Luther's remark is not entirely accurate, but it
does point strongly to the intermediate position of Meissnisch.
The country east of the Saale, where the language originated,
was colonial territory. Until the middle of the twelfth century
it had been inhabited exclusively by the Wends, a Slavonic
people, but by 1300 intensive immigration from various
districts in the west had largely Germanized the area. The
new vernacular which emerged from this linguistic melting-pot
was a High German of a predominantly Central type, known
technically as East Central German. As a recent creation, it
was still flexible and naturally embodied a number of linguistic
compromises. This is strikingly apparent in the phonetics. In
the modern Bavarian dialects, the medieval (Middle High
German) diphthongs *ie*, *uo*, and *üe* are preserved as such, but
in all Central German dialects they were monophthongized and
became long *i*, *u*, and *ü* respectively. The traditional Central
German dialects of the west retain the MHG long vowels *î*,
û, and *iu* [y:], but Bavarian diphthongizes these sounds, turning them into *ei* (*ai*), *au*, and *eu* (*äu*) respectively. In this case,
however, East Central German follows the south and uses the
Bavarian diphthongs.

But if Luther adopted as his own the principal phonetic
compromises present in Meissnisch—and thereby helped to
ensure that they should survive in Modern Standard German
—he also showed a fair degree of independence from his model.
Initially, in keeping with chancery usage, he wrote *eu* for the
MHG diphthong *ou* ('houbet' = 'heupt'), but subsequently
preferred the Upper German form in *au* ('haupt'). Similarly he
abandoned his earlier preference for East Central German *i* in
declined forms ('Gottis', 'fragist'), and though the established
Kanzleisprache was close to his native speech and convenient for
his polemical and pastoral purposes, it does not follow that
Luther's contribution to the German language was negligible.
In linguistic as in ecclesiastical matters, Luther was led, almost
against his will, to become a reformer. The Bible was the only
rule of life for Christians and must accordingly be made available in the vernacular, but to do this adequately necessitated a

creative approach to language such as was only possible to a
man of natural poetic gifts—and it is in the poetic quality of his
language rather than in minor details of syntax, morphology,
or accidence that Luther's ultimate importance lies. Luther
took over almost unchanged the orthography and inflexions of
an administrative language of limited application, but enriched
it with the vivid idiom of everyday speech, as quickened by his
own linguistic sensitivity, in order to fashion a vehicle for the
word of God. The result was a linguistic monument which,
even over a gap of four centuries, has lost nothing of the magnificent strength and dignity with which Luther originally
endowed it.

In translating the Bible Luther was no doubt materially
aided by the circumstance that East Central German had
already been developed by the Thuringian mystics, who in
their striving to express the ineffable had considerably increased
the German word-stock and rendered the language more pliant.
Luther prized these mystical works highly and had himself in
1518 edited one of the most famous, the *Theologia Deutsch* of the
mystic known as 'Der Frankfurter'. Whereas the mystics were
concerned to describe emotional experiences, so that their contribution to the German lexicon lies in the creation of words
such as 'einbilden', 'Einkehr', 'gelassen', 'Ichheit', etc., Luther
is above all a man of the real world and his vocabulary and
imagery are characterized by a strictly concrete and visual
quality. A considerable number of his coinings are still part of
everyday speech: one thinks of proverbial expressions like
'Bleibe im Lande und nähre dich redlich' (Ps. 37: 3; the
Authorized Version has 'So shalt thou dwell in the land and
verily thou shalt be fed'), or colourful popular images like
'durch die Finger sehen' (Lev. 20: 4; A.V.: 'hide their eyes'),
'Ein Dorn im Auge' (Num. 33: 55; A.V.: 'shall be pricks in
your eyes'), or 'mit seinem/meinem/fremdem Kalb pflügen'
(Judg. 14: 18; A.V.: 'Plough with my heifer'), etc. Equally it
is thanks to Luther's Bible that words like 'Bubenstück' (Ps.
41: 9; A.V.: 'Devise my hurt'), 'Denkzettel' (Matt. 23: 5; A.V.:
'phylacteries'!), 'Fallstrick' (Job 40: 24; A.V.: 'snares'), etc.,
have passed into the modern language.

But even if the outstanding qualities of Luther's Bible gave great
impetus to the establishment of a written standard and provided

a model of truly poetic stature to which generations of writers could turn for inspiration and linguistic sustenance—so much so that Jakob Grimm was moved to remark that modern standard German was a 'Protestant dialect'—the traditional claim that Luther was the father of the modern language needs to be treated with circumspection. By no means all the words and phrases which appear in Luther's translation passed into the standard German: many, like the striking 'Sie haben ihren Lohn dahin' of Matt. 6: 5, were destined to become living fossils. Others, like the 'Unrat' of which Luther makes mention in the *Sendbrief von Dolmetschen* (cf. p. 29) as a translation of 'perditio' (Matt. 26: 8), lost their original meaning in spite of Luther's championship, and had to be replaced by other synonyms after Luther's death (here, 'Vergeudung'). Similarly, the common preterite ending in 'e' ('ich sahe', etc.), or his use of traditional preterite forms such as 'schreib' (cf. 'Da schreib ich einen brieff', p. 10), did not find a place in the standard language. Nor is it always certain how much 'Lutheran' language is strictly personal to Luther. This is, of course, in itself unimportant when considering the impact of the writings bearing his name, but it is interesting to note that, like all his generation, Luther exhibited an indifference to the form in which his writings were presented to the public such as would be inconceivable in a modern author. Until the mid twenties Luther never read proofs of his works, so that it was the printer and professional proof-reader who decided the orthographical shape of his language. Luther was concerned only with the content and its accurate reproduction, not with questions of morphology and orthography; as his manuscripts show, he was as idiosyncratic as the rest of his generation in these matters. In editing the Bible translation, Luther did indeed, as he tells us in the *Sendbrief von Dolmetschen* and as the minutes of the editorial committee testify, lavish great care on the form the text was to take, but here again his efforts were directed to the accuracy of the translation and its euphonious expression; it was men like Georg Rörer and Christoff Walther, the proof-readers in Lufft's printing establishment, who decided the shape of the words on the printed page. Further, like the polemical works bearing his name, many Lutheran Bibles circulated in dialectally coloured reprints—a phenomenon which became all the more evident in the sixties, when the centre of the Bible-printing industry shifted from Wittenberg to Frankfurt am Main.

Reservations such as these emphasize the self-evident truth that Luther did not 'create a new language'. His historic significance lies rather in the tremendous impetus he gave to the hesitant and fumbling movement towards a German standard which was already discernible before 1517. His impact was, of course, by no means the same in all German lands, and, like their educated counterparts, some 'mothers in the home' and some 'common men in the market place' naturally found Luther's quickening of the German language more acceptable than others. As a Central German dialect, Luther's German naturally found ready acceptance in Central German areas. Equally, though sermons long continued to be preached in Low German in the northern parts of the country, it was Luther's language which filled the gap caused by the regression of Low German consequent on the decline of the Hansa as a political and economic force: the new Low German Bibles were henceforth a translation of Luther's version, and the last edition before modern times appeared in Goslar in 1621. In Upper Germany, by contrast, partly for linguistic, partly for confessional reasons, Luther's language met with greater resistance. Adam Petri, the Basel printer who published an edition of Luther's New Testament in 1522, for instance, found it necessary to explain for the benefit of his Alemannic public that by 'Lippe' Luther meant 'Leftze', by 'Ziege' 'Gaiß', by 'Ufer' 'Gestad', by 'Hügel' 'Bühel', by 'harren' 'beiten', by 'fühlen' 'empfinden', etc. Significantly, Johann Eck used many of these terms in his Upper German Catholic Bible of 1537 (cf. p. 34) and, not less significantly, his rendering met with only qualified success and served merely to delay rather than turn the Lutheran tide: where his vocabulary differed from Luther's, it has tended to remain dialectal, or to be accepted only in highly specific contexts.

The process of standardization and accommodation to something approaching a Lutheran norm embraces accidence, syntax, and vocabulary, but since the modification of the vowel system of medieval German is the hallmark of modern German, a glance at the way vowels are treated in the texts assembled in this anthology will conveniently illuminate the way in which progress towards a measure of uniformity was by no means systematic or solely due to Lutheran influence. If we look at the texts from the Alemannic area, for instance, we find that in Basel in 1494 Bergmann von Olpe's compositor in setting Brant's *Narrenschiff* (p. 92) preserves intact the vowel system inherited from the Middle Ages ('myn', 'syn', 'win', 'dût', 'gût', etc.), as well as a variety of Alemannic peculiarities ('rott' = 'Rat', 'noch' = 'nach', etc.). Hans Grüninger's edition of *Hug Schapler* (p. 192), printed in Strassburg in 1500, similarly retains the old long vowels ('myn huß', 'hût' = 'mein haus', 'heute', etc.) and diphthongs ('ysenhût', 'bûlen', etc.) and incidentally, like Brant's text, the final dental of the third person plural present indicative ('gehortendt', 'warendt', etc.) which, together with the *uo* diphthong, was long to be a characteristic feature of Alemannic texts. This same final dental did not appear in the edition of *Eulenspiegel* (p. 225) which Grüninger printed some fifteen years later, however, and the long *î* regularly appears as *ei* ('sein', 'mein', 'leib', etc.), although long *û* is retained unchanged ('lut', 'daruff'). Yet only three years earlier, in printing Thomas Murner's *Narrenbeschwörung*, Matthias Hupfuff, also of Strassburg, had conscientiously preserved both the final dental and the full medieval vowel system. By contrast, in the edition of 1518 printed in Strassburg by Johannes Knobloch (p. 105), we find that a fair number of the long vowels have been diphthongized, albeit in a rather haphazard fashion: Hupfuff had printed—and Murner had almost certainly written—'Das ich *myn* ort nit het versessen', which Knobloch sets as 'Dz ich *meī* ort nit het versessen', but he is not consistent and prints a little further on 'Wer wolt *mein* ôrt*lin yn* han genûmen' (the bar over the *u* indicates the omission of a following *m*). Similarly, he prints both 'wyt' and 'weit', 'Pfeyff' and 'pfiffer', 'zytig' and 'zeit', preferring on the whole to retain the long vowels ('Dyn', 'syn', 'fyn', etc.) together with the traditional diphthong ('gût', 'thût', etc.). Grüninger is somewhat more systematic in his edition of Murner's *Von dem großen Lutherischen Narren* of 1522: he follows the pattern set in his edition of *Eulenspiegel* in that the diphthongization of *î* is common (although forms such as 'ynher', 'schâflin' also occur), while the old *iu* is retained as *û* ('lûten' = 'läuten'), and long *û* survives unchanged ('vß', 'vff'), as does the old diphthong *uo* ('můß', 'zů'). Grüninger still retains the final dental of the third person plural of the verb, but in printing Hutten's *Gesprächbüchlein* (p. 134) a year earlier, Peter Schott had not seen fit to impose it on Hutten's text, while long *û* now regularly appears as a diphthong ('auß', 'auff', 'trawrig'), as does long *î* ('feynd', 'sein'), although the inevitable exception does occur also ('jnher', 'diewyl'). The old and the new vowel systems long continued to coexist: Bartholomeus Grüninger in 1533 in his edition of Pauli (p. 228) still prints 'vß' as well as 'aus', 'sin' as well as 'sein', along with the *û* diphthong, but the tendency to Bavarian diphthongization is predominant. By 1557 in the edition of *Von Gûten vnd bôsen Nachbaurn* (p. 200), printed by Georg Messerschmidt who took over the Knobloch establishment in about 1541, the old long vowels survive only in an occasional 'vff', and in the edition of *Flôh Haz*, printed by Bernhart Jobin in 1578 (p. 121), they have disappeared completely, although the characteristic South German diphthong *û* remains. This last document shows, in the spellings in *ai* ('main', 'bain'), Bavarian influence—possibly due to a passing fashion or the presence of some wandering journeyman. At any rate it is uncharacteristic and by 1590 has disappeared in the 'Ausgabe letzter Hand' of Fischart's *Geschichtklitterung* (p. 208) and similarly does not occur in the *Lalebuch* of 1597 (p. 232), which appeared without imprint, but is usually ascribed to Alsace. This latter work even abandons the *û* diphthong and presents a text which, apart from certain vagaries of spelling, is recognizably modern.

In the High Alemannic region the modernization of the vowel system did not begin quite so early. As late as 1527, when many authorities tell us the Zürich printers went over to the new diphthongs, Froschauer was printing Zwingli's pamphlet on the Eucharist (p. 56) with the non-diphthongized long *î* ('din', 'zyt', 'glych', etc.) and the old *û* diphthong such as Zwingli had probably written. Even in Zürich, however, Zwingli's Bible was printed with the new diphthongs in the next decade in the interests of a wider market.

Similar developments were taking place elsewhere in German-speaking lands. In Nürnberg, for instance, the anonymous printer of Sachs's dialogue of 1524 (p. 142) uses the new diphthongs and the old Upper German *û*, and regional influence is sufficiently strong the following year for the anonymous printer of our version of Luther's pamphlet against the peasants (p. 73) to impose on his East Central German original the Bavarian spellings in *ai* ('oberkayt', 'dreyerlay', 'wayß', etc.) and the *û* diphthong ('thût', 'gût'). In the version of the *Tannhäuserlied* published in Nürnberg about 1530 (p. 244), however, the Bavarian spellings have largely disappeared ('ayd' is the only example to set against 'eyn', 'meyn', 'weyb', etc.), but the *û* diphthong is retained ('hûb an zû grûnen'). By 1559, in the edition of Forster's *Frische Teutsche Liedlein* printed by Johann vom Berg, this diphthong has disappeared, although one case of Bavarian spelling ('schaiden') does occur in our example (p. 250). A similar approximation to the new norm may be observed in the edition of Hans Sachs printed by Christoff Heussler in 1560 (p. 150), although a number of contracted and distorted forms ('erlieden' = 'erlitten', etc.) often make understanding difficult.

But lest we should now conclude that the vowel system was by this time standardized throughout Germany, the *Faust-Volksbuch* printed in Frankfurt in 1587 retains *û* ('mûste', 'bûbisch', etc.). Even the odd item of Upper German vocabulary occurs, in spite of the fact that, according to many reference books, it had long been replaced by Lutheran German: Helen has 'Lefftzen', not 'Lippen', and the Pope drinks out of 'Kanten' rather than 'Kannen'! This concrete example causes us to look rather more closely at the often-quoted remark of Sebastian Helber, the grammarian and lawyer of Freiburg, who in 1593 claimed to discern three main German dialects: *Mitter Teütsch* (as printed in Leipzig, Erfurt, Cologne, Frankfurt(!), Nürnberg, Mainz, Speyer, and Strassburg), *Donawisch* (as printed in Bavaria and Swabia), and *Höchst Reinisch* (as printed in Switzerland). But though German was still far from unified, and even as a literary language needed the combined efforts of two centuries of grammarians and theorists to make it so (Opitz, Schottel, Gottsched, Adelung, etc.), the preponderance of *Mitter Teütsch* in Helber's list is a clear indication of a tangible degree of standardization and more than a hint of the shape of things to come.

I · THE REFORMATION

PROBABLY the most important of the factors which helped to bring about the Reformation was the loss of moral authority on the part of the Church in late medieval times. The Great Schism—when Christian Europe had been forced to witness the disgraceful spectacle of two and even three rival popes laying claim to the throne of St. Peter and hurling imprecations at each other—had severely weakened the claims of the papacy to speak with quasi-divine authority, and the emergence of proto-protestant heretics such as John Wyclif and John Huss bears eloquent witness to the widespread dissatisfaction with prevailing ecclesiastical conditions and a corresponding desire to turn from an obviously corrupt institution to the 'simple purity' of the Scriptures. Nor, after the healing of the Schism in the early fifteenth century, had the majority of popes, with their worldly ambitions and the scandalous nature of their lives, done much to restore the respect which their office had traditionally enjoyed. The Borgia Pope, Alexander VI (1492–1503), 'father, husband, and father-in-law' to the infamous Lucretia, was but a striking example of the moral decay which seemed to have attacked the whole system and which, at the popular level, manifested itself in the prevalence of abuses such as the trade in indulgences, the 'sale' of dispensations in respect of plurality of benefices, or the payment of 'Hurengeld' by priests who found the celibate state burdensome. Money seemed to be the measure of all things in the Church and religion itself—at least in its official manifestations—appeared equally to be a matter of mechanical forms and external observances, the worship of relics, the observation of feast-days and the like, rather than an inner thing of the spirit. This was, however, still an age of faith in which religion had an importance and a grip on men's minds scarcely conceivable in the mid-twentieth century; far from occasioning a significant growth of paganism or a general loss of faith, the failure of official Christianity simply brought forth an insistently expressed demand that the Church set its house in order, and for decades before the emergence of Luther the cry for a 'reformation in head and members' had echoed through Christian Europe.

That other pillar of medieval Europe, the Holy Roman Empire of the German nation, had similarly fallen on evil days, and the once powerful office of emperor was now little more than an empty dignity which, no matter how jealously sought—the office was freely elective, although after 1438 the Habsburg candidate was always elected—proved generally to be more of a liability than an asset and saddled its holder with no more than a theoretical authority with which to discharge his numerous official responsibilities. Real political power had long since devolved on to the individual territorial princes, who in their own domains exercised virtually sovereign authority. This political fragmentation of the Empire had not only denied to the Germans the reality of that national unity which the English and the French were—however tentatively —beginning to enjoy, but also thwarted the development of any national church policy and prevented the establishment of that degree of autonomy within the Roman Church—and the consequent freedom from the latter's financial exactions—which the Statutes of Mortmain and Praemunire or the Pragmatic Sanction of Bourges had assured for the English and the French. To the rage and embitterment of all good patriots, German gold continued to fill the papal coffers—a state of affairs which, as late as 1521, enabled Luther to appear as the defender of the 'national interest' against the rapacity of an Italianate hierarchy.

Intellectually the most important development of the age was the rise of humanism. The movement—in essence the manifestation of the spirit of the Renaissance in the intellectual sphere—began in Italy about the middle of the fourteenth century and only gradually penetrated northern Europe. As its name implies, humanism saw its ideal in the *humanitas* of classical antiquity, but far from being pagan or unchristian in outlook, the best representatives of the movement were concerned to restore piety and morals along with good learning and to use learning to penetrate to the essence of religion: the human spirit was a reflection of the divine and man's task was to develop it to the full. This, it was held, could best be achieved by the study of the classics, in which the human spirit had expressed itself with unparalleled excellence. The whole movement is thus characterized by a deliberate turning back to the sources of European civilization, and by the end of the fifteenth century scholars all over Europe were hard at work collecting, collating, and editing manuscripts containing classical and patristic texts. This return *ad fontes* and the resultant tendency to question established authority in the light of the testimony the sources bore was to have repercussions in all spheres of intellectual life, but it was in theological studies that its immediate impact was greatest. The veneration of classical, pagan antiquity in itself represented a challenge to the Church's claims to a monopoly of authority, but more important than this was the application of humanist philological techniques to the sacred books from which the Church drew its authority: inevitably the return to the sources led the humanists to look at the Bible with new eyes and compare the ideal they found there with the ecclesiastical reality which surrounded them.

This characteristic combination of a critical attitude to the Church and a concern with the Scriptures, in which pious and philological motives were equally represented, is shared by a variety of European humanists, but it was in Erasmus of Rotterdam (1467–1536) that these tendencies gained their supreme expression. His *Enchiridion militis christiani* (1503) proclaims the value of the classics as a preparation for the revelation of God in the Scriptures, rejects the externalizing of late medieval religion with its emphasis on 'works', and declares religion to be the expression of a right attitude of mind. The *Praise of Folly* (1509) touches on these topics from the satirical angle and pours scorn on the corruptness and hollowness of current religious practice before celebrating the sublime 'folly' of the true Christian. It was, however, his edition of the Greek New Testament (1516)—an obvious expression of the desire to return *ad fontes*—which presented the greatest challenge to the authority of the Church. For centuries St. Jerome's Latin translation of the Bible, the 'Vulgate', had been regarded as authoritative and free from error by the Church; now, however, the new science of philology was able to demonstrate that as a rendering of the sources it left much to be desired and that the 'authoritative' text needed to be read in the light of texts possessed of greater authority! Significantly, although Erasmus's edition was itself not free from error, it was to constitute an invaluable aid for the Protestant Bible translators of the next generation, so that in this respect at least Erasmus and the humanists, as the sixteenth-century *bon mot* put it, 'laid the egg which Luther hatched'.

Within the Empire itself the authority of the Church amongst intellectuals was further undermined by the great scandal associated with the name of Johann Reuchlin (1455–1522), who is usually regarded as one of the greatest of the North European humanists and the first important non-Jewish Hebrew scholar of modern times. In 1510 a converted Jew named Pfefferkorn had, with the backing of the Dominicans of Cologne, obtained an imperial mandate directing him to destroy all Hebrew books and documents in the Empire. Only the books of the Old Testament were to be spared the burning. As the foremost Hebraist of his day Reuchlin had protested against this startling piece of obscurantist vandalism. This had led him into conflict with the Dominican order, in whom the

Inquisition was vested, and had subsequently involved him in a long and unedifying lawsuit which culminated in appeals by both sides to Rome. The leading humanists, for whom the case symbolized the Church's incapacity and unwillingness to come to terms with the 'New Learning', rallied to Reuchlin's defence, and a collection of their letters, assuring him of their support, was published under the title *Clarorum virorum epistolae* (1514). This suggested the most celebrated satire of the age, a volume entitled *Epistolae obscurorum virorum*, which purported to be a collection of letters written by obscure monks and priests to a leading Dominican assuring *him* of *their* support. In reality the letters came from the pens of humanist friends of Reuchlin (Crotus Rubeanus and Ulrich von Hutten) who thus let the representatives of the old order speak for themselves, as it were, in order to pillory their barbarous Latin and their ignorance, stupidity, and immorality.

Such academic jokes as these, however, like the whole literary and philological culture from which they sprang, scarcely touched the broad mass of the people. Intellectuals might laugh at the obscure men and prosperous bourgeois might complain about the greed of the clergy and return *ad fontes* via the numerous vernacular editions of the Scriptures which began to appear in the closing decades of the fifteenth century, but it does not follow from this that disaffection was rife—most people, after all, could not afford to buy books and were in any case unable to read them. There was, it is true, an undercurrent of discontent which occasionally gave religious overtones to agrarian revolt or expressed itself in the mystical tradition deriving from Tauler and Seuse which taught that the essence of religion lay in personal experience of God and thus tended to exclude the Church and its priests from the believer's spiritual life. In the main, however, even where congregations felt that the moral and pastoral standards of their priest left much to be desired (and, as the example of Luther shows, the common Protestant picture of the priesthood as a collection of corrupt lechers is grotesquely untrue), they were content to grumble, while continuing to pay their tithes, worship the saints, and observe the hundred and sixty fast days each year. From the dying Middle Ages they had inherited a very real fear of Hell which was heightened in the early sixteenth century by a widespread mood of apocalyptic expectation, and this alone—quite apart from the force of habit and tradition—was sufficient to keep the vast mass of the population loyal to the Church. In the context of the Reformation the fact that superstition was rife and that the practice of religion was often crudely externalized is far less important than the fact that there was in the people as a whole a very real interest in things religious and a very real desire for the certainty of salvation. Only because it seemed to offer the certainty of salvation was the Reformation able to establish such a firm hold on the minds of men.

But even after all the political, intellectual, and religious factors have been taken into account, the Reformation remains to a surprising extent the work of one man—Dr. Martin Luther (1483–1546). It was Luther's personal struggle for the certainty of salvation which gave Protestantism its central doctrines, and it was Luther's obstinate courage in the face of overwhelming odds which, combined with his skilful exploitation of the new mass medium of the printing-press, enabled these doctrines to survive in the early years of the controversy. From the time he published his ninety-five theses on indulgence on 31 October 1517 (tradition has it that he nailed them on to the door of the Schloßkirche in Wittenberg, where he held the chair of Biblical studies at the newly established university) until his death in 1546 he exercised immense authority within the movement he had called into being: even the greatest and most self-willed Protestant princes sought his advice and approval, and, with the possible exception of Zwingli, all the Reformers, Bucer, Bugenhagen, Melanchthon, and even Calvin, regarded themselves as Luther's pupils.

In 1505 Luther, although destined for the Law, on a sudden impulse entered the monastery of the Augustinian Eremites in Erfurt. As a novice and as a young priest Luther was tortured by an obsessive scrupulosity arising from his sense of his own unmitigated sinfulness and his attendant concern for the salvation of his soul. Faced with the awful majesty and justice of God, Luther became convinced that he could never justify himself before God by his own merits. Further, there was no means by which he could even cleanse himself of sin, since the sacrament of penance presupposed that the sins of the penitent were confessed, and Luther felt he could never be sure that he had confessed all the sins he had committed. In any case, the sacrament did not remove the sinful nature of mankind and so, as it were, simply cured the symptoms and left the disease untreated. Accordingly, it seemed to Luther that he could not escape damnation. Luther eventually found relief from the intense anguish engendered by this train of thought in such Pauline texts as Romans 1: 17 and Romans 3: 28 ('The just shall live by faith', 'We conclude that a man is justified by faith without the deeds of the Law'). The solution did not lie in the attempt to justify himself before God by trying to do 'the deeds of the Law', the solution lay in an unreserved acceptance that he was sinful and had deserved damnation, and in an unconditional trust that God of His great mercy would not punish the sinner according to his merits, but because of this trust in His goodness regard the sinner as being sinless. This is what Luther means when he speaks of Justification by Faith: the faith he postulates is fiduciary faith (*fides fiducialis*) and has little to do with faith in the sense of an acceptance of the historicity of the miracles or the teaching of the Church (*fides dogmatica, theoretica*). Since, however, faith is a gift of God, since man cannot choose to do good but must do evil (Luther is convinced of man's 'Unvermögen zum Guten', cf. p. 21), since God is under no obligation or compulsion to bestow grace on the sinner, it follows that man is subject to predestination: God treats us according to His own volition and may well choose to damn the sinner—indeed He has already decided the sinner's fate long before the sinner was born! The Catholic Church, by contrast, while laying due emphasis on the primacy of God in the process of justification, had always maintained the possibility, or rather the necessity, of co-operation between man and God, God rewarding or punishing the individual according to the good works and moral efforts he had made during his life on earth.

The Reformation made public property of Luther's unorthodox solution of his personal anguish, and it was no accident that it was precisely on the question of indulgences that he came into conflict with the Church in 1517. His condemnation of indulgences is not merely a complaint against the excesses of Tetzel and his like, or a protest against the externalizing and commercializing of the sacrament of penance, as might appear to be the case from Luther's own account (p. 8). Luther was in fact protesting against the whole penitential system of the Church and against the traditional teaching that man could oppose his 'merits' to the justice of God and so in a way justify himself before his Maker. Precisely because the sale of indulgences was an abuse, however, the essential challenge represented by the ninety-five theses tended to be obscured. Initially Luther seems to have thought his position to be orthodox, and was rather taken aback to find that his academic gesture of inviting fellow theologians to dispute with him on technical matters of mutual concern should produce such a storm of controversy and that he should on the one hand be fêted as the liberator of Germany from the monstrous tyranny of Rome and, on the other hand, be reviled as an enemy of the Christian Church and a limb of Satan who was reviving the teachings of condemned heretics such as Wyclif and Huss. Only gradually, largely thanks to polemical attacks and meetings with opponents (Cajetan, Miltitz, Eck, etc.), did Luther come to see how alien to his own dearest convictions the official view of the Church really was.

By 1520 the breach with the Church was complete and Luther's great treatises of that year, *De captivitate babylonica ecclesiae, An den Christlichen Adel deutscher Nation von des Christlichen Standes Besserung,* and *Von der Freiheit eines Christenmenschen,* gave a firm theological basis to the evangelical movement, which in three short years had assumed national and international proportions. The new teachings revolved around four cardinal doctrines: (1) the Scriptures, not Popes and Councils, were the supreme authority and rule of life for Christians; (2) the distinction between clergy and laity was artificial and unevangelical: all believers were in fact priests and such power as the priest might have was delegated to him by the Christian community; the claim that the Church was entitled to arbitrate in affairs of state was thus a fiction; (3) men were justified before God not by virtue of their own merits, but by virtue of the fiduciary faith that was within them; (4) the sacraments did not operate 'magically' (*ex opere operato*), but were dependent for their efficacy on the faith of the participant (*ex opere operantis*).

The efforts of both Church and State to crush Luther (the Pope excommunicated him in 1520, and after his refusal to recant at the Diet of Worms (1521), he was put under the ban of the Empire) proved to be vain. Paradoxical as it may seem in view of its fundamentally pessimistic view of man, the new teaching was widely experienced as a tremendous liberating force which gave men new hope and courage and enabled them, if not to shake off, at least to disregard the oppressive burden of sin and the attendant fear of Hell-fire they had inherited from the dying Middle Ages. Almost equally important was the fact that the incidental protest against abuse and corruption in the Church and the rejection of the economic exploitation of German believers by an Italianate hierarchy appealed to sentiments that had been rife in Germany for decades. Further, quite apart from such considerations, many of the princes and municipalities, who in view of the constitution of the Holy Roman Empire in practice enjoyed absolute power in their own territories, rapidly acquired a vested interest in the survival of Lutheranism by virtue of their secularization of Church lands. The international situation was also uniquely favourable to the new teaching. In 1520 and again in 1529 the Turks carried their Holy War to the gates of Vienna, and the quarrels of Habsburg and Valois involved the good Catholic Emperor, Charles V, in almost continuous wars with the Most Christian king of France.

Equally, the administrative tasks produced by the size and complexity of Charles's empire, which included most of Italy, Spain, the Netherlands, and the Americas, meant that he could never fully devote his energies to his declared intention of extirpating the Lutheran heresy: significantly he left Germany after the Diet of Worms and did not return during the next nine vital years. The Lutheran party naturally took full advantage of these circumstances: the growth of the Protestants' numbers and the readiness of their leaders to enter into 'unpatriotic' alliances with foreign powers combined with the ineptitude of their enemies to give them a political importance which not even their defeat in the civil war of 1547 seriously impaired and which ultimately enabled them to gain legal recognition for their faith in the Religious Peace of Augsburg (1555).

For Luther himself, the years after 1521 were largely devoted to defending, confirming, and strengthening the evangelical faith, be it by translating the Scriptures (New Testament, 1522; Old Testament, 1534) and providing a German liturgy and order of service (his Catechism appeared in 1529), or advising fellow Lutherans on theological and moral problems and continuing to remind them of the need for constant vigilance against the Roman Antichrist.

1. Luther as an old man recalls the outbreak of the Reformation

Wider Hans Worst (1541)

Wider Hans Worst is one of a series of savagely polemical pamphlets produced during the quarrels of Henry, Duke of Braunschweig-Wolfenbüttel (the Hans Worst of the title), Philip, Landgrave of Hesse, and Johann Friedrich, Elector of Saxony, and constitutes Luther's defence of himself and his electoral master against the attacks of Duke Henry. Our extract concerns only the events of 1517, and is taken from the edition of 1541, printed by Hans Lufft of Wittenberg.

Es geschach im Jar da man .17. schreib / das ein Prediger Münch mit namen Johannes Detzel / ein grosser Clamant / Welchen zuuor Hertzog Friderich hatte zu Jnspruck vom Sacke erlöset / Denn Maximilian hatte jn zur erseuffen geurteilt / in der Jhn (kanst wol dencken vmb seiner grossen tugent willen) Vnd Hertzog Friderich lies jn des erinnern / da er vns Wittemberger also anfieng zu lestern / Er bekandte es auch frey. Der

selbige Detzel fûret nu das Ablas vmb her / vnd verkaufft gnade
vmbs Gelt / so thewr oder wol veil er aus allen krefften ver-
mocht. Zu der zeit war ich Prediger allhie im Kloster vnd ein ₁₀
junger Doctor / newlich aus der Esse komen / hitzig vnd lûstig
in der heiligen Schrifft.

Als nu viel Volcks von Wittemberg lieff dem Ablas nach gen
Jûtterbock vnd Zerbest etc. Vnd ich (so war mich mein HERR
Christus erlôset hat) nichts wuste was das Ablas were / wie es
denn kein mensch nicht wuste / fieng ich seuberlich an zu
predigen / man kôndte wol bessers thun / das gewisser were /
weder Ablas lôsen / Solche predigt hatte ich auch zuuor gethan
hie aufm Schlosse / wider das Ablas / Vnd bey Hertzog Friderich damit schlechte gnade verdienet / Denn er sein Stifft auch ₂₀
seer lieb hatte. Nu das ich zur rechten vrsachen des Luthe-
risschen Lermens kome / lies ich alles also gehen wie es gieng.
Jn des kômpt fur mich / Wie der Detzel hette geprediget grewlich schreckliche Artickel / der ich dis mal etliche wil nennen /
Nemlich.

Er hette solche Gnade vnd gewalt vom Bapst / wenn einer
gleich die heilige Jungfraw Maria Gottes Mutter hette ge-
schwecht oder geschwengert / so kûndte ers vergeben / wo der
selb in den Kasten legt / was sich gebûrt.

Jtem / das Rote Ablas Creutz mit des Bapsts wapen / in den ₃₀
Kirchen auffgericht / were eben so krefftig / als das Creutz
Christi.

Jtem / Wenn S. Peter jtzt hie were / hette er nicht grôsser
Gnade noch gewalt weder Er hette.

Jtem / Er wolte im Himel mit S. Peter nicht beuten / Denn
er hette mit Ablas mehr Seelen erlôset weder S. Peter mit
seinem Predigen.

Jtem / Wenn einer Gelt in den Kasten legt fur eine Seele im
Fegfewr / so bald der Pfennig auff den boden fiel vnd klûnge /
so fûre die Seele heraus gen Himel. ₄₀

Jtem / Die Ablas gnade / were eben die Gnade / da durch der
Mensch mit Gott versûnet wird.

Jtem / Es were nicht not / Rew noch Leide oder Busse fur
die Sûnde zu haben / wenn einer das Ablas oder die Ablas
Brieue kauffet / (ich solt sagen / lôset) vnd verkaufft auch
kûnfftige Sûnde. Vnd des dings treib er grewlich viel / vnd war
alles vmbs geld zu thun.

Jch wuste aber zu der zeit nicht / wem solch gelt solte / Da
gieng ein Bûchlin aus / gar herrlich vnter des Bisschoffs zu
50 Magdeburg wapen / darin solcher Artickel etliche / den Que-
storn geboten wûrden zupredigen. Da kams erfûr / das Bisschoff
Albrecht / diesen Detzel gedinget hatte / weil er ein grosser
Clamant war / Denn er war zu Meintz Bisschoff erwelet / mit
solchem Pact / das er zu Rom das Pallium selbs solt keuffen
(lôsen sage ich) Denn es waren zu Meintz newlich drey Bisschoff / Berthold / Jacobus vnd Vriel kurtz nach einander
gestorben / das dem Bisthum vieleicht schweer war / so offt vnd
kurtz auff einander / das Pallium zu keuffen / welchs gestehet /
wie man sagt .26000. etliche sagen .30000. gûlden / Denn so
60 thewr kan der Allerheiligst Vater zu Rom flachsfaden (der
sonst kaum sechs Pfennig werd ist) verkeuffen.

Da erfand nu der Bisschoff dis fûndlin / vnd gedacht das
Pallium den Fockern zu bezalen (denn die hatten das geld
fûrgestreckt) mit des gemeinen mans Beutel. Vnd schickt diesen grossen Beuteldrescher in die Lender / Der drasch auch
weidlich drauff / das es mit hauffen begonst in die Kasten zu
fallen / zu springen / zu klingen. Er vergas aber sein selbs da
neben nicht. Es hatte dazu der Bapst dennoch die hand mit im
Sode behalten / das die helfft solt gefallen zu dem gebew S.
70 Peters Kirchen zu Rom. Also giengen die gesellen hinan mit
freuden vnd grosser hoffnung vnter die Beutel zu schlahen vnd
zu dresschen. Solchs sage ich / wuste ich dazu mal nicht.

Da schreib ich einen brieff mit den Propositionibus / an den
Bisschoff zu Magdeburg / vermanet vnd bat / Er wolte dem
Detzel einhalt thun / vnd solch vngeschickt ding zu predigen /
wehren / Es môchte ein vnlust draus entstehen / Solchs gebûrte
jm als einem Ertzbisschoffe / Den selben brieff kan ich noch
auff legen / Aber mir ward kein antwort. Des gleichen schreib
ich auch dem Bisschoff zu Brandenburg / als Ordinario / An
80 dem ich seer einen gnedigen Bisschoff hatte. Darauff er mir
antwortet / Jch griffe der Kirchen gewalt an / vnd wûrde mir
selbs mûhe machen / Er riete mir / ich liesse dauon. Jch kan wol
dencken / das sie alle beide gedacht haben. Der Bapst wûrde
mir solchem elenden Bettler viel zu mechtig sein.

Also giengen meine Propositiones aus wider des Detzels
Artickel / wie man im gedrûckten wol sehen mag. Die selbigen
lieffen schier in vierzehen tagen durch gantz Deudsch land.

Denn alle welt klagt vber das Ablas / sonderlich vber Detzels Artickel. Vnd weil alle Bisschoue vnd Doctores still schwigen / vnd niemand der Katzen die Schellen anbinden wolte (Denn 90 die Ketzer meister / Prediger Ordens / hatten alle welt mit dem Fewr in die furcht geiagt / Vnd Detzel selbs auch etliche Priester / so wider seine freche predigt gemuckt hatten / eingetrieben) Da ward der Luther ein Doctor gerhůmet / das doch ein mal einer komen were / der drein griffe / Der Rhum war mir nicht lieb / Denn (wie gesagt) ich wuste selbs nicht was das Ablas were / vnd das lied wolte meiner stimme zu hoch werden.

Dis ist der erste rechte grundliche anfang des Lutherischen Lermens / . . .

Der ander anfang dieses Lermens ist der Heiligst Vater Bapst 100 Leo / mit seinem vnzeitigen Bann / da zu holffen / Doctor Saw vnd alle Papisten / auch etliche grobe Esel / da jderman wolt Ritter an mir werden / schrieben vnd schrien wider mich / was nur feder regen kundte. Jch aber hoffete / der Bapst solte mich schützen / Denn ich hatte meine Disputation also verwaret vnd gewapent mit schrifft vnd Bepstlichen Drecketen / das ich sicher war / der Bapst wůrde den Detzel verdamnen vnd mich segenen / schreib jm auch zu / die Resolution mit einer demütigen schrifft / Vnd gefiel solch mein Buch auch vielen Cardinalen vnd Bisschouen seer wol. Denn ich dazu mal besser Bepstisch 110 war / weder Meintz vnd Heintz selbs je gewest sind noch werden můgen / Vnd die Bepstlichen Drecketen klerlich da stunden / das die Questores die Seelen nicht aus dem Fegfewr mit Ablas lösen kůndten. Aber da ich des segens wartet / aus Rom / da kam Blitz vnd Donner vber mich / Jch muste das schaff sein / das dem Wolffe das wasser betrůbt hatte / Detzel gieng frey aus / ich must mich fressen lassen.

Da zu giengen sie mit mir armen so fein Pepstisch vmb / das ich zu Rom wol .16. tage verdampt war / ehe die Citation mir zu kam. Aber da der Cardinal Caietanus auff dem Reichstage 120 zu Augspurg komen war / Erlanget Doctor Staupitz / das der selb gute Fůrste / Hertzog Fridreich / selbs zum Cardinal gieng vnd erwarb / das mich der Cardinal hören wolt / Also kam ich gen Augspurg zum Cardinal / Der stellet sich freundlich / Aber nach vielen hendeln erbot ich mich hinfort zu schweigen / so fern mein wider teil auch schweigen můste. Da ich das nicht erlangen kundte / Appellirt ich vom Bapst zum Concilio / vnd

zoch dauon / Also ist die sache hinfort auch auff die Reichstage
komen / vnd offt gehandelt / dauon jtzt nicht zu schreiben /
130 Denn die Historien ist zu lang / Jn des giengs mit schreiben
widernander auffs hefftigst / bis es nu da hin komen ist / das
sie das Liecht vnuerschampt schewen / Ja viel dings selbs jtzt
leren / das sie zuuor verdampt / dazu nichts zu leren hetten /
wenn vnser Bůcher thetten.

Jst nu ein Lermen hieraus komen der jnen weh thut / Des
můssen sie jnen selbs dancken / Warumb haben sie die sachen
so vnuernůnfftig vnd vngeschickt getrieben wider alle Recht /
Warheit / Schrifft vnd jr eigen Drecketen? Sie důrffens keinem
andern schuld geben / denn jnen selbs / Wir wőllen jres klagens
140 in die faust lachen / vnd jr zum schaden spotten / vnd vns
trősten / das jr stůndlin komen sey. Denn sie auch noch heutiges
tags nicht auff hőren / als die verblenten / verstockten / vnsinnigen
narren / die sache also zu handeln / als wolten sie mutwilliglich
zu grund gehen / Gottes zorn ist vber sie komen / Wie sie
verdienet haben.

2. Luther explains the issues at stake in the indulgence controversy

Eyn Sermon von dem Ablaß vnnd gnade (1518)

The ninety-five theses were intended to stimulate learned discussion amongst academic theologians, and Luther was initially rather concerned at the amount of attention they attracted in lay circles. *Eyn Sermon von dem Ablaß vnnd gnade*, which may have been preached as early as 31 October 1517 but which was not published until the following year, is an attempt to give vernacular expression in a form suitable for a lay audience to the point of view which underlies the Theses. In its printed form, the *Sermon* is not so much a piece of continuous prose as a series of notes, and its disjointedness makes it rather difficult to understand, even when it is read—as it must be read—in conjunction with the Theses themselves. Stylistically and in its insistence on a problem which today is largely of historical interest, it is not calculated to have an immediate appeal for the twentieth-century reader. Amongst Luther's contemporaries, however, it enjoyed tremendous success, passing through twenty-two editions in two years, and its status as a best seller of the early Reformation period bears eloquent witness to the passionate involvement of wide sections of the contemporary public in the indulgence controversy.

Our text is that printed by Georg Rhaw of Wittenberg in 1518, and is notable especially for its retention of Chancery spelling.

*Eyn Sermon von dem Ablaß vnnd gnade | durch deñ wirdigeñ
doctorñ Martinum Luther Augustiner zu Wittenbergk geprediget.*

Czum Ersten solt yr wissen / das eczlich new lerer / als Magister
Sentē. S. Thomas vñ yhre folger gebē d' puß drey teyl / Nemlich
die rew / die peycht / die gnugthuung / Uñ wiewol dißer vnderscheyd nach yrer meynung / schwerlich adder auch gar nichts /
gegrundet erfunden wirt in der heyligenn schrifft / noch in den
alten heyligen Christlichen lererñ / doch wollē wir das yczt ßo
lassen bleyben / vnd nach yrher weyß reden.

Czum andernñ sagen sie / der ablaß nympt nycht hynn das   10
erst adder ander teyll / das ist / die rew adder peycht / sunderū
das dritt / nemlich die gnugthuung.

Czum Driten. die gnugthuung wirt weyter geteylet in drey
teil / das ist / Beeten / vastē / almußē / also / das beetē begreyfft
allerlei werck der seelē eygē / als leßē / tichten / horen gottes
wort / predigen / leeren vnd d' gleichen. Uasten begreiff allerlei
werck der casteyūg seins fleyschs / als wachen / erbeiten / hart
lager / cleider etc. Almußē begreyff allerlei gute werck der lyeb
vñ barmherczickeyt gegen dem nehsten.

Czum Uierden / Jst bey yhn allē vngeczweyfelt / das der   20
ablas hin nympt die selben werck der gnugthuūg / vor die sund
schuldig czuthun adder auffgeseczt / dann ßo er die selben
werck solt all hin nehmen / blieb nichts gutes mehr da / das wir
thun mochtenn.

Czum Funfften. Jst bey vielē gewest eyn große vñ noch vn-
beschloßene opiny / Ab der ablas auch etwas mehr hynnehme /
dañ solche auffgelegte gute werck / nemlich / ab er auch die
peyne / die die gotlich gerechtigkeyt / vor die sunde / fordert /
abnehme.

Czum Sechsten. Laß ich yhre opiny vnuorworffeñ auff das   30
mal / Das sag ich / das mā auß keyner schrifft bewerenn kañ /
das gottlich gerechtigkeyt etwas peyn adder gnugthuung begere
adder fordere / vonn dem sunder. Dañ allein seyne herczliche
vnd ware rew adder bekerūg myt vorsacz hynfurder / das Creucz
Christi czu tragenn / vnnd die obgenanten werck (auch von
nyemāt auffgeseczt) czu vben / Dañ ßo spricht er durch Ezechie.
Man sich der sunder bekeret / vñ thut recht / so will ich seyner
sunde nicht mehr gedencken. Jtem also hatte er selbs all die
absoluirt. Maria Magda. den gichtpruchtigē. Die eebrecherynne

40 &c. Uñd mocht woll gerne horen wer das anders bewerē soll.
Unangesehen das eczlich doctores ßo gedaucht haben.
Czum Sibenden. Das findet man woll / das gott eczlich nach
seyner gerechtigkeyt straffet / Ader durch peyne dringt czu der
rew / wie ym .88. p̄s. Szo seyn kinder werden sundigen / will ich
myt der ruthen / yhre sunde heym suchen / Aber doch meyn
barmherczickeyt nit vonn yhnn wendē. Aber diße peyne /
stehet in nyemandes gewalt nachczulassen / dañ alleyne gottis.
Ja er will sie nit lassen / sūder vorspricht / er woll sie auflegē.
Czum Achten. Der halbē ßo kann man der selbē gedunckten
50 peyn / keynen namen geben / weyß auch nyemant / was sye ist /
ßo sie diße straff nyt ist. auch dye guten obgenanten werck
nit ist.
Czum Neunden. Sag ich / ob die Christenliche kirch noch
heut beschluß / vnd auß ercleret / das der ablas mehr dañ die
werck der gnugthuūg hyn neme / ßo were es den nocht tausent-
mal besser / das keyn Christenmensch den ablas loßet oder
begeret / sunderñ das sye lieber die werck thetten vnnd die peyn
litten / dañ der ablas / nit anderst ist nach mag werden / dañ
nachlassung gutter werck / vnnd heylsamer peyn / die man
60 billich solt erwellē dañ vorlassen / wiewol etlich d' newen
prediger zweyerley peyne erfunden / Medicatiuas Satisfactorias /
das ist etzlich peyn czur gnugthuung / eczlich czur besserung /
Aber wir haben mehr freyheyt czuuorachten (got lob) sulchs
vnnd des gleychen plauderey / dañ sie haben czu ertichten /
dañ alle peyn / ya alls was gott aufflegt / ist besserlich vnd tzu
treglich den Christen.
Czū czehenden / Das ist nichts geredt / das der peyn vnnd
werck czu vill seynn / das der mensch sye nit mag vol brengen /
der kurcz halben seyns lebens / Darumb yhm nott sey der
70 Ablas. Antwort ich das / das keyn grundt hab / vñ eyn lauter
geticht ist / Dañ gott vnnd die heylige kirche / legen nyemand
mehr auff / dañ yhm czu tragē muglich ist / als auch .S. Paul
sagt / das got nit leßt vorsucht werden yemand / mehr dañ er
mag tragen / vnd es langet nit wenig czu der Christenheyt
schmach / Das mā yhr schuld gibt / sye lege auff mehr / dañ wir
tragen kunen.
Czum eylfften. Wann gleych die puß ym geystlichē recht
geseczt / iczt noch ginge / Das vor ein yglich todtsund / syeben
iar puß auffgelegt were / Szo must doch die Christenheyt / dye

selbē gesecz lassen / vñ nit weyter aufflegen / dañ sye eynem 80
yglichen czu tragē warē. Uil weniger / nu sye iczt nicht seyn/sall
mā achtē / das nicht mehr auffgelegt werde dañ yederman wol
tragē kan.

Czum czwelfftē. Man sagt wol / das der sunder mit der
vberingen peyn / inß fegfewr oder czum ablas geweyset sall
werdenn / aber es wirt wol mehr dings / an grundt vnd bewerung
gesagt.

Czum Dreyczehendē. Es ist eyn großer yrthū das yemādt
meyne / er wolle gnugthun vor seyne sundt / so doch got die
selbē alczeyt vmb sunst / auß vnscheczlicher gnad vorczeyhet / 90
nichts darfur begerend dā hynfurder woll leben. Die Christen-
heyt fordert wol etwas / also mag sie vnd sall auch das selb
nachlassen / vnnd nichts schweres adder vntreglichs auflegen.

Czum Uierczehendē. Ablaß wirt czu gelassen vmb der vnuolkōmen vnd faulen Christen willen / die sich nit wollen kecklich
vben in guten wercken / oder vnleydlich seyn / dañ ablas
furdert nyeman czum bessern / sundern duldet vnnd zuleßet yr
vnuolkōmen / darumb soll man nit wider das ablas redenn /
man sall aber auch nyemand darczu reden.

Czum Funffczehenden. Uill sicherer / vnnd besserer thet 100
der / der lauter vmb gottes willen / gebe czu dē gebewde .S.
Petri / ader was sunst genāt wird / Dan das er ablas darfur
nehme / dañ es ferlich ist / das er sulch gabe vmb des ablas
willē vñ nit vmb gottz willē gibt.

Czum Secheczehendē. Uill besser ist das werck eynen
durfftigen erczeygt / dan das czum gebewde geben wirt auch
vill besser / dan der ablas dafur gegebē / dan wie gesagt. Es ist
besser eyn gutes werck gethā / dañ vill nach gelassen. Ablas
aber / ist nachlassung villgutter werck / ader ist nichts nach
gelassen. 110

Ja das ich euch recht vnderweise. ßo merckt auff / du salt
vor allenn dingen (widder sanct Peters gebewde noch ablas
angesehen) deynē nehsten armē geben / wiltu etwas geben. Wan
eß aber dahyn kumpt / das nyemandt yn deyner stat mehr ist
der hulff bedarff (das ob gottwil nymer gescheen sall) dañ saltu
geben ßo du wilt tzu den kirchen / altarn / schmuck / kelich /
die in deyner stadt seyn. Und wen das auch nu nit mehr not
ist / Dañ aller erst / ßo du wilt / magstu geben zu dē gebewde
.S. Peters adder anderwo. Auch soltu dennoch nit das vmb

120 ablas willen thun. dañ sant Paul spricht Wer seynē hauß
genoßē nit wol thut / ist keyn Christē vnd erger dañ ein heyde /
vñ halts dafur frey / wer dir āders sagt / der vorfurt dich / adder
sucht yhe dein seel in deynem Beutell vnd fund er pfenning
darinne / das were ym lieber dañ all seelē. Szo sprichstu. Szo
werd ich nymer mehr ablas loßen. Antwort ich / das hab ich
schon obē gesagt / Das meyn will / begirde / bitt vñ ratt ist / das
nyemandt ablas loße / laß die faulen vnd schlefferigen Christen /
ablas loßen / gang du fur dich.

Czum Sibenczehenden. Der ablas ist nich geboten auch nicht
130 geratē / sunderñ von der dinger czall / die czu gelassen vñ
erleubt werdē. darumb ist es nit eyn werck des gehorsams / auch
nit vordinstlich / sūderñ eyn außczug des gehorsams. Darumb
wiewol man / nyemant weren soll / den czu loßen / ßo solt mā
doch alle Christē daruon cziehen / and zu den wercken vñ
peynen / die do nachgelassen / reyczen vnd sterckenñ.

Czum Achtczehendē. Ab die seelen auß dē fegfewr geczogen
werden durch den ablas / weyß ich nit / vñ geleub das auch
noch nich / wiewol das eczlich new doctores sagen / aber ist
yhn vnmuglich czubeweren / auch hat es die kirch noch nit
140 beschlossen / darumb czu mehrer sicherheyt / vil besser ist es /
das du vor sie selbst bittest vñ wirckest / dan diß ist bewerter
vñ ist gewiß.

Czum Neunczehendē. In dissen puncten hab ich nit czweyffel / vnnd sind gnugsam in der schrifft gegrund. Darumb solt
ir auch keyn czweyffel haben / vñ last doctores Scholasticos /
scholasticos sein / sie sein alsampt nit gnug / mit yhren opinien /
das sie eyne prediget befestigenn soltenn.

Czum czwenczigsten. Ab etzlich mich nu wol eynen keczer
schelten / den solch warheyt seer schedlich ist im kasten. Szo
150 acht ich doch solch geplerre nit groß / sintemal das nit thun /
dañ eczlich finster ghyrne / die die Biblien nie gerochē / die
Christenlichē lerer nie geleßē yhr eigen lerer nie vorstanden /
sundern in yhren lochereten vnd czurissen opinien vill nah
vorwesen / dā hetthen sie die vorstanden ßo wisten sie / das sie
nyemādt solten lestern / vnuorhort vñ vnuberwundē / doch got
geb yhn / vnd vns rechten sinn. Amen.

Getruckt Nach Christ geburt Tausent funff hundert
vñ ym achczehenden Jar.

3. Luther expounds the doctrine of Justification by Faith

Von der freyheyt eynes Christen menschen (1520)

Von der freyheyt eynes Christen menschen is the last of the three great Reformation treatises published in 1520. The other two, *An den Christlichen Adel deutscher Nation* and *De captivitate babylonica ecclesiae praeludium*, are essentially polemical pamphlets, the work of a man who was protesting at the prostitution of religion in a Church which he had come to regard as being almost totally corrupt. The first deals with the unbiblical nature of the claims made in support of papal authority, asserts that all believers are priests through baptism, and proposes a whole series of ecclesiastical and religious reforms; the second attacks the current theory and practice of the sacraments and reduces the seven sacraments of the Roman Catholic Church to three (baptism, communion, and penance). By contrast, *Von der freyheyt eynes Christen menschen* is devotional rather than polemical. It was written at the instigation of the papal nuncio, Karl von Miltitz, who was concerned to patch up the quarrel between the Church and Luther and in the course of their meeting at Lichtenberg in October 1520 persuaded Luther to write to the Pope and explain his position—a course of action which was also advocated by influential members of Luther's order, as well as the advisers of Frederick the Wise, who were all naturally anxious to avoid an open breach with the papacy. Luther responded to these various pressures by writing the tract on Christian liberty together with a prefatory letter to Leo X, which, in spite of its apparently respectful attitude to the Pope himself, was barely calculated to placate the latter in view of its swingeing attack on the corruption of the curia. The essay on Christian freedom appeared in both Latin and German, but it was the shorter German version which was published first and almost immediately established itself as one of the classic statements of the Lutheran faith. The initial paradox—inspired by 1 Cor. 9: 19—of the simultaneous freedom and servitude of the Christian is quite characteristic of Luther's antithetical, dialectical mode of thought and is used as a basis from which to explore the nature of Justification and the relationship of Faith and Works. Accordingly, the pamphlet expounds views which are implicit—and often explicit—in everything Luther wrote. This is, however, probably the most personal of all Luther's theoretical works. Luther is here presenting us with the solution to the problems which tortured him during his noviciate and early priesthood, and he does so not in the high-flown language of the professional theologian, but in the simple language of immediate religious experience: the whole work is redolent of Luther's awareness of his own sinfulness and utter inadequacy before God and proclaims his sense of relief at the realization that God did not require him to do the impossible and justify himself by his own works, but simply to trust in Him. The distinction which Luther makes between the inner and the outer man, between body and soul, is perhaps sharper than most twentieth-century readers would be inclined to accept—indeed, some of

Luther's contemporaries, notably the leaders of the Peasants' Revolt of 1524–5 (cf. p. 63), were unable to accept it either; but the assertion that mankind cannot be saved by its own efforts, but only by the action of freely bestowed grace operative in the faithful believer, and the affirmation of the Christian life as a life of active service to one's fellow men, are as valid for the modern Protestant as they were when Luther wrote in the prefatory letter that 'it is only a little book if you count the pages, but to grasp its meaning is to understand the whole sum of the Christian life'.

Our text is taken from the edition which was printed anonymously in Wittenberg in 1520.

Jhesus.

Zvm ersten / Das wir grundlich mugē erkennen was ein Christen mēsch sey / vnd wie es gethan sey vmb die freyheit / die ym Christus erworben vnnd geben hat / dauon sant Paulus vil schreybt / wil ich setzen diße tzwen beschluß.

Eyn Christen mensch ist eyn freyer herr vber alle ding / vnd nymandt vntterthan.

Eyn Christen mensch ist eyn dienstpar knecht aller ding / vnd yderman vntterthan.

10 Diße tzwen beschluß sein klerlich sant Paulus i. Cor .xij. Jch bin frey in allē dingē / vñ hab mich eins ydermā knecht gemacht. Jtē Ro .xiij. Jr solt nymandt etwas vorpflichtet sein / den das yr euch vnttereinander liebet. Lieb aber die ist dienstpar / vnd vntterthan dē das sie lieb hat. Also auch von Christo Gal .iiij. Got hat seinen son außgesandt vō einē weib geborē / vñ dē gesetz vnd'thā gemacht.

Czū andern / Diße tzwo widerstendige rede der freyheit vñ dienstparkeit tzuuornemen / sollen wir gedēckē / dz ein yglich Christē mēsch ist tzweierley natur / geistlicher vnd leyplicher. 20 Nach der selen wirt er ein geistlich / new / ynnerlich mensch genennet / nach dem fleisch vnd blut wirt er ein leyplich / alt vnd eusserlich mēsch genēnet. Vnd vmb dises vntterschides willē / werdē vō ym gesagt in der schrifft / die do stracks widernander sein / wie ich ytzt gesagt von der freyheyt vnd dienstparkeyt.

Czū drittē / so nemē wir fur vns den ynwendigē geistlichē mēschē / tzu sehē was dartzu gehore das ein frum / frey Christē mēsch sey vnd heysße. So ists ofenbar dz kein eusserlich dīg mag in frey noch frum machen / wie es mag ymmer genennet 30 werdē. dan sein frūmigkeyt vnd freyheyt / wider umb sein

boßheyt vnd gefencknis / sein nicht leyplich noch eusßerlich.
Was hilffts die selen / das der leyb vngefangē / frisch / vnd
gesundt ist / ysßet / trinckt / lebt wie er wil? Widerumb was
schadt das der selen / das der leyb gefangen / kranck vnd madt
ist / hungert / durstet vnd leydet / wie er nicht gerne wolt?
Dißer ding reichet keynes biß an die selen / sie tzu befreyhen
oder fahen / frum oder boße tzu machen.

Czum vierden / also hilffet es die sele nichts / ob der leyb
heilige kleyder anlegt / wie die priester vnd geistlichen thun /
auch nit ob er in den kirchen vnd heiligen stetten sey. Auch 40
nicht ob er mit heiligen dingen vmbgehet. Auch nicht ob er
leyplich bette / faste / walle / vnnd alle gute werck thue / die
durch vnd in dem leybe geschehen mochten ewigklich. Es muß
noch alles etwas anders sein / das der selen bringe / vnd gebe
frumigkeyt vnnd freyheyt. Dan alle diße obgenanten stuck /
werck / vnd weyßen / mag auch an sich haben vnnd vben eyn
boßer mensch / eyn gleyßner vnd heuchler. Auch durch solch
weßen keyn ander volck / dann eyttel gleißner werden. Widerumb schadet es der selen nichts / ob der leyb vnheilige kleyder
tregt / an vnheiligen orten ist / yßt / trinckt / wallet / bettet nicht / 50
vnnd lesßet alle die werck onstehen / die / die obgenanten
gleyßner thun.

Czum funfften / hat die sele kein ander ding / wyder in hymel
noch auff erden / darinnē sie lebe / frum / frey / vn̄ Christen sey /
dan das heilig Euāgeliū / das wort gottes von Christo geprediget.
Wie er selb saget Johan .xi. Jch bin das leben / vnd aufferstehung /
wer do glaubt in mich / der lebet ewigklich. Jtem .xvij. Jch bin
der weg / die warheyt / vnd das leben. Jtem Math .iiij. Der
mensch lebet nit allein von dem brot / sonder von allen wortten
die do gehen von dem mundt gottes. So muessen wir nun gewiß 60
sein / das die sele kan alles dings entperen / on des wort gottes /
vn̄ on das wort gottes / ist yhr mit keynem ding beholffen. Wo
sie aber das wort hat / ßo darff sie auch keines andern dings
mehr / sonder sie hat in dem wort gnuge / speiß / freud / frid /
liecht / kunst / gerechtigkeyt / warheyt / weißheyt / freyheyt /
vnd alles gut vberschwengklich . . .

Czum sechstē / fragestu aber / welchs ist dan das wort / das
solch grosse gnad gibt? Vnnd wie sol ichs gebrauchen? Antwort. Es ist nit anders / dann die predigt von Christo geschehen / wie das Euangelium ynnehelt. Welche sol sein / vnnd ist 70

alßo gethan / das du horest deinen got tzu dir reden / wie alle
dein leben vnd werck nichts sein vor got / sonder muesßest mit
allen dem das in dir ist ewigklich vorterben. Welchs so du
recht glaubst / wie du schuldig bist / so mustu an dir selber
vortzweiffeln / vnd bekennen das war sey der spruch Osee. O
Jsrael in dir ist nichts dan dein vorterbē / allein aber in mir
stehet dein hulff. Das du aber auß dir vnd von dir / das ist auß
deinem vorterben kūmen mugest / so setzt er dir fur seinen
lieben son Jesum Christum / vnd lesset dir durch sein lebendigs
80 trostlichs wort sagen / du solt in den selbigē mit festem glauben
dich ergeben / vnd frisch in yn vortrawen. So sollen dir vmb
desselben glaubēs willen alle deine sund vorgeben / alle dein
vorterben vberwundē sein / vnd du gerecht / warhafftig /
befridet / frum / vnd alle gepot erfullet sein / vō allen dingen
frey sein. Wie sant Paulus sagt Ro .i. Ein rechtfertiger Christen
lebt nur von seinē glauben. Vnd Ro .x. Christus ist das ende
vnnd fulle aller gebot / denen die in yn glauben.

Czum sibenden / darūb solt das billich aller Christen eynigs
werck vnd vbūg sein / das sie das wort vnd Christum wol in sich
90 bildeten / solchen glauben stetig vbeten vnd sterckten. dan kein
ander werck mag eynen Christen machē. Wie Christus Joan
.vi. tzu den Juden sagt / da sie yn fragten / was sie fur werck
thun solten / das sie gotlich vnd Christlich werck theten. Sprach
er. Das ist das eynige gotlich werck das yr glaubt in denen den
got gesandt hat / welchen got der vatter allein auch dartzu
vorordnet hat. Darumb ists gar ein vberschwencklich reichtumb / ein rechter glaub in Christo / den er mit sich bringt alle
seligkeit / vnnd abnympt alle vnseligkeit. Wie Mar. vlt. Wer
do glaubt / vñ tauft ist / der wirt selig. Wer nit glaubt der wirt
100 vordampt . . .

Czum achten / Wie gehet es aber tzu das der glaub alleyn
mag frum machen / vnnd on alle werck so vberschwencklich
reichtumb geben / ßo doch souil gesetz / gebot / werck / stendt /
vnd weyße vns furgeschriben sein in der schrifft? Hye ist fleissig
tzumercken / vnd yhe mit ernst tzubehaltē / das allein der
glaub on alle werck frum / frey / vnd selig machet / wie wir
hernach mer horen werden. Vnd ist tzuwissen das die gantz
heylige schrifft wirt in tzweyerley wort geteylet / welche sein /
gebot oder gesetz gottes / vnd vorheyschen oder tzusagunge. Die
110 gepot leren vnnd schreyben vns fur mancherley gutte werck /

aber damit sein sie noch nicht geschehen. Sie weyßen wol / sie
helffen aber nicht / lernen was man thun sol / geben aber keyn
sterck dartzu. Darumb seyn sie nuhr dartzu geordenet / das
der mensch darynnen sehe sein vnuormugen tzu dem gutten /
vnnd lerne an yhm selbs vortzweyffeln. Vn̄ darumb heissen sie
auch das alte testament / vnnd gehoren alle ynß altte testament.
Als das gepot / Du solt nit boß begird haben / beweyßet das wir
allesampt sunder sein / vnd kein mēsch vormag tzu sein on boße
begirde / er thue was er wol / darauß er lernet an ym selbs
vortzagen / vnnd anderßwo tzu suchen hulff / das er on boße 120
begirde sey / vnd also das gebot erfulle / durch eynen andern /
das er auß ym selb nicht vormag. alßo sein auch alle andere
gebot vnns vnmuglich.

Czum neunden / wen nun der mensch auß den gebotten sein
vnuormugen gelernet / vnd entpfunden hat / das ym nun angst
wirt / wie er dem gebot gnug thue: Seyteinmal das gebot muß
erfullet sein / oder er muß vordampt sein: Szo ist er recht gede-
mutigt / vnd tzu nicht worden / in seinen augen / findet nichts in
yhm / damit er mug frum werden. Dan so kumpt das ander
wort / die gotlich vorheischung vnd tzusagung / vnd spricht / 130
wilt du alle gebot erfullen deiner boßen begirde / vnd sund
loß werden / wie die gebot tzwingē vnd fordern / Sihe da / glaub
in Christum / in welchem ich dir tzusag / alle gnad / gerechtigkeyt / frid / vnd freyheyt / glaubstu / so hastu / glaubstu nit / so
hast du nicht. Dann das dir vnmuglich ist mit allen wercken der
gebot / der vil vnd doch keyn nutz sein mußen / das wirt dir
leicht vnd kurtz / durch den glaubē. Dan ich hab kurtzlich in
den glaubē gestellet alle ding / das / wer yn hat / sol alle ding
haben / vnd selig sein: wer yn nit hat / sol nichts haben. Also
geben die tzusagung gottes / was die gebot erfordern / vnd 140
vorbringen / was die gebot heyssen / auff das es alles gottes
eygen sey. Gebot vnd erfullung er heysßet alleyn / er erfullet
auch alleyn. Darūb sein die tzusagung gottes / wort des newē
testaments / vnd gehorē auch yns newe testamēt.

Czum tzehenden / Nun sein diße vnnd alle gottes wort /
heilig / warhaftig / gerecht / fridsam frey / vnnd aller gute vol /
darumb wer yn mit einē rechten glauben anhangt / des sele
wirt mit yhm voreinigt ßo gantz vnnd gar / das alle tugent
des worts / auch eygen werden der selen. Vnnd alßo durch
den glauben die sele von dem gottes wort / heylig / gerecht / 150

warhafftig /fridsam / frey / vnnd aller gute vol / eyn warhafftig kind
gottes wirt / wie Johan .i. sagt. Er hat yn geben / das sie mugē
kinder gottes werden alle die yn seinen nahmen glauben . . .
Czū .xij. Nit allein gibt d' glaub souil dz die seel dē gotlichē
wort gleich wirt aller gnadē vol / frey / vñ selig / sond' voreinigt
auch die sele mit Christo / als eine braut mit yrē breutgā. Auß
welcher ehe folget / wie sant Paul sagt / dz Christus vñ die seel
ein leib werdē / so werdē auch beyd' gutter fal / vnfal / vñ alle
ding gemein / dz was Christus hat / dz ist eygē d' glaubigē sele /
160 was dy sele hat wirt eigē Chr̄i. So hat Christus alle guter vñ
seligkeit dy sein d' selē eigē / so hat die seel alle vntugēt vñ
sund auff yr die werdē Christi eigē. Hy hebt sich nū d' frolich
wechsel vñ streit / die weil Christus ist got vñ mēsch / welcher
noch nie gesundigt hat / vñ sein frūmigkeit vnuberwītlich /
ewig vñ almechtig ist / so er dē d' glaubigē selē sund durch yrē
brautring / dz ist / d' glaub im selbs eigē macht / vñ nit anders
thut dā als het er sie gethā / so mussen die sund in ym vor-
schlundē vñ erseufft werdē. Dā sein vnuberwīdlich gerechtigkeit
ist allē sundē tzu starck / also wirt dy seel vō allē yrē sundē laut-
170 terlich durch yrē malschatzs / dz ist des glaubēs halbē ledig vñ
frey / vnd begabt mit d' ewigē gerechtigkeit yrs breutgams
Christi. Jst nun dz nit ein froliche wirtschaft da d' reiche /
edle / frum̄ breudtgā Christus dz arme vorachte boses hurlein
tzu d' ehe nīpt / vñ sie entledigt vō allem vbel / tziret mit allē
gutern. So ists nit muglich dz die sund sie vordāme / dā sie ligē
nun auf Christo / vñ sein in ym vorschlūdē / so hat sie so ein
reiche gerechtigkeit in irē breutgā / dz sie abermals wid' alle
sund bestan mag / ob sie schon auff yr ligē. Dauō sagt Paulus .i.
Cor .xv. Got sey lob vñ danck d' vns hat gegebē ein solch
180 vberwindūg in Christo Jesu in welcher vorschlūden ist der
todt mit der sund . . .
Czum neuntzehenden / das sey nun gnug gesagt von dem
ynnerlichen mēschen / von seiner freiheit / vnd der heubt
gerechtigkeyt / welch keynes gesetzs noch guten wercks bedarff /
iha yr schedlich ist / so ymandt dardurch wolt rechtfertig tzu
werden sich vormessen. Nun kūmen wir auffs ander teyl / auff
den eusserlichen menschen. Hye wollen wir antwortten allen
denen / die sich ergern auß dē vorigen reden / vnd pflegen
tzusprechen / Ey so dan der glaub alle dingk ist / vnnd gilt
190 allein gnugsam frum tzu machen / warumb sein dann die gutten

werck gepotten? so wollen wir gutter ding sein / vñ nichts thun.
Neyn lieber mensch / nicht also. Es wer wol also / wen du allein
ein ynnerlich mensch werest / vnd gantz geystlich vnd ynnerlich
wordē / welchs nit geschicht biß am iungsten tag. Es ist vnd
bleibt auff erden nur ein anheben / vnd tzunemen / welchs wirt
in ihener welt vorbracht. Daher heisset der Apostel primitias
spiritus / das sein die ersten frucht des geists / darūb gehort
hyeher das daroben gesagt ist / Ein Christen mensch ist ein
dienstbar knecht / vnnd yderman vntterthan / gleich / wo er
frey ist / darff er nichts thun / wo er knecht ist / muß er allerley   200
thun. Wie das tzugehe wollen wir sehen.

Czum tzwentzigsten / Ob wol der mēsch ynwendig nach der
selen durch den glaubē gnugsam rechtfertig ist / vnd alles hat
was er haben sol / on das der selb glaub vnd gnugde muß
ymmer tzunemen biß in yhenes leben / so bleibt er doch noch
in dyßem leyplichen leben auff erden / vnd muß seinen eigen
leyp regirn / vnd mit leuthen vmbgehen. Da heben sich nun
die werck an / hye muß er nicht mussig gehen / da muß furwar
der leyb mit fastē / wachen / arbeyten / vnd mit aller messiger
tzucht getriben vnnd geubt sein / das er dem ynnerlichen   210
menschen / vnd dem glauben gehorsam vñ gleichformig werde /
nit hyndere noch widerstreb / wie sein art ist / wo er nit ge-
tzwungen wirt. dan der ynnerliche mensch ist mit got eynes /
frolich / vnd lustig / vmb Christus willen / der ym souil than
hat vnd stett alle sein lust darin / dz er widerūb mocht got auch
vmbsunst dienen in freyer lieb / ßo findt er in seinem fleisch
eynen widerspenstigen willen / der wil der welt dienen / vnd
suchen was yn lustet. Das mag der glaub nit leyden / vnd legt
sich mit lust an seinen halß yn tzu dempffen vnnd weren. Wie
sant Pauls sagt Ro .vij. Jch hab eyn lust in gottes willen nach   220
meinem ynnern menschen / ßo find ich eynen andern willen in
meinem fleisch / der wil mich mit sunden gefangen nemen.
Jtē ich tzuchtige meinen leyb / vnd treyb yn tzu gehorsam auff
das ich nit selbs vorwerflich werde / der die andern leren sol.
Jtem Gal .v. Alle die Christū angehoren / creutzigen yr fleisch
mit seinen boßen lusten.

Czū .xxi. Aber die selben werck mussen nit geschehen in der
meynung / das dardurch d' mēsch frum werd vor got / dann
die falsch meynung kan der glaub nit leyden / der alleyn ist /
vnd sein muß die frūmigkeyt vor got / sonder nur in der meinūg   230

das der leyb gehorsam werde / vnd gereynigt von seinen boßen
lusten / vnnd das aug nuhr sehe auff die boßen lusten sie
auß tzutreyben. Dan die weil die seel durch den glauben reyn
ist / vnd got liebet / wolt sie gern das auch alßo alle ding reyn
weren / tzuuor yr eygē leyb / vnd yderman got mit yr liebt vnd
lobt. So geschichts das der mensch seins eygen leybs halben nit
ank mussig gehen / vnnd muß vil gutter werck darober vben /
das er yn tzwinge / vnnd doch die werck nicht das rechte gut
sein / davon er frum vnnd gerecht sey vor got / sonder thue sie
240 auß freier lieb vmbsunst / got tzugefallē / nichts daryn anders
gesucht noch angesehen / dann das es got alßo gefellet / welchs
willen er gerne thet auffs allerbeste. Darauß dann eyn yglicher
kan selbs nemen die maß vnd bescheydenheyt den leib tzu
casteyen / dan er fastet / wachet / arbeyt / souil er siecht dem leyb
nodt sein / seinen mutwillen tzu dempffen. Die andern aber die
do meynen mit wercken frum tzu werden / haben keyn acht
auff die casteyung / sonder sehen nur auff die werck / vn̄ meynen
wen sie der selben nur vil vnd groß thun / so sey es wol than /
vnd sie frum worden / tzu weylen tzu brechen die kopff / vnd
250 vorterbē yr leyb daruber / das ist eyn grosse torheyt / vnnd
vnuorstandt Christlichs lebens vnd glaubens / das sie on glauben
durch werck frum vnd selig werden wollen . . .
Czum drey vnd tzwentzigsten / darumb sein die tzwen spruch
war / Gutte frume werck machē nymmer mer eyn guten
frūmen man: sonder eyn gut frum man macht gutte frume
werck. Boße werck machen nymmer mer eyn boßen man /
sond' ein boßer man macht boße werck: also das alweg die
person tzuuor muß gut vnd frum sein vor allen guten wercken /
vnnd gute werck folgen vnnd außgehen / von der frūmen guten
260 person. Gleich wie Christus sagt. Ein boßer bawm tregt keyn
gutte frucht. Ein gutter bawm tregt keyn boße frucht. Nun ist
offenbar / das die frucht tragen nicht den bawm / so wachssen
auch die bawm nit auff den fruchten / sonder widerumb / die
bawm tragē die frucht / vnd die frucht wachssen auff den bawmē.
Wie nun die bawm muesßen ehe sein dann die frucht / vnd die
frucht machen nit die bawm wid' gutte noch boße / sonder die
bawm machen die fruchte. Also muß der mēsch in der person
tzuuor frum oder boße sein / ehe er gutte oder boße werck thut.
Vnd seine werck machen yn nit gut od' boß / sond' er macht gute
270 oder boße werck . . . Aber der glaub gleych wie er frum macht /

so macht er auch gute werck. So dan die werck nymāt frum
machē / vn̄ der mēsch tzuuor muß frum sein ehe er wirckt / ßo
ists offenbar das allein der glaub auß lauttern gnaden / durch
Christū vnd sein wort die person gnugsam frum vnd selig
machet. Vnnd das keyn werck / keyn gepot eynē Christen nodt
sey tzu der seligkeyt / sonder er frey ist von allen gepoten / vnd
auß lautterer freyheyt vmbsunst thut / als was er thut / nichts
damit gesucht seines nutzs oder seligkeit. Dan er schon sat vn̄
selig ist durch seinē glaubē / vn̄ gottes gnadē / sond' nur got
darinnē gefallē.   280

Czum .xxiiij. Widerumb dem der on glauben ist / ist keyn
gut werck furderlich tzu der frummigkeyt vnd seligkeyt /
widerūb keyn boße werck yn boße vnd vordāpt machen / sonder
der vnglaub der die person vnd den bawm boß macht der thut
boße vnnd vordampte werck. Darumb wen man frum oder
boße wirt / hebet sichs nit an dē werckē an / sonder an dem
glauben. Wie der weyße man sagt. Anfang aller sund ist von
gotte weichen vnd ym nicht trawen. Also leret auch Christus /
wie man nicht an den wercken muß anheben / vn̄ sagt. Entweder
macht den bawm gut / vn̄ seine frucht gut / oder macht den   290
bawm boße / vnd sein frucht boße. als solt er sagen / wer gutte
frucht habē wil muß tzuuor an dem bawm anheben / vnd den
selben gut setzen. Also wer do wil gutte werck thun / muß nicht
an den wercken anheben / sonder an der person die die werck
thun sol. Die person aber macht nymandt gut / dan alleyn der
glaub / vnnd nymandt macht sie boße / dan alleyn der vnglaub.
Das ist wol war / die werck machen eynen frum oder boße fur
den menschen. das ist / sie tzeygē eusserlich an / wer frum oder
boße sey. Wie Christus sagt Math .vij. Auß yren fruchten sollet
yr sie erkennen . . .   300

Czum .xxvi. Das sey von den wercken gesagt in gemeyn /
vnd die eyn Christen menschē gegen seinem eygen leybe vben
sol. Nun wollen wir von mer wercken sagen / die er gegen
andere menschen thut. Dan der mensch lebt nit allein in seinem
leybe / sonder auch vntter andern menschē auf erden. Darūb
kan er nit on werck sein gegē die selben / er muß yhe mit yn
tzureden vnnd tzuschaffen haben / wie wol ym der selbigen
werck keins nodt ist tzu der frūmigkeyt vnd seligkeyt. Darumb
sol seine meynung in allen wercken frey / vnd nur dahyn
gericht sein / das er andern leuttē damit diene vnnd nutz sey. 310

Nichts anders ym furbilde / dann was den andern nodt ist. das heysset den ein warhafftig Christen leben / vnnd da gehet der glaub mit lust vnd lieb ynß werck / als sant Paulus leret die Galatas . . .

Czū .xxx. Auß dem allē folget der beschluß / das eyn Christen mēsch lebt nit in ym selb / sond' in Christo / vnnd seinē nechsten / in Christo durch den glaubē / im nechstē durch die liebe: durch den glaubē feret er vber sich in got / auß got feret er wider vntter sich durch die liebe / vnd bleibt doch ymmer 320 in got vnnd gotlicher liebe. Gleich wie Christus sagt Johan .i. Jr werdet noch sehen den hymel offen stehen / vnd die engel auff vnd absteigen vber den son des mēschen. Sihe das ist die rechte geistliche / Christliche freyheyt / die das hertz frey macht / von allen sunden / gesetzen / vnd gepotten / welch alle andere freyheit vbertrifft / wie der hymel die erden. Welch geb vns got recht tzuuorsten vnnd behalten. Amen.

4. Luther explains his approach to the task of translating the Bible

Ein Sendbrieff / von Dolmetschen / vnd Fürbitte der Heiligen (1530)

Luther's translation of the New Testament appeared in 1522 (Old Testament in 1534). Although it was only one of a number of translations which were published in Germany in the later fifteenth and early sixteenth centuries (twenty-two vernacular editions between 1483 and 1522), Luther's version naturally attracted immediate attention, partly because of its undoubted linguistic power, but primarily because of Luther's status as a reformer and arch-heretic. Amongst the numerous criticisms which Roman Catholic theologians, notably Cochläus, Faber, and Emser (whose own 'orthodox' translation of 1527 was in fact considerably indebted to Luther's), levelled against Luther's translation was the assertion that Luther had deliberately twisted the meaning of the original in order to make it fit in with his own preconceived ideas. In this connection it was pointed out that he had rendered the text of Romans 3: 28, which in the Latin ran: 'Arbitramur hominem iustificari ex fide absque operibus legis', by 'Wir halten / daß der Mensch gerecht werde on des Gesetzs werck / allein durch den Glauben'. In view of the importance which attached to the relative roles of faith and works in Reformation controversy, this text naturally assumed special significance, and since there was in neither the Latin nor the Greek text an equivalent for '*allein* durch den Glauben', his opponents argued—not without a certain justification—that Luther was perverting the meaning of St. Paul's text. The *Sendbrieff von Dolmetschen* contains Luther's reply to these charges. It was written in 1530 at the Veste Coburg, where Luther had taken up residence in order to be as near as possible to Augsburg during the meeting of the Imperial Diet: as an outlaw he could not safely leave Saxon territory, but in view of the importance of the proceedings (it was here that the famous *Confession*, a succinct statement of the Lutheran position from the pen of Melanchthon, was presented to the emperor), he needed to be available for consultations. The form of the pamphlet—a letter in which Luther explains to a friend his reasons for departing from the strict letter of the original text—is almost certainly not just an essayist's device; such a device would have been foreign to Luther's nature, and we must see in the letter a genuine answer to an actual query, whose propagandist possibilities were exploited only as an afterthought. Rather surprisingly, Luther does not, in the main, base his case on the theology of Justification, but defends his 'mistranslation' in terms of a relativist philosophy of language which, in its exposition of the distinct nature and different spirit of German from Latin, in its assertion that the translator must translate the sense rather than the individual words, and in its establishment of the speech of the common people as the only valid criterion of natural language, constitutes a revolution in linguistic thinking.

Our extract is drawn from the middle section of the pamphlet, after the opening polemic on the theme that 'Papist und Esel sei ein Ding', and before Luther begins to argue *analogia fidei*. The text is that printed by Georg Rhaw of Wittenberg in 1530.

Euch aber vnd den vnsern wil ich anzeigen / warûmb ich das wort (Sola) hab wôllen brauchen / Wiewol Roma .iij. nicht Sola / sondern solum odder tantum von mir gebraucht ist / Also fein sehen die Esel meinen Text an. Aber doch hab ichs sonst anderswo / sola fide gebraucht / vnd wil auch beide Solum vnd Sola haben. Jch hab mich des gevlissen jm dolmetschen / das ich rein vnd klar deudsch geben môchte. Vnd ist vns wol offt begegenet / das wir .xiiij. tage / drey / vier wochen / habē ein einiges wort gesucht vnd gefragt / habens dennoch zu weilen nicht funden. Jm Hiob erbeiten wir also / M. Philips / 10 Aurogallus vnd ich / das wir jnn vier tagen zu weilen kaum drey zeilen kundten fertigen. Lieber / nu es verdeudscht vnd bereit ist / kans ein jeder lesen vnd meistern / Leufft einer itzt mit den augen durch drey odder vier bletter / vnd stôsst nicht ein mal an / wird aber nicht gewar / welche wacken vnd klôtze da gelegen sind / da er jtzt vber hin gehet / wie vber ein gehoffelt bret / da wir haben mûst schwitzen vnd vns engsten / ehe denn wir solche wacken vnd klôtze aus dem wege reumeten / auff das man kûndte so fein daher gehen. Es ist gut pflûgen / wenn der acker gereinigt ist. Aber den wald vnd die stôcke ausrotten / 20 vnd den acker zurichten / da wil niemand an. Es ist bey der

welt kein danck zu verdienen / Kan doch Gott selbs mit der
sonnen / ja mit himel vnd erden / noch mit seines eigen sons
tod / keinen danck verdienen / sie sey vnd bleibe welt des
Teuffels namen / weil sie ja nicht anders wil.

Also habe ich hie Roma .iij. fast wol gewust / das jm Lateinischen vnd Griechischen Text / das wort (Solum) nicht stehet /
vnd hetten mich solchs die Papisten nicht dûrffen leren. War
ists. Diese vier buchstaben S o l a stehen nicht drinnen / welche
30 buchstaben die Eselskôpff ansehen / wie die kue ein new thor /
Sehen aber nicht / das gleichwol die meinung des Texts jnn
sich hat / vnd wo mans wil klar vnd gewaltiglich verdeudschen /
so gehôret es hinein / deñ ich habe Deudsch / nicht Lateinisch
noch Griechisch reden wôllen / da ich deudsch zu reden jm
dolmetschen furgenomen hatte. Das ist aber die art vnser
Deudschen sprache / weñ sich ein rede begibt / von zweien
dingen / der man eins bekennet / vnd das ander verneinet / so
braucht man des worts solum (allein) neben dem wort (nicht
odder kein) Als weñ man sagt / Der Bawr bringt allein korn
40 vnd kein gelt / Jtem / ich hab warlich itzt nicht gelt / sondern
allein korn / Jch hab allein gessen vnd noch nicht getruncken /
Hastu allein geschrieben vnd nicht vberlesen? Vnd der gleichen
vnzeliche weise jnn teglichem brauch.

Jnn diesen reden allen / obs gleich die Lateinische odder
Griechische sprache nicht thut / so thuts doch die Deudsche /
vnd ist jhr art / das sie das wort (Allein) hinzusetzt / auff
das / das wort (nicht odder kein) deste vôlliger vnd deutlicher
sey / Deñ wiewol ich auch sage / Der Bawr bringt korn vnd
kein gelt / So laut doch das wort (kein gelt) nicht so vôllig vnd
50 deutlich / als wenn ich sage / Der Bawr bringt allein korn
vnd kein gelt / vnd hilfft hie das wort (Allein) dem wort (kein)
so viel / das es ein vôllige Deudsche klare rede wird / denn
man mus nicht die buchstaben jnn der Lateinischen sprachen
fragen / wie man sol Deudsch reden / wie diese Esel thun /
Sondern man mus die mutter jhm hause / die kinder auff der
gassen / den gemeinen man auff dem marckt drûmb fragen /
vnd den selbigen auff das maul sehen / wie sie reden / vnd
darnach dolmetschen / so verstehen sie es denn / vnd mercken /
das man Deudsch mit jhn redet.

60 Als wenn Christus spricht / Ex abundantia cordis os loquitur.
Wenn ich den Eseln sol folgen / die werden mir die buchstaben

furlegen / vnd also dolmetschen / Aus dem vberflus des hertzen redet der mund. Sage mir / Jst das deudsch gered? Welcher deudscher verstehet solchs? Was ist vberflus des hertzen fur ein ding? Das kan kein Deudscher sagen / Er wolt denn sagen / es sey das einer allzu ein gros hertz habe / oder zu viel hertzens habe / wiewol das auch noch nicht recht ist / Denn vberflus des hertzen ist kein deudsch / so wenig / als das deudsch ist / Vberflus des hauses / vberflus des kacheloffens / vberflus der banck / Sondern also redet die mutter jm hause vnd der gemein man / Wes das hertz vol ist / des gehet der mund vber / das heist gut deudsch geredt / des ich mich gevlissen / vnd leider nicht allwege erreicht noch getroffen habe / Denn die Lateinischen buchstaben hindern aus der massen seer / gut deudsch zu reden.

Also / wenn der verrheter Judas sagt / Matthei xxvj. Vt quid perditio hec? vnd Marci .xiiij. Vt quid perditio ista vngenti facta est? Folge ich den Eseln vnd buchstabilisten / so mus ichs also verdeudschē / Warûmb ist diese verlierung der salben geschehen? Was ist aber das fur deudsch? Welcher deudscher redet also / Verlierung der salben ist geschehen? Vnd wenn ers wol verstehet / so denckt er / die salbe sey verloren / vnd mûsse sie etwa widder suchen / Wiewol das auch noch tunckel vnd vngewis lautet. Wenn nu das gut deudsch ist / warûmb tretten sie nicht erfur / vnd machen vns ein solch fein / hûbsch / New deudsch Testament / vnd lassen des Luthers Testament ligen? Jch meine ia sie solten jhre kunst an den tag bringen / Aber der deudsche man redet also / Vt quid etc. Was sol doch solcher vnrat? odder was sol doch solcher schade? Jtem / Es ist schade vmb die salbe / Das ist gut deudsch / daraus man verstehet / das Magdalene mit der verschûtten salben sey vnrethlich vmbgangen / vnd habe schaden gethan / das war Judas meinung / denn er gedacht bessern rat damit zu schaffen.

Jtem / da der Engel Mariam grûsset vñ spricht / Gegrûsset seistu Maria vol gnaden / der Herr mit dir. Wolan / so ists bisher schlecht den Lateinischen buchstaben nach verdeudschet / Sage mir aber / ob solchs auch gut deudsch sey? Wo redet der deudsch man also / du bist vol gnaden? Vnd welcher Deudscher verstehet / was gesagt sey / vol gnaden? Er mus dencken an ein fas vol bier / odder beutel vol geldes / Darûmb hab ichs verdeudscht / du holdselige / damit doch ein Deudscher / deste

mehr hin zu kan denckē / was der Engel meinet mit seinem
grus. Aber hie wöllen die Papisten toll werden vber mich / das
ich den Engelischen grus verderbet habe / Wie wol ich dennoch
damit nicht das beste deudsch habe troffen. Vnd hette ich das
beste deudsch hie sollen nemen / vnd den grus also verdeudschen / Gott grûsse dich du liebe Maria (denn so viel wil der
Engel sagen / vnd so wûrde er gered haben / wenn er hette
wöllen sie deudsch grûssen) Jch halt sie solten sich wol selbs
110 erhenckt haben fur grosser andacht / zu der lieben Maria / das
ich den grus so zu nichte gemacht hette.

Aber was frage ich darnach? sie toben odder rasen / Jch wil
nicht wehren / das sie verdeudschen was sie wöllen / Jch wil
aber auch verdeudschen / nicht wie sie wöllen / sondern wie
ich wil / Wer es nicht haben wil / der las mirs stehen / vnd halt
seine meisterschafft bey sich / denn ich wil jhr widder sehen
noch hôren / sie dûrffen fur mein dolmetschen nicht antwort
geben / noch rechenschafft thun / Das hôrestu wol / Jch wil
sagen / Du holdselige Maria / du liebe Maria / vnd lasse sie
120 sagen / Du vol gnaden Maria / Wer Deudsch kan / der weis
wol / welch ein hertzlich fein wort das ist / Die liebe Maria / der
liebe Gott / der liebe Keyser / der liebe Fûrst / der liebe man /
das liebe kind. Vnd ich weis nicht / ob man das wort liebe /
auch so hertzlich vnd gnugsam jnn Lateinischer odder andern
sprachen reden mûge / das also dringe vnd klinge jns hertz /
durch alle sinne / wie es thut jnn vnser sprache . . .

Doch hab ich widderûmb / nicht allzu frey die buchstaben
lassen faren / Sondern mit grossen sorgen / sampt meinen
gehûlffen drauff gesehen / das / wo etwa an einem wort gelegen
130 ist / hab ichs nach den buchstaben behalten / vnd bin nicht so
frey dauon gangen / Als Johan .vj. da Christus spricht / Diesen
hat Gott der Vater versiegelt / da were wol besser deudsch
gewest / diesen hat Gott der Vater gezeichent / odder / diesen
meinet Gott der Vater / Aber ich habe ehe wöllen der deudschen
sprache abbrechen / deñ von dem wort weichen / Ach es ist
dolmetschen ia nicht eines iglichen kunst / wie die tollen heiligen
meinen / Es gehôret dazu ein recht / frum / trew / vleissig /
furchtsam / Christlich / geleret / erfaren / geûbet hertz / Darûmb
halt ich / das kein falscher Christ / noch rotten geist / trewlich
140 dolmetschen kônne / wie das wol scheinet / jnn den Propheten
zu Wormbs verdeudschet / darin doch warlich grosser vleis

geschehen / vnd meinem deudschen fast nach gangen ist / Aber
es sind Jûden dabey gewest / die Christo nicht grosse hulde
erzeigt habē / sonst were kunst vnd vleis gnug da . . .

5. Luther as a practising translator

The Gospel according to St. Matthew 6: 1–7; Psalm 23; The
First Epistle to the Corinthians 13

The general significance of Luther's translation of the Bible has already been
noted (p. xv). The five versions of Matthew 6 reproduced here are intended
to provide an indication of the way Luther translated and the degree to
which his language developed and found acceptance during his lifetime.
Passage (a) reproduces the text of the Vulgate. Passage (b) reproduces the
text published by Anton Koburger of Nürnberg in 1483; it derives from the
first German printed Bible published by Johann Mentel of Augsburg in
1461, which in turn derives from a late fourteenth-century rendering. As a
piece of German, it is clumsy and clings anxiously to the Latin to the point
where it does violence to the German: 'facis elemosynam, noli tuba canere
ante te' becomes 'so du thust eī almusen. nit wolst singen vor dir mit dem
horn', 'in abscondito' becomes 'ī verborgen', etc. By contrast Luther's
Septembertestament of 1522 (passage (c)) moves freely and naturally: idioms
such as 'noli tuba canere ante te' are not merely transposed, but are replaced
by a German equivalent 'solltu nitt lassen fur dyr posaunen' and the needs
of German grammar and syntax are observed, as well as the euphony and
balance of the sentence—even to the point of inserting words: 'wirt dyr*s*
vergelten *offentlich*' = 'reddet tibi'. Passage (d) is taken from the 'Ausgabe
letzter Hand' of Luther's translation (1545) and does little more than
modernize the orthography—although the two modifications ('an den ecken
auff den gassen' becomes 'an den ecken *vnd* auff den Gassen' and 'bete zu
deynem vater verporgen' becomes 'bete zu deinem Vater *im* verborgen') bear
witness to that never-ceasing concern with the minutiae of sense and sentence rhythm which elsewhere was to produce more striking changes.
Passage (e) is taken from Johann Eck's translation, which was published in
Ingolstadt in 1537. It was based to a certain extent on Emser's 'orthodox'
translation of 1527—which in turn drew on Luther's (cf. p. 34). This is not
to say, however, that it does not exhibit a certain independence from Luther.
As well as differing from Luther in its Upper German forms (*ů* and the
spellings in *ai* are retained, as is 'stand' = 'stehen', while 'vil geschwâtz
treiben' is preferred to 'plappern', etc.), it offers a number of alternative
renderings not conditioned by dialectal considerations. In preferring 'kain
lohn haben' to the more euphonious 'den lohn dahin haben', for instance,
Eck was nearer to modern usage than his rival, and his 'Sehet euch für' is
also probably a better equivalent for 'attendite' than Luther's 'Habt acht'.
Significantly, however, Eck prefers 'gleißner' as an equivalent for 'hypocritae', whereas Luther's 'heuchler' was to become standard. Equally

significant is Eck's literal approach, which can produce un-German expressions, and his corresponding unwillingness to insert words and fill out his text in the interests of style: he retains the literal and somewhat unnatural 'gerechtigkait nit thût' as an equivalent for 'justitiam faciatis' (although 'gerehtecheit' in MHG *could* mean a legally fixed financial contribution), and there is in his version no equivalent for Luther's 'offentlich'. Where there is no risk of adding to or modifying the scriptural text, Eck has, however, tended to succumb to Luther's influence. It is highly unlikely that he would have arrived independently at such renderings as 'solt du nit lassen vor dir pusanen: wie die gleißner thô in jhren schûlen' or 'dan sie mainen / sie werden erhôret / wan sie vil wort machen', and in spite of their South German garb few passages in Eck's New Testament can deny their indebtedness to Martin Luther.

Luther's claim to unique greatness as a Bible translator does not rest so much on the influence he exerted on others, however, as on the excellence of his translation as a work of literature in its own right, and passages (*f*) and (*g*), which reproduce the 23rd Psalm and 1 Corinthians 13 from the edition of 1545, exemplify Luther's ability to write prose which, in its rhythm and balance, in its dignity and euphonious strength, has been equalled by very few German writers and surpassed by none.

(*a*) Attendite ne iustitiam uestram faciatis coram hominibus ut uideamini ab eis: alioquin mercedem non habebitis apud Patrem uestrum qui in caelis est.

Cum ergo facis elemosynam, noli tuba canere ante te, sicut hypocritae faciunt in synagogis et in uicis, ut honorificentur ab hominibus: amen dico uobis, receperunt mercedem suam. Te autem faciente elemosynam nesciat sinistra tua quid faciat dextera tua: ut sit elemosyna tua in abscondito: et Pater tuus qui uidet in abscondito reddet tibi.

10 Et cum oratis non eritis sicut hypocritae, qui amant in synagogis et in angulis platearum stantes orare, ut uideantur ab hominibus: amen dico uobis, receperunt mercedem suam. Tu autem cum orabis, intra in cubiculum tuum: et clauso ostio tuo ora Patrem tuum in abscondito: et Pater tuus qui uidet in abscondito reddet tibi. Orantes autem nolite multum loqui sicut ethnici: putant enim quia in multiloquio suo exaudiantur. Nolite ergo adsimilari eis: scit enim Pater uester quibus opus sit uobis ante quam petatis eum.

(*b*) Hutet euch. das ir ewere gerechtigkeit icht thut vor dē mēschen. das ir werdt gesehē vō in. oder ir habt nit lons bey ewerm vater. der in den hymeln. ist.

darūb so du thust eī almusen. nit wolst singen vor dir mit dem

horn. als die gleychsner thun in den synagogen. vñ in den gassen.
das sy werden geeret von den menschen. Fûrwar sag ich euch.
sie haben empfangen iren lon.
wañ so du gibst eī almusen. Es sol nit wissen deī lincke hand. was
dings thu dein gerechte. das dein almusen sein in verborgen.
vnd dein vater. der es siht in verborgen. d' vergilt dir.   10
Vñ so ir betetet nit werdet als die gleychsner. die da lieb haben
steend zubeten in den synagogē. vñ in dē winckeln der gassen.
daz sie werden gesehen von den mēschen. Fûrwar sag ich euch.
sy habē empfangen irē lone.
Aber so du betest. so gee in dein kamer. vñ beschlewß dein tûr.
vnd bet zu deim vater in verborgen. vñ dein vater. der es siht ī
verborgen. vergilt dir.
Vñ so ir betet. nicht wôlt vil reden als die ethnici thun. wañ
sie wenen. dz sie werden erhôrt in irē vil reden.
darūb nicht wôlt ī werden gleych. wañ ewer vater weyst. wz 20
euch not ist. ee deñ ir in bittet.

(c) Habt acht auff ewr almoßen / das yhr die nitt gebet /
fur den leutten / das yhr vonn yhn gesehen werdet / yhr habt
anders keynen lohn bey ewrm vatter ym hymel / wenn du nu
almosen gibst / solltu nitt lassen fur dyr posaunen / wie die
heuchler thun yn yhren schulen vñ auff den gassen / auff dz sie
von den leutē gepreysset werden / warlich / ich sage euch / sie
haben yhrn lohn dahyn.
Wenn du aber almosen gibst / so laß deyne lincke hand nitt
wissen / was die rechte thut / auff das deyn almosen verporge
sey / vñ deyn vatter / der ynn das verborgen sihet / wirt dyrs 10
vergelten offentlich.
Vnnd weñ du bettist / soltu nitt seyn / wie die heuchler / die da
gerne stehen vnnd beten ynn den schulen / vnd an den ecken
auff den gassen / auff das sie von den leuten gesehen werden /
warlich / ich sage euch / sie habē yhrn lohn dahyn /
Wenn aber du bettist / so gehe yñ deyn kemerleyn / vnnd
schleuß die thur zu / vnnd bete zu deynem vater verporgen /
vnnd deyn vatter / der yn das verporgen sihet / wirt dyrs
vergelten offentlich.
Vnnd wenn yhr betet / sollt yhr nitt viel plappern / wie die 20
heyden / deñ sie meynen / sie werden erhoret / weñ sie viell
wortt machē /

darumb solt yhr euch yhn nit gleychen / Ewer vatter weyß /
was yhr bedurfft / ehe dann yhr yhn bittet /

(*d*) Habt acht auff ewer Almosen / das jr die nicht gebt fur den
Leuten / das jr von jnen gesehen werdet / Jr habt anders keinen
Lohn bey ewerm Vater im Himel.
Wenn du nu Almosen gibst / soltu nicht lassen fur dir posaunen /
wie die Heuchler thun / in den Schulen vnd auff den gassen /
Auff das sie von den Leuten gepreiset werden / Warlich ich sage
euch / sie haben jren Lohn dahin.
Wenn du aber Almosen gibst / So las deine lincke hand nicht
wissen / was die rechte thut / Auff das dein Almosen verborgen
10 sey / vnd dein Vater / der in das verborgen sihet / wird dirs
vergelten öffentlich.
Vnd wenn du betest / Soltu nicht sein wie die Heuchler / die da
gerne stehen vnd beten in den Schulen / vnd an den ecken vnd
auff den Gassen / Auff das sie von den Leuten gesehen werden.
Warlich ich sage euch / sie haben jren lohn dahin.
Wenn aber du betest / So gehe in dein Kemmerlin / vnd
schleus die thür zu / vnd bete zu deinem Vater im verborgen
vnd dein Vater / der in das verborgen sihet / wird dirs vergelten
öffentlich.
20 Vnd wenn jr betet / solt jr nicht viel plappern / wie die Heiden /
Denn sie meinen / sie werden erhöret / wenn sie viel wort
machen.
Darumb solt jr euch jnen nicht gleichen / Ewer Vater weis /
was jr bedürffet / ehe denn jr jn bittet.

(*e*) Sehet euch für / das jhr ewer gerechtigkait nit thüt vor den
menschen / auf das jhr võ jnē gesehen / sunst werdet jhr kain
lohn haben bei ewerm vater / der im himel ist.
Darum so du almůsen gibst / solt du nit lassen vor dir pusanen:
wie die gleißner thõ in jhren schůlen / vnd auf den gassen / auf
das sie von den leütten gepreißt werden / Warlich sag ich euch /
sie haben jhren lohn schon eingenumen.
Du aber wan du almůsen gibst / so laß dein lincke hand nit
wissen was die rechte thůt / auf das dein almůsen verborgen sei /
10 Vnd dein Vater / der in das verborgen sihet / würdt dirs vergelten.
Vnd so jhr båtet / solt jhr nit sein wie die gleißner / die
da gern stand / vnd båten in den schůlen / vnd an den ecken

der gassen / auf das sie von den leüten gesehen werdē / Warlich
ich sag euch / sie haben jhren lohn schon empfangen.

Du aber / wan du bâtest / so gang in dein kâmerlein / vñ
schleüß die thür zů / vnd bâte zů deinem vater verborgen / vnd
dein vater der in das verbor(gen) sihet / würdt dirs vergelten.

Wan jhr aber bâtet / solt jhr nit vil geschwâtz treiben / wie die
Haiden / dan sie mainen / sie werden erhôret / wan sie vil wort 20
machen /

darum solt jhr euch jhn nit gleichen / Dann ewer vater
waißt / was euch von nôten ist ee dan jhr jhn bittet /

(*f*) Der HERR ist mein Hirte / Mir wird nichts mangeln.
Er weidet mich auff einer grûnen Awen / Vnd fûret mich zum
frisschen Wasser.
Er erquicket meine Seele / er fûret mich auff rechter Strasse /
Vmb seines Namens willen.
Vnd ob ich schon wandert im finstern Tal / fûrchte ich kein
Vnglûck / Denn du bist bey mir / Dein Stecken vnd Stab
trôsten mich.
Du bereitest fur mir einen Tisch gegen meine Feinde / Du
salbest mein Heubt mit ôle / Vnd schenckest mir vol ein.   10
Gutes vnd Barmhertzigkeit werden mir folgen mein leben lang /
Vnd ich werde bleiben im Hause des HERRN jmerdar.

(*g*) Wenn ich mit Menschen vnd mit Engel zungen redet / vnd
hette der Liebe nicht / So were ich ein donend Ertz oder eine
klingende Schelle. Vnd wenn ich weissagen kûndte / vnd wûste
alle Geheimnis / vnd alle Erkentnis / vnd hette allen Glauben /
also / das ich Berge versetzte / vnd hette der Liebe nicht / So
were ich nichts. Vnd wenn ich alle meine Habe den Armen
gebe / vnd liesse meinen Leib brennen / vnd hette der Liebe
nicht / So were mirs nichts nûtze.

Die Liebe ist langmûtig vnd freundlich / die liebe eiuert
nicht / die liebe treibt nicht mutwillen / sie blehet sich nicht / sie 10
stellet nicht vngeberdig / sie sûchet nicht das jre / sie lesset
sich nicht erbittern / sie tracht nicht nach schaden / sie frewet
sich nicht der vngerechtigkeit / sie frewet sich aber der warheit /
Sie vertreget alles / sie gleubet alles / sie hoffet alles / sie duldet
alles. Die Liebe wird nicht mûde / Es mûssen auffhôren die
Weissagungen / vnd auffhôren die Sprachen / vnd das Erkentnis
wird auch auffhôren.

Denn vnser wissen ist stückwerck / vnd vnser Weissagen ist
stückwerck. Wenn aber komen wird das volkomen / so wird
20 das stückwerck auffhören. Da ich ein Kind war / da redet ich
wie ein kind / vnd war klug wie ein kind / vnd hatte kindische
anschlege. Da ich aber ein Man ward / that ich abe was
kindisch war. Wir sehen itzt durch einen Spiegel in einem tun-
ckeln wort / Denn aber von angesicht zu angesichte. Jtzt er-
kenne ichs stücksweise / Denn aber werde ich erkennen gleich
wie ich erkennet bin. Nu aber bleibt Glaube / Hoffnung / Liebe /
diese drey / Aber die Liebe ist die grössest vnter jnen.

6. The reaction to Luther

(i) Hieronymus Emser rejects the doctrine of the Priesthood of
All Believers and Luther's view of the papacy

*Wid' das vnchristenliche buch Martini Luters Augustiners / an den
Tewtschen Adel außgangen* (1521)

Although not as forceful as Johann Mair von Eck, who wrote mostly in
Latin, or as penetrating as Thomas Murner (cf. p. 45), Hieronymus Emser
(1477–1527) is usually held to be one of the most effective spokesmen of
the Roman Catholic Church during the early years of the Reformation. He
was born at Ulm and studied classics, law, and theology at Tübingen and
Erfurt, before moving to Leipzig as secretary to the reigning Duke George.
(Saxony was divided between two branches of the Wettin family, the older
branch holding the electoral dignity, the younger simply bearing the ducal
title. The former was to become Protestant, the latter remained Catholic.)
Emser knew Luther personally and until 1519 apparently enjoyed good
relations with him. The public disputation held between Eck and Luther
at Leipzig in that year, however, marks a turning-point in their relationship,
and when Emser, following Eck, suggested in an open letter that Luther was
supporting the Hussite cause, Luther responded with a polemic which led
to an exchange of increasingly acrimonious pamphlets. Luther's appeal to
the secular authorities in *An den christlichen Adel* (1520) precipitated a further
series of exchanges on the subject of the Priesthood of All Believers, the
primacy of the Pope, and the nature of the mass, in which Emser, although
outclassed, doggedly continued to defend the Roman position. It was, however, as a result of his attacks on Luther's translation of the New Testament
(1522) that Emser achieved a measure of permanent fame. He claimed to
have found no less than 1,400 errors in Luther's version, and at the suggestion of his princely patron, Duke George, proceeded to publish his own
translation in 1527. In spite of the efforts of certain modern scholars to
justify him as a translator, there is no doubt that his rendering is heavily

indebted to Luther's (cf. Eck's version (p. 34) which follows Emser), a fact which Luther duly and contemptuously recorded in the *Sendbrieff von Dolmetschen.*

Our extract is taken from *Wid' das vnchristenliche buch Martini Luters,* which constitutes Emser's reply to *An den christlichen Adel.* Emser's technique is simple: he lets Luther speak for himself, quoting verbatim, and then produces his own counter-arguments.

The text is taken from the edition of 1521, which appeared in Leipzig under a fictitious imprint.

Luter.

Die Romanisten haben drey mauren mith grosser behendigkeyt vmb sich getzogen / da durch sie sich her beschûtzt / das sie nyemandt hat môgen reformiren / dadurch die gantze Christenheit greulich gefallen ist.

Emßer.

Was die vrsach sey darumb die Christenheit ßo greulich gefallen / hab ich obangeregt / als nemlich das dye gôttlich forcht / Bruderliche lieb vnd trau / so gar bey vns allen erloschen ist / wyr seyen geistlich oder weltlich Edel oder vnedel / Das aber Luter hie vorwendet von dreyen maurn d' Romanisten hatt er fulleycht genomen auß Virgilio dem heidischen Poeten / der von der helle saget Eneidos .vi. triplici circundata muro / Dann in der heiligen schrifft / find ich von den mauren nicht / die er mauren getoeffet hatt / Wol weiß ich ein spruch des Herren do er saget Esaie lxij. vber deyne Mauren Jerusalem hab ich gesatzt huter / den gantzen tag vnnd die gantzen nacht werdenn sie nicht stilschweigen Disen hutern oder wechtern / das ist den heiligen Enngeln getraw ich wol sie werden die Mauren der Christenheit vor Lutern wol bewaren Vñ dem Romischē stul sampt gemeyner pristerschafft yr freyheit / macht / vnd oberkeyt / die ynen Got selber gegeben / so gantz nicht entfrombdē lassen / Das sie aber tzimlicher weiß reformirt werden / ist mir ouch nitt entgegen / vnd (die warheit tzubekēnen) gemeyner Christenheit gros von nôten / . . .

Luter.

Man hats erfunden das Bapst / Bischoff prister / Clostervolck wirt der geistlich stand genant / Fursten / Herrē / Hantwerchleut vnd ackerleut / der Weltlich städt wôlchs gar eyn feyn coment oder gleyssen ist. Doch soll nyemant darub schuchter

werden / dann alle Christen seint warhafftig geistlichs standes /
vnnd ist vnter yn keyn vnderscheid / dan des amptshalben.

Emßer.

30 Hie betriegt Luter die eynfeltigen leyen mit der Logica / in
dem wortlin geistlich / wolches equiuocum ist / vnd auß mangel
Teutschen getzeinges / aleyn / dreierley bedeutung tragen muß /
deren yetwedern ym latein ein sunder wortlin auffgesatzt / als
namlich ecclesiasticus / spiritalis / vnd religiosus / Dann deren
yetweders / wyrt vorteutschet geistlich secundum cōmunem
vsum loquendi Germanorum omniū. Es ist aber gar ein grosser
vnterscheyd / Dann / ecclesiastici synt die geystlichen / die der
kirchen heupter / glider vnd dyner synt / von der kirchen yren
enthalt / vnd was die kirchē belangt tzuorden / gebieten vñd
40 vorbieten / tzu binden vnd entbinden haben / als Bapst /
Bischoff / prister vnd alle geweichten personē der kirchen / vnd
der bedeutung nach ist Luters beschlus falsch vnd comittirt
fallaciam equiuocationis so er spricht es seyen alle Christen
warhafftig geystlich oder geystlichs standes / Dann es synt vill
Chrysten vñ namlich alle leyen dy yn der kirchen vñ was die
selbē belanget weder tzu binden noch tzuentbinden / weder
tzu thon noch tzu schaffen haben / vnd yn dem fall nicht
vor geistlich sonder vor weltlich personen gehalten werdē /
wolches nit eyn coment oder gleissen / sonder der gemeyn
50 altherkomen / brauch ist in der Christenlichen kyrchen / darauff
alle Bepstliche vnd keyßerliche Recht sich grunden / vnd
tzwischen dißen beiden stenden tzu erhaltung frides vnd
bruderlicher eyntracht vnderschidlich ordnung vnd satzungen
gestalth haben / Wie dann Christus dißen vnterscheyd selber
ouch gemacht / in dem / das er den Aposteln hohern gewalt /
andere gebot / vnd mher heymlichs vorstandes vnd außlegūg der
schryfft dann dem gemeinen volck gegeben hat / wie ich yn
meiner vorred angetzeyget vnd der heylig Matheus betzeuget
eiusdem xiij. Derhalben nicht alleyn amptzhalbenn ßonder
60 auch des stādes halbē der do stat auff pristerlicher wyrd vnd
weichung von got selber eingesetzt (wo wyr anders der Chri-
stēlichen kirchen gleuben vñ vns die ketzer nit vorfūren lassen
wollen) gar eyn mercklich vnderscheyd ist tzwischen den
geystlichen vnnd den weltlichen / Dann das ampt volget dem
stand / vnd nicht der stant dem ampt / vñ ist eyn ytzlicher tzu

dem ampt vorpflicht / das sein stand eruordert als die prister
tzu beten / der adel tzu beschutzen / vñ das gemein volck tzu
arbeiten . . .

Luter

Darumb so ist des Bischoffs weyhen nit anderst dann als wen
er an stat vnd person der gantzen Samlung eynen auß dem 70
hauffen nheme / die all geleiche gewalt haben vñ ym beuelhe
die selbē gewalt vor die andern außtzurichten /

Emser

Hie setzt Luter aber tzwen grobe feler / Orstlich das d'
bischoff die prister weyhe an der Stat vnd person der gantzē
gemeyn oder Samlung / Czum andern das die auß der samlung
desselben aleinn durch yren beuel all gleichen gewalt haben
weliches beyder seyt erlogen ist Dann der bischoff weyhet die
prister nitt an stat der gemeyn / sonder an Gotes stadt / dartzu
ist nye gehort noch erfaren vō der tzeit Christi bis auff disen tag
das die leyen einichen prister gemacht / oder tzu weihen macht 80
gehabt hetten / Sonder Cristus als der oberst vnd orste prister
des nawen testaments von dem Wie oben vormeldet all pristerschafft herflußt / hat orstlich geweyhet die heiligen Apostel /
Die apostel Mathiam / Paulū / Policarpū / Jgnatiū / vnd ander /
Paulus Dionysiū Titum / Thimotheū vñ ander / darnach ye
einer den andern bis auff dise stund / das die leyen nye nichtzit
damit tzu thon gehabt . . .

Luter

Die ander mauer ist noch loser vnd vntuchtiger / das sie alein
wollen meister in der schrifft sein / ob sie schon yr lebē lang
nichtzit darynn lernen. 90

Emßer.

Diße mawer ist ßo starck vnd grundtfest / das sie weder Luter
noch lucifer vmbstossen wirt / Dann wann ein ytzlicher fantast
die schrifft seins gefallens deuten mocht wie er wolt / wurd sie
mehr synn kriegen / dann hydra heupter hat / vñ wyr der
sachen nymͪer eins werden / das aber Luter die tzu Rom so vor
vngelert halt macht alleyn seyn hochtrabender geist der in also
vorwenet hat / als wer er allein der klugest auff erden . . .

Luter

Darumb ists ein freuel erdicht fabel vnnd mogen ouch keinen
buchstaben auffbringen / damit sie bewerē das des bapsts alein
100 sey die schrifft außtzulegen / oder yr außlegūg tzu bestetigen /
Sie haben ynen die gewalt selbs genomen /

Emßer

Diße fabel das nyemant die schrifft außlegen soll dann der
Bapst / hat Luter selber erticht / dann die Christenliche kirch
weret keynem die schrifft aus tzu legen der das tzil der alten
Christenlichen lerer nicht vberschreit / Also betzeuget Augu-
stinus epl'a lix ad paulinum / vnd spricht Es ist nutz das vber
die finsterheit der heyligen schrifft / die got vns zu vbung (also
tunckel vnd vorborgen haben wollen) vilerlei meinungen gefunden werden / So eyn yeder seyn beduncke sagt / Doch das
110 yr aller meynung dem glauben vnd Christenlicher ler nicht
entgegen sey / Dergleiche schreybt auch Gregorius in registro
li. iij. cap. ci. also sprechende / in dem vorstand der heyligen
schrifft soll nichtzit vorworffen werden / das dem rechten
Christenlichen glouben nicht wider ist / Dann gleich wie aus
eim einige gold / einer guldin kette der ander ring oder ander
geschmuck macht / also findenn ouch die außleger / aus einer
schrifft manicherlei vorstand die do al diene tzu schmuck vn
tzier der braut Cristi dz ist d' heylige christeliche kirche Doch so
sol keiner sein selbs meynug oder außlegūg vor die best halte /
120 sie werde dan vo der Christenlichen kirchen vor gut erkent vnd
angenome Der halben so haben die Christelichen lerer / so yn
was tieffs in der schrifft vorgefallen / dasselbig alwegen dem
Romische stul vorbehalten / Oder so sie gleich was da vo
geschribe / der Romischen kirche vnderworffen / als der meister-
in vn regel des gloubens / die ouch Ciprianus lib. iiij. epl'a. viij.
nennet ein mutter vnd wurtzel der Christelichen kirchen /
wolchen gewalt ym der Bapst nicht selbs genomen sonder von
got hat . . .

Luter

Es ist offenbar gnug / das die schlussel nith alien Sant Petro /
130 sonder der gantzen gemeind geben sint /

Emßer

Sie sint der gantzen gemeind tzu trost vnnd tzu gut geben /

das ynen damit allen der himel auffgeschlossen werden sol. Aber nit / das sie ynen selbs auffschliessen / sollen oder mugen / als wenig als sich die schaff / on ein hirtten selbs weyden mogen / Das aber Christus nicht aleyn vor Petrum sonder vor vns all gebeten hab / das konnen wir al wol erleyden vnd hor niemant der das anfecht /

Luter

Denck doch bey dir selber Sie mussen bekennen das frõme Christen vnder vns sein / Warumb wolt man den der selben wort vnd vorstand vorwerffen.   140

Emßer

Jst doch ein Esel ouch from / man trawet ym aber dan nocht nit vber die silberkamer / sonder stelt yn in ein stall / Also wiewol ich weiß das ouch etzliche leyen in der heiligē schrifft bas erfarn sint dann mancher prister oder Doctor der Theologey Noch weißt vns Got nit an die leyen / sonder an die prister Malachie .ij. Die lyppen des pristers bewaren die kunst / vnd sie sollen das gesetz fragen oder lernē auß seynem mundt / dan er ist ein engel der spitz des herrē /

Luter

Es muß ye nicht aleyn der Bapst recht haben / ßo der artickel recht ist Jch glewb ein heilige Christēliche kirchē /   150

Emßer.

Die weil der Bapst das oberste glid der Christenlichē kirchē / so darff man (ßo mā die Christelich kirch geleubt) in bapst nicht sonder gleuben / dann wo die fies sint do ist ouch das haupt / vnd wo die Christenlich kirch / do ist der bapst mit eingetzelt quia vbi totū ibi etiā pars est Darūb so trißhet Luter hie ein ler strou . . .

Luter

Die dritte mauer fellet von yr selber nider / wo dise orste tzwu fallen /

Emßer

Dise maur haben vil ersteigen wollen / die den hals dar uber abgefallen sint / Doch gleich wie Lutter beschliesset / wo die andern tzwu fallen / so falle die võ yr selber hynach / Also wil 160

ich a contrario wider yn beschliessen / Die weil die andern
tzwu maurn noch nith gefallen / vnd nyᵐher mher fallen werden
mogen / ẞo bleibt dise ouch wol bestendigk /

Luter

Sie haben ouch keynen grund der schrifft das aleyn dem
Bapst gepurt ein cōciliū tzu beruffen dan alein yr eigē gesetz.

Emßer.

Es beruffet nyemandt die reichsteg dann der Keißer / so ist
nichtzit bindig was eyn Rat beschußt / es werde dann vom
Fursten bestet vnd bekrefftiget / Warumb solt dann d' Bapst an
Gotes stat die macht ouch nicht haben bey den Concilien?
170 Oder warumb solten der geistlichen recht nith gelten darumb
das sie die selber gesetzt / so doch ein ytzliche stat macht hat yr
selbs eigen recht vnd weychvild tzu setzē tzu dem ẞo geben die
geistlichen recht tzu wo sich ein Bapst forchtet vor eim concilio vnd wolt das nicht beruffen / das als dann die Cardinel das
tzu beruffen macht haben / wye dñs Alexandrinus post alios
saget in c. si Papa di .xxxx.

Luter.

So lesen wyr actuū quinto das der Apostel cōciliū nith Sant
Peter hat beruffen Sond' all apostel vñ die eltisten.

Emßer.

Luter thut der geschrifft hie gewalt / Dann der text nith sagt
180 wer das concilium beruffen hab / Sond' das ein tzweyung tzu
Antiochia vnder denn brudern erwachsen sey von wegen der
beschneydung / Derhalben sich Paulus vñ Barnabas erhaben
vnnd gen Jerusalem kōmen die Apostel da selbst rattzufragen
wie sie sich in dem halten solten / vō welchen sie empfangen /
vnd als sie bey einander versamelt geweßt / die Apostel vnd
eltisten / Haben etzlich pharisey geraten mann sol die Heiden
ouch beschneyden / Do sey Petrus auffgestanden vnd angefangen
tzu reden / wie do selbs der text meldet / vnd darnach Jacobus
sant Peters meynung tzugefallē vñ die bekrefftiget mit der
190 schryfft. Dieweil dan in eim itzlichē rat der ẟrstlich redet der
den Rat beruffet / als der Burgemeister in eyner stat / Od' eyn
Furst an seym hoff So er seine Ret tzu samen vordert / vnnd yn

orstlich ertzelet warumb er sie beschickt vnd was die sach sey /
Szo ist mher tzu glouben / Das sant Peter der tzum ŏrsten auffgestanden vnd von der sach beschließlich geredt / das concilium
auch tzusamen gevordert hab / Dann das Luter ab auctoritate
negatiue sagt / Sant Peter hab es nicht beruffen / vnd ym fal ob
das gleich Jacobus als der bischoff des ortes beruffen / so het
er doch das vngetzweiuelt gethan auff beuelh Petri als des
obersten / Welches auß dem erscheynet / das Petrus die ersten 200
stym gehabt / vnd Jacobus erst nach Petro sein meynung dartzu
gesagt / Wie der text clerlich außdruckt / Darumb so ist der
selbs ein Ertzketzer / der sagen darff / wo es sant Peter beruffen
het wer es nith ein Christēlich concilium sonder ein ketzerisch
conciliabulum gewest / Dann Gerson der beweist / klarlich das
Petrus sein primat vnd oberkeit nith von den aposteln sonder
von Gott gehabt / Darumb yn dann alle lerer krichisch vñ
lateinisch nennen ein fursten der apostel / Warumb solt das
dann ein ketzerisch conciliabulū sein / das er alß der furst der
andern beruffen het? . . . 210

Luter

Auch wann ich ansehe die concilia die d' Bapst gemaht hat /
fint ich nicht sonders das darinnen ist außgericht.

Emßer

Wan die Bepst in yren concilien nicht mher aus gericht dann
das sie ßo mancherley teufelischler ketzerey außgeroden / ßo
hetten sie der Christenheit nicht wenig gefrommet. Aber ketzerey
ist nichtzit ßonders bey Lutern / dann er von iuget damit vmb
gegangen / vnd das gifft lang vorhin bey ym vorsamelt hat / sust
wer ym ouch vnmoglich souil ketzerischer bucher auff ein
hauffen herauß tzuschutten . . .

(ii) Albrecht Dürer bewails the alleged death of Luther

Tagebuch der Reise in die Niederlande (1521)

Albrecht Dürer (1471–1528) is remembered primarily as the greatest of the
German Renaissance painters, but he also produced a considerable body of
writings, including a few lyric poems, numerous letters, and a number of
technical works on draughtsmanship and aesthetics. Our extract is taken
from the journal he kept during his visit to the Netherlands (1520–1). The
purpose of the journey was to appeal to the new Emperor, Charles V, for

the renewal of the pension granted to him by Maximilian I (d. 1519), but the richness of Dutch painting and the royal welcome extended to him, as well as his own interest in new countries, prompted him to stay longer than was absolutely necessary for the accomplishment of his purpose.

Our text is that established by H. Rupprich, *Dürer: Schriftlicher Nachlaß* (Berlin, 1956).

17.5.1521 Jtem am freÿtag vor Pfingsten im 1521 jahr kamen mir mehr geng Antorff, das man Marthin Luther so verrätherlich gefangen hett. Dann do in des kaisers Carols herolt mit dem kaÿserlichen glait war zu geben, dem ward vertrauet. Aber so bald in der heroldt bracht beÿ Eÿßenach in ein unfreundlich orth, saget [er], er dörffte sein nit mehr, und ritt von ihm. Als bald waren 10 pferd do, die fürten verrätherlich den verkaufften frommen, mit dem heÿligen geist erleuchteten mahn hinweg, der do war ein nachfolger Christj vnd deß wahren christlichen
10 glaubens. Und lebt er noch oder haben sie jn gemördert, das ich nit weiß, so hat er das gelitten umb der christlichen wahrheit willen und umb das er gestrafft hat das unchristliche pabstumb, das do strebt wieder Christus freÿ lassung mit seiner grossen beschwerung der menschlichen gesecz, und auch darumb, das wir unsers bluth und schweiß also beraubt und außgezogen werden und daselb so schandlich von müssiggehendem volck lesterlich verzehret wird, und die durftigen krancken menschen darrumb hungers sterben müßen. Und sonderlich ist mir noch das schwerest, das uns gott villeicht noch unter ihrer falschen
20 blinden lehr will lassen bleiben, die doch die menschen, die sie vätter nennen, erdicht und auffgeseczt haben, dardurch uns das göttlich worth an viel enden fälschlich außgelegt wird, oder gar nichts fürgehalten . . . Darumb sehe ein jeglicher, der do Doctor Martin Luthers bücher list, wie sein lehr so klar durchsichtig ist, so er das heilig evangelium furth. Darumb sind sie in grosen ehren zu halten und nit zuverbrennen; es wer dann, das man sein wiederpahrt, die alle zeit die wahrheit wieder fächten, jns feuer würff mit allen jhren opinionen, die do auß menschen götter machen wollen, aber doch, das man
30 wieder neuer luterische bücher truck hett. O Gott, ist Luther todt, wer wird uns hinfürt das heilig evangelium so clar fürtragen! Ach Gott, was hett er uns noch in 10 oder 20 jahrn schreiben mögen! O ihr alle fromme christen menschen, helfft mir fleissig bewainen diesen gott geistigen menschen und ihn

bitten, das er uns ein andern erleuchten mann send. O Erasme
Roderadame, wo wiltu bleiben? Sieh, was vermag die vngerecht
tÿranneÿ der weltlichen gewahlt vnd macht der finsternüß!
Hör, du ritter Christj, reith hervor neben den herrn Christum,
beschücz die warheit, erlang der martärer cron! Du bist doch
sonst ein altes meniken. Jch hab von dir gehört, das du dir selbst 40
noch 2 jahr zugeben hast, die du noch tügest, etwas zu thun.
Die selben leg wohl an, dem evangelio und dem wahren christlichen glauben zu gut, und laß dich dann hören, so werden der
höllen porten, der römisch stuhl, wie Christus sagt, nit wieder
dich mügen. Und ob du hie gleich förmig deinem maister
Christo würdest und schand von den lügnern jn dieser zeit
leidest und darumb ein klein zeit desto eher stürbest, so wirstu
doch ehe aus dem todt ins leben kommen und durch Christum
clarificirt. Dann so du auß dem kelch trinckest, denn er
getruncken hat, so wirstu mit ihm regiren und richten mit 50
gerechtigkeit, die nitt weißlich gehandelt haben. O Erasme,
halt dich hie, das sich gott dein rühme, wie vom Davidt
geschrieben stehet; dann du magst thun, und fürwar, du magst
den Golliath fellen. Dann gott gestehet beÿ der heÿligen christlichen kirchen, wie er ja unter den Römischen stehet, nach
seinem göttlichen willen. Der helff uns zu der ewigen seeligkeit,
gott vatter, sohn und heiliger geist, ein einiger gott. Amen.

(iii) Thomas Murner mocks Luther's view of the sacraments

*Von dem grossen Lutherischen Narren wie in doctor Murner beschworen
hat* (1522)

Amongst the numerous Roman Catholic replies to Luther which sought to
refute his errors point by point—often at great length and with a formidable
display of learning—perhaps the most appealing, and certainly the most
amusing, is that contained in Thomas Murner's satire *Von dem grossen
Lutherischen Narren wie in doctor Murner beschworen hat*. Here Murner abandons
the learned style and the subtle arguments which characterize his numerous
anti-Lutheran pamphlets (32 between 1519 and 1522) for the robust laugh-
ter of his earlier moral satires (cf. p. 105). Difficulties with the printer and
the Strassburg censors prevented the poem from achieving the popularity
it deserved, but the work subsumes most of the attitudes of Roman theologians, albeit in a somewhat scurrilous fashion. This scurrility is, however,
not untypical of much sixteenth-century controversy.

Murner's sprawling mock epic, rich in references to the author's previous
career and to contemporary controversy, falls into three main parts. In the

opening chapters Murner appears as the learned exorcist of the *Narren-beschwörung* who conjures the follies of the Great Lutheran Fool, an allegorical figure in whom the 'errors' of Lutheranism are embodied. In the second part, strikingly prophetic in its anticipation of the Peasants' War of 1525 and the political consequences of the Reformation, Murner describes the looting hordes of Lutherans who lay waste the countryside and sack churches and monasteries, and then, in an image dear to his heart, sees himself as the defender of the castle of the Old Faith against the assaults of the Lutheran cohorts. Finally, in the closing chapters, he yields to Luther's blandishments and compromises with Lutheranism, going through a form of marriage with Luther's fictive daughter (the reformed faith?), until, finding in the bridal chamber that she suffers from impetigo, he rejects her, since marriage is after all not a sacrament in the Lutheran view! Luther is so upset at this that he dies, refusing extreme unction, and is buried to the accompaniment of a cats' chorus in the latrine. The Great Fool, by contrast, recants on his death-bed and is given more suitable interment. Throughout the work, which in the fashion established by Brant is richly illustrated with woodcuts, Murner appears as a tom-cat dressed in a monk's cowl (a reference to the ironical pun on his name 'Murrnarr' = 'tom-cat'+'fool') and, in quite characteristic fashion, finally claims the cap of the Great Fool as his due.

Our extract is taken from the final section and in effect constitutes a discussion of Luther's attitude to the sacraments. In one of the great Reformation treaties of 1520, *De captivitate babylonica ecclesiae praeludium*, Luther had launched a full-scale attack on the sacramental system of the Roman Church arguing that the abuses introduced by the Papists had made a Babylonian captivity out of what should have been perfect freedom. Of the seven sacraments of the Roman Church he is prepared to allow only three as being evangelical: baptism, penance, and communion (with the important reservation that the mass is not a sacrifice and that it is unevangelical to withhold the cup from the laity). The other four sacraments (orders, confirmation, matrimony, and extreme unction) are rejected as failing to conform to his requirement that a sacrament should be instituted by Christ and should contain both a sign and a promise of the grace the believing participant receives. (Cf. the definition in the Book of Common Prayer, which in this follows Luther: 'An outward and visible sign of an inward and spiritual grace given unto us, ordained by Christ himself as a means whereby we receive the same and a pledge to assure us thereof'. Aquinas's definition is simpler and 'unevangelical': 'The sign of a sacred thing in so far as it sanctifies men'.) Murner had early seen that Luther's position represented a major breach with tradition and had translated the Reformer's technical Latin work into German (rather to Luther's initial embarrassment) in order to reveal the extent of his heresy. In much the same way he sprang to the defence of Henry VIII in the latter's quarrel with Luther consequent on the publication of Henry's (probably ghosted) reply to *De captivitate*, *Assertio septem sacramentorum*—the pamphlet for which the Pope awarded Henry the title, still borne by English monarchs, of *Fidei Defensor*.

In view of this background, it is not surprising that the question of the sacraments should occupy a considerable place in Murner's satire, and behind its coarse humour our extract expresses one of Murner's deepest concerns. Luther is sick unto death and Murner offers him the sacraments which for centuries—'evangelical' or not—have brought comfort to generations of Christians. Luther, however, in the self-willed, perversely destructive fashion which Murner regards as typifying the Wittenberger's whole relationship with the Church, refuses this comfort and dies as he has lived, a negative and divisive force who obstinately refuses to recognize the truth and seeks to rob religion of much that is beautiful and has the power meaningfully to console mankind in his greatest need.

The text is that of the edition of 1522, printed in Strassburg by Johannes Grüninger.

Luther.

O Murner mein die stund ist kumen
　　Das ich mein tag hab ein genumen
Hie endt sich gotz barmhertzikeit
　　Sein rechtlichs vrteil ist bereit
Meins lebens ist nit me vff erden
　　Es můß ietzund gestorben werden
Das aller grusampst ist der dot
　　Menschlichem gschlecht die grôste not
So ich mich nun entsetz darab
　　Wa ich dich ie erzürnet hab　　　　　10
Jst mein hôchste bit an dich
　　Mir das verzeihen gnedigklich
Darzů an meinem letsten end
　　Mit deinem trost nit von mir wend
Des bit ich got im himelreich
　　Das er dir solchs mit lon vergleich.

Murner.

Wer ist vff erden der nit hat
　　Mitleiden so es vbel gat
So nun dir kumpt dy letste not
　　Vnd dich dein geist vf erd v'lot　　　20
So verzeihe dir auch got
　　Vnd ich verzeihe dirs alles sandt
Was ir nur ie begangen handt
　　Das selbig als verzigen ist
Durch den lieben reichen crist
　　Das er mir auch mein sünd verzeihe
Vnd vätterliche gnad verleihe

So du aber begerst damit
Das ich in trost verlaß dich nit
30   So sei meins trosts der anefang
Dich zů sumen hie nit lang
Dein sünd zů beichten rat ich dir
Es kumpt dir wol ia folgstu mir
Du hast ein widerwertigkeit
Gerüstet vff der cristenheit
Das laß dir sein von hertzen leidt
So rat ich dir zům andern mol
Dich vff den weg zů speisen wol
Mit dem heiligen sacrament
40   Das got dir geb ein seligs endt
Dir günnen wôl das himelbrot
Zů stür vnd hilff vß aller not
Zům dritten lůg vnd selbs erwôl
Das sacrament vnd heiligs ôl
Das du in krafft der dreier ding
Von hinnen farest leicht vnd ring
Kein andern trost kan ich dir geben
Am letsten end in disem leben
Vnd weitern trost erwart von got
50   Den er dir geb nach diser not.

Luther.

Got wôl dir dancken ewigklich
Das du in dem erleichtrest mich
Vnd all mein vbeldat laßt ligen
Ja dir gethon hast gar verzigen
Das ich sol aber beichten mit
Thů ich vff diser erden nit
Die pfaffen den man beichtet hie
Die hat doch got erstifftet nie
Jrem priesterthům der tüffel hat
60   Vff diser erden geben stat
Der selb hat es auch als erdicht
Darumb ich inen beichte nicht
Doch wil ich got mein sünd veriehen
Der würt mir sie wol vbersehen

Wan sie mir sein von hertzen leid
　Durch sein gruntloß barmhertzigkeit
Das heilig brot vnd sacrament
　Das wil ich nit an meinem ent
Das euwere priester geopffert hent
70　Dan ich haltz nur für ein testament
Die ölung die du mir wilt geben
　Die nim ich nit / dan merck mich eben
Das ist kein sacrament fürwar
　Jetz diser zeit vnd was nit vor
Der pfaffen geit vnd wůcherei
　Die hon die ding erstifftet frei
Vff das in iren seckel kum
　Alle güter vmb vndumb
　So machen sie kein menschen frum.

Murner.

80　Es gilt warlich nit diputieren
　Von sacramenten reden fieren
Der dot ist hie gib kurtzen bscheidt
　Jst es dir von hertzen leit
　Die vffrůr in der cristenheit
Vnd zwitracht die du hast gemacht
　Sprich ia vnd nein hie kurtz bedacht
Wiltu dan beichten zů dem dot
　Begerst das sacramentisch brot
Vnd die ölung auch darzů
90　So wil ich lůgen das ichs thů
Darin die gemein cristenheit
　Jr hoffnung setzt vnd seligkeit
Als von cristo selbs erstifft
　Lut der heiligen gotz geschrifft
Woltstu die selben nit erkennen
　Vnd schiedst on die sacrament von dennen
Vnd meinst du woltst ir nit bedörffen
　Jch wolt dich in ein scheißhuß werffen
Vnd mit luter dreck begraben
100　Da andere keiben ligen vergraben
　as möcht ich thůn mit billicheit
DSo dir dein sünd nit weren leit

Vorab das du die sacrament
  Hast abgethon darzů geschent
  Darin wir vnser hoffnung hent
Doch rieff die můter gottes an
  Das sie dir wŏl ietzund bei stan
  Es wil doch an ein scheiden gan.

Luther.

Kurtz ab ich scheid von diser welt
  Der sacrament mir keins gefelt   110
  Die du mir oben hast erzelt
Jch halt nichtz druff vnd wil ir nit
  Mariam auch darzů nit bit
Sie ist ein mensch als andere sint
  Ob sie schon auch ist gottes frint
Als andere heiligen alle sant
  Was künnen sie mir thůn beistant
Jch ken kein heiligen me dan got
  Daruff nim ich ietzund mein dot
  Nim her mein seel in diser not   120
Alde far hin du ŏde welt
  Bei got erhoff ich widergelt.

Murner.

Es můß billich gescheiden werden
  Wie ein mensch hie lebt vff erden
Der luther hat kein andere freit
  Dan die fridsam cristenheit
Jn ein solchen zwitracht bringen
  Nun hat er lon der bŏsen dingen
Als ins scheißhuß mit dem man
  Der kein sacrament wil han   130
  Vnd fart vngleubig hie von dan
Jns scheißhuß hŏrt ein solcher keib
  Dem nie kein boßheit vber bleib.

(iv) Thomas Müntzer castigates Luther as a cowardly braggart and a lackey of the princes

Hoch verursachte Schutzrede | vnd Antwwort | wider das Gaistloße Sanfft | lebende fleysch zů Wittenberg . . . (1524)

Luther's main concern was with the relationship of the individual to God, and although he frequently pronounced on social questions, from the need to maintain adequate schools to the rate of interest a banker might properly pocket without damage to his soul, these were of distinctly subordinate interest to him. In the main he was content to let the State and society look after themselves, so long as they did not impinge on matters of doctrine, and even when they did do so, he was loath to put himself in opposition to the secular authorities which, as St. Paul taught, had been instituted of God. This position was naturally welcomed by the authorities, and it was not accidental that the Lutheran reformation was often introduced by the head of state or the local city council as a policy decision—a process which was to be given striking legal recognition by the clause in the Religious Peace of Augsburg (1555) which is usually summed up in the tag 'cuius regio, eius religio'. The role ascribed by Luther to secular authority as the divinely appointed guardian of the Christian community, which in turn owed obedience to authority, made Lutheranism an ideal state religion and inevitably invited the rebuke that Luther was a 'Fürstenknecht', a princes' lackey, who materially, by conniving at the secularization of Church lands, and morally, by conferring a divine blessing and effective episcopal authority on many a manifestly godless government, bound the human spirit with chains stronger than those he had burst by his protest against Rome. By removing the checks and balances inherent in the traditional rivalry between Church and State, it is argued, Luther amongst other things permanently thwarted the growth of a democratic Germany and prepared the way for the emergence of absolutist Prussia and ultimately of Nazi Germany. Such a view ignores the fact that the greatest absolutist powers in Europe were Catholic France, Spain, and Austria, while the Scandinavian countries —all of which were Lutheran—did not develop as Prussia did. Further, it was in the Lutheran Church that the Nazis found some of their most effective opponents. Even so, the charge that Luther betrayed the Reformation to the princes is still raised repeatedly—especially in eastern Europe—and in its simplest form is not easy to dispute. One of Luther's earliest critics in this respect was Thomas Müntzer (1490–1525).

Müntzer was an early convert to Lutheranism, and it was on Luther's recommendation that he was appointed preacher in Zwickau in 1520. In this centre of the Saxon weaving industry, traditionally radical in religious matters, Müntzer came under the influence of the group of religious enthusiasts who were latterly to be known as the 'Zwickau Prophets' and whose puritanism, chiliasm, and replacement of external authority by the 'inner voice'—they in effect constituted the native German variety of the Anabaptist movement—appealed strongly to his own mystically oriented outlook. Quarrels with the more orthodox clergy forced the extremists to leave Zwickau, the Prophets going to Wittenberg, where the threat they posed to Luther's tentative reformation caused the latter to return home hot-foot from his exile and labours as a Bible translator at the Wartburg, where he had been in hiding since the Diet of Worms. Müntzer, after some months of wandering, found a refuge in the mining town of Allstedt. Here, in anticipation of Luther, he married an ex-nun, and, again in anticipation of Luther, produced a German liturgy. Up to mid 1524 Müntzer was apparently ready to collaborate with instituted authority, but throughout his obviously deeply felt, though often very obscure, pronouncements there runs an 'anabaptistic', apocalyptic note characterized by the insistence on the need for a radical re-ordering of society, an assertion that the 'inner light' is the only valid guide to truth, and a conviction of the implacable hostility of the world to the true believer, whose suffering is tantamount to a sign of salvation. After his unsuccessful attempt to convince the Saxon princes of the rightness of his position in July 1524, the violent revolutionary element becomes more pronounced and is accompanied by a primitive communism and an assertion of faith in the common people as a 'collective Messiah' which would establish the New Jerusalem on earth.

This quickening of political and social problems with theology was anathema to Luther, but to make matters worse Müntzer opposed to the Wittenberger's biblicism and doctrine of Justification by Faith a belief in direct inspiration by the Holy Ghost ('Was Bibel, Bubel, Babel', he once exclaimed, 'man muß auf einen Winkel kriechen und mit Gott reden!') and his own peculiar conviction of the near-impossibility of faith: the actively borne cross of suffering, not 'faith', was the *sine qua non* of justification. In a famous polemic, *Brieff an die Fürsten zu Sachsen von dem auffrurischen geyst* (1524), in which his contempt for the 'Schwarmgeister', or enthusiasts, and his fear of civil disorder are faithfully reflected, Luther roundly condemned Müntzer as a Satan who was perverting the Gospel in order to spread sedition amongst the common people. The unmitigated contempt which speaks from the title of Müntzer's reply, *Hoch verursachte Schutzrede | vnd Antwwort | wider das Gaistloße Sanfft | lebende fleysch zů Wittenberg*, is entirely characteristic of his view of the 'Wittenberg Pope', as he called Luther. The latter is in his eyes a corrupt creature who for the sake of an easy life has put the Gospel in the service of the princes, an Esau who has sold his birthright for a princely pottage.

The subsequent course of Müntzer's life was brief and tragic. Driven from Allstedt by the animosity of Luther and the suspicion of the Saxon authorities, he found refuge in Mühlhausen. The following year (1525), when the peasants of central and southern Germany, in the last of a series of peasant revolts, rose against their feudal overlords, Müntzer inevitably became one of their leaders, quickening the peasants' more or less traditional agrarian demands with a sense of religious urgency and God-willed purpose and vainly trying to impose on the restricted, local aims of the peasants a wider, grander design. In the wave of repression which followed the defeat of the peasants at Frankenhausen in May 1525, Müntzer was one of the first victims. He was tortured, made a full confession, and was beheaded on 27 May 1525.

Our text is that of the edition which was printed anonymously in Nürnberg in 1524.

Der arme schmeichler wil sich mit Christo in getichter gûtigkeit decken / wider den text Pauli .j. Timoth .j. Er saget aber im̄ bûch võ kauffßhandelũg daß die Fürsten / sõllen getrost vndter die diebe vñ Rauber streichen. Jm selbigen verschweigt er aber den orsprung aller dieberey. Er ist ein Heerholt / er wil danck verdienen / mit der leüthe blûtuergiessen vmb zeitlichs gûts willē / welches doch got nit auff seine maynung befolhen. Sich zû / die grundtsuppe des wûchers der dieberey / vñ Rauberey / sein vnser herrn vñ Fürsten / nemen alle creaturen zum aygen-
10 thumb. Die visch im̄ wasser / die võgel im̄ lufft / das gewechß auff erden mûß alles jr sein. Esaie .v. Darüber lassen sy dann gottes gepot außgeen vnter die armen / vnd sprechen. Got hat gepoten. Du solt nit stelen / es dienet aber jn nit. So sye nun alle mēschen verursachen / den armen ackerman / handt werckman / vnd alles das da lebet / schinden vnnd schaben. Michee .iij. ca. So er sich dann vergreifft am aller geringesten / so mûß er hencken. Do saget deñ der Doctor Lûgner. Amen. Die herren machē das selber / daß jn der arme man feyndt wirdt / dye vrsach des Auffrûrß wõllen sye nit weg thûn / wie
20 kañ es die lenge gût werdē? So ich das sage / mûß ich auffrû-risch sein / wolhyn . . .

Schâme dich du Ertzbûbe / wiltu dich mit der jrrenden welt heüchlen zû flicken. Luce .ix. vñ hast alle menschē wõllē rechtfertigē. Du waist aber wol wen du solt lestern / die armen Münch vnd pfaffen vnd kaufleüth / kõnnen sich nit weren / darumb hast du sye wol zûschelten. Aber die gotlosen Regenten soll nyemandt richten / ob sye schon Christum mit fûssen treten. Daß du aber den pawrn setigst / schreibest du / die Fürsten werden durch das wort gotes zû scheytern gen / vñ sagest in
30 deiner gloß vber das newlichiste Kayserlich Mandat. Die Fürsten werden von dem stûl gestossen. Du sichst sye auch an vor Kauff lewth. Du soltest deyne Fürsten auch bey der nasen rucken / sy habēs woll vil hõher / dañ villeicht dye anndern verdienet / was lassen sye abgen? an jren zynsen vnd schynderey &c? Doch das du die Fürsten gescholtē hast / kanstu sy wol wider mûts machen / du newer Pabst / schēckest jn klõster vñ kirchē / do sein sy mit dir zû fryden . . . Du hast die Christen-heyt mit einem falschen gelauben verwerret / vnnd kanst sy /

nun die noet heer geet / nit berichtē. Darumb heüchelstu mit
den Fürsten / du meynst aber es sey gůt worden / so du einen 40
grossen namen vberkomē hast / vnd kummest ane ende wie du
zů Leiptzgk vor der aller ferlichisten gemayn gestanden pist /
was wilt du dye leüte blindt machen? Dir war also woll zů
Leyptzgk / fůrest du doch mit någelen krentzlen zum thor
hynauß / vnd trunckest des gůten weyns zum Melchior Lother.
Das du aber zů Augspurg warest / môchte dyr zů keyner fer-
lichkeyt gelangen / dann Stupicianum / Oraculum stundt hart
bey dir / er môchte dyr wol helffen / aber yetzt is er von dyr
abgewichen / vnnd ein Abt wordē. Jch hab sicherlich sorg du
werdest jm volgen / der Teüffel stet warlich nit in der warheyt / 50
er kann seyner tück nit lassen. Doch er forchtet sich im bůchlein
vom auffrhůr / vor der prophecey seines greüels. Darumb saget
er vō den newen Propheten / wie die schrifftgelerten wider
Christum. Johannis .viij. c. Darumb hab ich fast das ganntz
Capitel zum gegenwertigen vrteyl genützt Paulus sagt von
propheten .j. Corint .xiiij. Ein rechter prediger můß ja ein
prophet sein / wann es die welt noch also spôttisch duncket / es
můß dye gantz welt prophetisch sein / soll sye anders vrteylen
vber die falschen propheten / wie wilt du die leüthe vrtaylen / so
du dich im Münch kalbe des ambts eüßserst? Daß du sagest wie 60
du mich ynß maul geschlagen hast / redest du die vnwarheyt.
Ja du leügst in deinen halß / spieß tieff / pin ich doch in Sechs
oder Syben Jaren nit bey dir gewesen. Hastu aber die gůten
brůder zů narren gcmacht / die bey dir gewesen / das můß
frcylich an tag kommen / es wirt sich auch annderst nit reymen /
du soltest die klaynen nit verachten. Matthei .xviij.
   Vber deinem rhümen / môchte einer woll endtschlaffen / vor
deiner vnsynnigen torheyt. Daß du zů Worms vorm Reich
gestanden pist / danck hab der Teütsch adel / dem du daz maul
also wol bestrichen hast / vnd hônig gegeben / dann er wenethe 70
nit annderst / du würdest mit deinem predigen / Beheymische
geschenk geben / Clôster vnd Stifft. Welche du ytzt den Fürsten
verheyssest. So du zů Worms hettest gewanckt / werest du ee
erstochen vom Adel worden / dann loß gegeben / weyß doch
ein yeder / Du darffst warlich dir nit zů schreiben / du woltest
dań noch ein mal dein Edels blůt / wie du dich rhůmest /
darumb wagen / du geprauchest do selbst mit den deinen wilder
tück vnnd lyste. Du liessest dich durch deinen rath gefangen

nemen / vñ stellest dich gar vnleydlich / wer sich auff deyne
80 schalckheyt nit verstünde / schwŭr woll zun heyligē / du wårest
ein frümmer Mertin. Schlaff sanfft liebes fleisch. Jch rüche dich
lieber gepraten in deinem trotz durch gotes grym̄ im̄ hafen
oder topff peym fewr. Hierem̄. j. Dann in deinem aygen
sŏtlein gekocht / solte dich der Teüffel fressen Ezechielis .xxiij.
Du pist ein Eselisch fleisch / du würdest langsam gar werden /
vnd ein zåchs gerichte werden deinen milch meülern.

(v) Huldrych Zwingli deprecates Luther's boastfulness and
intemperance and rejects his teaching on the sacraments

*Das dise wort Jesu Christi / Das ist min lychnam der fŭr ŭch hinggeben
wirt / ewigklich den alten eynigen sinn haben werdēd* (1527)

Huldrych (Ulrich) Zwingli was born in 1484 of peasant stock at Wildhaus
(Toggenburg) and studied at Basel, Bern, and Vienna, before becoming
parish priest at Glarus (1506–16). Although he subsequently claimed that
he began preaching the evangelical faith in 1516, it was not until the years
1522–3, when Luther's doctrines were already popular in Switzerland, that
he emerged as the Reformer of Zürich, where he had been 'Leutprediger'
at the Großmünster since 1519. In this capacity he had, however, from the
first shown himself sympathetic to the reformed teaching. A keen disciple
of Erasmus, he had early been drawn to the latter's Christian humanism,
which saw Christianity above all in ethical terms, and from Erasmus too he
had learnt to criticize the abuses from which the Church suffered and to see
in the Scriptures the only valid rule of life for Christians. Probably under
Luther's influence he came to recognize that the humanist belief in the
possibility of reform consequent on the spread of enlightenment was inadequate, but, at least originally, his Protestantism was almost as much political
as religious in nature. Luther was essentially unpolitical in outlook and the
emergence of Lutheranism as an ideal state religion is a paradoxical result
of its founder's basic indifference to political questions, but the reformation
which Zwingli inaugurated tended—perhaps because of the more democratic traditions of the Swiss cantons—to reflect Zwingli's political attitudes
and his belief that the duly elected authorities must take over the task of
reforming the Church. Thus his fight against Bernhard Samson, the local
indulgence-seller, was probably more a protest against the economic
exploitation of the Swiss than an attempt to prevent the prostitution of the
sacrament, and constitutes an ecclesiastical counterpart to his campaign
against the sale of mercenaries for service in the Italian Wars (he had himself served in Italy as a chaplain in 1513 and again in 1515). Similarly, in
contrast to Luther, it was not to the members of the republic of letters that
he appealed in the disputations of 1523, but to the Zürich town council, and
it was the latter which declared him to be the victor and at whose behest
the new faith was established in the canton. Equally, his death on the battle-

field of Kappel (1531) in the course of a civil war with the Catholic cantons bears witness to his belief in the necessity of spreading the new faith by 'political' means.

Like all the founding fathers of Protestantism, Zwingli owes a profound debt to Luther and subscribes to all the fundamental Lutheran doctrines: Justification by Faith, the Priesthood of All Believers, the sole authority of the Scriptures, etc., but his reformation was far more consistent than Luther's and is characterized by a thorough-going puritanism: the vestments and ceremonies, even the music of the old faith, were banished, the altar became a plain wooden table, and paintings and statues were removed or whitewashed. These external differences were of small significance compared with their differing view of the nature of the sacraments, however, Luther retaining the traditional view that the sacraments constituted vehicles of divine grace, Zwingli seeing them as confessions of faith on the part of the participants and signs of their commitment and calling—baptism, for instance, he likened to the Jewish rite of circumcision. It was on the question of the nature of the Eucharist that this difference was to manifest itself most sharply. Luther retained the Roman doctrine of the 'real presence' of Christ in the bread and wine of the Eucharist; in contradistinction to the Roman teaching that the substance of the elements underwent a complete change (transubstantiation), however, Luther advocated a doctrine of 'consubstantiation', i.e. the substance of Christ and the substance of the elements were mingled, 'as fire enters into iron when it is heated'. Zwingli, by contrast, denied the real presence and saw in the Eucharist a commemorative act and an affirmation of the brotherhood and community of the participants.

The incapacity of the reformers to compromise on this issue poisoned the relationship between Wittenberg and Zürich throughout the twenties, and in 1529 led to the breakdown of the talks between Luther and Zwingli at Marburg, a breakdown which finally confirmed the division of German-speaking Protestantism into two bitterly hostile camps. After Zwingli's death (which Luther characteristically declared to be a judgement on his false teaching), his south German followers tended to be absorbed by Lutheranism, but in Switzerland itself Zwingli's reformation was taken over and expanded by Calvin and thereby, in an indirect way, ultimately achieved a wider currency than its German rival.

Zwingli emerges from his writings as a man possessed of a rather dry, practical mind. He never shared Luther's profound religious doubts nor, so far as one can judge, his exuberant, exultant faith, and what he wrote— characteristically he produced no single outstanding statement of faith or work of edification—is generally lacking in the power and emotional vigour we find in Luther. His style is that of a scholar rather than of a popular reformer—Luther's proverbs significantly tend to be replaced by classical allusions. All his writings do, however, bear witness to his shrewdness and the outstanding clarity of his intellect and more often than not he seems to have the advantage of his opponents.

Our extract is taken from the second pamphlet written by Zwingli in the course of the arguments and recriminations which preceded the deadlock of

1529. It is Zwingli's reply to Luther's tract *Daß diese Worte Christi* (*Das ist mein Leib, etc.*) *noch fest stehen widder die Schwermgeister,* and was to provoke Luther to write his famous *Bekenntnis vom Abendmahl Christi* of 1528. The text is that of the edition of 1527, printed by C. Froschauer of Zürich.

Jch verschon din hie / lieber Luter treffenlich / dañ du in vil gschrifften / durch sandbrieff vnd sust / noch vil stôltzer dich gerûmpt hast / darum man dich wol solt erstouben / aber wir wellend / ob Gott wil / maaßhaltē / vñ dich einen menschē lassen blybē. Dañ in der warheyt / so weystu wol / das zů der zyt / du dich harfür stalltist / gar ein grosse menge dero was / die in dem lesen vnd spraachen gar vil geschickter warend weder du / wiewol sy vß forcht / vñ dz sy Gott nit erwackt vnd mañlich macht / sich nit harfür staltend Jsrael zeschirmen / vnd wid'
10 den grossen Goliath vō Rhom zefechten (Jetz volgt ouch din lob) Aber du wurdt in dem allem vō Gott berûfft nit anderst / weder Dauid: stalltist dich dem fyend engegen so trostlich / dz alle die vor ouch angsthafft warend / wie der schmåchlich Antichrist hin wurd genomē / gesterckt wurdēd / sprungend dir zů / also / daß das Euangeliū in einen treffenlichen vfgang kam. Darum wir Gott billich dancken sôllend / dz er dich erweckt hat / do es nieman waagen dorfft. Vnd dich als ein nutzlich gschirr in eeren habē. Als wir ouch gern thůnd / ob du glych das selb in vil weg verkerest . . . Vnnd ob du glych yetz
20 vss zornes anfechtung tobist / woltend wir dir gernn vmb vordriges dienstes wegen übersehen / so wilt du es nit erkennen. Das du aber yetz vss zorn tobist / kanst ob Gott wil / nit lôugnen / wenn du nun din eygen bůch lisest / dann die vnzal der scheltworten vnnd verkerten meinungen / als wir håll machen werdend / kan vss liebe vnd wolbetrachtung nit kumē. Dann besich alle die vss bittergheyt ye geschribē habēd / wo ye gheiner jm selbs so gar engangen sye als du dir selbs in dem bůch engangen bist. Vñ solt man das in eynen geyst kônnen rechnen? oder wider dich nit reden? oder der jrrung wychen?
30 Saul was zum ersten milt / vnd Gott lieb / vnd gschickt / aber do er hochmůtig ward vnnd tyrannisch / ließ jn Gott tåglich toub werdē / nam jm vnerbere ding für / solt es darumb recht gewesen sin / drum dz er einist geschickt gewesen? . . . Darumb verman ich dich by dem Gott / der dich vnnd mich geschaffen hatt / du wellest in dich selb gon / vnd anderlüt lassen vō dir singen vnnd sagen / deß du vilicht wol wert bist. Dann was

hast du / das du nit von Gott empfangen habist? Hastus aber
empfangen / worumb růmst du dich? I. Corinth .4. Vnnd mag
dz alles nit helffen / so wil ich dir dich selbs eigenlicher in aller
gůte zů erkennen geben. Du wilt ye gsehen sin / sam du die 40
ban des Euangelij allein gerütet habist / darinn ich dir vast vil
zůgib. Aber ich wil dir für die ougen stellē / das du den wyten
herrlichen schyn des Euangelij nie erkennt hast / du habist
dann deß selben widrum̄ vergessen. Also: . . . Du hast dem
Fegfhür allweg (ists als man sagt) etwas zůgegeben: Welches
aber das Euangeliū nit erliden mag. Dañ wer im gloubē ab-
stirbt / der ist heil / vnd kūpt in ghein vrteil noch verdam̄nuß /
sunder ist vss dem tod ins lebē gangē / Jo .5. Vnnd můßtind
wir gnůg tůn für vnser sünd od' selbs reinigē / so wer Christus
vergebē gstorbē. Gal. 2. Darzů ist vor Christo ghein fegfhür 50
gewesē / vñ es sôlt erst gebuwē sin / nach dē die bezalung für
die sünd schon bar gezelt ist? Jtem / du hast dem fürbitt der
sâligē die im him̄el sind / etwas zůgegebē / one grund der
gschrifft / so wir doch nun einē mitler habēd / fürbitter vñ be-
zaler / etc. Gal. 3. vñ .I. Timo. 2 vnd .I. Jo. 2 . . . Jtem / in dem
span der Bilderen / entscheydestu die sach also: Das vss dem
gsatzt Mosis / vns allein das antreffe / das mit dem Gsatzt der
liebe des nechsten gemessen werd. Nun werdind die Bilder nit
da hingerechnet / darumb môg man sy haben oder nit. Als ouch
Paulus meinung sye / da er .I. Corinth. 8. also spricht: Wir 60
wüssēd dz der gôtz nüt ist in der welt. Jn welcher diner ent-
scheydung / zum ersten also jrrest / dz man es nit lidē sol / dañ
es strytet din Canon oder schnůr wider Gottes wort. Dañ
Christus spricht Matth. 22. Jn denen beden gebottē hanget dz
gantz gsatzt vñ die prophetē. Also můssend wir ye alles so im
altē testamēt stadt / nach den beden gsatzten ermessen / namlich
nach der eer vnd liebe Gottes / vñ nach der liebe des nechsten.
So wir nun die Bilder nach dem ersten gsatzt der eer vnd liebe
Gottes messend / so sind sy schnůrrichtig wid' Gott / dann die
bilder sind zůuereerung vfgericht nach dem wir die / denen sy 70
dar gestelt sind / für helffer vnnd Gôtt vfgenom̄en habend. Vnd
kurtz / es sol vnd mags der gloub nit erliden / das man bilder
hab / die man verere / oder die in so gwüssem anzug vñ gefar
der vereerung stond / als sy in den templē werdend fürgestelt /
als Exod .20. wol verstanden wirt. Spricht yeman / so aber
nun hinfür so starck vnd eigenlich gelert wirt / das man sy nit

vereeren sôlle / so ligt nit daran / man lasse sy in den templen
ston oder nit / so redt der vss sinem duncken: vnd trachtet aber
nit dz Gott / der die ewig wyßheit vnnd fürsichtigkeyt ist / wol
80 hatt gewüßt was vss dem fürstellen der gôtzen kum̃en wurd / ob
glych syn wort schrüwe: Du solt sy nit vereeren noch jnen
dienen / oder zucht embieten / vnd hats verbotten. Darum̃
sôllend wir nit wyser wellē sin weder Gott / vñ sagen: Wir
wellend oder môgends haben / so wir sy nit vereerend / etc.
dañ lassend wir sy ston: gebend wir allen Gottlosen hoffnung
den vngloubē wider zebringen / vnd vrsach / das die jugēd vnd
nachkom̃en für vnd für môgēd / wo ein kleine zyt das wort
vnderlassen wurd / widerum̃ mit den gegenwürtigen Gôtzen in
abgôttery gefûrt werden . . .

90   Dise ort habe ich dir / hochgeachter Martine Luther /
darumb für die ougen gestelt / das du sehist / das du nit an
einem ort verschossen bist / sunder an vilen / vnnd dich für hin
des hohen rûmens vnder den Christen mâssigest / sam du es
allein alles gethon habist. Welches wir dir gar wol gunnen
môchtind / so verr jm also wer. Aber du bist allein ein redlicher
Aiax oder Diomedes / vnder vil Nestoren / Vlyssen / Menelaen.
Thû gmach / laß dich das klein glid / von dem Jacobi am dritten
capitel geschriben stat / nit überylē. Wir wüssend den rûm
Pauli wol / vnnd Demosthenis by den Athenernn / ouch
100 Ciceronis by den Rhômeren / aber es ist vns allweg zebesinnen.
Erstlich / wer die sygind / die vns lobind / demnach ouch
eigenlich besehen / ob wir also sygind / als man vns lobt. Dañ
wir warlich in dinem anfang wol gesehen / wo es dir faalt /
habend doch gûtlich darzû geschwigen / dines namens halb /
vnnd aber die leer dariñ du nit recht wandletest / mit trüwen on
vnderlaß getriben / damit aller wenigost verletzung beschehe . . .

Das du aber sagst / wir sygind des einträchtig / Christum zû
durâchten: wellend wir dem rechten Richter befelhen / der
weißts ob jm also sye: es wirdt ouch hinfür in vnserer Antwurt
110 wol erlernet / wer Christū allermeist durâchte . . .

Wir verbütend ghein leer für die Kilchen zebringen / sy sye
Bâpstisch / Luter / Trûb / oder vnsauber: wir stond aber denn
mitt dem Pflegel Gottes worts darüber: fûrennd ouch den
vßtrettenden Ochsen darüber / vnd erstoubends recht wol: denn
vallt von etlicher so vil hin / als wenn bôse jar sind / vnnd gheyn
Korn in der sprüwer ist. Dine bede bûcher von Bilderen vnnd

Nachtmal Christi / wider die schwermer / hat mā by vns fry
gelesen / vñ demnach mit ernst vßgetrôschen / ist nüts da bliben
dann *inanes Paleae* / lår strow / so vil die meynung antrifft / das
ist nützid anders weder schyn der klůgen worten: vnd ist der 120
fygenboum / der allein bletter hatt . . .

Jetz můß ich ein mal dine eygne wort setzen. Luther. a. am .4.
andren teyl: Eben der selbige teufel ists / der vns yetz durch
die Schwermer anficht mit lesterunge / des heiligen hochwirdigen Sacraments vnsers Herren Jesu Christi / darauß sie
wôllen eitel brod vnd weyn zū malzeichen oder denckzeichen
der Christen machē / wie es yhn treumet vnd gefellet. &c. Zürn
nit lieber Luther / ich můß dise wort wol erstouben vnnd
wannen / allein zů einer prob / das du sehist wie es dem gantzen
bůch gon wurde / wo mans sôlt recht zerzeysen. Erste. Wie 130
kumpts das dirs yetz der arm Tüffel můß alles gethon haben /
wie in minem huß der Nieman. Jch wond der Tüffel wer schon
überwunden vnnd gricht. Jst nun der tüffel ein gwaltiger Herr
der welt / als du glych dauor geredt hast / wo blybt dañ das
alle ding durch Gottes fürsichtigheyt gehandlet werdennd?
Sprichst: Er würckt aber durch den Tüffel in üch. So sag an /
môgend wir darwider oder nit? Jch meyn nein. Was bist dann
du für ein Christ / das du mit vns so gar ghein erbårmd hast / so
du sichst das Gott dem tüfel so vil gwalt hat über vns geben?
Bsinn dich / vnd frag den tüfel bas / ist er dir so wol erkant / was 140
gilts er wirt dir sagē dz alle valsche leer erst recht zegrund gon
wirt / weñ alle die hoffnung die du vñ andre one gottes wort
verheyssend / hingenoͤmen wirt / denn werdend wir erst recht
onhåblingē lernen gon . . . Schwermer nennestu vns / vnd
weyß ich nit eygenlich was Schwermer heyßt. Jsts als vil als
ein touber / narr / oder ein nårrischwyser / kan ich mich nit
erweren / můß etwas an mir erkennē / so gemein vnnd früntlich
ist min gnådige frow Stultitia allen mēschen / vñ mir besunder.
Aber ich denck Luther / nit dz du vns daher schwermer namp-
tist / oder aber du schultest vns alleyn mit dem das allen 150
menschen gemein ist. Oder ist es als vil / als *praestigiator* /
Fanaticus / Latinisch: welchen wir wol môchtind in Tütsch einen
Betrieger / Zoubrer / Fantasten / oder tollen nennen: so sich
eygenlich vf welche die tôlleren sygind / Die da erkennend das
kein ander essen des lychnams Christi sin mag / weder dz
geistlich / welches allenthalb by der geschrifft eynhålligheyt

beston mag: Oder die / jn lyblich essen wellend / vnd sinen
lychnam / wider alles vermôgen sines eygnen worts / vßtennēd
nach der gottheyt / wellēd jn doch gantz vn̄ gar ins menschē
160 mund essen / vn̄ wer sôlchs nit nachlaßt / d' ist ein schwermer /
narr / tôrpel / ja tüfel: môrd' vn̄ seelen verderber. Mit lestrunge
des heiligen hochwirdigen sacraments vnsers Herren Jesu
Christi . . . Die lestrend aber die heiligen sacrament / die jnen
zûgebend das sy nit habend / vnd den sacramenten die nützid
anders sind / weder zeychen heyliger dingen / zû gebend / sy
sygind das heilig ding selb. Die creatur dem schôpffer glych
machēd / welches nit allein ein lestrung der sacramenten /
sunder gottes selbs ist / als vß Ro .I. wol ermessen wirt. Daruß
sy wellend ytel brot vn̄ wyn (sprichstu) zum malzeichē oder
170 danckzeichē der Christē machē. Jn den wortē machstu dich
selb lieber Luter / so argwônig / ja in allem dem bûch / dz ein
wund' ist: dan̄ du glycherwyß klagst als die Bâpstler: vm̄ ding
die du nit hast / vn̄ dir nie verheisē sind: dan̄ wz ist vns verheißē
so wir den lychnā Christi lyblich âssind? So aber du vns gût
bâpstisch fürdichtest / wie die sünd durchs lyblich essē verzigen werdind / der gloub beuestet / vnnd der lychnam zû der
vrstende erhalten / etc. Alles one Gottes wort / was thûstu
anderst / weder der Bapst? Der dichtet ouch das gsâgnet ôl
machte heylig / neme die sünd hin / vnd wychte. Vnd do du
180 jm die büchs vmbkartest / schrey er nit ouch also? Die wellend
vns die heyligen sacrament nem̄en? Was nimpt man dir / lieber
Luther? so man vô den sacramēten lert haltē / wie Christus vnd
die apostel dauon gehaltē habend? Nützid anders / weder das
man din wort nit für Gottes wort annimpt. Hie by / thûstu vns
gwalt vnd vnrecht / das wir ytel win vn̄ brot wellind vß dē
sacrament machē. Dan̄ so verr du vô der gantzen dancksagung
redst / so haltēd wir / das diß zemenkummen also sol gestaltet
werdē / das alle die den Herren Christum Jesum verjehēd / jren
Heiland sin / hie danck sagind / vm̄ den tod den er für vns
190 erlidten hat / vnnd miteinander das war zeychen / damit vns
Paulus lert zû einem lychnam vn̄ brot / doch ouch nun bedütlich
werden / essind. Daran du sichst / das wirs nit ein ytel gemein
brot machēd / deß bruchs halb: dann es ein verzeichenlich brot
vnnd mass ist / als nit wir / sunder Paulus lert .I. Corinth .10.
Warumb schiltestu dan̄ dise wort / dāckzeichen malzeichen (so
verr malzeichen zû gûtem genom̄en wirt) vnnd warzeychen?

Hôrstu nit das er spricht: Ein brot vnd ein lychnam sind wir die menge / darumb das wir von einē brot essend? Wiltu aber allein von der substantz oder materi reden / ob es brot sye oder das fleysch Christi / so gib du dir selbs antwurt: dann du hast 200 gelert das es ein brot sye / vnd sye nit der lychnam Christi / vnnd das an so mengem ort / daß nit not ist zů erzellen. Aber in dem brot werde der lychnam Christi geessen. Also hast du ytel brot vnnd wyn daruß gemachet / nitt wir: dann sichst du den bruch an / so hôrstu wol das wirs nit als eynualtig brot bruchend vnnd haltend im Nachtmal / sunder für ein war vnnd pflicht oder eynigung zeychen. Sichst du aber die materi oder sub- stantz an / so hast du gelert / es sye nützid anders dann brot. Das ander / da du sprichst / Aber in dem brot werde der lych- nam Christi geessen / bringstu vß dem dinen / nit von Gott: 210 dann er spricht: Das ist min lychnam. Nit: Jn dem brot ist min lychnam. Warumb legst du nun vff vns das du gethon hast / oder missest vnns zů argem mitten zů / das du redest?

7. The Peasants' War

(i) The peasants state their aims

Dye Grundtlichen Vnd rechten haupt Artickel / aller Baurschafft vnnd Hyndersessen der Gaistlichen vñ Weltlichen oberkayten / von wôlchen sy sich beschwert vermainen (1525)

The outbreak of the series of peasant uprisings in central and southern Germany in 1524 and early 1525 suggests in its quickening of social and economic grievances with evangelical teaching an obvious parallel with the revolt of the English peasants in 1381, and the more recent activities of the Taborites in Bohemia. Yet, like Wyclif and Huss before him, Luther did no more than give added emphasis and scriptural authority to the protest against grievances which for the greater part of a century had from time to time erupted in peasant violence: characteristically the peasants of 1525 adopted as their device the *Bundschuh*, or peasant's shoe fastened with a long leather thong, which had first appeared in a revolutionary context in the *Bundschuh* uprising of 1493.

The economic position of the peasants varied considerably, but, whether prosperous or not, the peasant was traditionally regarded as the milch cow and the beast of burden of the whole community. The fifteenth century had seen a worsening of the peasants' position in that with the end of the great period of colonization in the east, surplus population was no longer exported and the average peasant holding grew smaller as it was divided amongst a number of children. Further, the decline in the position of the lesser nobility caused these to extort more rent and services from their tenants—a lead which the greater landowners were not slow to follow. Few peasants were allowed to retain more than a third of the crops they produced and were in addition compelled to work a varying number of days for the overlord without wages. Within living memory, although clearly the lot of the peasant varied according to local tradition, the fertility of the soil, the personality of his overlord, and his own social position (whether serf or bondsman), many traditional rights and privileges in respect of hunting and fishing had been eroded, so much so that peasants could not even defend their crops against the inroads of game, while increasingly heavy taxes, especially death duties, and the sequestration of common grazing land and forest in many areas reduced the smaller peasants to extreme poverty. The replacement of native German law, by which a man was judged by his equals, by Roman law, by which he was judged by jurists and which substituted the concept of slavery for that of serfdom, was a further grievance, while the increasing tendency on the part of overlords, consequent on the steady process of inflation, to refuse to allow tenants to commute feudal services to a money rent also contributed to the prevailing unrest.

In these circumstances it was hardly surprising that Luther's message of Christian freedom, especially when misinterpreted by visionary preachers such as Müntzer and the Prophets of Zwickau and quickened by a widespread mood of apocalyptic expectation (a Second Flood was commonly expected to take place in 1524), should produce an unusually violent upheaval. Beginning in Stühlingen near Schaffhausen in June 1524, the unrest spread rapidly, sweeping south and west through the Black Forest and the Breisgau as far as Switzerland and Alsace and north and east through Franconia, Hesse, and Thuringia. The peasants were by no means leaderless—the Anabaptist preacher Hubmaier (cf. p. 76), the imperial knights Götz von Berlichingen and Florian Geyer, the famous wood-carver and mayor of Würzburg Tilman Riemenschneider, and the revolutionary theologian Thomas Müntzer (cf. p. 52) all exercised command in their various areas—but leadership tended to be highly localized and the movement as a whole suffered from an almost total lack of any sense of direction, organization, or discipline. After considerable initial local successes and the alienation of moderate opinion consequent on the looting and killing in which many 'Haufen' freely indulged, the Thuringian peasants suffered a crushing defeat at Frankenhausen in May 1525, while the rebels in Württemberg, Franconia, and Alsace met a similar fate in the battles of Böblingen, Königshofen, and Scherweiler. In the savage reprisals and repression which now followed, it has been estimated that—apart from the uncounted thousands who were wantonly blinded or otherwise maimed—some 100,000 peasants were put to death.

The 'Twelve Articles' of Memmingen are variously attributed to the Anabaptist preacher, Balthasar Hubmaier, a Memmingen tanner named Sebastian Lotzer, and a Memmingen preacher called Christoph Schappeler. Although officially the manifesto of the Upper Swabian peasants who gathered at Memmingen in mid March 1525, the Articles may be taken as representing the broad mass of peasant opinion: they passed through at least twenty-three editions and clearly enjoyed wide dissemination.

For a revolutionary manifesto, the Articles are surprisingly moderate in tone and touchingly naïve in the arguments advanced. Down to our own day Christ has commonly appeared to unsophisticated minds as the advocate of a communistic way of life, or at least as the champion of those who 'travail and are heavy laden', and so it was with the peasants of 1524–5. From Luther they had learnt to appeal to scriptural authority, had heard that they were all priests and inheritors of the freedom of the Christian man, and the manifest inequality in their own society seemed to be in obvious conflict with the apparent message of the Gospels. Accordingly society must be changed. This attempt to christianize the world by basing the law on the Gospel was, however, in striking contrast to Luther's highly sophisticated concern to distinguish between the 'two kingdoms' and between inner and outer freedom (cf. p. 18), and the peasants' suggestion that Luther might act as a judge of the rightness of their cause is striking testimony to the extent to which they had misunderstood his teaching. Not that Luther refused to draw certain social conclusions from biblical precedent, of course: he argued, for instance, that slavery was permissible since Abraham had kept slaves, and even justified the bigamous marriage of Philip of Hesse in similar terms; but the attempt to make a programme of social reform from the Gospels constituted in his eyes a perversion of the Word of God, and he was shortly to emerge as the peasants' sternest opponent.

Our text follows the Wolffenbüttel copy of the edition of the Articles printed by Melchior Ramminger of Augsburg in 1525.

Hye nachuolgent die Artickel.

DER ERST ARTICKEL.

Zvm ersten ist vnser diemůttig bytt vñ beger / auch vnser aller will vñ maynūg / das wir nun fürohin gewalt vnd macht wõllen haben / ain gantze gemain sol ain Pfarer selbs Erwõlen vnd kyesen. Auch gewalt haben den selbigen wider zůentsetzen / wañ er sich vngepürlich hieldt / Der selbig erwõlt Pfarrer soll vns das hailig Euangeli lauter vñ klar predigen one allen menschlichē zů satz / leer vnd gebot / dañ vns den waren glaubē stetz verkündigen / geyt vns ain vrsach got vnd sein gnad zů bitten / vnns den selbygen waren glawben einbylden vnd in vns bestetten / Dann wann seyn genad in vnß nit ein gepyldet wirdt / so bleyben wir stetz fleysch vn blůt / das dañ nichts nutz ist / wie klårlich in der geschrifft stat das wir allain durch den waren glauben zů got kom̄en kinden / vnd allain durch seyn barmhertzigkait sålig můssen werden / Darumb ist vns ain sõllicher vorgeer vñ Pfarrer võ nõtten vñ in diser gestalt in d' geschrifft gegrindt.

Marginal references: 1 Thim. 3 · Titon. 1 · Actuū. 14 · Deutro. 17 · Exodi. 31 · Deutro. 10 · Johann. 6 · Gallata. 2

DER ANDER ARTICKEL.

Wie dann Zům andern nach dem der recht Zehat auff gesetzt ist im 20
die ganntz alten Testament vnd im Neuen als erfüldt / nichts destminder
Epistel zů
den Hebr. wŏllen wir den rechtē korn zehat gern gebē / Doch wie sich
saget. gebürt / dem nach man sol in Got geben / vñ den seynen
Psal. 109 mitaylē / gebürt es ainem Pfarrer so klar das wort gots verkindt /
Seyen wir des willen hinfüro disen zehat / vnser kirch Brŏpst so
Genesi. 14 dañ ain gemain setzt / Sollen einsemlen vnd eynnemen / daruon
De. 18. 12 ainem Pfarrer so vō ainer gantzen gemain erwŏlt wirt / seyn
zymlich gnůgsam auffenthalt geben / jm vnd den seynen /
Deutro.25 nach erkantnus ainer gantzen gmain / vnnd was über bleybt
sol man (armen dürfftigen / so im selbē dorff verhandñ seynd) 30
1.Thim. 5 mittailen / nach gestalt der sach vñ erkantnus ainer gemain /
Math. 10 was über bleybt soll man behaltten / ob man Raysen můßt von
1. Chor. 9 lands not wegen / Darmit man kain landts steüer dürff auff den
armen anlegen / Sol manß von disem überschuß außrichten /
Auch ob sach were daz ains oder mer dŏrffer weren / die den
Ein christ zehenden selbs verkaufft hettent auß ettlicher not halbē / die
liche selbigē so darumb zů zaigen / in der gestalt haben von aynem
erpiet
tung gantzen dorff der sol es nit entgeltñ / Sond' wir wellen vns
Luce. 6 zymlicher weyß nach gestalt vñ sach mit im vergleychen / jm
Math. 5 sollichs wider mit zymlicher zyl vnd zeyt ablassen / Aber wer 40
Mā sol nie vō kainem dorff sollichs Erkaufft hat vñ jre forfaren jnen selbs
māt nichs solchs zůgeaygent haben / wŏllen vnd solen vnd seynd jnen
nemen.
nichts weyters schuldig zůgeben / alain wie obstat vnsern
Erwŏltē Pfarrer darmit zů vnderhalten / Nachmalen ablesen /
oder den dürfftigē mittailen / wie die hailig geschryfft innhŏlt /
Sy seyen gaistlich / oder welttlich den klaynen zehat wŏllen wir
gar nit geben / Dañ Got der herr hat dz vich frey dem menschen
Genesis. 1 beschaffen / das wir für ain vnzymlichñ zehat schetzen / den
die menschen erdicht haben / Darumb wŏllen wir jn nit weytter
geben.   50

DER DRIT ARTICKEL.

Zům dritten / Ist der brauch byßher gewesen das man vns für
Esaie. 53 jr aigen leüt gehalten haben / wŏlch zů erbarmen ist / angesehen
1.Petri. 1 das vns Christus all mitt seynem kostparlichen plůtvergůssen /
1. Chor. 7 erlŏßt vnnd erkaufft hat / Den Hyrtten gleych alls wol alls Den
Roma. 13 hŏchsten / kain außgenommen / Darnmb erfindt sich mit der
Sapien. 6 geschryfft das wir frey seyen vnd wŏllen sein / Nit dz wir gar
1. Petri. 2

frey wôllen seyn / kain oberkait haben wellen / Lernet vnß
Gott nit / wir sollen in gepotten leben nit yn freyem fleysch- Deut. 6
60 lichen mûtwilen. Sonder got lieben jn als vnserrn Herren. jn Mathei. 4
vnsern nechsten erkennen / vnnd alles das so wyr auch gern Luce. 4
hetten / das vnns Got am nachtmal gepotten hat zů ainer letz / Luce. 6
Math. 5
darumb sollen wir nach seinem gepot leben zaigt vnd weißt Johan. 13
vns diß gepot nit an das wir der oberkkait nit korsam seyen /
nit allain der oberkait / sunder wir sollen vns gegen jederman
diemûtigñ / das wir auch geren gegen vnser erwelten vnd Roma. 13
gesetzten oberkayt (so vns von Got gesetzt) jn allen zimlichen Actuū. 5
vñ Christlichen sachen geren gehorsam sein seyen auch Ain Christ
liche
onzweyfel jr wedendt vnß der aigenschafft als war vnnd recht erbiet
70 Christen geren endtlassen oder vns jm Euangeli des berichten tung
dz wirß seyen.

DER VIERT ARTICKEL.

Zum vierten ist bißher jm brauch gewesen / dz kayn armer
man nit gewalt gehabt hatt / das willpret gefigel oder fisch jn
fliessenden wasser nit zů fachen zů gelassen werdē / welchs
vns gantz vnzymlich vñ vnbrůderlich dunckt / sunder aigen-
nützig vñ dem wort Gotz nit gemeß sein / Auch in etlichen
ortern die oberkait vns dz gewild zů trutz vnd mechtigem
schaden habē / wil vns dz vnser (so Got dem menschen zů nutz
80 wachsen hat lassen) die vnuernüfftigen thyer zů vnutz verfretzen Gene. 1
mûtwiligklich / leydē můssen / dar zů stillschweigen das wider Actuū. 10
1 Timo 4
Gott vnd dem nechsten ist / Wañ als Gott der herr den men- 1 Cor. 10
schen erschůff / hat er jm gewalt geben vber alle thier / vber den Coloss. 2
Ain christ
fogel im lufft vnd vber den fisch jm wasser. Darumb ist vnser liche erbie
begeren wañ ainer wasser hette dz ers mit gnůgsamer schriff tung
beweysen mag das man das wasser vnwyssenlych also erkaufft
hette / begeren wir jms nit mit gewalt zů nemen Sunder man Ein chri-
mûst ain Christlich eynsechen darynnen habē vō wegen stliche erbietung
brůderlicher lieb / aber wer nit gnůgsam anzaigen darum kan
90 thon / solß ainer gemayn zymlicher weyß mittailen.

DER FUNFFT ARTICKEL.

Zum fünfften seyen wir auch beschwert der beholtzung halb / Wie oben
im ersten
Dañ vnsere herschafften habend jnenn die hôltzer alle allain cap. des. 1
geaignet / vñ wañ der arm man was bedarff můß ers vmb zway bůch Mosi anzaigt
geldt kauffen / ist vnnser maynung was für hôltzer seyen / Es ist.

habens geistlich oder weltlich jnnen die es nit erkaufft haben /
sollen ayner gantzen gemain wider anhaim fallen / vñ ainer
gemayn zimlicher weiß frey sein aim yetlichē sein noturfft jnß
hauß zů brēen vm̄ sunst lassen nemen / auch wañ vō nôten sein

Hierauss wurde zů zym̄ern auch vm̄ sunst nemē / doch mit wissen der 100
nitt auss- so vō d' gemain darzů erwelt werdē. So aber kains verhandñ
rayttung
des holtz wer / dañ das so redlich erkaufft ist wordenn / Sol man sich mit
geschehen den selbigen briederlich vñ Christelich vergleichen / Wañ aber
wirt, ange-
sehen die das gůt am anfang auß jnen selbs geaygnet wer worden vnd
verordnet nachmals verkaufft worden / Sol man sich vergleichen nach
ē Ain crist
liche gestalt der sach vñ erkantnuß briederlicher lieb vnd heiliger
erbiet
tung geschrifft.

DER SECHST ARTICKEL.

Zům sechstcn ist vnser hart beschwerung der dyenst halben
wôlche von tag zů tag gemert werden vnd teglich zů nemen / 110
Roma. 10 begeren wir das man ain zimlich einsehen dar ein thů / vnß
der massen nit so hart beschweren / Sonder vns gnedig hier
jnnē ansehen wie vnser Eltern gedient haben allain nach laut
des wort gots.

DER SYBENT ARTICKEL.

Zům sibendē dz wir hinfüro vns ain herschafft nit weyter
wôlle lassen beschwerē / sond' wieß ain herschafft zymlicher
weiß aim verleycht also sol erß besitzen laut der verainigůg des
herren vñ bauren / Der herr soll jn nit weiter zwyngen noch
Luce. 3 dryngen mer dyenst noch anders von jm vmb sunst begeren / 120
1. Tessa. 4 Darmit der Baur solych gůtt onbeschwert also rüeblich
brauchen vnd niessen müg / ob aber des herrē dienst von
nôtten weren / sol jm der baur willig vñ gehorsam für ander
sein / doch zů stund vnd zeyt / das dem bauren nit zů nachtail
dyen / vnnd jme vmb aynen zymlichen pffenning deñ thůn.

DER ACHTET ARTICKEL.

Zům achten sey wir beschwert / vñ der vil. so gůter jnnen
haben / das die selbigen gůter die gült nit ertragen kindē vnd
die Bauren das jr darauff einbiessen vñ verderben. das die
herschafft dieselbigen gůter / Erberleüe besichtigen lassen / vñ 130
nach der billikayt ain gylt erschöpff / damit der baur sein
Math. 10 arbait nit vmb sunst thye / dañ ain yetlicher tagwercker ist
seyns lons wirdig.

DER NEUNDT ARTICKEL.

Zům neünten seyen wyr beschwertt der grossen frefel / so man Esaie. 10
Epheß. 6
stetz new satzung macht / nit dz man vnß strafft nach gestalt
der sach / sunder zů zeyten auß grossem neyd / vnd zů zeytten Luce. 3
auß grossem gunst / Jst vnser maynung / vns bey alter ge- Jhere. 26
schribner straff straffen / darnach die sach gehandelt ist / vnd
140 nit nach gunst.

DER ZEHENT ARTICKEL.

Zům zehenden sey wir beschwert / das etlich haben jnen Wye oben
zůgeaignet / wisen der gleichē ecker / die dañ ainer gemain zů Luce. 6
geherendt / Dieselbigen werden wir wider zů vnsern gemainen
handen nemen / Es sey dann sach das mans redlich erkaufft Christlich
hab / wañ mans aber vnbillycher weyß erkaufft het / Sol man erbietung.
sich gůtlich vnnd briederlich mit ainander vergleychen nach
gestalt der sach.

DER AYLFFT ARTICKEL.

150 Zům ailften wellen wir den brauch genant den todt fall gantz
vñ gar abthůn habñ / Den nimer leidē noch gestatten / das Deutro.18
man witwen waisen das jr wider Got vñ eerē / also schentlich Math. 8
nemen berauben sol / wie es an vil ortten (menigerlay gestalt) Esaie. 10
geschehen ist / vñ von den / so sy besitzen vnd beschirmen
solten / hand sy vns geschunden vnnd geschaben / vnd wañ sy
wenig fůg hettendt gehabt / hettendt diß gar genomen / dz Got
nit mer leidē wyl / sunder sol gantz absein / kain mensch nichts
hinfiro schuldig sein zů geben / weder wenig noch vyl.

BESCHLUß.

160 Zům zwelften ist unser beschluß vñ endtlyche maynůg / wann
ainer oder mer Artickel alßhie gesteldt (So dem wort Gotes nit
gemeß) weren / als wir dañ nit vermainen die selbigen artickel / Die weyl
wo man vns mit dem wort Gots für vnzimlich anzaigen / wolt el im wort
wyr daruon abston / wañ mans vns mit grnndt der schrifft Gotes be
erklert. Ob man vns schon etlich artickel yetz zů lyeß / vñ seyen.
hernach sich befendt das vnrecht weren / sollen sy von stundan Christ-
todt vñ absein. nichts mer gelten / der gleichen ob sich in der liche er-
schrifft mit der warhait mer artickel erfunden / die wider Got bietung.
vnd beschwernus des nåchsten weren / wôll wir vnns auch
70 vorbehalten / vnnd beschlossen haben / vnnd vns in aller

Christlicher leer yeben vnd brauchen / darumb wir **Gott den herren** bitten wöllen / der vns das selbig geben kan vnnd sunst nyemant / Der frid Christi sey mit vns allen.

(ii) Luther changes sides

(a) *Ermanunge zum fride auff die zwelff artikel der Bawrschafft ynn Schwaben* (1525)

(b) *Wider die mordischen vñ Reubischen Rotten der Bawren* (1525)

When the peasants named Luther as an arbiter of the rightness of their cause, they put him in a position where he must inevitably be the loser: if he decided in favour of the peasants, he would alienate the landowners and the bourgeoisie; if he rejected the peasants' claims as unjustified, he would naturally lose the support of the great mass of the rural population. In the light of Luther's undoubted courage in defence of the truth as he saw it, it is probably a mistake to see his ultimate condemnation of the peasants as evidence of a basely calculating mind. Luther was motivated by the biblically founded belief (Rom. 13: 1–7) that all authority was instituted of God and that even when authority acts immorally, the Christian should not resist outrage, but suffer it. Further, he was fundamentally out of sympathy with programmatic attempts to alleviate material hardship, since these always tend to deflect human endeavour from what he would regard as humanity's real purpose in life: material conditions, as he explained in the opening paragraphs of *Von der Freiheit eines Christenmenschen* (cf. p. 18), have nothing to do with the state of a man's soul. Even so, Luther's dealings with the peasants constitute one of the most unhappy episodes in the Reformer's career, although it is important not to attribute to him more than a moral responsibility for the events of the Peasants' War—the peasants would probably have risen without his preaching, just as the princes would have butchered them without his encouragement.

Initially Luther's reaction to the peasants' demands was not entirely unfavourable. His regard for authority notwithstanding, Luther's violent temper and personal knowledge of princely oppression, also no doubt a measure of pique at the refusal of many princes to listen to evangelical truth, led him in his reply to the Twelve Articles, *Ermanunge zum fride auff die zwelff artikel der Bawrschafft ynn Schwaben* (passage (a)), to rebuke the princes for their godless oppression of their subjects. The peasants, by contrast, are addressed as 'liebe herren vnd brüder' and gently reminded that violence and rebellion, however justified, are contrary to the will of God. The pamphlet was written in mid April 1525, but before it had left the presses, Luther changed sides. Frustration and pique at the failure of his preaching mission to the rebel peasants of the Harz, anger at the increasing influence of Müntzer and the *Schwarmgeister*, and annoyance at the vacillation of the new Saxon Elector (Frederick the Wise died early in May convinced that the rebellion was a judgement on him for having failed to embrace the reformed faith more warmly), combined with genuine outrage at the news of the peasant excesses

—which opponents naturally attributed to his influence—to produce the savage and intemperate outburst known as *Wider die mordischen vñ Reubischen Rotten der Bawren* in which he declared the peasants to be limbs of Satan and exhorted all right-minded men to kill them like so many mad dogs (passage (*b*)).

Not unnaturally this change of front caused Luther's opponents considerable satisfaction and his admirers equally great embarrassment. Even in an age of intemperate polemics and public cruelty, the violent and unchristian nature of Luther's language and the brutality with which the princes acted on his advice shocked public opinion. Luther's position might be theologically sound, but his admirers could scarcely shield him from the charge of a monumental lack of charity. It was to refute such a charge that Luther wrote *Eyn Sendebrieff von dem harten buchlin widder die bauren.* Here he deprecates unnecessary cruelty, such as the rape of Müntzer's pregnant widow by one of the conquering noblemen, sets forth his—not entirely convincing—distinction between God's kingdom, where mercy prevails, and the kingdom of the world, which is a place of anger and punishment, and then, in a fashion which epitomizes the dogmatic cruelty which in Christian Europe has so often gone hand in hand with religious conviction, stands by what he previously wrote against the peasants: 'Wer Gottes wort nicht will hören mit güete / der mus den hencker hören mit der schärpfe . . . Barmhertzig hyn / barmhertzig her / wyr reden itzt von Gottes wort / der will . . .'.

The lot of the peasants who survived the holocaust was in most cases probably not noticeably worse than before, but in other respects the Peasants' War represents an important turning-point in German history. The legitimate aspirations of large sections of the German people for a voice in the ordering of their own affairs had been brutally suppressed; the authority of the princes had been correspondingly strengthened and the inherent tendencies towards fragmentation into petty absolutist states confirmed. Lutheranism was still to achieve some notable successes in northern Europe, but 1525 none the less marks the turning of the Lutheran tide, which had previously seemed destined, in Germany at least, to sweep all before it. With Luther's 'betrayal' of the peasants, the Reformation ceased abruptly to be a national German movement and the great mass of the rural population of southern Germany either returned to their old Roman allegiance or sought solace in more radical forms of Protestantism. Thus to the political fragmentation of the Holy Roman Empire was added a deep religious division which has haunted the course of German history down to our own day.

Passage (*a*) is taken from the edition printed by Georg Rhaw of Wittenberg in 1525, passage (*b*) from the anonymously printed edition which appeared in Nürnberg in 1525.

(a) An die Fürsten vnd Herrn

Erstlich mûgen wir niemand auff erden danckē solchs vnradts vnd auffruhrs / denn euch Fûrsten vnd herrn / sonderlich euch blinden Bisschoffen vnd tollen Pfaffen vnd Mûnchen / die yhr noch heuttigs tages verstockt / nicht auffhôret zu toben vnd

wůten widder das heilige Euangelion / ob yhr gleich wisset das
es recht ist / vnd auch nicht widderlegen kůndet / Dazu ym
welltlichen regiment nicht mehr thut / denn das yhr schindet
vnd schatzt / ewern pracht vnd hohmut zu furen / bis der arme
10 gemeine man nicht kan noch mag lenger ertragen. Das schwerd
ist euch auff dem halse / noch meynet yhr yhr sitzt so feste
ym Satel / man werde euch nicht můgen ausheben / Solche
sicherheyt vnd verstockte vermessenheyt wird euch den halls
brechen / das werdet yhr sehen. Jch habs euch zuuor viel mal
verkůndigt / yhr solltet euch hůten fur dem spruch / Psalm.
104. Effundit contemptum super principes. Er schůttet verach-
tung vber die Fůrsten / Yhr ringet darnach / vnd wóllet auff
den kopff geschlagen seyn / da hilfft keyn warnen noch vermanen fur.
20   Wolan / weyl yhr denn vrsach seyt / solchs Gottes zorns /
wirds on zweiffel auch vber euch ausgehen / wo yhr euch noch
nicht mit der zeyt bessert. Die zeychen am hymel vnd wunder
auff erden gelten euch lieben herren / keyn guts deutten sie
euch / keyn guts wird euch auch geschehen. Es ist schon des
zorns eyn gros teyl angangen / das Gott so viel falscher lerer
vnd propheten vnter vns sendet auff das wyr zuuor mit yrthum
vnd Gottes lesterung reichlich verdienen die helle vnd ewige
verdamnis. Das ander stuck ist auch fur handen / das sich die
bawren rotten / daraus / wo Gott nicht weret / durch vnsere
30 busse bewegt / folgen mus / verderben / verstórung vnd ver-
wůstung Deutsches lands / durch grewlich / mord / vnd blut
vergiessen.
    Denn das sollt yhr wyssen / lieben herrn / Gott schaffts also /
das man nicht kan / noch will / noch solle ewr wueterey die
lenge dulden. Yhr můst anders werden / vnd Gotts wort
weichen / Thut yhrs nicht durch freundliche willige weyse / so
můst yhrs thun / durch gewelltige vnd verderbliche vnweise.
Thuns diese Bawren nicht / so můsens andere thun. Vnd ob
yhr sie alle schlůgt / so sind sie noch vngeschlagen / Gott wird
40 andere erwecken / Denn er will euch schlagen vnd wird euch
schlagen. Es sind nicht bawren / lieben herren / die sich widder
euch setzen / Gott ists selber / der setzt sich widder euch /
heymzusuchen ewer wueterey. Es sind etliche vnter euch / die
haben gesagt / sie wóllen land vnd leut dran setzen / die
Luterische lere auszurotten / Wie důnckt euch? wenn yhr ewr

eygen prophetē weret gewesen / vnd were schon land vnd leut
hynan gesetzt? Schertzt nicht mit Gott / lieben herrn / Die
Juden sagten auch wyr haben keynen Kŏnig / vnd ist eyn
solcher ernst worden / das sie ewiglich on kŏnig seyn mŭssen.

(b) Wider die stŭrm̄enden Bawren Martinus Luther.

Dreyerlay grewliche sünden wider Got vnd menschen laden
dise bawrn auff sich / daran sie den todt verdienet haben an
leybe vñ seele manigfeltiglich. Zum ersten / das sie yhrer
oberkait trew vñ hulde geschworen haben / vnderthenig vnd
gehorsam zŭsein / wie solchs Got gebeut / da er sprichtt/ Gebt
dem Kayser / was des kayers ist / Vñ Roma .xiij. Jcderman sey
der oberkait vnderthan etce. Weil sie aber disen gehorsam
brechen mŭtwilliglich vnnd mit freuel / vnd darzŭ sich wyder
jre herren setzen / haben sie damit verwirckt leyb vnnd seel / 10
als die trewlose meynaydige lugenhafftigē / vngehorsamen
buben vñ bŏßewicht pflegen zŭthŭn . . .

Zum andern / das sie auffrŭr anrichten / rauben vnd plun-
dern mit freuel Clŏster vnd Schlŏsser / die nicht jr seyndt / da
mit sie / als die offentlichen strassenreuber vnd mŏrder / allein
wol zwyfeltig den tod an leyb vnd seele verschulden. Auch ein
auffrŭrischer mensch / den man des bezeugen kan / schon ynn
Gottes vñ Kayserlicher acht ist / das / wer am ersten kan vnd
mag / den selben erwürgen / recht vnd wol thŭt / Denn vber
eynen offentlichen auffrŭrigen ist ain yeglicher mēsch baide 20
oberrichter vnd scharffrichter / gleych als wenn ain feür angeet
wer am ersten kann leschen / der ist der beste / denn auffrŭr
ist nicht ain schlechter mord / sondern wie ain groß feur / das
eyn land anzündet vñ verwŭstet / also bringt auffrŭr mit sich
ayn land vol mords / blŭtuergiessen / vñ macht witwen vñ
waisen vnd verstŏret alles / wie das aller grŏssest vnglück /
Drumb sol hie zerschmeyssen / würgen vñ stechen / haymlich
oder offenlich / wer da kan / vñ gedenckñ das nicht gifftigers /
schedlichers / teuffelischers sein kan / deñ ain auffrŭrischer
mēsch gleich als wenn man ainen tollen hund todschlahen 30
mŭß / schlegstu nicht / so schlecht er dich vñ ain gantz land
mit dir.

Zum dritten / das sie solliche schreckliche / grewliche sŭnde /
mit dem Euangelio decken / nennen sich Christliche Brŭder /
nemen ayd vnd hulde / vñ zwingen die leutte / zŭ solchen

greweln / mit jnen zů halten / damit sie die allergrôsten
Gotßlesterer / vñ schender seines hailigen namens werden /
vñ eeren vñ dienen also dem teuffel / vnder dem schein des
Euangelij / daran sie wol zehen mal den tod verdienen an
40　leyb vnd seele / das ich heßlicher sünde nye gehôrt habe. Vnd
achte auch / das der teuffel den jungsten tag empfinde dz er
solch vnerhorte stuck fürnimpt / als solt er sagen / Es ist das
letzte / drumb solt es dz ergste seyn / vñ will dye grundsuppe
rûren vnd den boden gar außstossen . . .

Aber die ôberkayt so Christlich ist / vnnd das Euanngelion
leydet / derhalben auch die bawern keynen schein wider sie
haben / sol hie mit forchten handeln. Vnnd zum ersten die
sachen Got heymgeben / vnd bekennen / das wir solchs wol verdienet haben / Dazů sorgenn / das Got villeicht den Teuffel also
50　errege zů gemayner straff Deutschs lands. Darnach demûtig-
lich bitten wider den Teuffell vmb hulffe / Denn wir fechtenn
hie nicht allein wider blůt vnd flaysch / sondern wider die
geystlichen bôßwicht in der lufft / welche mit gebet mûssen
angegriffen werdenn. Wenn nu das hertze so gegenn Got
gerichtet ist das mann seinen gôtlichen willen lest walten / ob
er vns wôll oder nicht wôlle zů Fürsten vnd herrn haben / sol
man sich gegen den tollen pauren zum yberfluß (ob sy es wol
nicht werdt sind) zů recht vnd gleichem erbieten Darnach wa
das nit helffen wil / fluchs zum schwert greyffen.
60　Dann ein Fürst vnd herre mûß hie gedencken / wie er Gotes
amptman vnd seins zorns diener ist Roma. am xiij. dem das
schwert vber solch bûben beuolhen ist Vnd sich ebenn so hoch
für got versündigt / wo er nicht strafft vnnd weret / vnnd seyn
ampt nicht volfürt / als wann einer mordet / dem das schwert
nicht beuolhen ist. Dañ wa er kan / vñ strafft nit / es sey durch
mord oder blůtuergiessen / so ist er schuldig an allem mord
vnd vbel / das solche buben begeen / als der da mûtwiligklich
durch nachlassen seines gôtlichen beuelhs / zůlest solche
boßhayt zůûben so ers wol weren kan vnd schuldig ist / Darumb
70　ist hie nicht zů schlaffen. Es gilt auch nicht hie gedult oder
barmhertzikayt / Es ist des schwerts vnd zorns zeyt hie vnnd
nichtt der genaden zeyt.

So sol nu die ôberkayt hie getrost fort dringen / vnd mit
gutem gewissen drein schlahen / weyl sie ein ader regen kan /
dañ hie ist das vrtayl / das die baweren bôse gewissen vnd

vnrecht sachen haben / vnd welcher bauer darüber erschlagen wirdet mit leib vnd seel verloren vñ ewig des teüffels ist. Aber die oberkayt hat ein gůt gewissen vnd recht sachen / vnd kan zů got also sagen mit aller sicherhayt des hertzens / Sihe / mein got / du hast mich zum Fürsten oder herrn gesetzt / daran ich 80 nicht kan zweyffeln / vnnd hast mir das schwert beuolhen vber die vbeltheter Roman .xiij. Es ist dein wort vnnd mag nicht liegenn. So můß ich solchs ampt / bey verlust deyner gnaden / außrichten / So ist es auch offenlich / das dise bauern vilfaltig vor dir vnd vor der welt den tod verdient / vnd mir zů straffen beuolhen. Wilt nu mich durch sie lassen tôdtenn / vnnd mir die ôberkayt wider nemen vnd vnter geen lassen / wolan so gesche dein will / So stirbe ich doch vnnd gee vnter inn deynem gôtlichen befelh vnnd wort / vnnd werd erfunden im gehorsam deynes befelhs vnnd meines ampts. Darumb wil ich straffenn 90 vnnd schlahen so lang ich eine ader regen kan / du wirst wol richten vnnd machen.

Also kans dann geschehen / das / wer auff der oberkeyt seytē erschlagen wirdt / ein rechter merterer vor got sey / so er mit solchem gewissenn streyt / wie gesagt ist Denn er geet inn Gôtlichem wort vnd gehorsam Widerumb was auff der baweren seyten vmbkompt / ein ewiger hellebrandt ist / denn er fůret dz schwert wider gottes wort vnnd gehorsam / vnd ist ein teuffels glid Vnnd obs gleich geschehe / das die bawern oblegenn da got fur sey / denn got sein alle ding müglich / vnd wir nicht 100 wissen / ob er villeicht zum vorlauff des Jungstē tags / welcher nicht ferne sein wil / wôlle durch den teüffel alle ordnung vnd oberkayt zů stôrenn vnd die welt in einen wůstē hauffen werffen / So sterben doch sicher vnd geen zů scheyttern mit gůtem gewissenn die inn jrem schwerd ampt funden werdenn vnnd lassen dem teüffel das weltlich reych / vnd nemen darfür das ewige reych Solch wunderliche zeyttē seind yetzt / dz ein Fürst den himel mit blůtuergiessen verdienenen kan / bas dann anndere mit beten . . .

Drumb lieben herren loset hie / retet hie / helfft hie / erbarmt 110 euch der armen leute / Steche / schlahe / würge hie wer da kan bleybstu drůber tod / wol dir / seligklichern tod kanstu nymmer meer vberkom̄en. Denn du stirbst in gehorsam gôtt- lichs wortes vnd beuelhs Roma .xiij. vnnd im dienst der liebe den en nechsten zurretten auß der hellen vñ Teuffels banden.

So bitte ich nu / flyehe von den bawren wer da kan / als vom teuffel selbs. Die aber nicht fliehen / bitte ich got wolte sye erleüchten vnd bekeren. Wólche aber nicht zůbekeren sind / da gebe got / das sy kain glück noch gelingen haben můssen Hie sprech ain yeglicher frummer Christ / Amen. Deñ das gebet ist recht vnd gůt vnd gefellet got wol / das wayß ich. Dunckt das yemandt zů hart der denck das vntreglich ist auffrůr vnnd alle stunde der welt verstôrung zů warten sey.

120

8. The sectarian legacy of the Reformation

(i) Balthasar Hubmaier preaches Anabaptism

Ain Suͫ ains gantzen Christenlichen lebens (1525)

Amongst the numerous radical sects which emerged in German-speaking lands in the wake of the Lutheran reformation, probably the most important and certainly the most appealing was the movement known as Anabaptism. The earliest Anabaptists were followers of Zwingli in Zürich who in 1523 broke with the Swiss reformer on account of the latter's readiness to compromise with the secular authorities on the question of how quickly the new evangelical teaching on the ecclesiastical use of pictures and the new form of the Eucharist should be implemented. The 'splinter group', led by a certain Conrad Grebel, thus from the very start showed itself to be in opposition to instituted authority and this attitude was to condition the outlook of the Anabaptists for decades to come. The question of adult baptism, from which the movement was to get its name, was not merely an academic issue. Most of the Reformers, with their emphasis on faith as a precondition to the operation of the sacraments (as opposed to the Roman doctrine of *ex opere operato*, i.e. that the action of the priest 'created' grace irrespective of the faith of the participants), had inclined to question the appropriateness of baptizing infants and had resorted to various subterfuges to retain it—Luther, for instance, postulated a dormant faith in the infant similar to the faith of a sleeping man. In rejecting infant baptism in favour of the 'baptism of faith' administered to those who had reached the years of discretion, the Anabaptists made baptism a symbolical act by which the individual left the wider state-community and became a member of a small dedicated band of consciously Christian believers. This was more important than might appear at first sight: in effect, the age-old concept of the *corpus Christianum*, the identity of the Christian community and the 'Christian' State, was questioned and the interests of the former seen to be different from, if not hostile to, the latter. Not surprisingly, the State reacted savagely to the questioning of its authority: adult baptism was proscribed and those preaching it subjected to a merciless persecution which succeeded only in spreading the teaching from its original home to the furthest corners of the Empire. By virtue of their physically scattered nature and the avoidance of a centralized organization, the Anabaptists tended to split into a number of sects, each emphasizing different aspects of the central doctrines: thus the Melchiorites (followers of Melchior Hoffmann) in north-west Germany tended to a chiliastic, revolutionary antinomianism which in 1534–5 culminated in the disastrous attempt to establish the Kingdom of God in Münster; the Mennonites (followers of Menno Simons) in the Low Countries, by contrast, were puritanical and pacifist in outlook, while the Hutterer (followers of Jakob Huter) preached a primitive communism within a tightly organized social framework. With other Protestants the Anabaptists share a Christocentric biblicism, and it was above all the central position given to the community and the attempt to put into practical effect the precepts of the Sermon on the Mount and to practise a literal *imitatio Christi* in a life of service to one's fellow men which united them in a recognizable 'movement'. Concomitant with the emphasis on their own community was a certain isolationism *vis-à-vis* the outside world, which was to be converted, but in which believers—who refused to hold office, take oaths, or sit in judgement on their neighbours—could not participate fully. In spite of the savage persecution to which the Anabaptists were subjected they were never stamped out completely, and in an indirect way they contributed considerably to the development of the Protestant ethic and, especially in England, Canada, and the United States, where they still flourish, to the establishment of a Free Protestant Church.

Balthasar Hubmaier (b. *c.* 1482 near Augsburg) came under the influence of Zwingli in the early 1520s, while he was parish priest at Waldshut. In the fashion of the Reformers he began to hold services in German, rejected the ecclesiastical use of pictures, and married. By 1525 his early sympathy with Zwingli had disappeared and he adopted an increasingly Anabaptist position. Driven from Waldshut by the change in political circumstances consequent on the defeat of the peasants in 1525, he fled to Zürich, where he was imprisoned and recanted his Anabaptism. Almost immediately he withdrew his recantation, but after a further period in gaol was allowed to go free on condition he left the city. In 1526 he settled in Nikolsburg (Moravia) where he gained a considerable following. In most respects his teachings were close to those of the 'Swiss Brethren', except that he did not share their pacifism, hence the designation of his followers as 'Schwertler' (in contradistinction to the Swiss 'Stäbler'). The open hostility of the Austrian rulers of Moravia to the Anabaptists on both political and religious grounds caused the movement to be outlawed. Hubmaier was arrested in July 1527 and taken to Vienna. Here he was subjected to the customary torture, but refused to recant and was burnt at the stake on 10 March 1528. Three days later his wife was executed by drowning in the Danube.

Our extract was published as an independent pamphlet in 1525, appearing also in slightly modified form as Chapter VII of Hubmaier's *Von dem Christenlichen Tauff der glaübigen* of the same year, and is the earliest published statement of the Anabaptist position. The basic view of man as a creature of sin in whom there is no health and who must despair of his salvation is strikingly similar to that of Luther (cf. *Von der Freiheit eines Christenmenschen,* pp. 21 f.)—even the point of departure from Mark 1: 15 is the same as that of the ninety-five theses. It is the consequence which Hubmaier and his followers draw from the common premiss which is different—the assertion that the believer must signify his change of heart by being baptized and becoming a member of a distinct community. Luther equally taught that true Christians would always be in a minority in a distinctly wicked world, but his followers were never allowed to 'contract out'; worldly authority, Luther taught, was instituted by God for the protection of the community and it is a 'work of love' to honour and respect it. For the Anabaptists, however, the world and all in it—including the State—were sinful and of the Devil, something with which the believer could not compromise and which would of necessity persecute him as it had persecuted Christ. Hubmaier's teachings on the Eucharist, which take up the second half of the pamphlet, show a close kinship with those of Zwingli (cf. p. 57).

Jn Summa.

Zům ersten / Christus / do er leeret ain Christenlichs leben / Sagt er / Enderend oder besserend ewer leben / vnd glaubend dem Euangelio / Nun zů der enndrung deß lebens gehört / das wyr yn vnns selbs gangen / vnd erynneren vns vnsers thons vnnd laßsens / so befynden wir / das wyr thond wider Gott / vnd lassen / das er vns hat beuolhen / Ja wir befynden kayn gsundthayt in vns / sonder gyfft / verwundung vnd alle vnrainigkayt / die vns von anfang anhangt / wir seynd darinn
10 entpfangen vnd geboren / Also beclagt sich Job / Dauid / Hieremias / Joannes vnd ander gotselig menschen / Nun vber das befyndt der mensch in im auch weder hylff / trost oder ertzney / darmit er im selbs helffen möge / darumb so můß er an im selbs verzweyflen vnnd verzagen / wie der mensch / so do war in die morder eingefallen / Also ain ellennd dyng ist es vmb ayn menschen / der sich selbs hinderdenckt vnd erkennet.

Für das ander / So můß der Samaritan kommen / das ist Cristus / der bringt mit im ertzney / nåmlich wein vnd öl / vnd geüsts dem sünder in die wunden / Wein / er gibt dem
20 menschen ain rewen / das im seyn sünd layd seyen / vnnd öl / mitt wellchem er den schmertzen vertreybt vnd miltert / vnd spricht / Glaubend dem Euangelio / das klarlich anzaygt / das ich der artzt sey / der komen ist in dise welt / den sünder gerecht vnd fromb zemachen / Das Euangelium leert auch / das ich bin der ainig gnådiger / versöner / fürbitter / mitler / vnnd fridmacher gegen Got vnserm vatter / wer in mich glaubt / der würt nit verdampt / sonder hatt das ewig leben / durch

solliche trostwort würt der sünder widerũ erkickt / kombt zů
im selbs würt frölich / vnd ergibt sich füran an den artzt / also
das er im all sein kranckhait beuilhet / haimsetzt / vertrawet / 30
will sich auch / als vil ainem verwůten müglich / in seinen
willen ergeben / vnd růfft in an vmb gesundtmachung / darmit
was der verwundt auß aygem vermögen nit vermag / das im
der artzt radte / helffe vnd fürdere / darmit er seynem wort
vnnd bevelch volgen möge / Nun die leeren all / so die kranck-
hayt anzaygen / oder auff den artzt weisen / ee vnd sy glaubt
werden / seind sy ain bůchstab vnd tödtendt / aber im glauben /
macht sy der gayst Gottes lebendig / das sy anfahen leben /
grůnen vnd frücht bingen / also würt das wasser im glauben
zů wein auff d' hochzeit / vñ můß mã zůuor den rauhē rock 40
Joañis anlegen / ee vnd man das waich / lind vnd senfftmůtig
lemblin Christum Jesum möge vberkommen / Vñ yetz ergibt
sich der mensch inwendig im hertzen vnd fürsatz / in ain neu
leben / nach der regel vnd leer / Christi deß artzts / der in hat
gsund gemachet / vnnd von dem er hatt / das leben / Also
bekennt Paulus offentlich / das er nit lebe / sonder Christus
lebe in ym / derselb sey in im das leben / vnd ausserhalb deß
Christi / bekennt er sich vnnd seyne werck / eytel / zenichtig vnd
ain vnsåligen sünder.

Zům dritten. Nach dem vnd nun sich der mensch inwendig 50
vnd im glauben / in ain new leben ergeben hat / bezeügt er
auch das außwendig / offenlich vor d' Christenlichen kirchen /
in dero gmainschafft er sich lasset verzaychnen / vnnd einschrey-
ben / nach der ordnung vñ einsetzung Christi / Gibt derhalb
der Christenlichen kyrchen / das ist / allen schwestern vnd
brüdern / die da leben im glauben / in Christo / zů erkennen /
das er dermassen im wort Christi inwendig vnderricht / vnd
gesyñet seye / das er sych schon ergeben hab / nach dem wort /
willen vnd regel Christi füran zeleben / sein thon vnd lassen /
nach im schlichten vnd richten / auch vnder seinem fenlin 60
kempfen vnd streyten biß in den tod / vñ lasset sich tauffen mit
dem außwendigen wasser / in wellchem er offenlich bezeüget /
seinen glauben vnd fürnemen / Nemlich das er glaube / das er
ain gnådigen / gůtigen vnd barmhertzigñ Got vnd vatter habe
im himel / durch Jesum Christum / mit dem sey er wol daran /
vnnd zůfriden / Er hab im auch fürgesetzt / vnd sich inwendig
schon verpflicht / das er füran seyn leben enndern vnd bessern

welle / Er bezeüge auch solchs offenlich mit der entpfahung
deß wassers / Ob er füran mit offentlichen vnd ergerlichen
70 sünden den glauben vñ namen Christi beschwertzen oder
tadelen wurde / das er sich hiemit verpflichte vnd ergebe in
brůderliche straff nach der ordnung Christi. Matth. 18.

Zům vierten / Die weyl aber der mēsch wayßt vñ bekennt /
das er von natur ain bôser / wurmstichiger vnd vergiffter baum
ist / vnd kan noch mag auß ym selbs kayn gůte frucht bringen /
geschicht derhalb dyse pflicht / zůsagung vñ offenliche zeugknuß nit auß menschlichen krefften oder vermôgen / dañ das
wer ain vermůttung oder mennschliche vermessenhayt / sonder in dem namen Gottes vatters vnd sons vnd deß hailigen
80 gaysts / Oder in dem namen vnsers herren Jesu Cristi / dz ist /
in der gnad vñ krafft Gotes / dañ es ist als nun ain krafft /
auß dem allē eruolget / das der außwenndig tauff Christi
nichs anders ist / dann ain offenliche zeugknuß der inwen-
digen pflichten / mit der sich der mensch bezeugt vnnd vor
mengklich sich anzaygt / das er sey ain sünder / gibt sich
deßselben schuldig / doch darbey glaub er gentzlich / das
Christus im sein sünd durch seinen tod verzigē hab / vnd durch
seyn vrsteend in fromb gemacht / vor dem angesicht Gotes /
vnnsers himelischen vatters / Derhalb hab er schon bewilligt
90 für hin den glauben vnd namen Jesu Christi vor mengklich /
vnnd offentlich zů bekennen / habe sich auch verpflicht vnd im
fürgesetzt / nach dem wort vnd beuelch Chrysti füran zeleben /
aber das nit auß menschlichem vermôgen / darmit im nit beschehe wie Petro / dann on mich môgt ir nichts thůn / spricht
Christus / sonder in der krafft Gotes vatters vnd deß sons vñ
deß hailigen gaists / Yetz bricht der mensch auß im wort vñ
werck / verkündet vnd macht groß den namen vnd lob Christi /
darmit auch ander durch vns haylig vnd selig werden / wie wyr
durch ander / die vns Christum vor gepredigt / auch seynd zům
100 glauben komen / auff das / das reych Christi gemeert werde.

Hie volgt / veruolgung / das creütz / vnd alle trůbseligkayt /
von deß Euangelions wegen in der welt / die dañ hasset das
liecht vnd leben / vnd hatt lieb die finsternuß / Die welt will
nit ain übelthâtterin seyn / sonder fromb vñ gerecht in aygnen
wercken / macht ir selbs satzung vnd regel / dardurch sy
vermaynt sâlig zůwerden / verachtet die vnansehenlichen /
schlechten / ainfeltigen regel Christi / Hie springt herfür der

alt Adam / das ist / die vergifft natur / wie wir seyen in můtter-
leyb entpfangen vnd geboren / der selb lasset sein alt thück nit /
er reget die oren / er braucht seyn angeborne art / vnd wider- 110
strebt dem gayst ym menschen / das er nit thůdt / was er wille /
nach dem wort Gottes / da solle das flaysch getôdt werden / vnd
wil aber es nun leben vnnd regieren / nach seynen lüsten / Hie
liget ob vnnd syget der gayst Christi vnd bringt der mensch
gůt früchten / die nun zeügknuß gebennd ains gůten baums /
vnd yebt sich tag vnd nacht / yn allem dem / so das lob Gottes
antrifft / vnd brůderliche liebe.

Das ist ain summ vñ rechte ordnung ains gantzen Christenlichen lebens. Das do anfahet im wortt Gotes / darauß eruolgt
erkanntnuß der sünden vnd verzeyhung der selben im glauben / 120
Der glaub geett nit můssig / sonder ist arbaitsam in allen gůtten
Christenlichen werckē / Das seind aber allain gůte werck / die
Got selbs vns gehayssen hat / vnd vm̃ die er rechnung eruordern
wirt / am jüngsten tag. Math. 26. c.

Zům fünfften / Nach dem wir nun in dem glauben auß dem
wort Gottes / hell vnd clar erkennt haben / die vberschåtzlichen /
vnausprechenliche gůthait gotes / sollen wir darum̃ danckbar
sein / Got vnserem hymelischen vatter / welcher ye die welt
also ynbrünstigklich geliebt hat / das er seines aingebornē Sons
nit verschonet / sonder dē für vns dar gestreckt biß in tod / Ja 130
in den tod deß aller schendtlichsten creützes / darmit wyr selig
wurden / Hatt demnach Christus Jhesus vnser hayland selbs /
ain schône gedåchtnuß geordnet vnd eingesetzt / in seynem
letsten nachtmal / auff das wir sein nit vergessen / Dann als er
vnd seyne Jünger mit ainander assen / nam er das brott vnnd
saget wol / vnd sprach / Nement vnd essend / Das ist mein leyb /
der für euch geben würdt / das thůnd inn meyner gedåchtnuß /
Dergleych name er das drinckgeschirr / vnnd gab yn allen
zůtrincken / vnnd saget / Nemend vnd trinckend / Das ist
meyn blůt / das für euch vergossen würt / Zů verzeyhung der 140
sünden / das thůnd in meyner gedåchtnuß. Hie syhet mengklich
das brot / brot ist vnd wein / wein / wie ander brot vñ wein /
aber doch also eingesetzt / von Christo / Zů ainer ermanung
vnnd widergedåchtnuß / Als offt wir das brot mit aynander
brechen / außthaylen vnd eßßen / das wyr sollen seyns gebro-
chnen leybs für vnns an dem creütz / vñ außgethaylt / allen
denen / so in essen vñ nyessen im glaubē / yngedenck seyn /

da greyfft man augenscheynlich / das das brott nitt ist der
leyb Christi / sonder allayn ain ermanung desselben / Deß-
150 gleych ist der wein nit das blůt Christi / sonder auch ain
gedåchtnuß / das er sein blůt vergossen / vnd außthailt hab am
creütz / allen glaubigen / zů abwåschůg irer sünden / wie auch
der rayff vor dem wirtzhauß / nit weyn ist / sonnder ain gedåchtnuß desselben / Der gůthayten sollen wyr billich ingedenck
seyn / vnd nit vergessen / sonder die verkünden / auß schreyen
vnnd darum̄b danckbar sein in die ewigkait / Deß ermanet vns
Paulus gar ernstlich / do er schreybt zů den Corinthern .1.
Corinth. 11. cap. Als offt ir essend das brot (merckend / er
nemmets brot / vnd ist brot) vnnd ir trinckend das trinckgschir /
160 das ist den wein. (merckend / es ist weyn / dz man trinckt) sollen
ir deß herren tod verkünden / biß er kom̄t / Merckend / er
spricht / Biß er kombt / So hôrend wir wol das er nit da ist /
sonder er würdt erst kommen zů der stund deß jüngsten ge-
richts / in seyner grossen mayesteet vnd herrlykait / offenlich /
wie der blitz von Orient / biß gen Occident scheynende.

Hierauß eruolget vnd würdt grundtlich erlernet / das das
nachtmal nichts anders ist / dañ ain widergedåchtnuß deß
leydens Christi / der sein leyb von vnsert wegen dargestreckt /
vnd seyn rosenfarb blůt am creütz vergossen / zů abwåschůg
170 vnserer sünden / Auß dysem nachtmal habñ wir bißher ain
bern mose gemacht / die sach mit mum̄len vñ brum̄len außgericht / vnd die selben vmb groß gůt vnd gelt verkaufft / vnd
woltens füran noch gern thůn / das es got klagt sey / Welcher
mensch nu das nachtmal Cristi dermassen begeet / vnd
betracht das leyden Christi / in ainem vesten glauben / derselb
würdt auch Got vmb dyse genad vnnd gůthayt danck sagen /
sych in den willen Christi ergeben / der dañ ist / wie er vns
gethon hab / das wir auch also vnserem nåchsten thůn sollen
vnd vnser leyb / leben / gůt vnd blůt von desselben wegen dar
180 spañen / das ist der wil Christi / vnd die weyl vns solchs abermals
vnmüglich ist / sollen wir zů got růffen emssigklich vmb gnad
vnd krafft / das er vns die mitteyle / auff das wir also seinen
willen verbringen môgen / dañ wo er nit gnad gibt / so ist es
vmb vnns schon verloren / wir seind menschen vnd waren
menschen / vnd werden menschen / byß in den tod bliben.

O lieben herrn / freünd vnd brůder / nemendt zů hertzen / wz
ich eüch gesagt hab / vnd drachtent nach dem hellen / claren /

luteren wort Christi / daruß allain eüch / der glaub kumbt / in
dem wir miessen selig werden / dañ die Axt ist an die wurtzel
des boms gestelt / ist nichts verhanden / dañ dz er abgehauen 190
werde. Jch sag eüch fürwar / Fürchtendt jr den reyffen hie
zeitlich / Es wirdt der schne ewiger kelten vff eüch fallen /
Fürchtendt jr die kolen / Jr werdēt gar in dz feŭr fallen / dañ
Christus sagt mit heyttern worten / Welcher mich bekeñt vor
den mēschen / den wil ich bekennen vor gott meinem vatter /
welcher mich verleügnet vor den menschen / des will ich vor
gott verleügnen / fürchtent nit die / so euch den lib (der mer ist
dañ das gŭt) nemēn mŏgen / sond' fürchtent den / der eüch
lib vnd seel nemmen mag vnd werffen in die ewigen verdam-
nuß / wer oren hab / der here / das hŏrt vñ streng vrteyl gotes / 200
über die / stillschweiger vnd verleügner seins worts / wer nit
hŏren will / den erleücht vnser herr Got. Amen.

Hiemit seind got beuolhē.

Gebē zŭ waldshŭt Sambstag nach Petri vnd Pauli. Anno etc.
jm xxv.

(ii) Sebastian Franck condemns a literal approach to the
Bible, rejects all institutionalized religion, and preaches the
Church Spiritual

Paradoxa (1534)

The Anabaptists were only the largest recognizable group amongst the sectarians who made up the 'left wing' of the Reformation. Scholars differentiate
between 'enthusiasts' ('Schwärmer'), 'spiritualists', and 'anti-trinitarians',
but these minor groups tended to shade into each other and never constituted religious movements of a rigid or unified kind: certainly none
established 'churches' in the conventional sense. They did, however, represent a 'third force' which, for all its relative lack of denominational cohesion,
is of considerable importance and interest, and it is amongst the members of
this 'third force' that some of the most remarkable men of the age are numbered. Men like Paracelsus, Hans Denck, Sebastian Franck, Valentin Weigel,
Caspar von Schwenkfeld, Thomas Müntzer, and Andreas Carlstadt are
incapable of neat systematization: often their only real point of contact lies
in their 'extra-ecclesiastical' position and their allegiance to a loose tradition
of unorthodox thought which links the mystics and heretics of the Middle
Ages with Jakob Böhme and more modern philosophers. Each must be taken
on his own terms. In the general context of the Reformation, however, it is
important to remember that they represent only the visible tip of an iceberg
of considerable size and that their dissatisfaction with the orthodoxies of
Lutheran and Catholic is also an expression of the inarticulate dissatisfaction

of the generations of humbler men who sought a personal and private path to God outside the established confessions.

Sebastian Franck (1499–*c.* 1543) achieved prominence in a number of fields—as historian, geographer, pacifist, and as the compiler of a famous collection of proverbs—but it is as the leading spiritualist of his age that he is chiefly remembered. He studied at Heidelberg, was ordained as a Roman Catholic priest in 1524, but shortly afterwards was converted to Lutheranism and for a time was active as a Lutheran preacher at Gustenfelden, near Ansbach. Shortly after his conversion, he came under Anabaptist influence and left the Lutheran ministry to settle in Nürnberg, where he married in 1528. Like all sectarians Franck was, however, never tolerated for long in any one place, and in the course of the next ten years he lived in Strassburg, Esslingen, Ulm, and Basel, variously employed as a soap-maker, printer, and free-lance writer, but always persecuted by the local Protestant clergy as a man who posed a serious threat to their own narrow orthodoxies.

As a thinker Franck stands in the tradition established by the late medieval mystics and carries their spiritualization of religion to its ultimate conclusion. His views are expressed primarily in the long history of the world he published in 1531 under the title *Chronica Zeytbuch vnd geschycht bibel* and in the *Paradoxa* of 1534 (second extended edition, 1542), in which he develops in a series of some 280 paradoxes his views on the mysterious and esoteric nature of religion. Religious orthodoxies and all forms of organized religion he regards as barriers between the believer and God. Since God is a spirit, he will speak to his children in spirit and has no need of other channels of communication or revelation, whether they be priests or Scriptures. The Bible does indeed contain the word of God, but the latter is only to be understood in the light of direct personal revelation, which is not to be achieved by listening to preachers or reading commentaries—these simply confuse and obscure the truth—but by the operation of the divine spirit in the 'gelassen' heart of the believer. (Characteristically, Franck is fond of this mystical term.) Further, the world is material by nature and thus is entirely incompatible with the spirit of God and consequently needs must persecute or pervert true religion. Organized churches, being of the world, are thus not temples of God, but temples of the Devil, and the true believer cannot belong to any of these material churches, but is a member of the invisible community of the members of Christ, who are not, however, in a position to recognize and know each other. When compounded with Franck's natural charity and his view of the world as a place of inverted values, the tolerance and forbearance engendered by his position as a 'sectarian without a sect' was to give Franck as a historian and as a man a freedom from prejudice and a readiness to re-examine received opinions which were without parallel in an age of increasing intolerance.

Our extract is taken from the preface of the *Paradoxa*. The text is that of the edition published in 1542.

Nun hab ich diß mein Philosophei Paradoxa intituliert / vnd Paradoxum ein Wunderred / oder Wunderwort / verteutscht / Dieweyl die Theologey / der recht siñ der Schrifft (so allein

Gottes wort ist) nichts ist / dañ eyn ewig Paradoxum / wider
allen wahn / scheyn / glauben / vnd achtung der gantzen welt /
gewiß vnd war.

Dann es darff niemandt gedencken / daß das Euangelium
welt sey / oder das es die welt glaub / also halt / oder leyden
môg. Es haben alle botten Gottes ûber diser thôrechten vner-
hôrten Wunderred mûssen zû grund gehen / als ketzer vnd 10
bûben. Vnd das haben allweg die weysesten vnd frûmbsten der
welt gethan / vnd jnen ein gûten gnedigen / fleyschlichen Got
fürgedicht / der nit so narrecht / auch jnen nit so feindt sey /
das er solch ding beger / das eyner sich selbs hasse vnd abtôdte /
Es mûß der teuffel vnd nit Got seyn / der den leutten also ûbel
wil / vnd sie für narren helt. Auß mit disem feindtseligen Got /
der den menschen so ûbel will / vnnd jrem fleysch vnnd blût /
leib vnd leben / so feindt ist / das er dasselbig hassen / vnd ein
yeden sich seyner selbs verzeihen heißt / Es mûß gewiß der
Teuffel seinn / disser aber spricht die welt sey der almechtig / 20
gûttig / gnedig Got ein freundt vnd liebhaber der menschen /
der vns allein creutz trubsal vnd leyden abhilfft / vnnd nit
auflegt sonder vns glûck vnd heyl / gelt / ehr / gût / lang leben /
schon weib / kind / &c. verschaffet vñ darbey handthabet.
Aber das ist im neuwen Testament der teuffel / darumb helt
jhn die gantz welt fûr jhren Got vnd Fûrsten / wie jhn dann die
schrifft der welt Fûrsten vnd Got nent / den sie liebt / lobt / vnd
anbett in jrem hertzen / Joh. am 12.14.16 2. Corinth. am 4.
Widerumb was der lebendig Got ist / Nemlich eyn Geyst / vnd
derhalb seyner art nach / wider das fleysch / spricht sie / es sey 30
der teuffel / Wie an Christo / Luc. 11. Matt. 12. John. 8. wol
schein ist. Darum̃ sagt die gantz welt in jrẽ hertzen / wie Dauid
Psal. 14. spricht vnd nit im mund (da sie vil von eynem geistlichen leben von Got sagẽt / nach dem wahn vñ dichtung jres
hertzens) es sey keyn got / Darumb ist jr Got eyn Abgot / der
Teuffel / vnd gedicht jres hertzens.

Daher kompt es / das auch Gottes wort nit bey jr fehet noch
stat hat / Jtem das sie die Schrifft (derenn rechter siñ eyttel
wunderred sind) nit verstehet / dañ sie lassen jnen diß nicht
eingehen / vñ sind vil anders gesinnet / Ja stracks des wider- 40
spils. Darum̃ bleibt jhnen diß bûch verschlossen mit siben
Sigeln / schlossen / vnd hindernûssenn / die vorhin weg gethan
werden / vñ auffgehen mûssen. Was die siben sigel sind / ist

itzt nit stat zů sagenn. Das wiß aber gewiß / das Got mit fleiß
ein sondere sprach / vñ in Parabolis mit den seinen redt / das
die gotlosen so draussen sind / nit verstehen / was er mit seinē
kindern red / oder wil / Wie Christus deutlich sagt / das er
darum̃ verdeckt in Parabolis / durch eyn Allegorische / ver-
wendte red (wie Pythagoras mit seynen jüngern) mit jnen
50 redt / das seyn geheymnus vnder dem vmbhang des Bůch-
stabens verdeckt / in der Schůl blib / vor den gotlosen zůge-
deckt / vnd allein seyne kinder vernemen / Matth. 12. Joh. 12.
Nit das jnen Got entgehe / sonder darumb / das er weyß / das
sie der warheit nit vǎhig vnd wirdig sind / Ja das sie sew vnd
hund sind / die nur mit fůssen darauff tretten. Derhalben hebt
erß vor jnen auff / vnd verbirgt den geyst / das gemůt Christi /
den verstandt der Schrifft (der alleyn Gottes wort ist) vnder
ein verwendeten / allegorischen bůchstaben / den niemandt sol
verstehen vnd wissen / dann die jenen denen er disen außlegt /
60 vnd in der schůl Christi leret. Darumb bleibt die schrifft ein
ewig Allegori / Wunderred / rhǎtterschafft / verschlossen bůch /
tȯtender Bůchstab / vnd ein vnuerstendigs Rotwelsch / allen
Gotlosen / vnd eyn sondere sprach der kinder Gottes. Darumb
ist der Bůchstab on das liecht des Heyligē geysts ein finstere
Latern / den Paulus den todt vnd fürhang nent / 2. Cor. 3.
welcher die Phariseer hindert / das sie Mosi nit vnder die augen
mochten sehen / wirt aber hinweg gezogē / so wir vns zum
Herren bekeren / Dann so wir seynen willen wȯllen thůn / also
daß wir auch sonst nichts mehr dañ seynen willen darin
70 sůchen / vnd vns ernst ist / so legt er vns den selben auß /
Joh. 7 . . .
Was macht alle ketzerey in der Schrifft / dañ das den vnge-
reimbten Bůchstabenn der schrifft einer da ansticht / der ander
dort für sich nimpt / vnnd der einhelligen außlegung vnd
verstandt des fridsamen geysts niemandt achtet / sond' jederman den selbigē für sein Apollinē / got / vñ gottes wort achtet /
So er doch nur ein krip Christi / der tod / finsternuß / monstrantz / arch / scheid / latern / zeugnus / schloß / verschlossen
bůch / ja kaum der vorhoff in das heyligthumb ist. Gots wort
80 aber ist / der H. geyst / das liecht / schlůssel / schwert / leben /
heyligthumb / brodt / vnd Christus selbst. Derhalb ist nichts
mer wider den siñ der Schrifft vnd nichts wenigers Gottes
wort / dann eben die Schrifft / so mann sie nach dem Bůch-

staben verstehet / sie ist ein ewig Allegori. Es ist nit zůsagen /
was thür man auffthůt aller ketzerey / vnnd teglich newen
Secten / wie sichs erfindt / Jtem was vngereimpts vnd vnfůgs
darauß folget / so man die schrifft nach dem todten bůchstaben
verstehet. Es mȯcht eyner schier Ouidium de Arte amandi / so
leicht verthedingen / dann so man der Schrifft allenthalben
nach dem Bůchstabenn wolt nachkommen. Die hend abhawen / **90**
die augen außstechen / Christi fleisch essen / vnd sein blůt
trincken / wider geborn werden / den tempel zů brechen / vnd
in dreien tagen / &c. Tu est Petrus / etc. Qui credit / non
moritur / &c. Gewalt an sich selbs legen / Den rock vm̄ ein
schwert geben / drein schlagen / wie der prophet Hiere.
Vermaledeit / der seyn hend vom blůt enthelt. Jtem keyn schůch
tragen / Niemandt grůssen vñ zůsprechen auff dem weg / Keyn
gold vnd silber haben / Alle ding verlassen / verkauffen / Sein
seel vnd leben hassen / Zů narren vnd kindern werden / So
můsten wir nackend vnd vnuerschampt in der stat vmblauffen / **100**
auff die tisch hofieren / nit recht reden / Nicht arbeitten / wie
die vȯgel vnd blůmen auff dem feld / das vȯgelein lassen
sorgen / Das geben hundertfeltig wider nemen / &c . . .

Auß disem folgt / das der Bůchstab vnd der Grammatisch
siñ der Schrifft / auch nit der probstein / vnd goldtwag der
geyster seyn kañ / sonder derselbē geyst / siñ / außlegung / vñ
verstandt ist allein / wie Gottes wort / also alleyn die prob der
geister / Der Bůchstab aber dar gegen eyn gewiß zeichen vnd
hoffarb des Antichrists / vnd eyn rechter Silenus Alcibiadis /
wie jhn Erasmus nent.   **110**

Demnach dieweyl der Bůchstab d' Schrifft gespalten / vñ mit
jm selbs vneyns ist / kom̄en alle Secten darauß / Der sticht den
todtē bůchstaben da an / diser dort. Der versteht jn / wie er da
laut / Jhener wie er dort klingt. Nun seindt gewiß alle Secten
auß dem teüffel / vnnd eyn frucht des fleischs / Gal. 5. an
zeyt / stat / person / gesatz / vnd element gebundē / Allein dz
frey / vnsectisch / vnpartheisch Christenthum̄ / dz an deren
dinge / keins gebundē ist / sond' frey im geist vff gottes wort
stehet / vnd mit glauben / vnd nit mit augen begriffen vnd
gesehen kañ werden / ist auß Gott / Deren frombkeit weder an **120**
Sect / zeyt / stat / gesatz / person / vnd element gebunden ist /
Vnd dieweil nun biß anß end / gůt vnd bȯß in eynem netz
vnd acker diser welt beyeinander seyn werdē / Matt. 13. vnd

Jerusalem mitten vnder den Heyden zerstrewet soll ligen /
Luce. 21. halt ich von keyner sunderung vnnd Sect nichts /
Eyn yeder kañ für sich selbs wol from̄ seyn / wo er ist / darff nit
eben hin vnd her lauffen / eyn sondere Sect / tauff / kirchen
sůchen / anrichten / vñ auff den hauffen sehen / vnnd seynem
anhang zů lieb glauben / from̄ seyn / vnd zů dienst heüchlen.

130   Dieweil aber der bôsen alweg mer seind / dan der frommen /
Ja das zurstrewt Jsrael vnder den Heyden vmbferet / wie eynn
kleynes überigs heuflin waytzen auff einem vnkrauttigē acker /
oder hauffen spreüe / so wirt eyn yeder das creütz wol bekommen von seynem nachbawren / weyb vnd kindt / das er dan
vmb Gottes willen leydenn soll / biß mañ jhn nimmer leyden
will / Matth. 10. Die Kirch vñ das creutz der Heyden ist
allenthalb / er darff jhm nit erst von weyb vnd kindt in frembde
landt nachlauffen / odder vil mer zů den seynen fliehen / vñ
also dem creutze empfliehē. Jch kan auch keyner newen /

140 sondern Kirchen / berůffs / Tauffs / sendung des Heyligen
Geysts / mer (wie jhr vil teglich) warten / dieweyl ich weyß /
das Christus nit teglich eyn newes anfâhet. Jtem / das die
Kirch auff den Felsen Christum gebawen / bißher auch mitten
vnder den feinden vnd Heyden bestandenn ist / widerr alle Porten der Hellē / Matth. 16. Vnd was eüsserlich den schlüsseln /
Sacramenten / &c. ist abgangen / vnd mißbraucht worden /
vnnd noch abgehet / dz der heylig geyst an den seynen nicht
hat verseumbt / vnd die innerlich im geist vnd der warheit
gebraucht / erstatet / vñ die seynen mitten inn Babylone ge-

150 teufft / gelert / mit dem leib Christi gespeyßt / vnd absoluiert
in jhren gewissen vnd hertzē in aller welt / wie er auch vnder
allen vôlckern dem zurstreweten / gefangē Jsrael thůn wirt /
biß anß ende / Dieweyl die Kirch nit irget eynn sonderer hauff /
vnd fingerzeyge Sect ist / an Element / zeit / person vnd stat
gebundē / sonder ein geystlicher / vnsichtbarer leib aller glider
Christi / auß Gott geborn / vnd in eynem siñ / geyst vnnd glauben / aber nit in eyner statt / odder irget an eynem ort eusserlich versamlet / das mann sie sehenn / vnd mit fingern môge
zeygen / sonder die wir glauben / vnd nit sehen / dann mit gleich

160 geystlichen augen des gemůts vnd innerlichen menschens /
Nemlich / die versamlung vnd gemeyn aller recht Gots frommen vnd gůthertzigen / newer menschen / in aller welt durch
den Heiligen Geist in dem frid Gottes mit dem band der lieb

zůsammen gegürtet ausser deren keinn heil / Christus / Gott /
verstandt der schrifft / Heilger geyst / noch Euangelium ist.
Jn vnd bey diser bin / ich zů der sehne ich mich in meynem
geyst / wo sie zerstrewet vnder den Heyden vnd vnkraut
vmbferet / vnnd glaub die gemeinschafft der heyligen / kans
aber nit zeygen / bin aber gewiß das ich in der kirchen byn / sey
wo ich wöll / sůch sie derhalben / wie auch Christum / weder 170
hie / noch dort. Dañ ich weyß nit eben / welche steinn an disem
Tempel / vnd korn auff dem acker seind / die kent Got allein /
darumb er auch die sonderung allein seyn Engelen befolhenn
hat / die Schaff von Böcken / das vnkraut vom waitzen zů
scheyden / vnd nicht vns / wiewol die lieb der zeüge / losung
hoffarb / vñ zeygfinger ist / darbey man einen Christen mañ
erkent / wie bey den früchten den baum / Joan. 13. So bringt
doch die gließnerey so schöne frücht / das wir offt im vrtheil
betrogen werden / Matt. 7. 13. Gott weiß aber am besten /
welche sein / vnnd stein an disem Tempel seindt / 2. Timoth. 2. 180
Jch bin von Gottes gnadē nit so partheisch vnd Sectisch / dz
ich nit eyn yeden meynen brůder / fleisch vnd blůt achte /
d' mich darfür acht / vnd sich nit von mir trent / Ja der nach
Got eyffert vnd fragt / gericht vnd gerechtigkeyt wirckt / odder
wie Petrus / auß erfarung sagt / der Got förcht / vnd recht
thůt / in der gantzen welt / Auch die aus schwachheyt (vnnd
nit freuentlich widder den Heiligen geyst zum tod) zu zeytē
irren / anfaren / vnd sündigē / Gewiß / dz der Got angenem
ist / dem Herrn felt aufferstehet / vnd ein glidt Christi ist /
Jn welchem ich auch mein felhe als in meynen fleysch vnd 190
eynem fürgestelten spiegel sihe / vñ für den zů bitten / aber
jn gar nit zů richten hab / Rom. 2. 14.

II · MORAL SATIRE

SATIRE is not a genre, but the expression of an attitude of mind, and as such is not confined to any one literary form: Sachs's *Fastnachtspiel, Der Pawr inn dem Fegfewer* (p. 150), the speech of the Nestor of Laleburg (p. 234), or Murner's evocation of Luther's last moments (p. 45) are every bit as satirical as Brant's attack on bibliomania (p. 94) or Rollenhagen's revelation of the wretchedness of man's estate (p. 126), and there is scarcely a single genre of sixteenth-century literature which was not made a vehicle for social, political, religious, or moral satire. The fundamental attitude of the satirist is one of disapproval and the expression of his disapproval is compounded of three main elements: ridicule, chastisement, and an improving aim. All three elements are closely connected, but in any given work any one of them can predominate to the virtual exclusion of the others. Traditionally ridicule was seen as a means of punishing the person ridiculed and of inviting both him and the reader to avoid similar errors in future—*castigat ridendo mores* has been used for centuries as a justification of the comic muse. Not infrequently, however, the ridicule emancipates itself from its moral purpose and becomes an end in itself: in our own day, many of the novels of Evelyn Waugh exemplify this tendency admirably, and although, in the heavily serious climate of the sixteenth century, satire which is intended for amusement only is rare, Fischart's *Geschichtklitterung* (p. 208) and perhaps *Flöh Haz* (p. 121) could be seen as cases in point. Far more characteristic of the satire of our period is the tendency for the humour and ridicule to be forgotten in the desire to castigate error and effect a moral improvement, so that satire becomes rather vinegary didacticism in the manner of Brant or outright vituperation such as we find in Musculus (p. 114), the intention being to scold and bully the victim into a better way of life. Following Schiller's celebrated analysis of satire in *Über naive und sentimentalische Dichtung*, it has long been customary to distinguish between 'laughing' and 'punitive' satire; in practice, however, it is often not very easy to say in which category a given satire belongs: Murner's satire of the dying Luther seems to combine both elements, while Sachs's treatment of the three cocks (p. 118) and Rollenhagen's analysis of the human condition (p. 126) both seem to be calculated to produce a wise smile or a knowing shake of the head rather than mirth or anger.

No matter whether the result of his labours can be classed as 'laughing' or 'punitive' satire, or put into some third indeterminate category, the satirist almost invariably works 'negatively' in the sense that he attacks human failings and abuses and teaches his readers what men should do by showing them doing what they should not do. Thus it is usually from the revelation of some incongruity that the satire derives its point. At its lowest level this may be no more than the simple revelation of a deviation from what is normal and natural such as we find in Brant's bibliophile or Musculus's 'Pluderhosen', albeit underpinned with theological arguments. Not uncommonly, however, the inadequacies of the real world are compared to an ideal possibility—either stated or implied: thus Hans Sachs's complaint over the perversity and hypocrisy of the world in the fable of the three cocks becomes a satire because of the postulated, but only tentatively expressed, ideal of a society where men would love and respect the truth and speak it openly without fear or detriment to themselves—as the story stands in Pauli (p. 228) it could legitimately be construed as being value-neutral or simply as conveying a sound piece of worldly advice. By contrast, the humorists Fischart and Rollenhagen in their animal satires exchange the sublime for the ridiculous and compare the life of man to that of humble and despised animals, the humour proceeding from the inappropriateness we sense in the anthropomorphism, however speciously expressed. For all the humour, however, the authors in question are very much aware of the inadequacies of mankind, and in asserting the similarity or even superiority of the animal kingdom they are in fact exhorting their readers to greater humility by showing the ill-founded nature of human self-esteem.

The preponderance of satire in sixteenth-century literature is a consequence of the historical circumstances and of the prevailing view of literature. The century inherited a certain tradition of satire from the Middle Ages, and this tradition was unexpectedly quickened by the researches of the humanists into the literature of classical antiquity and the example the humanists set in their own Latin works. The Reformation further tended to strengthen this tendency by drawing almost all writers into the religious controversy and making them propagandists rather than poets. For the sixteenth century, however, this did not represent a prostitution of the poet in the way it might appear to us. The typical sixteenth-century writer was happily unaware of the *malheur d'être poète*: like the great painters of the day, he was a craftsman rather than the high priest of a religion of art. Indeed, unlike contemporary painters, none of the writers was a professional: they were cobblers, lawyers, parsons, schoolmasters, and civil servants, whose literary pursuits were incidental to their real occupations. Writers were thus not 'peculiar people' set aside from other men, and literature was neither the blessing nor the curse it was to become in the later eighteenth century. This was the age of 'applied literature' in which emotion recollected in tranquillity, unique and private visions of the world, or even linguistic ingenuity had little part to play; in his writing the author did not seek to 'confess' or to explore the inner and outer world, but rather to spread a particular view of a given problem, to diagnose the ills of mankind and to prescribe a—usually traditional—cure. Given these factors and the heavily religious temper of the age, it is not surprising that literature should be developed as the servant of the theologian and the moralist, and that the latter at least should commonly see in a satirical approach the spoonful of sugar which proverbially helps the medicine go down.

1. Standard themes: Folly, Vulgarity, and the Devil

(i) Sebastian Brant: *Das Narren schyff* (1494)

The son of a prosperous innkeeper in Strassburg, Sebastian Brant (*c.* 1457–1521) was for many years Professor of Canon and Civil Law at the University of Basel and latterly 'Stadtschreiber' (town clerk) at Strassburg. He engaged in a variety of literary activities including the composition of original Latin poems and an edition of Freidank's medieval German didactic work, *Bescheidenheit*, but it is as the author of *Das Narrenschiff* that he is chiefly remembered. Not least because of its felicitous use of woodcut illustrations, in the production of which a number of artists including the young Albrecht Dürer collaborated, the work achieved immediate popularity: it was translated, adapted, and pirated innumerable times and inaugurated the great tradition of folly literature which persisted until the end of the seventeenth century.

Recent research has shown that the 112 chapters of the *Narrenschiff*, each of which—with the exception of the introduction and conclusion—deals with a specific 'folly', are not quite so haphazard and formless as has traditionally been assumed. Each chapter can be shown to possess a distinct rhetorical form (*ratiocinatio, expolitio*), and the whole work seems to have been conceived as an *oratio suasoria* (see further U. Gaier, *Studien zu Sebastian Brants 'Narrenschiff'*, Tübingen, 1966). It is, however, unlikely that most of Brant's contemporaries were aware that the *Narrenschiff* was constructed according to classical rhetorical principles, and next to the fascination of the illustrations one of the chief attractions of the work must have been that the short chapters could conveniently be read independently of the whole and positively invited the reader to 'dip and skip' as fancy took him: even the allegorical device of the ship as the collecting-point for the fools who are going to be transported to 'Narragonia' is not sustained and Brant probably never intended his work to be read from cover to cover.

Brant's purpose is didactic: drawing on the folly tradition of the later Middle Ages with its societies of fools and Shrovetide festivities in which folly figures often played a considerable role, he seeks to raise the moral standards of his contemporaries by castigating their failings as 'foolishness'. As the spokesman of the conservative south German bourgeoisie, he advocates a sound, middle-class ethic and in this connection does not distinguish between unwise behaviour and actual vices. All deviations from his own puritanical middle-class norm, whether it be ignoring doctor's orders, building without adequate financial backing, imposing on the faithful by selling forged relics, committing adultery, or refusing to listen to the word of God, are indiscriminately condemned as foolish. While folly is thus often synonymous with sin, there is in Brant a strong rational and practical streak and the common denominator of the follies he attacks is improvidence —either with regard to the world to come or with regard to economic and social prosperity here on earth.

Although he associated with humanists such as Locher and Wimpheling, Brant is relatively untouched by the spirit of the Renaissance. There is little trace of *joie de vivre* in his work or of that intellectual curiosity and readiness to challenge authority which is the hallmark of humanism. Quite the contrary! In almost every chapter Brant anxiously quotes examples from sacred and profane history in order to lend his argument conclusive weight and on occasion he specifically rejects the pursuit of learning for its own sake and the investigation of the physical universe as examples of frivolous curiosity. Nor, in spite of the intention to improve his fellow men, does a reading of the work convey the impression that Brant really felt that the fools and knaves who, in his view, constituted the greater part of humanity were really worth his efforts on their behalf.

Brant's rather humourless and pedantic strictures on the failings of humanity are scarcely calculated to amuse a modern audience; historically, however, they provide us with interesting evidence of the climate of contemporary middle-class opinion and, especially in their serious-minded concern with moral standards, their criticism of ecclesiastical abuses, and their pathetic complaints over the vanishing political unity of the medieval Empire, give us an insight into some of the forces that were to combine to bring about the Reformation.

Passages (*a*), (*b*), and (*c*) characterize Brant's middle-class commonsensical approach and his rather narrow puritanism. Passage (*d*) is an expression of his political views. The length of individual chapters, which are written in *Knittelvers* (rhyming couplets with lines containing four stresses), varies, but the standard disposition of the text was the three or four lines of the preamble above the woodcut, and the title and four lines of text beneath it on the left-hand page followed by thirty lines of text on the right-hand page. The relationship of the woodcut to the text is often tenuous and may be the illustration of an idea, idiom, or proverb expressed in the text (*a* and *d*), a specific example of the generalized folly to which the chapter is devoted (*b*), or the representation of a famous example of the folly itself (*c*).

Our text is that of the edition of 1494, printed in Basel by Bergmann von Olpe.

(*a*)

Den vordantz hat man mir gelan
Dañ jch on nutz vil bůcher han
Die jch nit lyß / vnd nyt verstan

Von vnnutzē buchern

Das jch sytz vornan jn dem schyff
Das hat worlich eyn sundren gryff
On vrsach ist das nit gethan
Vff myn libry ich mych verlan
Von bůchern hab ich grossen hort
10   Verstand doch drynn gar wenig wort
Vnd halt sie dennacht jn den eren
Das ich jnn wil der fliegen weren
Wo man von künsten reden důt
Sprich ich / do heym hab jchs fast gůt
Do mit loß ich benůgen mich
Das ich vil bůcher vor mir sych /
Der künig Ptolomeus bstelt
Das er all bůcher het der welt
Vnd hyelt das für eyn grossen schatz
20   Doch hat er nit das recht gesatz
Noch kund dar vß berichten sich
Jch hab vil bůcher ouch des glich
Vnd lys doch gantz wenig dar jnn
Worvmb wolt ich brechen myn synn
Vnd mit der ler mich bkümbren fast
Wer vil studiert / würt ein fantast
Jch mag doch sunst wol sin eyn here
Vnd lonen eym der für mich ler
Ob ich schon hab eyn groben synn
30   Doch so ich by gelerten bin
So kan ich jta sprechen jo
Des tütschen orden bin ich fro
Dañ jch gar wenig kan latin
Jch weyß das vinū heysset win

Den vordantz hat man mir gelan
Dann jch on nutz vil bůcher han
Die jch nit lyß/ vnd nyt verstan

Von vnnutzē buchern

Das jch sytz vornan jn dem schyff
Das hat worlich eyn sundren gryff

Gucklus ein gouch / stultus eyn dor
Vnd das ich heyß domne doctor
Die oren sint verborgen mir
Man såh sunst bald eins mullers thier

(b)

Wer buwen will / der schlag vor an
Was kostens er dar zů můß han
Er würt sunst vor dem end abstan

Von narrechtez anslag

Der ist eyn narr der buwen wil
Vnd nit vorhyn anschlecht wie vil
Das kosten werd / vnd ob er mag
Volbringen solchs / noch sym anschlag
Vil hant groß buw geschlagen an
10   Vnd můchtent nit dar by bestan
Der kunig Nabuchodonosor
Erhůb jn hochfart sich entbor
Das er Babylon die grosse statt
Durch synen gwalt gebuwen hatt
Vnd kam jm doch gar bald dar zů
Das er jm feld bleib / wie eyn ků
Nemroth wolt buwen hoch jn lufft
Eyn grossen thurn für wassers klüfft
Vnd schlůg nit an das jm zů swår
20   Sin buwen / vnd nit můglich wår
Es buwt nit yeder so vil vß
Als vor zyten dett Lucullus
Wer buwen will / das in nit ruw
Der bdenck sich wol / ee dann er buw
Dann manchem kumbt sin ruw zů spat
So jm der schad jnn seckel gat /
Wer ettwas groß will vnderstan
Der soll sin selbst bewerung han
Ob er můg kumen zů dem stat
30   Den er jm für genomen hatt
Do mit jm nit eyn gluck zů fall
Vnd werd zů spot den menschen all /

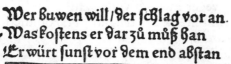

Wer Buwen will / der schlag vor an.
Was kostens er dar zů můß han
Er würt sunst vor dem end abstan

Von narrechtez anslag

Der ist eyn narr der Buwen wil
Vnd nit vorhyn anschlecht wie vil
Das kosten werd / vnd ob er mag
Volbringen solchs / noch sym anschlag

Vil weger ist / nüt vnderstan
Dann mit schad / schand / gespôt ablan /
Pyramides die kosten vil
Vnd Labyrinthus by dem Nyl /
Doch ist es als nûn langst do hyn /
Keyn buw mag lang vff erd hye syn /

(c)

Das best / am dantzen / ist das man
Nit yenierdar dût für sich gan
Vnd ouch by zyt vmb keren kan

Von dantzen

Jch hieltt nah die für narren gantz
Die freüd vnd lust hant jn dem dantz
Vnd louffen vmb als werens toub
Mûd fûß zû machen jnn dem stoub
Aber so ich gedenck dar by
10 Wie dantz / mit sünd entsprungen sy
Vnd ich kan mercken / vnd betracht
Das es der tüfel hat vff bracht
Do er das gulden kalb erdaht
Vnd schûff das gott wart gantz veraht /
Noch vil er mit zû wegen bringt
Vß dantzen vil vnratts entspringt
Do ist hochfart / vnd üppikeyt
Vnd fürlouff der vnlutterkeyt
Do schleyfft man Venus by der hend
20 Do hatt all erberkeyt eyn end /
So weys ich gantz vff erterich
Keyn schympf der sy eym ernst so glich
Als das man dantzen hat erdocht
Vff kilchwih / erste meß ouch brocht
Do dantzen pfaffen / mynch / vnd leyen
Die kutt mûß sich do hynden reyen
Do loufft man / vnd würfft vmbher eyn
Das man hoch sieht die blosßen beyn
Jch will der ander schand geschwigen
30 Der dantz schmeckt bas dann essen fygē

Das Beſt/am dantzen/iſt das man
Nit yenierdar dût für ſich gan
Vnd ouch by zyt vmß keren kan

Von dantzen

Ich hieltt naß die für narren gantz
Die freüd vnd luſt hant jn dem dantz
Vnd louffen vmß als werens touß
Müd fûß zů machen jnn dem ſtouß

Wann Kůntz mit Mâtzen dantzen mag
Jnn hungert nit eyn gantzen dag
So werden sie des kouffes eys
Wie man eyn bock geb vmb eyn geiß
Soll das eyn kurtzwil syn genant
So hab ich narrheyt vil erkant
Vil wartten vff den dantz lang zytt
Die doch der dantz ersettigt nit

(*d*)

Jch bitt üch herren groß / vnd kleyn
Bedencken den nutz der gemeyn
Lont mir myn narrenkapp alleyn

vō abgang des gloubē.

Wann ich gedenck sümniß / vnd schand
So man yetz spůrt / jn allem land
Von fürsten / herren / landen / stett
Wer wunder nit / ob ich schon hett
Myn ougen gantz der zåhern voll
10   Das man so schmåchlich sehen soll
Den krysten glouben nemen ab
Verzich man mir / ob ich schon hab
Die fürsten ouch gesetzet har
Wir nemen (leyder) gröblich war
Des krysten glouben nott / vnd klag
Der myndert sich von tag zů tag /
Zům ersten hant die kåtzer hert
Den halb zerrissen / vnd zerstört
Dar noch der schåntlich Machamet
20   Jnn mer / vnd mer verwůstet het
Vnd den mit sym jrrsal geschånt
Der vor was groß jnn Orient
Vnd was glöubig alles Asia
Der Mören landt / vnd Affrica
Jetz hant dar jnn / wir gantz nüt me
Es möcht eym hertten steyn thůn we / ...
On das man jnn Europa sytt
Verloren hat / jnn kurtzer zyt

Ich bitt üch herren groß/vnd kleyn
Bedencken den nutz der gemeyn
Lont mir myn narrenkapp alleyn

vō abgang des gloubē.

Wann ich gedenck sümniß/vnd schand
So man yetz spürt/in allem land
Von fürsten/herren/landen/stett
Wer wunder nit/ob ich schon hett.

s .iiij.

Zwey keyserthům / vil künig rich

30 Vil mechtig land / vnd stett des glich . . .

Der wolff ist worlich jnn dem stall

Vnd roubt der heiligen kyrchen schoff

Die wile der hirtt lyt jnn dem schloff

Die Rômsche kirch vier schwestern hat

Do man hielt Patriarchen stadt

Constantinopel / Alexandria

Jherusalem / Anthiochia

Die sindt yetz kumen gantz dar von

Es würt bald an das houbt ouch gon / . . .

40 O Rom / do du hatst künig vor

Do waßt du eygen / lange jor /

Dar noch jnn fryheit wardst gefůrt

Als dich eyn gmeyner rott regiertt

Aber do man noch hochfart staltt

Noch richtům / vnd noch grossem gwalt

Vnd burger wider burger vacht

Des gmeynen nutzes nyeman acht

Do wart der gwalt zům teil zergon

Zů letzst / eym keyser vnderthon

50 Vnd vnder solchem gwalt / vnd schyn

Bist funffzehen hundert jor gesyn

Vnd ståts genomen ab / vnd von

Glich wie sich myndern důt der mon

So er schwyndt / vnd jm schyn gebrist

Das yetz gar wenig an dir ist

Well gott / das du ouch grôssest dich

Do mit du sygst dem mon gantz glich /

Den dunckt nit / das er ettwas hab

Wer nit dem Rômschen rich bricht ab

60 Zům erst die Saracenen hant

Das heilig vnd gelobte landt

Dar noch die Turcken handt so vil

Das als zů zalen / nåm vil wile /

Vil stett sich brocht hant jnn gewer

Vnd achten yetz keyns keysers mer /

Eyn yeder fürst / der ganß bricht ab

Das er dar von eyn fåder hab / . . .

Durch gott / jr fürsten sehen an

Was schad / zů letst dar vß werd gan /
Wann joch hyn vnder kem das rich   70
Jr blyben ouch nit ewigklich /
Eyn yedes ding me sterckung hatt
Wann es bynander gsamlet stat
Dann so es ist zerteilt von eyn /
Eynhellikeyt jn der gemeyn
Vffwachsen die bald all ding macht
Aber durch mißhell / vnd zwytracht
Werden ouch grosse ding zerstȯrt /
Der tütschen lob was hochgeert
Vnd hatt erworben durch solch rům   80
Das man jnn gab das keyserthům /
Aber die tütschen flissen sich
Wie sie vernychten selbst jr rich
Do mit die stůdt zerstȯrung hab
Bissen die pferd jr schwåntz selb ab /

Worlich yetz vff den fůssen ist
Der Cerastes / vnd Basylist /
Mancher der würt vergyfften sich
Der gyfft dar schmeycht dem Rȯmschē rich
Aber jr herren / künig / land /   90
Nit wellen gstatten solch schand
Wellent dem Rȯmschen rich zů stan
So mag das schiff noch vff recht gan
Jr haben zwor eyn künig milt
Der üch wol fürt / mit ritters schiltt
Der zwyngen tůg all land gemeyn
Wann jr jm helffen wendt alleyn
Der edel fürst Maximilian
Wol würdig ist der Rȯmschen kron
Dem kumbt on zwifel jnn sin handt   100
Die heilig erd / vnd das globte landt
Vnd wůrt sin anfang thůn all tag
Wann er alleyn üch trüwen mag /
Werffen vō üch solch schmoch / vn̄ spot
Dann kleynes heres / walttet gott /
Wie wol / wir vil verlorn handt
Sindt doch noch so vil kristen landt
Frům künig / fürsten / adel / gmeyn /

Das ich hie ſitz der vordriſt dran
Das macht das ich beſchweren kan
Ob es nit yedem würt geſellen
Noch kan ich mich zum erſten ſtellen

Ich hett mein warlich ſchier
Dz ich mei ort nit het verſeſſen (vergeſſen
Ich bins der ſelbig geuckelman
Der vnſer narren bſchweren kan

Das sie die gantze weltt alleyn /
Gewynnen / vnd vmbbringen baldt 110
Wann man alleyn sich zamen haldt
Truw / frid / vnd lieb sich bruchen důt
Jch hoff zů gott / es werd als gůt /
Jr sindt regyerer doch der land
Wachen / vnd důnt von üch all schand
Das man üch nit dem schiffman glich
Der vff dem mer flißt schloffes sich
So er das vngewitter sicht /
Oder eym hund der bŏllet nicht /
Oder eym wåchter der nit wacht 120
Vnd vff syn hůtt hatt gantz keyn acht
Stont vff / vnd wachen von dem troum
Worlich / die axt stat an dem boum
Ach gott gib vnsern hŏubtern jn
Das sie sůchen die ere dyn
Vnd nit yeder syn nutz alleyn
So hab ich aller sorgen keyn
Du gebst vns sigk jn kurtzen tagen
Des wir dir ewig lob thůn sagen / . . .
Das schifflin schwancket vff dem mer 130
Wann Christus yetz nit selber wacht
Es ist bald worden vmb vns nacht
Dar vmb ir die noch üwerm stadt
Dar zů gott vsserwelet hatt
Das ir sŏnt vornan an die spytz
Nit lont / das es an uch er sitz
Důnt was üch zymbt noch üwerm grad
Do mit nit grŏsser werd der schad
Vnd gantz abnem die Sunn / vnd mon
Das houbt / vnd glyder vndergon / 140
Es loßt sich eben sŏrglich an
Leb ich / jch man noch manchen dran
Vnd wer nit an myn wort gedenck
Die narren kappen / ich jm schenck

(ii) Thomas Murner: *Doctor murners narrē beschwerūg* (1512)

Thomas Murner (1475–1537) entered the Franciscan order while in his
teens, and after studying and teaching at a number of universities gained

considerable fame as a preacher, moral satirist, and controversialist. A native of Alsace, he began with verse satires (*Doctor murners narrē beschwerüg*, 1512; *Der schelmen zunfft*, 1512; *Die Geuchmatt*, 1515), written under the influence of his great compatriot, Sebastian Brant, but in spite of his indebtedness to the latter—and in the *Narrenbeschwörung* he even borrows the woodcuts from the *Narrenschiff*—he is possessed of a much warmer personality and a more highly developed waggish sense of humour, and his treatment of traditional themes of moral satire exhibits a liveliness, and often a scurrility, of which Brant was only rarely capable. From Brant he takes over the equation of folly and moral failing, and many of his chapters are scarcely different in content from those of the *Narrenschiff*. Murner does not, however, share in Brant's narrow, pedantic rationalism and many of the follies he attacks are much more obviously sins in the strictly theological sense than those which fell under Brant's displeasure—so much so that a recent critic has spoken of his 'Verteufelung' of the folly motif. Similarly, his attacks on the abuses prevalent in the Roman Church are generally more savage in tone than those we meet from time to time in the *Narrenschiff*. But although Murner bitterly regretted the prevalence of abuses and at first was not unsympathetic to Luther's protest, he hoped—like Brant and Erasmus—for a reform within the framework of the established teaching of the Church and developed into one of Luther's most vocal opponents, when it became obvious that Luther was, in Murner's phrase, 'throwing out the baby with the bath water' and destroying the essential fabric of the faith. In a series of some thirty-two pamphlets, which grew steadily more acrimonious in tone as the Reformation gained in impetus, he opposed to Luther's insistence on the Scriptures the time-honoured traditions of the Church, regretted the public discussion of theological problems as being likely to confuse the simple believer, and saw in Luther's revolt the harbinger of political strife and civil war. These views gain their most effective expression in 1522 in the long satirical poem he directed against the 'folly' of the Protestant movement under the title *Von dem grossen Lutherischen Narren wie in doctor Murner beschworen hat*. (Cf. p. 45.)

Our text is taken from the edition of 1518, printed by Johannes Knobloch of Strassburg, in which the woodcuts of the *Narrenschiff* are replaced by original illustrations of inferior quality.

(a) Ein wechsen naß machen.

Das ich hie sitz der vordrist dran
Das macht das ich beschweren kan
Ob es nit yedem würt gefellen
Noch kan ich mich zum ersten stellen

Jch hett mein warlich schier vergessen
Dz ich meī ort nit het versessen
Jch bins der selbig geuckelman
Der vnser narren bschweren kan

Vnd der gschrifft ein nasen machen 10
Glosieren auch zů allen sachen
Weñ ich nit selber her wer kůmen
Wer wolt mein ŏrtlin yn han genůmen
Darumb bin ich ietz beneuenut
Vnd stell mich her in eygner hut
Man nent vns meister der geschrifft
Die heilig ist vnd sele antrifft
Darumb lond wir vns doctor schelten
Vnd wissent nit was die růben gelten
Wir dŏrfften bas eins narren bschwerers 20
Dañ der ley eins gůten lerers
Weñ wir vnser bibel lesen
Christi der zwŏlffbotten wesen
Der heiligen geschriff seindt wir so fro
Als weñ du küwtest bonenstro
Wir achtend nit das gŏtlich recht
Es macht vns im haubt schwampelecht
Wir seindt die ersten vndern gelerten
Die bŏsen valschen vnd verkerten
Vnd zeigendt dir das ewig leben 30
So wir weit louffen irr dar neben
Wir gloubend als das geschriben stat
Vnd handlent doch mit vnser that
Als ob daran kein zwifel were.
Es wer als sampt ein valsche lere
Wir seindt die ersten die verspotten
Das wir dich leren vnd dir roten
Got hat vns geben kunst vnd ere
Erkantnüß der gŏttlichen lere
Darumb wir meister seindt genant 40
Das wir dir geben ein verstandt
Dyns heils vnd vnser nit vergessen
So sindt wir auch mit narren bsessen
Wir wysent dich den rechten weg
Vnd lauffent wir den affen steg
Der selbig weg / die hymel stroß
Jetz ist er eng dañ ist er groß
Jetz ist er lang / yetz ist er wyt
Nach dem ein yeder opffer gyt

50 Dañ reden wir nach vnßerm bduncken
    Darnach wir etwan habent truncken
Wir hond sant peters schlüssel noch
    Wie wol das schloß hat aber doch
Got durch syn gwalt verendern lon
    Das selten me würt vffgethon
Got můß vns yetz barmhertzig syn
    Darnach erzürnent wir in fyn
Gůtter ding můß mit vns lachen
    Wir hondt beuelch in synen sachen
60 Was wir thůndt das ist gethon
    Vff erden vnd in hymels thron
Er wer vns gantz ein eben man
    Truwt er vns wol vnd schribs nit an
Wir vnd er sindt geschwister kindt
    Dan syner gschrifft wir meister sindt
So er offt ist vnser knecht
    Als das wir wendt ist mit jm schlecht
Der geschrifft mach ich ein wechsen naß
    Do ich vormals herr thoman was
70 Do bsorgt ich all zyt das ich hett
    Geprediget me / vnd me geredt
Dañ ich das selb geschriben fandt
    Mit flyß sůcht ich rechten verstandt
Jetz so ich doctor murner heiß
    Wañ ich schon ein ding nit weiß
So blemper ich do mit herfür
    Vnd lerne das ouch sag ich dir
Verlaß mich vff mein doctoradt
    Das hat mir offt vnd dick geschadt
80 Jch schetzt mich dick für ein doctor
    Do was ich ein narr noch als vor
Die warheit schwygen deller schlecken
    Vil lassen in der feder stecken
Wañ dich der dodt würt strecken baß
    Vor got must alles sagen das
Wir solten die vnwysen leren.
    Das irrendt schåflin wider keren
Zů des rechten hirten st
    So bringen wirs den wölffen all

Von got dem tüfel in syn huß
  Was wil zů letst doch werden durß
Jch wolt wer vns beuelhen wolt
  Syn sel das er auch selber solt
Darzů lůgen offt vnd dick
  Die tüfel sindt vns yetz zů geschickt
Das der für war einfeltig ist
  Dem durch myn ler ein sel entwischt
Es ist ein zytiger reg gewesen
  Die zecken mir ouch ab zůlesen

(b) *Zu dantz stellen*

Als man yetzund dantzen wil
  Lieffens also nach dem zil
Vnd kerten sich nit wider vmmen
  Rat du wañ wurdens wider kummen

Werent hie all gut gesellen
  So wotl ich nun zů dantz stellen
Solt ich so grosse arbeit han
  Ee ich bschwůre yederman
Vnd solt mir nit ein freüdlin machen   10
  Jch weinet offt so ich solt lachen
Pfeyff vff mach mir den dranraran
  Elßlin / gretdlin vornan dran
Die nit hübsch seindt laß dahinden
  Wir dantzen nit mit frummen kinden
Frumkeit hôrt nit an den reyen
  Es kum an dantz pfaff oder leyen
So hat die erberkeit ein endt
  Das kritzen krammen in der hendt
Das winckellouffen heimlich fragen   20
  Fründtlich grieß herwidersagen
Als ich verstandt vnd ist auch war
  Kein frumme tochter hôrt nit har
Nun die den knaben stüren kan
  Wañ er zů springen fahet an
So hebt sie in hoch vff entbor
  Lüg ich oder sag ich wor

Als man yetzund dantzen wil
Lieffens also nach dem zil
Vnd kerten sich nit wider vmmen
Rat du wañ wurdens wider kummen

Berent hie all gut gesellen
So wott ich nun zü dantz stellen
Solt ich so grosse arbeit han

Es ist kein scham noch zucht da bey
  Wañ sie die tŏchtern werffent frey
Vnd gredtlin sich hoch ynher bricht 30
  Das man ir weiß nit wo hin sicht
Wer sein tochter frum wil han
  Der laß sie an kein dantze gon
Der schåffer von der nüwen statt
  Maniches kindt verderbet hat
Geschendt vnd bracht vmb all sein eer
  Die yetzundt ein ee frauw were
Sunst sitzt sie in dem frauwen huß
  Vnd ist der ere der boden vß
O schåffer du vil ŏder man 40
  Was hast du schand vnd übels gethon
O schåffer du vil bŏses lied
  Du machst die tŏchtern offt so mied.
Vff die gůten heiligen tag
  Das keine got nit dienen mag
Vnd lieffent dir zů lieb ein iar
  Vnd sůchten gott nit vor dem thor
Vff suntag hondt sie dir gedient
  Vnd mit got sich nit versient
Der schåffer hat ir hertz besessen 50
  Das sie irs gots hondt gantz vergessen
Der schåffer ist ein werder man
  Das er so grossen dienst můß han
Schåffer hin vnd schåffer har
  Nym der schåfflin eben war
Jch fŏrcht es werd ein zeit her kummen
  Das dir die schåfflin werdē genůmen
Vnd an ein andern dantz gefiert
  Da bitterlichen wirt gehoffiert
Da wirt üch dañ dar nach ir ringen 60
  Vnd wirt eüch anders leren springen
Wañ es dar zů kummen ist
  Das dym dantz der pfiffer brist
Vnd dyne schåflin seindt geschoren
  Mit hut vnd har ewig verloren
Dañ wirt erst got die tŏchtern stellen
  Die ir nit dantzen lassen wellen

Die ir vmb ire zucht veracht
Solich werden dañ herfür bracht
70   Die selben werden vornan ston
Vnd mit maria dantzen schon

(iii) Kaspar Scheidt: *Grobianus | Von groben sitten | vnd vnhöflichen geberden* (1551)

Since Thomasin von Zerclaere had written *Der wälsche Gast* (1215–16), the *Betragensbüchlein* and the *Tischzucht* (books which gave instruction in polite behaviour and etiquette) had occupied a permanent, if modest place in the German literary tradition. Parodies of the *Betragensbüchlein*, which sought to quicken the heavy didacticism of the latter with satire by presenting the reader with a manual of bad behaviour and inviting him to laugh at a caricatured version of those things he should not do, were not unknown in the fifteenth century, but it was left to the sixteenth century to exploit the concept to the full in such works as Johann von Schwarzenberg's *Büchlein vom Zutrinken* (1512), Wilhelm Salzmann's *Grobianus Tisch zucht* (1538), and Friedrich Dedekind's famous *Grobianus sive De morum simplicitate libri duo* (1549). St. Grobianus ('grob' = rude, vulgar, coarse) had appeared first in Chapter 72 of the *Narrenschiff*, whence he had rapidly passed into popular mythology, and Dedekind's work gives an account of a day in the life of one of the saint's devotees. Being written in Latin, Dedekind's work could obviously never become really popular outside the academic public for whom it was written, and in 1551 Kaspar Scheidt (1520–65), a schoolmaster in Worms, published an augmented German adaptation, *Grobianus | Von groben sitten | vnd vnhöflichen geberden*, which in its enthusiastic and detailed description of loutish table-manners, dress, appearance, and behaviour (ostensibly in the hope that the reader would avoid committing the same errors) achieved immediate popularity, a popularity it retained for at least a century and a half, during which time it went through more than fifty editions, translations, and adaptations.

Our text is taken from the edition of 1551, printed in Worms by Gregorius Hoffmann.

Das erste Capitel | von auffstehen | anziehen | langem hare | vnd geelen zenen.

Hje lern ein jeder schůler mein
Der niemands wil gehorsam sein /
Noch thon was man jn weiß vnd sag /
Hierinn er bald ergreiffen mag
Was jm zu grobheit noch gebrist /
So er ein wenig fleissig ist.
Erstlich soll dir zun ohren gehn /
10   Wann du des morgens auff wilt stehn /

Das doch gar selten sol geschehen
Eh du den disch gedeckt magst sehen:
Den åltern wünsch kein gůten tag /
Der wunsch sie doch nichts helffen mag:
Vnd spar dein wort nach grobem sitt /
Blaß dann das kraut vnd můß darmit /
Das hembd thů an / vnd lauff daruon /
Das du nit můst am kalten ston.
Nim̄ fluchs die kleider an den arm /
Lauff in die stuben also warm /
Vnd zeuch dich bey dem offen an /
Da dir die kelt nit schaden kan.
Laß dich nicht hindern / ob dabey
Junckfrawen oder weiber sey:
Vnd mach dein fadenrecht für dich.
Laßt jemandt das verdriessen sich /
So sprich / Wer mich nit gern hie sicht /
Der geh hinauß vnd jrr mich nicht.
Auch wiltu vor junckfrawen brangen /
So laß ein weil die hosen hangen
Biß auff die schwartzen knie hinab /
Daß man dein auch zu lachen hab.
Dir werden die junckfrawen holt /
Ein jede dich gern haben wolt.
Nåm dich in solcher abenthewr
Ein reichs weib / wer dir auch ein stewr.
Kein gürtel bind nit vmb die lenden /
Man möcht dirs sonst zur hoffart wenden.
Das har strål nit / hůt dich bey leib /
Har auff zupflantzen zimpt eim weib.
Ein maußbild sol sich nit auffbutzen /
Als sich die jungen bůler mutzen.
Dir aber ists ein hoffzucht zwar /
Wann dir vol federn hangt das har /
Darauß kan jederman erwegen
Daß du nicht seist im stro gelegen.
Das har laß all zeit wachsen lang /
Daß es dir auff die achseln hang:
Obs schon dem scherer nicht gefelt /
Es ist dir gůt für winters kelt:

20

30

40

50

> Die alten trûgen auch vor zeitten
>   Dang har / wie das die bûcher deuten /
> Jn langen haren hettens ehr /
>   Jetz acht man keiner einfalt mehr.
> Auch zimpt es deinen sitten nicht /
>   Zu weschen hend vnd angesicht.
> Dann deiner grobheit wol anstat
>   So beides hangt vol wûst vnd kat.
> Laß weschen wem es wol gefelt /
> 60   Acht nit wie sich ein ander stelt.
> Wer vnlust hat an deiner weiß /
>   Der geh vom disch / such ander speiß.
> Spricht jemandt zu dir: Wâsch die zeen.
>   So sprich: Was thût es dich angehn?
> (Mit kaltem wasser ist nit gsundt
>   Zu wâschen deine zeen vnd mundt)
> Was hast an meinen zeenen feel?
>   Jst dann nicht auch der Saffran geel?
> Die farb hat auch das kôstlich Golt /
> 70   Dem jetzund sind all menschen holt /
> Das kôstlichst vnder alln Metallen /
>   (Drumb laß dir geele zeen gefallen.)

(iv) Andreas Musculus: *Vom zuluderten / zucht vnd Ehrerwegnen pludrichten Hosenteuffel* (1555)

The sermon preached by Andreas Musculus, General-Superintendent of Brandenburg, at Frankfurt (Oder) on 15 August 1555 and subsequently published under the title *Vom zuluderten / zucht vnd Ehrerwegnen pludrichten Hosenteuffel / Vormahnung vnd Warnung* is not a particularly inspiring example of the satirist's art. It is almost completely lacking in humour and is not cast in any recognizable literary form, yet, although its very claim to be regarded as satire thus rests on shaky ground, its publication was an event of considerable importance in the German satirical tradition.

Fashion in clothes and hair-styles has always been a bone of contention between the generations, and Musculus's diatribe against the fashionable *Pluderhosen*, the baggy, puffed-out trousers made of many yards of cloth and decorated with a variety of ribbons and slits which allowed the coloured lining or even the bare flesh to show through, rehearses many of the perennial complaints against new styles of dress. The new fashion, he suggests, is expensive and so causes foolish youths to waste their substance on frippery; the emphasis on the body and its decoration is inherently sinful, as it constitutes an invitation to sexual immorality (in view of the prominence given to the 'cod-piece' in the *Pludertracht* the charge is not entirely without substance!); clothes indicate the mentality of the wearer and the new fashion— a very familiar argument in our own day—is an indication of the loss of moral fibre in the younger generation when compared with their virtuous ancestors; being affected by all classes (they were introduced by the *Landsknechte* and constituted a sartorial revolution from below), they represented an offence against the sumptuary legislation which sought to uphold the divinely ordained social stratification by stipulating the amount and quality of cloth a man of a given social class might use for his garments.

Musculus's tract is not only important as a classic of anti-fashion literature, however; it also introduced a new conceit in sixteenth-century literature. Musculus's title reflects the current belief in the physical existence of the Devil, to which Luther had given such encouragement, and at the same time breaks with the tradition inherited from Brant which regarded moral failings as foolish aberrations. Under the influence of the Reformation, this essentially humane and rational conceit becomes increasingly less evident in Protestant lands, and human weaknesses are once again seen as damnable concessions to the Devil: Faust's pact with Satan in the *Volksbuch* of 1589 is only the culmination of a long process of which Musculus's pamphlet is the first important literary expression. (A Silesian preacher, Mattheus Friedrich by name, had in fact published a *Sauffteuffel* in 1551, whence Musculus probably derived his inspiration.) After 1555 the *Buhlnarr*, *Kleidernarr*, and all the other follies which derive from the *Narrenschiff* tend to disappear and are replaced by a host of corresponding devils. Musculus himself provided a *Fluchteuffel* and an *Eheteuffel* in 1556 as companions to the eminently successful *Hosenteuffel*, and thus inaugurated the outburst of devil literature which is a characteristic phenomenon of the later sixteenth century: in 1569 the Frankfurt (Main) publisher Sigmund Feyerabend was able to publish a *Theatrum Diabolorum* which brought together no fewer than twenty 'devil books', a number which increased to twenty-four in the second edition of 1575 and to thirty-three in the two volumes of the third edition in 1587.

Our text is taken from the edition of 1555, printed in Frankfurt a. d. Oder.

Die dritte sünde | des zulumbten hosen teuffels | wieder den bund | pflicht | vnd eid der heiligen Tauff.

Das wissen wir aus der heiligen schrifft / vnd vnser eigen erfarung / das wir in sünden entpfangen / geboren / vnd darinnen vnser leben zu bringen / zum bösen geneiget sein von jugent auff / wiewol solchs von allerley sünden geredt wird / so ist es doch an dem / das in vnserm fleisch vnd bluth / sonderlich regieret vnordentliche brunst vnd begirde zur vnkeuscheit / das auch im ehstand solche sünde mit vnterlaufft / vnd das vnrein machet vnd beflecket / das für dem erbfall / on alle sünde 10 vnd vnordentliche brunst zu gangen were / Adam hett solch

werck der merung one brunst begangen / aber wie oben vormeldet / bald nach dē falle / mercket vñ fůlet er solche brunst /
vñ seiner natur vorterbung / hůllet deswegen vnd decket zu /
das er nit durch entblôssung / solche bôse begirde erger mache
vnd mehr entzůnde. Demnach wie wir alle von Adam geborn /
solche schwacheit vnd vnordentliche lůste in vns befinden /
sagen wir zu vnd vorbinden vns mit Got in der Tauff / das wir
solchen bôsen lůsten in vnserm fleisch wiederstand thuen / vn-
20 seren leib tôdten vnd casteien / vnd vor allem hůtten wôllen /
was solche lůst in vns erregen / vorursachen vñ anreitzen môge /
Das wir auch nit ander leuten / mit worten / geberden vnd
kleidung / oder wo mit es sonst geschehen kan / wollen ergernis
geben / sonder wie Adam zudecket / vnd auch Gott selber Adam
mit dem ziegenbeltz bekleidet / das wir vns auch also erbarlich
vnd zůchtig mit kleidung vorhalten / vnd niemand zum bôsen
anreitzen wôllen / Das ist der bund den wir in der Tauff mit
Gott gemacht haben / darnach wir vns sollen halten vnd leben /
wie denn vnsere lieben vorfaren vnd groß eltern / bis auff diese
30 jetzige zeit / solcher erbarkeit in kleidung / sich beflissen haben /
vnd noch auff den heutigen tag / alle andere frembde Nationes
demnach / mit der kleidung also sich vorhalten / wie wir bald
wôllen weitleufftiger anzeigen . . .

*Die fůnffte Sůnde / des zuflambten hosen teuffels / wieder die
gewonheit / gebrauch vnd recht aller vôlcker auff erden.*

Das ist am tag / vnd erweiset es auch die gemeine erfarung /
das alle Vôlcker vnter dem Himel / nach eingebung der natur /
gleich wie Adam mit dem feigen blat / als oben vormeldet / sich
an dem teil des leibes / den jtzund vnsere jugent so vnzůchtig
40 entblôsset / auffs fleissigest bedecken vnd vorhůllen / das auch
die leut / so doch sunst der hitze halben in den heissen Lendern
gar nackent gehen / dennoch aus eingepflantzter zucht / scham
vnd erbarkeit / mit schůrtzen von schônen federn oder anderen
kôstlichen dingen / jre scham zudecken / Wir achten jtztiger
zeit fůr vns die Wenden etwas gering / noch sehen wir das bey
jn mehr erbarkeit vnd zucht ist / als bey vns / die wir doch
etwas besser sein wôllen / Du sichst keinen Wenden / so geringes
standes er ist / der mit so kurtzen vnd auffgethanen kleidern /
fůr jungfrawen vnd Frawen / forn gar blos vnd entdecket gehe /

der nit vmb seine lenden einen schurtz habe / vnd sich ehrlich 50
zudecke / Welche erbarkeit jtzunder gar vorgessen vnd hindan-
gesatzt ist / auch bey grossen leuten vnd Potentaten / die nit
allein fûr sich mit entdeckten hosen / fûr frawen vnd jeder-
menniglich gehen / sondern kônnen es auch leiden vnnd zusehen in jrem Frawenzimmer / das michs nit anders ansicht /
als sey alle erbarkeit aus Deutschland gewandert / vnd sich an
die stadt allenthalben der vnzûchtige vnnd vnsaubere teuffel
eingesatzt. Alle Nation / Walen / Spanier / Frantzosen / Polen /
Vngern / Tartern / Tûrcken / haben jre lange kleider / vnd
gewônliche zudeckung des leibs / wie sie es von jren Eltern 60
entpfangen / behalten / Allein Deutschland hat der vnuor-
schambte teuffel gar besessen vnd eingenomen / das jetzunder
mehr zucht / scham vnd erbarkeit im Venus berg / vnd vor
zeitten in den hinderheusern gewesen ist / als bey vns Deutschen / die wir doch vns alle jetzunder Erbar / Ersam / vnd Ernfeste / schreiben vnd nennen / vnd nit so viel Erbarkeit / Ehr
vnd zucht haben / als ein mucke mag auff dem schwantz weg
fûren . . .

Wiltu aber nit gleuben das dir solche kleidung vbel anstehe /
vnd dich vorstelle / so wende dich nur vmb / wenn du auff der 70
gassen so zuhackt vnd lumpicht rein gehest / vnd sich wie die
leut nach dir still stehen / dir nach sehen / vnd deiner vnmen-
schligkeit sich vorwundern / Sehen dir aber die Menschen nach /
pfuē dich an / so denck mit was augē dich Got viel mehr ansehe /
zornig vnd grimmig vber dich werde / Jch mein ja das heisse
sich schôn schmûcken / das mûgen ja schône hosen sein vnd
heissen / Aber hie hilfft kein sagen / der teuffel hat jetzunder die
jugent gar vorblendt / vn̄ sitzet jn mit gantzen Legion in den
lappen vnd lumpen.

Darumb wolt ich wûnschen / damit sie es doch môchten 80
erkennen / wie feine gesellen sie weren / vn̄ wie schôn jn die
hosen anstûndē / das die jungen auff der gassen sie mit dreck /
vn̄ die meid mit faulen eiern wûrffen / das sie es doch fûleten /
sintemal jn der teuffel die augen zugethā / das sie es nit sehen
kônnē.

Jch acht auch ein Obrigkeit thet nit vbel doran / wen̄ sie
sonst solch vnzucht nit straffen wolten / das sie bôse buben
bestelleten / die jn als Meerwundern vnd fasnacht narren nach
lieffen.

2. The fable and the animal epic

(i) Hans Sachs: *Die drey Hannen* (1557)

Traditionally the fable is a short anecdote in which animals are made to
behave as men in order to illustrate a 'moral'; the animal epic, by extension,
is often simply a fable writ large, or a collection of fables dealing with a
given theme in which the same animals reappear. Such an obvious didactic
vehicle was naturally very much to the taste of the sixteenth century:
translations of Aesop, Bidpai, and Cyrillus enjoyed great popularity, as did
the Low German version of the one great animal epic in European literature,
Reincke de Vos. Luther himself translated seventeen of Aesop's fables and
in this he was followed by two other Protestant divines, Erasmus Alberus
and Burkhard Waldis. Naturally, Hans Sachs, as one of the great popular moralists of his age, was very much attracted to the genre: he wrote
numerous fables and *Die drey Hannen* is one of the more interesting examples,
largely because of his development of the moral, in which one seems to
detect a certain loss of Sachs's usual crusading zeal.

Pauli (cf. p. 229) had presented his anecdote somewhat ambivalently
without drawing a moral, so that it could be understood simply as illustrating
the unwillingness of the world to hear the truth and as offering a sound piece
of advice in the light of the incident reported. When Sachs first treated the
anecdote in a *Spruch* of 1541, he had developed it into a moral complaint over
the perverse hostility of the world to truth. In this early version he does not
set out to give pragmatic advice as to the course of action the reader should
adopt in the light of the truth exemplified in the story, but to express his
sense of disgust at the hypocrisy and dishonesty of mankind and to call for
a radical change in human attitudes. The *Beschluß* of our version of 1557
modifies this position considerably: it retains a number of lines from the
conclusion of the earlier *Spruch*, but it is far from being just a complaint.
While subsuming the message of the version of 1541, it proceeds in the second
half to draw a somewhat immoral moral: the world should change its ways,
but it never will; those who wish to live successfully in the world will accept
that it is a corrupt place and keep quiet about its corruption, or even go so
far as to connive at that which they cannot alter.

The text is taken from the collected edition of Sachs's works printed in
1560 by Christoff Heußler of Nürnberg under the title *Sehr Herrliche Schöne
Tragedi | Comedi vnnd schimpf Spil.*

Schwanck | Die drey Hannen.

Es sthet im buch von Ernst vnd Schimpff
Ein Fabel doch mit feinem glimpff
Wie vor Jaren zu Meylandt saß
Ein alt Kauffman reych vbert maß
Der het ein junges schönes Weib
Doch sehr geil vnd fürwitz von Leib

Dieselbig einen Bulen het
Wenn der Kauffman außrayssen thet
Aufft Meß vnd Mårckt in frembde Landt   10
So schicket denn die Fraw zuhandt
Nach jrem Bulen hin jr Meyd
Die west vmb alle ding bescheid
Verporgen halff jr Bulerey
Die Meyd kunt auch viel Zauberey
Hie zu erzelen gar zu lang
Sie verstund aller Vôgel gsang
Das sie kund außlegen vernûnfftig
Was das bedeuten thet zukûnfftig
Nun sich auff einen Tag begab   20
Das der Herr wider ritte ab
Ein Monat nicht wider zukommen
Bald die Fraw solches het vernommen
Schuff sie das man den Bulen bracht
Der schlieff bey jr dieselben Nacht.
Nun het der Kauffman in dem Hauß
Drey guter Hannen vberauß
Vmb Mitternacht so hub ein Han
Vnter den dreyen Hannen an
Vnd sich mit seinen flûgeln schlug   30
Darnach kreet er mit vnfug
Mit heller stimm lautreisig gar
Viel mchr dcnn er gewonet war
Die Fraw lag munter hôret das
Des morgen frû sie fragen was
Jr Meyd / was der Han kreet het
Die der Frawen ansagen thet
Der Han het kreet im Hause hinn
Wohnt ein arge Ehprecherin
Weil der Herr ist geritten auß   40
Hat sie ein Bulen in dem Hauß
Das er sich mit den Flûgeln schlug
Darmit zeiget der Han genug
Das euch der Herr sol weidlich plewen
Euch vor der Bulerey zu schewen
Die Fraw thet zu dcr Meyde sagen
Ghe bald vnd schneid jhm ab den Kragen

Dieweil er mich gert zuuerrathen
Beide mit Worten vnd mit Thaten
50 Vnd wolt ein vnglůck mir zurichten
Sol lenger leben er mit nichten
Also dem Han sein Halß abschniet
Die Magdt / vnd jhn auff Mittag briet
Darnach allbeid zusammen sassen
Vnd jrn frommen Warsager assen
Zu nacht aber der ander Han
Fieng auch gar laut zu kråen an
Mit einer hohen hellen stim
Die Fraw lag vnd zuhôret jm
60 Zu morgens thet sie aber fragen
Jr Mayd / das sie jr auch solt sagen
Was der Han het zu Nacht thun kråen
Da thet die Meyd bald zu jr jehen
Der Han der kret es sey gestorben
Sein Gsell gar on vnschuld verdorben
Gestern / so bald es hab getaget
Drumb das er hab die warheit gsaget
Als die Fraw hôret diese wort
Jn zoren sie entrůst / rumort
70 Ghe bald vnd diesem Han gescheid
Den seinen Kragen auch abschneid
Auff das mein Handel bleib verporgen
Vnd ich nicht mehr auff jhn darff sorgen
Bald gieng die Meyd / den halß abschniet
Den andern Han / vnd jhn auch briet
Vnd assn den auch zu Mittag gar
Die dritten Nacht als aber war
Der Bul bey jr / da fieng auch an
Zu kråen lawt der dritte Han
80 *Audi vide & tace*
Vis viuere in pace
Die Fraw hôret das vnd thet auch fragen
Was thet der dritte Han heint sagen
Die Meyd sprach / dieser Han thet kreen
O du solt hôren vnd auch sehen
Vnd solt doch still schweigen darzu
Wilt anderst leben du mit rhu

Die Fraw antwort den weisen alten
Han / den wöll wir im Hauß behalten
Weil er kan sehen / hörn vnd schweigen   90
Mein heimligkeit nicht thut anzeigen
Bey dem bleibt alle ding verporgen
Jn rhu / vnd darff mich nichts besorgen
Das mein Bulerey komb an tag
Jch will ihn bhalten weil ich mag
Gib jhm gnug zessen / halt jhn wol
Weil er steckt solcher weißheit vol
Drumb sag ich dir bey meiner Ehr
Dieser Han gwint mit schweygen mehr
Denn die andern zwen mit jren Kråen   100
Ob sie gleich theten die warheit jehen

Der Beschluß.

Diese Fabel zeigt an mit klarheit
Wer noch der Welt saget die warheit
Der muß auch sehr viel darob leyden
Sie thut jhn schmehn / hassen vnd neyden
Tödten oder des Landts verjagen
Die Welt die hört nicht geren sagen
Die warheit / weil sie übel lebet
Jn aller vntrew oben schwebet   110
Drumb raumbt sie jr Warsager dann
Wie die Bulerin die zwen Hann
Vns zeigt aber der dritte Han
Wo in der Welt heutstags ein Man
Wil lebn in fried vnd stiller rhu
Der hör vnd seh / vnd schweig darzu
Oder aber thu der Welt heuchlen
Liebkosen vnd helff jr vermeucheln
Jr vnart vnd grundt böse stück
Dardurch mag er der Welt vnglück   120
Enttrinnen vnd viel vngemachs
Welt die pleibt welt / so spricht Hans sachs.

(ii) Johann Fischart: *Flöh Haz / Weiber Traz* (1573/7)

Fischart's treatment of the venerable theme of the mutual hostility of women
and fleas in *Flöh Haz / Weiber Traz* is in its good humour and uninhibited

exuberance probably the most attractive of all his satires and verse polemics: the metre skips along and incident follows incident with a liveliness worthy of the animals to whom the work is dedicated. The first part, which is heavily indebted to the version of Matthias Holtzwart, consists of a dialogue between a fly and a flea, in which the latter recounts the terrible fate which has overtaken his whole clan as a result of their attempt to implement his suggestion that they desert their previous sluttish host in favour of a more attractive, upper-class young lady. The complete destruction of his kith and kin, already anticipated in the fate of a similar expedition in which his father had participated as a youngster, and which the old man vainly recounts in an attempt to dissuade his son from this dangerous undertaking, moves the flea to appeal to Jupiter to forbid the genocidal activities of the human female with regard to his people. This introduces the more original but less interesting second part in which Fischart appears as the Flea Chancellor and emissary of Jupiter and announces the latter's verdict: fleas must expect women to act in self-defence and are told that they may in future only attack women when they are gossiping, dancing, or sojourning in the bath-house. (Bathhouses in the sixteenth century had an evil reputation as hotbeds of immorality.)

The element of social satire in Fischart's work has not uncommonly been exaggerated by interpreters who have suggested that the fleas are to be equated with the Imperial Knights or the Roman clergy in the German body politic, or that the fate of the fleas in trying to 'improve themselves' constitutes an affirmation of Fischart's support for the social *status quo*. It is improbable that Fischart had any such purpose in mind: the fleas may be massacred, but Fischart obviously sympathizes with them. He is writing in his most light-hearted mood and invites the reader to share his merriment, which speaks not only from the basic humorous conceit, but from a hundred and one inimitable touches (cf. the names of the fleas in our passage and the delightful comparison of one of the women to Count Dracula). This does not mean, of course, that Fischart's poem is lacking in satirical point. Fischart was no feminist and, with obvious delight in the lubricity of his subject, he mocks women for their alleged uncleanness and their love of gossip. But, unlike most other sixteenth-century satirists, Fischart is here basically not so much concerned with individual human failings as with the whole human condition, and his humorous anthropomorphism laughingly reveals the ultimate insignificance of human passions and aspirations by attributing them to such a humble and despised animal as the flea.

Our extract is taken from the first part of the poem: the flea is repeating his father's account of an attack on a group of market women in which he participated as a young man. The text is that of the edition of 1578, printed in Strassburg by Bernhart Jobin.

Da sah man ainen grosen streit /
Vnd der weiber sehr grosen Neid
Welchen zu vnserm gschlecht sie tragen /
Dan wiwol man pfleget zusagen /

Es hindert ståts / vnd sei nicht gut
Wann man zwo arbait ainsmals thut /
Jdoch die Weiber vns zu laid
Triben zugleich jr gschwetzigkait
Vnd auch jr giftig grimmig griff /
Man griff sie an hoch oder thif.   10
Vor zorn sie durch die zån auch redten
Wan sie ain zwischen fingern hetten /
Stellten auf andre zornig sich
Vnd mainten vns doch aigenlich:
Wie Pferd im Notstall stampften sie
Wan wir in sasen vnterm knie /
Sie stunden eh auf ainem fus
Das vns der ander reiben mus.
Aine erwischet ainsmals zwen
Zerknitscht sie auf dem Korb ganz hồn /   20
Vnd sprach dazu aus grosem grimm /
Die Toden / hồr ich / beissen nimm.
Ain andre hat gekaufet fisch /
Vnd drûber gossen Wasser frisch /
Als oft diselb mocht ain erwischen /
Warf sie in ins Wasser zun fischen /
Also im Wasser sterben thåten
Die nie kain Wasser betrubt håtten:
Vnd vnter in dein baide Vetter
Der Hochpliz vnd der Wollenschreter.   30
Aine ain Någlinstock het kauft /
Als diselb der Hundshummel rauft /
Fing sie in / steckt in inn den scherben /
Mußt da lebend begrabend sterben.
Ain andre stund da inn der Metzig /
War wie ain Guckgauch grindig / kråtzig /
Als jr ain Floh kroch vbern Rucken
Thet sie sich an ain pfosten schmucken /
Vnd rib sich wie ain ander Sau /
Vnd da plib des Hundshummels frau.   40
Aine sas dort / vnd hatte fail /
Zu deren nischt auch ain gut thail /
Die losung war jr nicht dermasen
Hoch anglegen / das sies konnt lasen

Zugreifen zwischen baide bain /
Sonder griff ernstlich flugs hinein
Vnd jaget das Schwarze Wildprett
Das sich im forst gesammlet het /
Sie wußt kain ort sie zu erschlagen /
50   Zu lezt richt sie sie auf dem Schragen:
Die hisen Schlizscheu / Supfloch / Schratter /
Vnd waren trei brüder vom vater.
Es het aine ainen gefangen /
Aber er war jr da entgangen.
Da wurf sie jr Schlapphaub nach im /
Vnd all jr Schlüssel vngestümm.
Ain andre dort zu Mittag as.
Vnd als der Filzfloh ir hart mas /
Fuhr sie hinein mit Schmutzig hånden /
60   Tapt so lang an den schmutzigen wånden /
Biß sie ertappet jren queler /
Da richtet sie in auf dem Teller /
Bei wein vnd brot / die man solt ehren
Vnd nicht mit Plutverguß vnehren:
Da dacht ich an den Traculam
Der sein Mal vntern toden nam.
Ain Magt zu ainem Pronnen kam /
Derselben eilends ich warnam /
Gedacht / da hastu gute weil /
70   Dan weil sie schöpfet inn der eil /
Kanstu jr plut die weil auch schöpfen:
Vnd dich nach aller gnüg bekröpfen:
Der Aimer war nicht halb heruf /
Da gab ich jr ain satten puff /
Nah bei der Waich / da es was süs /
Den Aimer sie bald laufen lis /
Vnd hub sich schnell auf hinden / biß
Man jren sah die Kerb gewiß /
Jch markt den bossen / sprang hindan /
80   Da kam sie ainen andern an /
War seiner Muter ainzig kind
Vnd his mit Namen PfezsieLind /
Der mußt das Junge leben sein
Da lasen auf dem kalten stain.

(iii) Georg Rollenhagen: *Froschmeuseler* (1595)

Like *Flôh Haz*, *Froschmeuseler* is a derivative work: it is an adaptation of the
classical Greek *Batrachomyomachia*, a mock epic in pseudo-Homeric style in
which the heroes of the Trojan War are replaced by mice and frogs, but in
spite of occasional truly delightful touches, such as the vision of the Animals'
Hell in Book I, the work is generally lacking the sharp wit and genial good
humour which made Fischart's epic so appealing. Rollenhagen is a poly-
math and a schoolmaster whose stated purpose is to provide a thoroughly
moral and useful alternative to the *Schwankbücher* of the time, and on to his
central theme is grafted a whole mass of extraneous material, some of which
is amusing—the intrigues and adventures of Reinke de Vos bulk large in
Book I, for instance—but which is often disturbingly obvious in its didactic
intent and which all too often creates the impression of uncontrolled garrulity,
in so far as it rapidly causes us to lose sight of the original subject-matter.
Judged as a whole, indeed, the work is not so much an epic as a collection
of fables on certain central themes. In many respects Rollenhagen is a conventional spokesman of his age: the citizen should be content with his lot and
obey the instituted authorities (who should, however, be bound by written
laws!), but his work is also conditioned by a certain rationalistic quality (cf.
his debunking of the human condition in passage (*a*)) and by a highly
developed interest in social and political matters. He is unique amongst
sixteenth-century satirists in that he does not judge men as moral beings to
be measured against absolute standards, but as social beings to be judged in
their relationship to society. Thus the whole of Book II is devoted to an
exploration in fable terms of the relative merits of the democratic, oligarchic,
and monarchic forms of government (after much debate Rollenhagen comes
down in favour of constitutional monarchy). Similarly Book III is largely
given over to an examination of the citizen's responsibilities in times of war.
Perhaps most remarkable of all is the advanced nature of Rollenhagen's
views on the relationship of Church and State. Book II with its allegorical
account of the Reformation, in which the corrupt Frog Pope, Beißkopff, is
finally vanquished by Luther in the shape of a valiant young frog called
Elbmarx, leaves us in no doubt where the author's sympathies lie, but unlike
most of his contemporaries Rollenhagen can contemplate with equanimity
and even advocate a strict division of Church and State and is quite
prepared to tolerate—though not to condone—the superstitious errors of
Beißkopff, so long as the latter does not try to extend his religious authority
into the political sphere.

Passages (*a*) and (*b*) illustrate respectively Rollenhagen's moral rationalism
and his political interests. The first is a story told by the Frog King Baußback
in honour of his guest Bröseldieb, Prince of the Mice; the second is put in the
mouth of the noble councillor Graukopff, as evidence of the weaknesses
inherent in any democratic state.

The text is taken from the edition printed in Magdeburg in 1595 by
Andreas Gehn.

(a)

Darauff wird Vlysses gewahr /
Das deins Geschlechts einer da war /
Der hůpffet jhm auff seine schuh /
Als ob er jhm wolt sprechen zu.
Dabey er merckt es wer sein Knecht /
Wiewol ers nicht kont wissen recht.
Vnd rhůrt jhn an mit Circes ruth /
Fragt was jhm dauchte lieb vnd gut.
Ob er nicht widder Mensch wolt sein?
10   Er wer ja seiner diener ein.
Der antwortet / er wer der Held /
Der vor auff kuntschafft war bestelt.
Die er kont meisterlich erfahren /
Wie sehr sie auch verborgen waren.
Nun wolt er bleiben eine Mauß /
Vnd wohnen in der Circe hauß.
Lieber im fried die brocken essen /
Der sie von der speiß kônt vergessen.
Denn nach so vielen Kriegs jahren /
20   Mit gefahr auff dem Meer vmbfahren.
Vlysses sprach / Es ist mir leid /
Deine grosse vnsinnigkeit.
Weistu nicht / das der Katzen orden
Die Meuß bey tag vnd nacht ermorden?
Das man sie mit den fallen fengt /
Erwůrgt / odr im wasser ertrenckt.
Das auch des Gifftes ist sehr viel /
Damit man sie tôdt ohne ziel.
Es gehet also in dieser welt /
30   Eim jedem seine weiß gefelt.
Sprach die Mauß / biß ers lernet baß.
Bey Menschen mir viel vbler was.
Jch must bey Tag vnd Nacht vmb kriechen /
Bey allen Menschen hôren / riechen /
Was sie fůr rahtschleg vorgenommen /
Vns zu schaden jhnen zu frommen.
Vornemlich bey der feinde schar /
Da ich alzeit hatt todts gefahr

Von Pfeylen / Schwertern / spieß vnd stangē /
Vnd bin kaum lebendig entgangen. 40
Von Lewen / Beeren / Wolffen / Hunden /
Dern jeder mich gern hett geschunden.
Jtzt fůrcht ich nur der Katzen zeen /
Den ich im loch wol kan entgehen.
Des Menschen Schiff sind vberall /
Auch gefehrlichr denn die Meußfall.
Da rhůmt man jhn ein hand voll ehr /
Ein wenig geld / vnd anders mehr.
Damit macht man sie so verwent /
So vnsinnig / so gar verblend / 50
Das sie auff solch stelhőltzlein mausen /
Da widder wind vnd wasser brausen.
Dauon auch keiner kan entlauffen /
Bis sie mit jhrm Meister ersauffen.
Es ist auff Erden auch kein gifft /
Das nicht den Menschen mehr betrifft
Denn eben sonst die andre Thier /
Wie denn ist widderfahren mir.
Wenn ich nicht wer ein Mensch gewesen /
Jch hett fůr Circe wol genesen. 60
Darumb bleib ich itzt der ich bin /
Fahr du mit guter wolfahrt hin.

(*b*)

Es gschach im Herbst / da der Nordwind /
Sehr kůhl vber die stoppeln gieng /
Vnd nach der warmen Ernt gar bald /
Sein fortrab schickt der Winter kalt /
Mit regen / schlossen / Hageln / krachen /
Vnd die Beum mit geschrey zubrachen /
Das bey der nacht im finstern thal /
Die Affen suchten vberall /
Wo sie ein sicher stethlein fůnden /
Daran sie sich verbergen kůnten. 10
Vnd krochen endlich all zusam /
Vnter ein holen Eichebaum /
Daselbst biß auff den tag zu lauschen /
Liessen den Wind fůr vber rauschen.

Als aber einer von dem hauffen /
Ein wenig weich Moß wolt außrauffen /
Darauff zu ruhen warm vnd lind /
Vngfehr ein kleines Würmlein find /
Das im finstern bey der nacht zeit /
20　Wie ein fůncklein schien in der Heyd.
Vnd rufft er hab ein fewr vernommen /
Die Affen all gesprungen kommen /
Blasen alle mit vollem mund /
So viel ein jeder blasen kunt /
Etliche lasen auch důrre bletter /
Damit fewr zu machen im Wetter.

Ejn Turteltaub saß an dem stam /
Wie die nun diß wesen vernam /
Flog sie auch zu den Affen hin /
30　Rieff in dem Wind mit lauter stim /
Das sie all miteinander jrrten /
Sich in vergebne erbeit fůhrten.
Es wer ein Wurm / vnd gar kein fewr /
Das blasen kem Niemand zu stewr.
Aber da war keiner der hort /
Der Turteltaubn rathsame wort /
Sie waren kalt / vnd suchten werm.
Das war die summ im gantzen lerm /
Das keiner sich abdringen ließ.
40　Einer den andern tratt vnd stieß /
Das sie auch noch zusammen satzten /
Feindlich sich bissen vnd zu kratzten.
Des wundert sich die Taub gar sehr /
Vnd rieff jhnen noch zu viel mehr.
Vnd ob gleich einer von den Alten /
Jhr rieth sie solt nur stille halten.
Das Affen Volck hôrt keinen Rath /
Ehe denn es kommen wer zu schad.
Wolt doch der Turteltauben Trewe /
50　Die Warheit reden ohne schewe.
Vnd schrie / vnd rieff: biß einer kam /
Der sie auß zorn beim kragen nam /

Zu jhrem grossen vngelůck /
Vnd zerriß sie auff kleine stůck.

. . .

Hjeran jeder zu lernen hat
Das guter Rath findt selten stath /
Den gleich die allr weisesten geben /
Es stehe darauff gut / Ehr vnd leben.
Wo Herr *Omnis* mit seinen Leuten /
Alles mag seins gefallens deuten. 60
Vnd Niemand fůrchtet vberall /
Wie es geraht in solchem fall.

III · DIALOGUE AND DRAMA

SINCE both dialogue and drama work through the medium of reported or invented speech, they often tend to be indistinguishable one from the other. The traditional distinction, that a dialogue aims at discussing ideas and is intended to be read or declaimed, while a drama represents conflict and action and is intended to be performed, is probably as sound a differentiation as we shall find; it is, however, important to remember that such textbook definitions are often more theoretical than practical: notoriously many dramas aim at ventilating ideas and are produced on the stage only incidentally—the plays of Hochhuth are a good modern example of this tendency—while many a dialogue is full of dramatic life and can readily be performed. Certainly for most sixteenth-century writers there was no real difference between the two genres: thus the humanist, Heinrich Bebel, in 1501 wrote a *Comoedia seu dialogus de optimo studio iuvenum*, while Wimpheling launched his comedy *Sylpho* (1480) by declaiming it to a university audience, and the play had to wait another twenty-five years to be performed. Conversely, Lucian, one of the greatest Greek dialogue writers, was regarded as a dramatist and his dialogues were regularly performed.

The philosophical dialogue, such as had been used by Plato, was little more than a conceit by which philosophical statements could be cast in a slightly more intriguing form than that of the treatise. Augustine's treatment of certain theological matters in dialogue form had given the genre currency in the Christian tradition, and in the Middle Ages it had been used by both the mystics and the scholastics, for whom it represented an obvious literary equivalent for the oral disputation. The sixteenth century saw two notable developments of this traditional genre. On the one hand, the dialogue as a pedagogic aid was developed by Erasmus (*Colloquia familiaria*, 1518 ff.) from a device intended to teach schoolboys Latin grammar into a vehicle by which he could put forward, often in delightful genre pictures, his own views on such diverse matters as the obligation on mothers to feed their own children and the nature of true Christianity. It was, however, in the vernacular Lucianic dialogue that the genre was to achieve its greatest importance as one of the principal polemical weapons of the reformed faith. For the controversialist every bit as much as for the philosopher, the dialogue was eminently suited to the exposition of a particular point of view by the process of question and answer, while for many a reader (and since the practice of reading aloud was widespread, for many a listener) the dramatic possibilities inherent in the dialogue gave it a greater realism and consequently a greater impact than more static literary forms: one could, as it were, participate in the great debate of the age, hear the advocates of the new or old faith put their case (suitably emasculated or distorted by the author, of course, lest the reader draw the wrong conclusion) and see how 'Truth' conquered 'Falsehood'.

The revitalization of the dialogue as a polemical weapon was an indirect consequence of the humanists' interest in the literature of classical antiquity. One of the most interesting writers redis-covered by the humanists was the rhetorician Lucian of Samosata, a Syrian Greek of the second century A.D., who had been virtually unknown in the Middle Ages, but now with the revival of learning rapidly established himself as one of the most popular of Greek authors. He was edited by Erasmus about 1500, was translated into the vernacular by more humble hands, and in spite of a certain scurrility which offended the pious, finally achieved 'set book' status in many a sixteenth-century grammar school. Lucian, as one of his recent translators tells us (P. Turner, *Satirical Sketches*, Penguin Classics), combined in his dialogues 'the philosophical dialogue used by Plato with the fantastic, farcical comedy of Aristophanes and the more realistic comedy of Menander' in order to pour scorn on the dishonesty and presumption of contemporary philosophers, the fatuity of humanity, and the hollowness of Greek religion. Lucian's style and attitudes thus provided a model which could readily be adapted in order to denigrate the Old Church and its representatives, and his popularization at the hands of Ulrich von Hutten inspired the host of polemical dialogues which accompanied the progress of the Reformation down to about 1525, when, with the hardening of the denominational fronts, the output of polemical literature began to subside.

Much of the drama written in the sixteenth century in Germany shared the learned origins of the dialogue; it was written in Latin and was intended to be acted by schoolboys as a means of cultural refinement and as an exercise in public speaking. These Latin 'school dramas' tended at first to be imitations of the comedies of Terence and Plautus, which were themselves also frequently pro-duced. Under the influence of the Reformation, however, and possibly influenced to a certain extent by the native religious drama, the school drama increasingly began to treat biblical subjects, such as the parable of the Prodigal Son, or the stories of Rebecca, Susanna, Tobias, etc. Since the audiences at these performances included people who had no Latin, it was quite common to provide a German synopsis or even to follow the Latin performance with a full German version, until latterly the custom arose of producing genuinely German school dramas. In spite of their popularity at speech-days and similar occasions, these heavily moralistic vernacular school dramas never in fact replaced in popular esteem the latter-day descendants of medieval religious drama. These again treated biblical topics—the Passion was the most popular theme—and had evolved originally from the 'dramatization' of the Gospel story by having different priests read the various 'parts'. As obvious attempts to make the Bible story 'come alive', they tended to be epic rather than dramatic and were often more by way of being festivals than performances, commonly running to inordinate length (Jörg Wickram's *Tobias*, which lasted for two whole days when produced in 1551, was by no means exceptional), but the festive spectacle they presented never lost its appeal and, in Catholic lands at least, long survived in the dramatic productions of the Jesuits.

The other type of drama which the sixteenth century inherited from the Middle Ages was the *Fastnachtspiel*, which in spite of its secular content also had its origins in religious ceremony, albeit of a pagan nature. Where the Church could not suppress heathen festivals and customs, it had usually succeeded in Christianizing them, and the *Fastnachtspiel*—the name derives originally from 'faseln' (= to talk nonsense) rather than 'fasten' ('Fastnacht' = Shrove Tuesday, the eve of the Lenten fast)—represents the accommodation of the spring-time fertility cults of the pre-Christian era to the festivals of the Church.

The spring festival probably consisted of a procession which carried fertility symbols round the fields to the accompaniment of chants and dances and culminated in the beating, burning, or drowning of an allegorical figure who represented Winter. These pagan rituals survived in a variety of forms—the maypole has persisted longer than most—but the most celebrated historical example is the masked procession or *Schembartlaufen* which took place annually in Nürnberg, where members of the local guilds and patriciate dressed in green and used green twigs to beat a figure clad in straw and moss. Such processions were naturally not limited to this one action, however, but included a variety of *tableaux vivants* mounted on drays, and the first 'plays' probably resulted from an innovation by which the participants explained themselves and their actions—a device which lives on in thinly disguised form in the review technique of many a literary *Fastnachtspiel*. The play soon liberated itself from the procession, however so that in Nürnberg, for instance, as early as 1500, the *Schembartlaufen* and the *Fastnachtspiel* were felt to be rivals. One consequence of this divorce of procession and play was that in the latter new dialogue tended to be imposed on actions whose ritual significance was now no longer understood. Thus the joy at the rebirth of nature is translated into the general sense of slapstick jollification and tomfoolery which is now seen as a last fling before the abstentions enjoined on the faithful during Lent. Similarly, the frequent obscenity and preoccupation with sexual matters probably constitutes a misunderstood survival of the original fertility cult, and by the sixteenth century the latter is often no more than an interest in the problems of married life. In much the same way the predilection for law-court scenes derives not only from their inherent dramatic possibilities, but from the competitions and judging of competitors which presumably played a part in the original celebrations. So, too, does the ritual beating out of Winter and his evil followers survive in the obvious love of horseplay and rough houses of one kind and another. The cult significance of the beating is, however, often rationalized into social satire, which embraces all classes but, in view of the urban origin of most of the *Fastnachtspiele* which have survived, tends to be directed especially against the peasantry.

The staging of these various types of play varied considerably according to the play, the people—invariably amateurs—acting in it, and the support they got from local organizations. The *Fastnachtspiel*, in keeping with its unpretentious nature (it seldom had more than six or eight characters or exceeded 400 lines of doggerel verse in length), could be produced almost anywhere: it did not even need a platform stage—a cleared space in a church or an inn would do if need be. The school drama, by contrast, with its greater length and larger cast, needed a stage of some kind, usually in a church or municipal hall, and tended to divide the audience from the players in the modern fashion. The religious 'spectacular', on the other hand, continued to use the 'simultaneous' stage of the Middle Ages, by which various parts of the 'stage', be it church or market-place, were made to represent a particular place: Heaven was at one end of the square, Hell at the other, Gethsemane on the right, etc. The audience, in so far as they did not have a place at a convenient window, often moved about from the scene of one action to the next.

None of the three main types of play which flourished in the sixteenth century was destined to develop into a national drama. The religious spectacle was absorbed into the drama of the Jesuits, or, like the Oberammergau passion-play (which dates from the early seventeenth century, but is based on earlier models), survived as a curiosity. The *Fastnachtspiel* tended to be frowned on in Protestant lands as a 'Catholic' genre and in any case was ousted by the theatrically more effective plays of the English strolling players who visited Germany at the end of the century and established a vulgarized type of Shakespearian drama. The school drama continued to be popular—amongst schoolmasters—and in a way may be regarded as the ancestor of the 'Kunstdrama' of Gryphius and Lohenstein, but these dramatists equally remained essentially literary phenomena and exercised little abiding influence on the development of the German theatre.

1. Ulrich von Hutten

Die Anschawenden (1519)

The earliest and perhaps the most able exponent of the satirical dialogue in Germany as a polemical instrument was the Franconian scholar knight, Ulrich von Hutten (1488–1523). Hutten was estranged from his family while still a youth because of his unwillingness to enter the Church, and led an uncertain and adventurous life as a wandering scholar and soldier, courtier and diplomat. A devotee of the 'New Learning', he was in contact with most of the leading German scholars of his day and studied at a number of German and Italian universities before emerging as one of the leading controversialists of his age. In his subordination of purely religious to political considerations Hutten is a somewhat anomalous figure in the early sixteenth century: his enthusiasm for Lutheranism lasted only so long as it seemed the evangelical movement might serve his own political aims, and similarly, one feels, he shared the humanists' concern with ethical behaviour only so far as his opponents' alleged immorality presented him with a convenient stick with which to beat them. Hutten dreamed of a strong united Empire in which his own knightly class would once again play a leading role, and it was in pursuit of this anachronistic concept that he participated in the abortive Revolt of the Imperial Knights under Franz von Sickingen in 1522, as a result of which he was forced to go into exile (C. F. Meyer paints a somewhat romanticized picture of his exile and death in *Huttens letzte Tage*). Concomitant with Hutten's ideal of a rejuvenated Empire was a passionate conviction that the Roman Curia was hostile to the best interests of the German nation and that Germany could never be strong so long as an Italianate Church was allowed to exploit her economically.

Hutten's publicistic crusade against the papacy began in 1517, when he brought out an edition of Lorenzo Valla's *De donatione Constantini magni* in which Valla had demonstrated the spurious nature of the Pope's claim to secular authority by showing that the Constantine donation (the document by which Constantine allegedly placed the greater part of western Europe under the authority of the Pope) was a forgery. In 1517 also Hutten par-

ticipated in the Reuchlin controversy by contributing a second volume of
Epistolae obscurorum virorum (see Introduction, p. 4). It was, however, his
naturalization of the Lucianic dialogue in Germany which gave him his
most effective weapon in his fight against Rome. Far from being regarded
as a sin in the sixteenth century, what we would call plagiarism was both
natural and expected, and Hutten uninhibitedly borrowed techniques,
situations, and even the odd title from his Greek model in order to satirize
his own particular *bêtes noires*. But whereas Lucian was probably not committed on a deeply personal level to the issues raised by his dialogues, which
were often by way of being rhetorical exercises, Hutten was passionately
involved in the question of the pernicious influence of the Church in Germany, and his dialogues are the work of a consciously political propagandist,
rather than of a littérateur or rhetorician. It was for this reason that he
deserted the exclusively Latin medium of the true humanist and translated
his savage attacks on the rapacity and dishonesty of the Roman clergy into
German, so that they would be available to all his fellow-countrymen. The
Gespräch büchlin of 1521 contained the German versions of four of his most
successful dialogues: *Febris prima, Febris secunda, Vadiscus sive Trias Romana,* and
*Inspicientes (Feber das Erst, Feber das Ander, Vadiscus oder die Römische dreyfaltig-
keit, Die Anschawenden).* Coming at a time when the credit of the papacy was
at a very low ebb, the volume constituted a major blow to the dignity of the
Roman Church and her representatives in Germany and provided a model
for the numerous anti-Roman dialogues which the next few years were to
bring forth. But the shift from Latin to German in Hutten's dialogues is
of far greater importance than the mere naturalization and popularization
of a humanist, neo-classical form, and is in its own way as significant as
Luther's own readiness to appeal to the general public in the vernacular,
to which it provides an obvious parallel. For almost the first time in the
history of western Europe, public opinion is being recognized as a factor of
immense importance with which emperors and popes need to reckon. More
important still, public opinion is shown to be something which the individual writer can, in the right circumstances and using the appropriate
techniques, mould to his own purposes.

Our text is that of the edition of 1521, printed in Strassburg by Peter
(? Hans) Schott.

P(haeton). Hilff gott / welh ein gepôlder vnd gereüsch / welhe
saufferey / wie groß vnd verdrießlich geschrey. Was ist aber
jhens für ein grosß menig volcks / das dort mitten jnhår gat?
Vnnd sag mir erstlich / wie heißt die statt?

S(ol). Die statt heisßt Augspurg / dahin versamelen sich die
Fürsten des Reichs / von grossen dingen sich zů beraten.
Aber die versamlung des volcks / ist ein procession vnnd fürt
den båpstlichen Legaten auß seiner herberg.

P. Welhen legaten vatter? oder wo fůren sye den hjn? Vñ
dieweyl du alle ding weisst / vñ dir niemant nichts verhålen   10

kan / so sag mir / was werden sye doch / weñ sye nun wol
beschenckt / vnd von dem wein erwõrmet seind ratschlagen?

S. Den Legaten fũren sye auff das Rathauß / da er inn auß
beuelh des Bapstes relation thũn würt. So ratschlagen sye / wie
man einen kryeg anfahe wider die Türcken. Welhen bapst
Leo der zehend / mitt verhoffnung eines gewiñs vndersteet /
vnd schicket darauff disen Caietanum dahin / zũ verschaffen /
damitt die Teütschẽ nichts anders / noch fürderlicher / dañ
den selbigen kryeg fürnemen.

20 P. Was gewiñes ist er dañ verhoffen? Würt villeicht mit gegen
dem Türcken zyehẽ / vñ verhofft etzwas daselbst zũ rauben?

S. Nichts. sonder von den Türcken redt er allein / sein gedãnckẽ
aber seind weyt von dannen. Dañ in rechter warheit / tracht
er nach der Teütschen gelt / hatt jm fürgenõmen / die zũ
plünderen / vñ was sye noch von gelt haben / abzũdringen.

P. Doran thũt er vnrecht. Württ er das aber auch vermõgen /
ein so streitbar vnd trãtzig volck?

S. Dz er solichs thũt / da hat er recht zũ. Er würt es auch
vermõgen / wiewol mit kunst / die er an statt des gewalts
30 brauchet.

P. Das verstehe ich nit.

S. Er gibt sich für einẽ hyrten auß / wie ettwã Christus gewest.
spricht / alle christen seyen seine schoff / zũuoran vnd mer
dañ andere diße Teütschẽ / zũ denẽ er yetzo dißen Leganten
schickt / jm sein schoff zũ scheren / vñ die wollen mit jm wider
über das gebürg zũ fũren. Hat er do vnrecht?

P. Bey glaubẽ vatter nein. wo sye anders seine schoff seind / vñ
er sye weydet.

S. Er weydet sye aber mit lauterer gõucherey / das sye doch ein
40 weyd sein bedunckt.

P. Jst dz aber genũg dz es sye also sein bedunckt?

S. Jnẽ ist es genũg.

P. So scher er sye / schynd sye auch wo es jm gefellt / diewyl sye
also gar dic geücherey annemẽ.

S. Er thũt es auch vñ yetzo schyrt er sye bitz auff das lebẽ / der
geytzig scherer.

P. Lassen sye sich aber also scherē / vnd schinden?

S. Fortan werden sye jnn nit mer wŏllen lassen. dann sich an /
wie sye jre grimmige augen auff jn geworffen. Vñ kenne ich
sye recht / so würt es nit weyt daruon sein / dz es jm übel   50
ergehe. Dañ sye seind jm feynd / vmb dz sye / seine boßheit
wissen / wiewol er sich gantz geystlich vnd bider / als ob er
das wår / dargibt.

P. Das thût er fürwar / der betriger / verwandlet sich wie ein
goŭckler / mit etzlichen verblendungen / also / das wer jn
sicht / nit dēcken mŏcht / er bŏß wår / dann er alle seine geberden / der fromkeit zŭ verglichen weysß / seine stirn /
augen / schültderen / red / ganck / vnd alles.

S. Noch werden sye jn nit leyden. Dañ vor jm haben vil der
glichen auch gethan. Darumb wiewol Teütschen von natur   60
einfaltige leütt seind / haben sye doch den trug so offt
befunden / das sye sich nun mer betrogen werdē verstehen.

P. So ist dißer scherer nit bey zeyten kōmen.

S. Wie du sagst. Dañ wår er zŭ rechter zeyt kōmen / mŏcht er
reych von dañen ziehen. Aber nun seind jm vil andere
vorkōmen / vnnd mag sein betrüglicheit nit stat habē . . .

P. Sag mir aber (bitte ich) ist er vō gŭtem geschlecht / oder
eines redlichen erbarn gemŭts / das in Rom vor andern
außschickt?

S. Von nŏten ist nit edel sein / wer zŭ Rom groß wurt / auch   70
nit von tugendē erleücht / sond' mag jn helffen / weiß er
sich mit betrug vnd bŏsen dücken herfür zŭ thŭn. Jch glaub
das dißer kaum seinē eygen vatter kenne / noch kompt er mit
einē sollichen gepreng vō Rom / über das gepürg / andere
sålig zŭ machen / hat vil aplaß bey sich geschürtzet / vñ låst
jm watsåckt vnnd gepåckt vol facultåt nachfŭren.

P. Drumb wurt er auch lår außgestossen werdē. Dañ ich
achte / ob schō Teütschē ir gelt gen Rom schicken wŏltē / dz
sye es dißem sŭn d' erdē nit vertrawē wurde.

S. Wie du sagst . . .   80

P. Ob er nun / dz alle vŏlcker gegē mitnacht / in den Türckischē
krieg einträchtiglich verwilligtē / erlangte / wurt er auch
weyter etzwz vnterstehen?

S. Er denckt doch vff nichtes weniger / dann den selbigen krieg
zů fůren. Es ist jm vmb golt zů thůn / dem thienet er / das
begeret er. Vnnd yetzo schwůr er / das selbig / wo man es jm
gebe / anders nit dañ vff den türckischē kryeg zů wenden.
Aber so bald er das hette (dann ich sag wie es die warheit ist)
so würd er es der Rômischen brasserey fürsetzen.

90 P. Lieber / so sag mir / wie lang würt er solichs spiles pflegen?

S. Bitz die Teütschen weiß werdē / die yetzo durch der Rômer
betrug gantz zů narren gemacht / vnd voller misßglauben
überredt seindt.

P. Jst es aber nahet dabey / dz sye weiß werden?

S. Nahet . . .

P. Also wôllen wir nun wider an den reychs tag / vnd des
Bapstes Legatē. Der selbig (nym war vatter) ist zů vnwillikeit
bewegt / vnd erhitzet durch zorn. Dañ er růfft etzwas auß der
procession herauff / vnnd ich glaub gântzlich / er sey über
100 vnß erzürnet. Dañ er sycht gegē vns . . .

C(aietanus). Gehestu zů letst ein mal herfür / du bôswicht? vñ
erschinest d' welt? der du soltest vff mein erstes winckē (ich
schweyg gebot) auch klarer vñ heller / dañ du pflagst /
erschinē.

S. Noch sehe ich nit / was ich übels gethan hab.

C. Sychstu es nit? der du in zehē gantzen tagē / nit einē strimen
deines scheyns bewisen / hast můtwilliklichē allē wolckē für
dich gezogē / als ob du d' welt dz liecht vergundest.

S. Dz ist d' Astrologē vñ sternēgucker schult / wo es and's
110 schult ist dañ die habē in jrē practiken also gesetzt / dz ich
diße zeyt nit scheinē sôll.

C. Du soltest aber mer gedocht haben / was eins Bapstes Legat
wôlle / dañ was den sternenguckern gefalle. Weystu nit do
ich auß Jtalien zohe / was ich dir trawet / wo du nit mit
grosser hitz Teütsch land / das zů vnzeyten kaltt ist / erwôr-
mest / vnd mir das gantz sumerisch mâchtest? vff dz ich nit
wider in Jtalien begetē dôrfft.

S. Gar nichts nam ich acht / was du mir gebotest / so hab ich
auch nit gemeynet / das ein tôdtlicher mensch über die
120 Sonnen gebyeten môg.

C. Hast du das nit gemeynet? vñ dir ist vnbekant / einen
Rỏmischen bischoff (der dann yetzo alle seine macht in mich
seinen Legaten / gegossen hat) in himelen vñ vff erden / was
er wỏll binden vñ lỏßen mỏgen?

S. Wol hab ich daruon gehỏrt / glaubt aber nit / dz es also
wår / wie er sich berủmpt. Dañ ich noch nye gesehē hab /
einen sterblichen menschen / etzwas hye oben verwandelē.

C. Wie? Glaubstu das nit? O bỏßer christ / den man vmb dz
du ein ketzer bist / verbånen / vnd dem teüfel geben soll.

S. Woltest du mich vom himel werffen / vnnd dem teüfel 130
geben? vñ (als man spricht) die Sonnē von der welt nemē?

C. Fürwar wil ich es thủn / wo du nit bald einem von meinen
schreiberen beychtest / vñ bittest ein absolutz von mir . . .
Dann wil ich dir ein bủsß auffsetzen / dz du ettwo mit vasten
erhungerest / oder yerget ein schwåre arbeit thủest. oder dich
mit walfart besủchung ermủhest. oder aber almủß gebest /
oder etzwas zủ dem Türckischen kryeg jnlegest. oder gelt
gebest in den Ablaß / daruon man sanct Peters münster / das
zủ Rom verfallen / widerumb bawen wil. oder wiltu das gelt
sparen / das du dich für deine sund lassest mit rủten schlagen. 140

S. Das ist ein harte sach. Was würstu aber darnoch mit mir
thủn?

C. Dañ werde ich dich vnschuldig sprechen / vnd gantz reyn
machē.

S. So würstu dem sprichwort nach / der Sunnē liecht geben?

C. Ja wie du sagst / wo es mir gefelt / auß krafft meyner
facultåten / die mir der zehend Lew gegebē hat.

S. Welche geücherey hỏre ich do. Meynstu yemant / auch von
den tỏtlichen menschen / so nårrisch sein / das er dich dißes
vermỏgē glaubt? . . . Laß dir ein purgatz von niswurtz eyn 150
geben. Dañ mich bedunckt / du werdest vnsinnig.

C. Vnsinnig? Du bist de facto im bañ. Dañ du hast vnersamlich
zủ des bapstes legaten geredt / darmit du in grosse vñ
vnaußlåschliche vermaledeyung gefallen bist . . .

S. Was sagstu heyliger vatter? Woltestu mich also vnverhỏrt
vnnd on schuld verdammen?

C. Wie ich gesagt. So låst man sye auch nit alle zů verant-
wortung kommen / die durch den Bapst vnd seine Legaten
verdampt werden.

160 S. Das wer aber vnrecht / weñ es nit von eüch beschåch. Aber
mir (bitt ich) wóllestu dißes mal genådig sein / vñ meyne sünd
vergebē.

C. Yetzo erst redestu recht. Dañ wer nit verdampt sein wil /
můsß genad biten. hyrumb gebiete ich dir / dastu mein
hinfür acht nemest / ich sey wo ich wóll. vnd yetzo / die weyl
ich in Teütsch land bin / so mach schöne tag / vnd mit krafft
deiner wórme treyb auß die kelt / die mich yetzo noch mitten
im heumonat anfichte . . .

S. Jch hette es vor langem gethan / so bedachte ich dastu vil
170 heymlicher ding beginnest / die du nit wóltest / das gemeyn
volck d' Teütschen von dir sehen. Der halben ich forchte / wo
ich klar erschine / vnd die selbigen deine heymlichkeiten /
den augen der menschen anzeygte / das es dir nit wol außginge.

C. Wie móchtestu mein heymlicheit andern anzeygen / so du
die selbst nit weyst.

S. So ich die nit weyß? Meynstu ich wisse nit / dz du yetzo
künig Carlen verhinderen wilt / dz er nit nach dem willen
seines Anherrē / zů Rómischem künig gewólet werde? Das
du dich auch sunst vil vnterwindest / das wo die Teütschen
180 wüsten / thåten sye nit mer darzů / würdē sye doch vffs
wenigst feyntlich hassē.

C. Lasß sye mich hassen / noch dannoch můssen sye mich dar
nebē fórchten. Wiewol ich nit haben wolt / das du solliche
ding offenbarest. Thůstu es daruber / so bisß im bann.

P. Welch einen tyrannen hóre ich da.

C. Auch gebiete ich dir / das du pfeil zů richtest / vnnd den
Teütschen pestilentz vnnd gehen tott zů schiessest. vff das
vil pfrůnden vnd geystlicher lehen ledig werden / damit
sich pension begeben / gelt geyn Rom gefalle / vnnd auch mir
190 alhie etzwas werde. Dann es seindt yetzo lange zeyt her nit
genůg pfaffen im Teütschē land gestorben. Hórestu wz ich
dir sage?

S. Fleyssiglich.

C. Aber erstlich scheüsß zů denn Bischôffen / das die Pallia ge-
kaufft werdenn. Vnd triff die prôbst vnnd reichen prelaten /
vff das die newen creaturē des Bapstes zů leben habē . . .

S. Sol ich dann pestilentz machen / so ist von nôten das ich ein
gewôlck einfůre / nebel über die erden sprenge / den lufft
betrůbe. derhalben ich fôrchte / dz vngewitter werd dir
misßfallē.   200

C. Am fürnemlichsten wil ich das pestilentz sey / damit
pfrůnden ledig werden . . .

P. Hôre mich du vnglückhafftiger man. Ein hirt sol seine schoff
weyden / nit ermorden.

C. Was sagest du kirchen diep? Was sagest du boßhafftiger
fůrman? Den ich mit vermaledeyung zertretten vnnd zerknitschen sol / bald yetzo . . . wie darfstu mir widerbellen? Jst
vnrecht / das ein hirt seine schoff schirt?

P. Das er sye schirt / ist nit vnrecht. Denn es thůnd es auch die
gůten hirten. aber die selbigē schinden vñ ertôdten die nitt. 210
Das magstu deynem bapst Leo sagen / vnd auch / wo er
nit vortan mâssigere legaten ins Teütschland schikte / werde
er etwa sehen ein zůsamen schwerung der schoff / wider ein
vngerechten / vngůtigen / vñ blůtdorstigen hirten . . .

C. Du meldest ding / von den man nit reden sol. hyrvmb bisß
verbannet. d
iße straff lege ich dir an vmb deine vnhôflüchē
vnversunnē red / die du mir gethan.

P. So schencke ich dich den Teütschen / die du beraubest / zů
einer spôtterey / das sye dich mit verspottung / gespey / vnd
verlachung von jnn iagen / villeycht auch übel tractiren. Vnd 220
dich dermassen halten / das alle nachkômen / eyn beyspil
von dir nemen. Bisß verspottet. Also wil ich dich gestrafft
haben.

S. Lasß von dem vnflat. Es ist zeyt / das wir den wagen abwertz
byegen / vnd dem abent sternen statt geben. Lasß jn liegen /
triegen / stelē / rauben vnnd plôndern / vff sein abentewer.

P. Der teüfel fůre jnn hin. Also treybe ich die pferde zů tal /
vnd fůre vnß gegen nidergangk.

Jch habs gewagt.

2. Hans Sachs

Disputacion zwischen ainem Chorherren vnd Schüchmacher | Darinn Das wort gotes vnd ain recht Christlich weßen verfochten wirtt (1524)

In spite of the obviously learned, humanist nature of the writings of Hutten and some of his imitators, with their Latin puns and classical allusions, the naturalization of the dialogue proceeded apace in the years immediately following the appearance of the *Gespräch büchlin*. Undoubtedly one of the most successful popularizers of the form was Hans Sachs, the cobbler-poet of Nürnberg (1494–1576). An artisan of little formal learning who during the course of a long life wrote prolifically in almost every contemporary genre (cf. pp. 118, 150), Sachs was one of the earliest literary advocates of the Reformation, and it was in no small measure due to his publicistic activity that the reformed religion succeeded in establishing itself in his native city. Throughout his life Sachs remained a staunch Lutheran, but he was never as blind to the problematical aspects of the Reformation as most of his contemporaries and in two of his dialogues he protested nobly against the intolerance and fundamentally unchristian outlook of certain of his co-religionists. The first of the four dialogues published in 1524, the *Disputacion zwischen ainem Chorherren vnd Schüchmacher* treats some of the central issues at stake in the Reformation controversy: the question of the relative authority of Pope and Scriptures, the relationship of priest and layman, and the right of the layman to interpret the Scriptures for himself. In order to ventilate these questions, Sachs takes up a standard device of the Reformation dialogue—a discussion between an educated representative of the Roman clergy and an unlettered Lutheran layman, who in the earnestness of his search for truth and his easy mastery of the Scriptures is more than a match for his opponent, whose knowledge of the Bible is shown to be sadly lacking. Usually the unlettered layman is a peasant—'Karsthans' or 'Jack Mattock' is the most celebrated of these Scripture-quoting representatives of the new faith—but Sachs as a city-dwelling artisan presents us in his dialogue with the shoemaker Hans, who is, of course, a thinly disguised version of himself. Normally in fifteenth- and sixteenth-century literature, representatives of the underprivileged classes are made to appear in an unfavourable light—the peasant particularly tends to be seen as a gross and brutal creature—and their positive role in Reformation dialogues is designed to illustrate a theological point, rather than to express some measure of social sympathy. Luther's assertion of the Priesthood of All Believers and of the right of the believer to interpret the Scriptures for himself had led to a positive cult of the 'biblefester Laie', the layman who had taken Christ's injunction to 'search the scriptures'(John 5: 39) to heart and knew his Bible well. Luther soon found it necessary to restrict the right of individual interpretation and to impose his own interpretations of Biblical texts on his followers, but in the early stages of the Reformation many theologians were anxious to abdicate their claims to specialist authority and it was not unknown for learned doctors like Andreas Carlstadt, a colleague of Luther's and sometime Dean of the Wittenberg theological faculty, to consult unlettered labourers on the meaning of Scriptural texts. Hans the shoemaker is an example of the 'bibelfester Laie': although a man of little formal learning who lives by the work of his hands, he is far better versed in the Scriptures than the gluttonous and card-playing canon of the Roman Church. Hans does not succeed in converting the canon to his evangelical faith—the canon's belly remains his God, as the citation of Philippians 3: 15 at the end is intended to show—but the dialogue's purpose is to communicate ideas rather than to represent significant or convincing action, and Sachs's hero effectively realizes his polemical function by revealing the ignorance of the representative of official Christianity and presenting to the reader the main doctrines of the Lutheran faith, supported by an overwhelming—and at times distinctly tedious—wealth of scriptural evidence.

Our text is taken from one of the two different editions printed anonymously in Nürnberg in 1524.

Bonus dies Kôchin.

Kôchin. Semper quies Seyt wilkuɱ mayster Hanns.

Schûster. Got danck euch / wa ist der herr?

Kôchin. Er ist im Suɱerhauß / Jch wil im rûffen / Herr / herr / d' Schûchmacher ist da.

Khorherr. A / Beneueneritis mayster Hanns.

Schûster. Deo gratias.

Khor. Was bringt ir mir die pantoffel?

Schûst. Ya / ich gedacht / ir werdt schon in die kirchen gangen.

Khor. Nayn / ich bin hindē im summerhauß geweßt / vnd hab 10 abgedroschen.

schûst. Wie hond ir gedroschen?

Khor. Ya / ich hab mein horas gebeet / vnnd hon alemit meiner nachtigal zû eessen geben.

Schûst. Herr was hond ir für eyn nachtigall / singt sye noch.

Khor. O nayn / es ist zû spate im jare.

Schûst. Jch waiß ein schûch macher / Der hat ain nachttigal / die hat erst angefanngenn zûsingen.

Khor. Ey der teuffel hol den schûster / mit sampt seiner Nachttigal / wie hat er den aller hayligisten vater den Bapst / 20 die hailign̄ våter / vnd vns wirdige herren außgeholhipt / wie ein holhipbûb.

schůst. Ey / herr fart schon / Er hat doch nur euern gotzdienst / leer / gebot vñ einkumen / dem gmainen man / angezaygt / vñ nur schlecht oben vberhyn / ist dañ solches ewer wesen / holhüpel werck.

Khor. Was geet es aber solchs vnser wesen den tollen schůster ane?

schůster. Es steet Exodi am .xxiij. So du deines feyndes Esel vnder dem last sihest ligen / nit laß in / sonder hilff im / Soll dann eyn getåuffter Crist seinem brůder nit helffen / so er in sech ligen inn der beschwert seiner gewissen?

Khor. Er solt aber die gaystlichen vnnd geweychten nit dareyn gemengt han (der Eselkopff) die wissen vor wol / was sünd ist.

schůst. Seyndt sye aber sündigen / so spricht Ezechiel .xxxviij. Syhest du deinenn brůder sündigen / so straff in / oder ich will sein blůt vō deinen henden fodern / Der halb sol vñ mů́ß ein getåuffter seinē sündigen brůder straffen er sey geweicht oder nit.

Khor. seyt jr Euangelisch.

schůst. Ya /

Khor. Habt ir nitt geleesen ym Euangelio Mathei am vij. richtet nit so werdt ir nit gerycht Aber ir Lutherischen nempt soliche sprüch nit zů hertzē / sůcht in auch nit nach / weñ sy sein wider euch.

Schůst. Straffen vnd richtten ist zwayerlay / wir vndersteen vnns nit zůrychtñ (welliches allain got zůgehŏrt / wie Paul' sagt zůn Rŏmern am xiiij. Nyemant sol einem andern seinen knecht richtñ &c.) Sonder ermanen vnd straffen / wie Got durch den prophetten Esaiam am lviij. sprichtt / Schrey / hŏr nit auff / Erhŏch dein stym̄ wie ein busan zůuerkündē meinem volck sein missethat &c.

Chor. Es stet auch Exodi .xxij / Du solt den obren nit schmehen in deinem volck.

Schůst. Wer ist dañ der oberst im volck / ist nit der Kaiser / vnd nachmals Fürsten Grauen mit sampt der Ritterschaft / vnd weltlicher oberhand?

Chor. Nayn / d' bapst ist eyn vicarius Christi / darnach die cardinel bischoffe / mit sampt dem gantzē gaistlichen stand /

vō dē steet in gaistlichen rechten. C. Solite. de maioritate et 60
obedientia Sy bedeüten die soñ / vnd der weltlich gewalt
bedeüt dē mon Deshalb ist der bapst vil mechtiger dañ d'
Kaiser / welcher im sein fůß küssen můß.

Schůst. Jst der bapst ein solcher gewelttiger herr / so ist der
gewißlich kain Stathalter Christi / wann Christus spricht
Joañ am .xviij. Mein reich ist nitt von dyser welt / vnd
Joañ .vj. Floch Cristus da man in zům künig machen wolt /
Auch sprach christus zů seinen junger / Luce .xxij. Die weltlichen künig herschen / vnd die gewaltigen haißt mā gnedige
herren / ir aber nit also / der grôst vnder euch soll seyn wie 70
der jüngst / vnd der fürnemest wie der dyener / Deshalb d'
bapst vñ ir gaistlichen / seyt nur dyener der christenlichenn
gemayn / wa ir anderst auß got seyt / d'halb mag man euch
wol straffen.

Khor. Ey der bapst vnd die seynen / sein nit schuldig gottes
gebotten gehorsam zůseyn / wie inn gaistlichen rechtñ steet.
C. Solite de maioritate et obedientia / auß dem schleüßt sich /
das der bapst kain sünder ist / sonder der allerhayligist /
derhalb ist er vnstraffpar.

Schůst. Es spricht Joañ .j. canonica .j. Wer sagt / er sey on 80
sünd / d' ist ein lugner / deshalb ist der bapst ein sünder oder
lugner / vñ nichtt der allerhayligest sonder zůstraffen.

Khor. Ey lieber / vnd wenn der Bapst so bôß wer / das er
vnzâlich menschenn mitt grossem hauffen zům teufel fůret /
dôrfft in doch nyemandt straffen / dz stet geschriben in
vnserm rechten / dis. xl. si papa / wie gefelt euch das

Schůst. Ey so steet im Euangelio Mathey .xviij. So deyn brůder
sündiget wider dich / so gee hin vnd straff in zwyschen dir vnd
im / hôrt er dich / so hastu sein seel gewunnen / Eussert sich
der bapst dañ solchs haylsamen wercks? 90

Khor. Jst dañ sollichs brůderlich gestrafftt / Also am tag
außzůschreyenn?

Schůst. Ey es volgt weitter im text / Wa dich dein brůd' nit
hôrt / so nŷm noch ein oder zwen zů dir / hôrtt er dich noch
nitt so sags der gemain / hôrt er die gemain auch nit / so laß
in geē wie ain hayden / wie da her domine?

L

Khor. Ey lieber wz ists dañ nutz / wenn ir vnns gleich lanng außschreyt? wir kern vns doch nichts daran / wir halten vns des Decretals.

100 Schûst. Es spricht Christus Mathei .x. Wa man euch nit hôrt / so schütlet den staub von ewern fûssen zû eyner zeugknus / das in das reich gotes nahent ist gewesen / den võ Sodoma vnd Gomorra wirt es treglicher sein am jungsten gericht / dann sollichem volck / wie wirt es euch dañ geen so ir kain straff wolt annemen.

Khor. Nu gib ich das nach wo es gelert / v'stândige leüt thâtñ / aber den layen zimpt es nycht . . . Eynem schûster zim̃ptt mitt leder vnnd schwertz vmbzûgeen / nicht mitt der hailigens geschrifft.

110 Schûst. Mit wôlcher hailiger geschrifft wolt yrs beybringen / einem getaufften cristen nit in der schrifft zû forschñ Leesen / schreiben? Dañ Christus sagtt Johannes .v. Durchsûcht die geschrifft / die gibt zeügknus vonn mir / so spricht der Psalmist .j. Selig ist der man der sich tag vnnd nacht yebett ym̃ gesetz des herren / so schreybt Petrus in der ersten Epistel am iij. seyndt alle zeytt vrbittig zûuerantwurttung yedermã der grund fodert die hoffnung die inn euch ist . . . Herr wie wurd wir beston / so wir nichts in der geschrifft westenn?

Khor. Wie die gens am wetter.

120 schûst. Jr spot wol dye Juden wissen ir gesatz vnd Propheten frey außwendig / sollẽ dañ wir cristen nit auch wissen das Euangeliũ Jhesu cristi wôlches ist die krafft Gottes / allen die selig sollen werden wie Paul' .j. Corinth .j. . . .

Khorherr. Lyeber was halt ir vonn dem Luther.

Schûster. Jch halt ynn für eynen Christenlichen leerer (wôllichen ich acht) Seytt der Appostel zeyt nye geweßt ist.

Khorherr. Lieber was nutz hatt er / doch geschafft inn der Christennhayt.

Schûster. Da hatt er ewer menschen gepot / leer / fund vnnd auffsatzung an tag gebracht / vnnd vns daruor gewarnet /
130 Zûm andern hatt er vnns in die hailigen geschrifft geweyset / dariñ wir erkennen das wir alle vnder der sünd beschlossenn vnd sünder seynndt Rômern .v. Zûm anndern / Das Christus

vnser aynige erlôsung ist wie zûn .j. Corinth .j. Vnd die
zway stuck treybtt dye schrifft schyer durch vnnd durch /
Darinn erleern wir vnnser aynige hoffnung / glauben vnd
vertrawen in Christo zûsetzen / wôllichs dañ ist dz recht
gôtlich werck vñ zû der seligkayt wie cristus spricht Johannis
am sechstenn.

Khor. darff man kains wercks dartzû / Spricht doch cristus 140
Matthey .v. Laßt ewer liecht leüchtñ vor den menschen / daz
sy ewer gûte werck sehen / vnd ewern vater ym hymmel
preysen.

Schûster. Paulus spricht Roma v. Wir halttenn das der mennsch
gerechtuertigt werd allayn durch den glaubcn / on zûthûûg
der werck des gesatz / Vnnd zûn Rômern am ersten / Der
gerecht würt seynes glawben lebenn.

Khorherr. Spricht doch Jacobus .ij. Der glaub on die werck
ist tod.

Schûster. Ein rechter gôtlicher glaub der feyret nit / Sonder 150
brinngt steets gûtte frücht / dañ Christus spricht Matthey
am .vij. Ein gûtter poum kan kayn bôse frucht bringen / Aber
solche gûtte werck beschehen nicht den himel zûuerdienen /
welichen vns Christus verdiennet hat / Auch nitt auß forchtt
der helle zû entpfliechen / vonn der vnns Christus erlôßt hat /
auch nit vmb eer / wann alle eer soll man Gott geben. Math.
an dem vierdten. Sonder auß gôtlicher lieb / Gott zû eyner
dancksagung vnd dem nechsten zû nutz / Wolan herr wie
gefelt euch nun des Luthers frucht.

Khorherr. Jst er dann so gerecht Wie das im dann so wenig 160
geleertter / vnnd mechttiger herren anhanngen? Allain der
grob vnuerstânndig hauff.

Schûster. Christo hyeng weder Pilatus / Herodes / Cayphas /
noch Annas ann / Auch nit die Phariseyer / Sonnder wider
stûnden im / allain dz gemain volck hyeng im an / Darumb
erfrewet sich Jhesus im gaist / Luce am zehenden / vnd
sprach / Vatter ich sag dir dannck / das du dise ding hast
verborgen vor den weysen diser welt / vnd hast sich
geoffennbart den klaynen.

Khor. Ey lieber / der gemayn hauff gybtt auch des weniger tayl 170
dem Luther recht.

Schůst. Das machen ewer luṁppenprediger / die schreyen es sey ketzerey vñ das on alle geschrifft / Christus hat aber den klainen hauffen verkündt Mat .v. Geet ein durch die eng pfort / wañ die pfort ist weyt / vnd der weg brayt der zů der verdaṁnus fůret / vnd ir seynd vil die darauff wandlen / vnd Math .xxij. Vil seyndt berůfft / aber wenyg außerwõltt . . .

Chor. Man leütet in Khor / Kechin lang den Korrock her Wolan lieber mayster zyecht hin im frid / es wirt leicht noch
180 als gůt /

Schůst. Ob gott will / wolan alde / der fryd sey mit euch lyeber herr hond mir nichts verübel / vnd verzeycht mir.

Khor. Verzeych vns got vnser sünd.

Schůster. Amen.

Khor. Secht nur an liebe Kõchin / wie reden die layen so gar freflich gegen vns geweychten / Jch mayn der teuffel sey ynn dem schůster verneet / er hat mich in harnasch geiagt / Vnnd wer ich nit so wol geleert / er het mich auff den esel gesetzt / Darumb wil im nicht mer zů arbaitten geben / sonder dem
190 hans Zobel / der ist ein gůts eynfeltigs mendlin / macht nit vil wort mit der hailigen gschrift / vnd Lutherischen ketzerey / wie dañ den layen nit zyṁlich ist / noch gepürt mit yren seelsorgern zů disputiern / wañ es sagt Salomon / Wõllicher eyn eynfeltig wandel fůrt / der wandelt wol / Ey disen spruch soltt ich dem dollē schůster fürgeworffen hon / so wer er villeicht darab erstumbt.

Kõchin. O herr / Jch hett ymmer sorg nach dem yr in mit der schrifft nit vberwinden kündt / ir wurd in mitt dem pantoffel schlahen.

200 Khor. Jch hab nur von der gemayn / eyn auffrůwr besorgt / sunst wolt ich im die panttoffel in sein antlitz geschmeist haben / im het Christus od' Paul' in dreyen tagen nit abgewischt / wie wol er all sein vertrauwen auff sye setzt . . . Vor zeyten het wir ein sollichen inn Bann verkündt / Aber yetzundt můssen wir von den layen hõren vñ lernen / wie die Phariseyer võ Cristo. Liebe kechin růff vnserem Calefactor / der lißt vil in der Bibel / vñ villeycht der gschrifft baß bericht ist dañ ich / Er můß mir von wunnders wegen etlich sprüch sůchen

Kechin. Heinrice / Heinrice. Gee herauf zů dem herren. 210

Calefactor. Wirdiger herr was wőltt jr?

Chorherr. Vnser schůster hat mich lang vexiert / vnd vil auß
der Bybel angetzaigt / wie dañ der Lutherischen brauch ist /
du můst im etlich Capittel nach sůchen / ob er gleich hab zů
gesagt / auff das ich in in der schrifft fahen mőcht.

Calefactor. Jr solt es billich selbs wissen / jr hond lang die ge-
weichttē examinieren helffen.

Cor. Ja daselbs brauchtt man nur schůllerische leer / was die
menschen haben geschriben vñ gemacht vnd gar wenig das
gaistlich recht / welchs die hailigen våtter in den Concilijs 220
beschlossen haben.

Calefactor. Es leg an dem nicht das die våter in Concilijs
beschlossen / vñ die mennschen so nach in kommen sein
geschriben vnd gehalten haben wa die selben gesetz / leer vñ
schrifft auß dem wort vñ gaist gotes weren wann die prophetten / Apostel vnd Euangelisten seind auch mennschen
geweßt.

Chor. Ey / so haben sy auch jrren mügen / Aber die Lutherischen wellen das nitt glauben.

Calefactor. Nayn / Wañ Petrus spricht .ij. Petri .j. Es ist noch 230
nye kain waissagung auß mennschlichem wyllen herfür
bracht / sonder die hailigen menschen gottes hand geredt /
getriben / von dem hailigen gaist / Vnd eben darnach verkündt Petrus / die falschen propheten / die vyl verderblicher
secktten ein werden fůren / Bedeut ewern gaistlichen stand /
Ordenn Regel vnd allen menschen find (ausserhalb dem
wort gotes) darmit ir yetz vmb geet.

Khor. Ya es ist aber auff vnns nit geredt / sonder auff die alten
vñ lengst vergangen.

Cale. O yr thoren vnd trågs hertzen zů glawben / alle dem / 240
das dye Propheten geredt haben Luce . xxiiij.

Kőchin. Herr haißtt euch den hanen meer krően / von mir lydts
irs nit.

Khor. O du laußiger bachant / wil du mich auch rechtuertigen
vnd leeren Bist auch der Lutherischenn bőßwychtter ainer /

Troll dich nur bald auß dem hauß / vnd kum̄ nit wider du
vnuerschamtes thyer.

Cale. Es thût euch anndt / das euch der schûster das rodt pyrrett
geschmeht hatt / Laßtt euch nit wunndern / wann im altten
250   gesatz / hat Gott die hirtten seyn wort lassen verkünden / also
auch mûssen (euch phariseyer) die Schûster leeren / Ya es
werden euch noch die stain in die oren schreyen Alde ich
schaid mit wissen.

Kôchin. Euch geschycht recht mich wundert das ir mit dem
groben fültzen reden mügt. Sy schonen weder euch noch der
hailigen weych.

Khor. Jch wil mich nun wol vor in hyettenn / verprents künd /
fürcht fewer Wollan ich wil inn Khor / so gee an marckt /
kauff ein krammet vogel oder zwelff / Es wirt nach eessen
260   meines gnedigen herren Caplon / mit etlichen herren kom̄en /
vnd ein panngett haltten   Trag die Bibel auß der stuben
hinauß / vnd sich ob die stayn vnd würffel all im bretspyl
seyn / Vnd das wir eyn frischen kartten oder zwû haben.

Kôchin. Es sol sein / Herr werdt ir vō stundt an nach dem vmbgang heymher gen.

Kor. Ya / schaw das eessen berayt sey.

Paulus
Yr bauch yr gott
M.D.XXiiij.

3. Hans Sachs

Der Pawr inn dem Fegfewer (1552)

Hans Sachs (1494–1576; cf. pp. 118, 142) wrote some eighty-five *Fastnachtspiele*, and *Der Pawr inn dem Fegfewer*, produced during the period of his greatest
activity during the fifties, is a characteristic example of his work in the genre:
naïve, but intensely alive, full of robust fun, yet free from the grosser
obscenities proper to the genre and concerned not simply to amuse the
spectator, but also to impart an eminently sound, if homely, piece of advice
on how he should order his life.

Although he produced six thousand separate compositions in almost every
contemporary genre except prose narrative, Sachs was not blessed with a
particularly inventive mind. He was, however, an assiduous plunderer of
other men's inventions: Terence and the Bible, the chivalresque novel and

the *Gesta Romanorum*, Pauli's *Schimpf und Ernst* and the *Eulenspiegel-Volksbuch*
all supplied him with material—indeed it is to no small extent in his function as a purveyor and popularizer of medieval, classical, and Renaissance
themes that his cultural and historical significance lies.

Der Pawr inn dem Fegfewer derives from a story by Boccaccio (*Decameron*,
Third Day, Novel VIII), which Sachs knew from Heinrich Schlüsselfelder's
translation. In Boccaccio's story the wife of a gentleman named Ferondo appeals to an allegedly saintly abbot to help her cure her husband of jealousy.
The abbot explains that he can cure Ferondo, his plan being to drug the
latter, confine him in a dungeon, and persuade him that he is in fact dead
and must be punished in purgatory for his jealousy, and then subsequently
to raise him from the dead again. The wife agrees to this plan and also to the
abbot's demand that she should become his mistress in return for the service
he performs in curing her husband. As a result of his ten months' incarcera-
tion in the abbot's dungeon, Ferondo is cured of his jealousy and on his
'resurrection' happily accepts as his own the child the abbot has fathered on
his wife, while the latter remains the abbot's mistress for a long time to come.

The drastic cure of the jealous husband fitted naturally into the *Fastnachtspiel* tradition, both in terms of the often cruel slapstick proper to the genre
and in terms of the equally traditional concern with problems of married
life (cf. p. 132). Accordingly Sachs retains the comic central situation of the
drugged and imprisoned husband purged of his jealousy by a horse-cure
administered by a monk in one of the abbey dungeons. Equally, some of his
best lines (the peasant's surprise at being dead, his inquiry about souls eating, his annoyance at having no candles and at the poor quality of the wine)
are developed from remarks in Boccaccio. In spite of the licence which the
Fastnachtspiel traditionally enjoyed in sexual matters, however, the licen-
tiousness inherent in Boccaccio's treatment of the theme was alien to Sachs's
devoutly Protestant moral outlook and there is in his play little trace of the
novelist's gallant satire of the cuckold husband, or of his mockery of the
'saintliness' of the clergy and the gullibility of the faithful. As a Protestant
polemicist of some standing Sachs was not averse to attacking the Roman
clergy, but unlike Boccaccio he was, in both theory and practice, a staunch
upholder of the institution of marriage (his first marriage lasted some forty
years and after the death of his wife he married again at the age of sixty-
seven). The sham of Ferondo's marriage would inevitably be distasteful to
him and, in contradistinction to Boccaccio's novel, Sachs's play is informed
by a conviction of the sanctity and honourable nature of the married estate
even though he is well aware of the latter's disadvantages and problems.
Accordingly, the whole emphasis of Boccaccio's story is shifted, with an
attendant heightening in the unity of interest, which is now concentrated
entirely on the cure of Heintz Düppel. Els, Düppel's wife, is unquestionably
faithful to him, and Boccaccio's incontinent priest survives as the wise abbot,
who is indeed vaguely unhappy with his celibate lot, but whose waggish cure
of Düppel testifies not only to a certain want of reverence, but also to a
pastoral concern for the welfare of the abbey's tenants.

Besides the satire of married life, the *Fastnachtspiel* was frequently used as
a vehicle for social satire. Partly for the same reasons as have always caused

the city-dweller to look down on his rural cousin, partly as an unconscious
exorcism of the very real urban fear of the peasantry (a legacy of the agrarian
revolts of the fifteenth and sixteenth centuries), the peasant was singled out
as the butt for the dramatists, who never tired of representing him as a
stupid, avaricious clodhopper, grasping, but gullible in the extreme and
an easy prey for any smart alec who came along. It is therefore not surprising
to find that Boccaccio's upper-class Ferondo has been translated into the
uncouth and stupid Heintz Düppel. Yet, as so often with Sachs, we are not
confronted with just a type, but with a genuine character, to whom the
author has given a number of individualizing traits which enable him to
exist for us as a person—one thinks of Düppel's malapropisms, his disin-
genuousness, his concern to get back his basket, or his self-pity and his
petulant recriminations against his wife when he finds himself in purgatory.
But it is above all the naïve good humour of Sachs's farce which gives it its
appeal, be it in the comic basic situation with the gullible and wretched
Düppel sitting opposite his 'Scheißkübel' in the darkness of his cell, or in the
incidental touches such as Gröltzenbrey's association of the evanescence of
human life with the memory of a recently consumed dish of buttermilk, or
Düppel's call to his wife to let him out of his prison, or his ungrateful remarks
about the wine and the candle.

It is this naïve and robust sense of humour combined with the dramatist's
sharp eye for the ludicrous and absurd aspects of human behaviour and his
ability to present a well-observed anecdote in convincing dramatic form
which have enabled Sachs's *Fastnachtspiele* to survive as living literature—
they are still successfully produced in his native Nürnberg—while his more
ambitious and pretentious works (sixty-four 'comedies' and sixty-one
'tragedies', which suffer from an almost grotesque incongruence between
theme and execution) survive only as names in the handbooks of literary
history.

Our text is taken from the edition of Sachs's collected works, *Sehr Herrliche
Schöne Tragedi / Comedi vnnd schimpf Spil*, published by Christoff Heußler of
Nürnberg in 1561.

Faßnacht spiel. Mit 6 Personen
Der Pawr inn dem Fegfewer.

Der Abt geht ein mit Herr Vlrich / vnnd spricht.

> O Glück wie bist so wunderbar
> Du gibst es keinem Menschen gar
> Das er mit warheyt möcht gesprechen
> Jch hab es gar als gebrechen.

Herr Vlrich spricht.

5
> Gnediger Herr jr seidt betrübt
> Das glück zu bschuldigen euch vbt

Hat es euch nit reichlich begabt
Das jr seidt ein gefürster Abt.
Hat euch das glück nit gnug gegeben.

Der Abt spricht.

Hat mir aber gnummen darneben 10
Auch den löblich / heyling Ehstandt
Das selbig thut mir weh vnd andt
Das also hie mein guter nam
Darzu mein gschlecht vnd alter stam
Gentzlichen abstirbet mit mir. 15

Herr Vlrich spricht.

Gnediger Herr was klaget jr
Solt euch nit wünschen in Ehstandt
Darinnen ist stetz vor der handt
Jammer vnd leid / forn vnd hinden
An kleinen vnd ahn grossen Kinden 20
Eins ist kranck / das ander vngratten
Beide mit worten vnd mit thaten
Darob so müst jr euch denn gremen
Schandt vnd vnehr von jn einnemen
Ergrifft jr denn ein zenckisch Weyb 25
Da würt erst peinigt ewer Leyb
Mit kiffen / zancken vnd mit nagen
Das ir kaum kündt die haudt ertragen
Dergleich het jr mit Megdt vnd knechten
Jm Hauß auch vbertag zu fechten 30
Es ist nit alles süs vnd gut
Was in der Eh geleissen thut
Die Eh hat viel heimliches leiden
Mit Eyffersucht / hassen vnd neyden
Solchs seidt jr hie entladen gar. 35

Der Abt spricht.

Ja Herr Vlrich es ist wol war
Sorg halber ich wol freyer bin
Nun wöl wir es gleych treiben hin
Wie wirs getrieben habn biß her
Jch hab gemeindt in der Eh wehr 40
Kein sawrs / nur küchel zu essen.

Herr Vlrich spricht.

Herr ewr gnad kan wol ermessen
Das sich gar viel vnrats zu trag
Jm Ehlichen standt vbertag
45   Weyl viel klag für euch kummen thut
Von den Ehleuten böß vnd gut.

Der Abt spricht.

Es kumbt je warlich vbertag
Für mich so manch wunderlich klag
Solt mir kaum also trawmen than
50   Hört / hört / geht / secht wer klopffet ahn
Jm Kloster an der fördern thür.

Herr Vlrich schaudt nauß / spricht.

Es steht ein Pewrin darfür
Heintz Düppels Weib von Milchtahl
Wirt euch klagen jren vnfahl
55   Sie hat ein grobn / dölpischen Man
Der nichtsen denn Eyfferen kan.

Der Abt spricht.

So geht hin vnd lasset sie ein
Last hören was jr klag wirt sein.

Herr Vlrich bringet die Pewrin / sie spricht.

Ach mein Herr Abt ich kum auff trawen
60   Zu raten mir betrübten Frawen.

Herr Vlrich spricht.

Sie ist gar einfeltig vber auß
Frumb / schlecht vnd ghrecht wie ein spitzmauß
Jr wert gar gute schwenck anhörn
Sie glaubt als / ist leicht zubethörn.

Der Abt spricht.

65   Sagt liebe Fraw was ligt euch ahn.

Die Pewrin spricht.

Mein Herr ich hab ein alten Man
Der Eyffert vmb mich tag vnd nacht
Hat mich schier in die schwintsucht bracht
Er lauschet mir nach vorn vnd hinden
Trodt an ein ketten mich zu binden 70
Das ich jm bleiben muß im Hauß
Vnd hat mit mir gar manchen strauß
Wenn ich ein andern ahn du sehen
Wenn ich schon nichts zu jm thu jehen
So heist er einen schlebsack mich 75
Schmecht vnnd schlecht mich auch hertiglich
Das ich es nit mehr leiden mag.

Der Abt spricht.

Mein Tochter auß deiner ansag
Merck ich / du bist vielleicht geneigt
Zu bulerey / hast jmbs erzeigt 80
Hat vmb sunst nit die Eyffersucht.

Die Pewrin spricht.

Nein mein Herr Abt in aller zucht
Hab ich mich je biß her gehalten
An dem Eyfrenden / groben alten
Derhalb mein trawen zu euch hab 85
Helfft mir doch dieses Eyffern ab
Wo nit so kumb ich von mein sinnen.

Der Abt spricht.

Kein bessern raht west ich darinnen
Denn das man den alten noch hewer
Ein Monat setzt in das Fegfewer 90
Das er sein Eyffern darinn bůst.

Die Pewrin spricht.

Mein alter aber sterben můst.

Der Abt spricht.

Ja / doch baldt er ins Fegfewr kôm
Die straff seinr Eyffersucht einnem

95 So wůrdt durch mein gebet jm geben
Wiederumb sein natůrlich leben
Denn wůrdt er der frůmbst Man auff erdē
Vmb dich nimmer mehr eiffern werdē

Die Pewrin spricht.

Ja lieber Herr so wŏl wirs than.

Der Abt spricht.

100 Mein Fraw / was wird deñ sein mein lahn
Wenn ich jm hůlff des Eyffers ab.

Die Pewrin spricht.

Mein Herr in meinem Kůsthal hab
Jch ein haffn mit pfenning eingraben
Den selben solt jr zu lohn haben
105 Wann mich bedůnckt in meinen sinnen
Es sinn bey sieben pfundt darinnen
Doch ich euch den nit bringen dar
Biß mein Mann ins Fegfewr fahr
Er sicht mir wol so důckisch drauff.

Der Abt spricht.

110 Nun sey beschlossen dieser kauff
Doch sag gar keim Menschen daruan
Schick in das Kloster heint dein Man
Das er zu schenck mir etwas bring
Kes / eyer oder ander ding
115 So wil ich durch mein kunst thewer
Hinab schicken in das Fegfewer.

Die Pewrin spricht.

Ja lieber Herr das wil ich than
Euch schicken heindt mein alten Man.

Die Pewrin geht ab.

Herr Vlrich spricht.

Wie gfelt ewer Gnadt die Pewrin
120 Jsts nicht / wie ich euch sagt vorhin.

Der Abt spricht.

Es ist gar ein einfeltigs Viech
Sie ist eben geleich für mich
Sie hat mich trewlich zu raht fragt
Vber jrs Mans eyffer geklagt
Jch sol jm den helffen vertreiben 125
Sie kůn sunst nit mer bey jm bleiben
Da hab ich geraten durch abentheur
Wir wóln jn setzen in das Fegfewr
Darinn sein Eyffersucht zu bůsen
Raht wie wir das angreiffen můssen 130
Das vns mit der sach můg gelingen
Den haffn mit pfenning zu wegn bringē
Vnd also mit dem groben alten
Auch samb ein Faßnacht spiel thun haltē

Herr Vlrich spricht.

Der kunst bin ich warlich zu schlecht 135
Wie man den Pawrn ins Fegfewr brecht

Der Abt spricht.

Den anfang wil ich euch wol zeygen
Doch thůt bey Leib vnd Leben schweigen
Die Pewrin wirt heindt ohn gefehr
Den Pawrn ins Kloster schicken her 140
Da wil ich jm den geben ein
Ein tolm in einem sůssen Wein
Als denn der schlaff jn vberwigt
Das er da wie ein todter ligt
Denn wóllen wir in legen ein 145
Jm Chor ins grab von Mermelstein
Wie es darnach sol weiter gehn
Laß ich euch darnach auch versthen
Diß tranck steht in ein schónen glas
Jn meinem kalter / wenn ich euch das 150
Heiß holen / so ergreifft das recht.

Herr Vlrich spricht.

Dort kumbt der Pawr einfeltig schlecht.

Der Pawr bringt birn inn einem Krebn / vnd spricht.

Da kum ich zu euch mein Herr Dabt
Mein Fraw vnd ich habn euch begabt
155 Mit diesen frischen schlegel birn
Bit wölt mein kreben nit verliern
Wil jn wol bey dem bendtlein kennen.

Der Abt spricht.

Du thust die bieren nicht recht nennen
Sůnder Regelbirn ist jr nam
160 Sie sindt noch zu herdt allesam
Důgen nit zu essen also.

Der Pawr spricht.

Mein Herr Dapt / legt sie in ein stro
So werden zwischen hie vnd Lichtmessen
Dreck weich / als denn můgt jrs wol essen

Der Abt spricht.

165 Es ist von birn geredt genunck
Herr Vlrich bringt dem Mann ein drunck
Jn der Abtey in meinem kalter.

Der Abt gibt jm ein schlůssel. Herr Vlrich geht ab / der Abt S.

Was thut dein Weyb mein lieber alter.

Der Pawr spricht.

Sie sitzt da heimen spindt vnd singt
170 Frölich / das es im Hauß erklingt
Jch weiß gar nit weß sie sich frewdt
Habs doch wol drey mal ghandelt heudt

Herr Vlrich kumbt / bringt das glaß mit tolm / vnd spricht.

Es sindt zwen Pawren auch danieden
Die ewr Gnad hat fůr jn beschieden.

Der Abt spricht.

175 Ja heisset die Pawren all zwen
Eilendt herauffer zu mir gehn.

Vlrich geht ab.

Der Abt spricht.

Du aber trinck / vnd setz dich nider
Darnach geheim zu Hausse wider.

Der Pawr trinckt es als auß / gibt dem Abt das glaß wider /vnd
spricht.

Herr Dapt das trûncklein schmeckt mir wol
Wolt Got das glaß wehr wider vol.   180

Die zwen Pawren kummen / der Abt spricht.

Warumb bringt jr nit ewer gûlt
Wenn ich euch gleich handelt vnd schûlt
Vnd legt euch in die Keichen schlecht
Meindt jr es gschech euch sehr vnrecht.

Eberlein Grôlzenbrey spricht.

Herr Abt last ewren zorn hoschen   185
So baldt wir haben außgetroschen
So wôl wir das gûlt Korn bringen.

Der Abt spricht.

So kumbt all beidt nach diesen dingen.

Heintz Dûppel felt auff der banck nider /Nickel Rubendunst
spricht.

Schaw / schaw wie felt vnsr nachtbawr nider
Kum laß jm baldt auff helffē wider   190

Heintz dûpl lest hent vnd fûs fallen sie rûtteln jn / Nickel
Rubendunst spricht.

Jch sorg ihn hab der schlag troffen.

Der abt schaut zu im.

Ja es ist anderst nicht zu hoffen
Secht ir nit wie er ist erblichen
All sein krefft sint von im gewichen

195 Secht nur wie sich anspitzt sein Nasen
Sein augen brechen jm der massen
Sein pulß schlecht nit / er ist schon todt

Eberlein Grölzenbrey spricht.

Bist du denn hin inn dieser noht.
Sey wir erst nechtn bey nander gsessen
200 Vnd haben ein putter Milch gessen
Wie baldt ists vmb ein Mensch geschehen

Nickel Rubendunst spricht.

Was wirt sein Weyb nur darzu jehen
Wenn wir jr heimbringen die mehr
Jm Kloster sey gestorben ehr
205 Eberlein wilt du jrs ansagen.

Eberlein Grölzenbrey spricht.

Ja sie wirdt nit viel darnach fragen
Weil er sie wol geblaget hat
Mit seinem Eyffern frü vnd spadt
Wie das jm Dorff weyß jederman.

Der Abt spricht.

210 Jr Pawren greifft den todten ahn
Tragt jn int Kirchen in den Chor
Da ist ein grab gehawen vor
Beim Sagra in ein Merbelstein
Da selb wöl wir jn legen ein
215 Mit dem Couendt vnd der Proces
Morgen halt wir jm ein Seelmes.
Solchs zeigt ahn seiner Frawen frumb
Das sie morgen zum Opffer kumb.

Sie tragen den Todten ab.

Der Abt vnnd Herr Vlrich kummen wider / der Abt spricht.

Den Pawren hab wir ins grab bracht
220 Nun geht jr hin bald / es wirt nacht
Vnd nembt jn heimlich auß dem grab
Schlept jn in die Presaun hienab

Last ligen jn biß auff mitnacht
Wenn er denn vom tholm aufferwacht
So schreidt jn denn ahn vngehewr 225
Er sey gstorben / sitz in dem Fegfewr
Thut jn weidlich mit ruten hawen
Drumb das er eyffert vmb sein Frawen
Treibt mit jm ein solch Affenspiel
Wie ich baß vnterrichten wil 230
Doch das sollichs als heimlich gschech
Das niemandt wiß / merck / hôr noch sech

Herr Vlrich spricht.

Bring ich den Pawren ins Fegfewr
Jch treib mit jm mein abentewr
Gieb vmb sein eyffern jm ein buß 235
Der er sein lebtag dencken muß.

Herr Vlrich geht ab.

Der Abt spricht.

Nun wil ich geren sehen zu
Wie sich der Pawer halten thu
Wenn jm Herr Vlrich saget frey
Wie das er jm Fegfewer sey 240
Wie wirt der Pawr klagen vnd achen
Wie wirt des schwancks so gut zu lachen

Der Abt geht ab.

Herr Vlrich bringt den Pawrn / legt jn nider / vnd spricht.

Wie ist Heintz Düppel also schwer
Laß schawen wenn er auffwachn wer
Jn der Presaun / was wirt er jehen 245
Wirt nit wissn wie jm ist geschehen.

Der Pawr rûmstert sich / steht auff vnnd greifft vmb sich an die vier ort / vnd spricht.

Botz Lung / botz Leber wo bin ich doch
Was ist das für ein finster loch
Sich vnd hôr nichts an disem endt
Jch greiff nichts / denn vier steiner wendt 250

M

Wie bin ich nur kummen herein
Jch wil schreien der Frawen mein
Els / Els / thu auff vnd laß mich auß.

　　Herr Vlrich mit grosser stůmb spricht.
Schweig du bist jetzt in nobis Hauß
255　　Du wirst noch ein weil hinnen sitzen
Bey andern armen Seelen schwitzen
Vnd mit jn leiden gleyche pein

　　　　Heintz Důppel spricht.
Botz leichnam angst wo mag ich sein.

　　　　Herr Vlrich spricht.
Du bist im Purgatorium.

　　　　Der Pawr spricht.
260　　Ach sag mirs teudsch / ich bit dich drum
Jch kan warlich kein Laperdein.

　　　　Herr Vlrich spricht.
Ach Pawer dein frewdt die wirt klein
Du bist ach in dem Fegfewer.

　　　　Heintz Důppel spricht.
O erst ist mir das lachen thewer
265　　Sag mir ahn bin ich denn gestorben.

　　　　Herr Vlrich spricht.
Ja du bist an eim trunck verdorben
Dein leyb ist schon begrabn auff erden

　　　　Der Pawr spricht.
Erst wil dem schimpff der bodn außwerden
So bin ich nur mein arme Seel.

Der Můnch nimbt jn beim halß / buckt jn vber benck / vnnd
spricht.
270　　Da buck dich / du must leiden quel
Des Fegfewrs pein must du entpfinden
Doch wil ich dich nur treffen hinden.

Der Pawr buckt sich vbert benck / der Münch haudt jn mit
ruten

Der Pawr spricht.

Auweh / auweh / thu mich bescheyden
Warumb ich diese pein muß leyden.

Herr Vlrich der Münch spricht.

Darumb das du dest vbel trawen   275
Vnd eyfferst vmb dein frumme Frawen
Dieweil du thest auff erden leben
Wirt diese straff dir teglich geben.

Heintz Düppel spricht.

Jch hab leider geeyffert sehr
Vmb mein Weyb ye lenger ye mehr   280
Wann ich het die Breckin sehr lieb
Das selb mich zu dem Eyffer trieb
Vnser Münch haben mir nie verkündt
Das Eyffern sey so ein grosse Sündt
Jch het es warlich sunst nit than   285
Jch bit dich wölst mir zeygen ahn
Bist ein Teuffl / oder wer bist du
Der mir setzt also hefftig zu.

Herr Vlrich spricht.

Jch bin kein Teuffel auß der Hel
Sonder bin gleych wie du ein Seel   290
Jch muß auch jm Fegfewer leiden.

Heintz Düppel spricht.

Lieber thu mich noch eins bescheiden
Sindt wir zwo Seel im Fegfewr allein.

Herr Vlrich spricht.

Ja wol du arme Seel nein / nein
Es sindt etlich tausendt Seel hinnen   295
Die also bratten vnd brinnen
Jedoch keine die ander nicht
Jm Fegfewer hört oder sicht.

Vlrich geht ab.

Heintz Dûpel spricht.

Hôr sey wir vnter dem Erdtrich vnden
300 Hôrst / ich merck die Seel ist verschwundē
Ach weh / weh / mir ellenden armen
Bin ich gestorbn ahn als erbarmen
Erst rewet mich mein Weyb vnd Kinder
Mein ecker / wisen / Sew vnd Rinder
305 Vnd auch mein eingegraben gelt
Das ich het oben in der Welt
Nun muß ich sitzen hie verflucht
Von wegen der schnôden Eyffersucht
Jst mir mein jung lebn worden abbrochen
310 Bin nur sechtzg jar auff erdn vmb krochē
Het noch wol acht Jar mûgen leben
Het ich mich nit auffs Eyffern geben.

Herr Vlrich kumbt bringet semel vnd Weyn / vnd spricht.

Js vnd trinck da hast Semel vnd Weyn
Welche dir heudt das Weybe dein
315 Geopffert hat zu den Seelmessen.

Der Pawr spricht.

Danck habs / hats mein noch nit vergessē
Sie hat mich dennoch ein wenglein lieb
Wiewol ich viel zanckens mit jr trieb
Sag mir essen die Seelen auch.

Herr Vlrich spricht.

320 O ja es ist jr alter brauch.

Der Pawr spricht.

Wie das mir kein Liecht opffern thet
Das ich darbey gesehen het
Weil es ist so stickfinster hinnen.

Herr Vlrich spricht.

Sie opffert eins / das thet verbrinnen
325 Dieweil man dir die Seelmeß sung.

Der Pawr spricht.

Ey schendt sie pox leber vnd Lung
Das liecht het mir viel nôter thon
Denn dem Mûnch der obn altar stohn
Der het wol von dem tag gesehen.

Herr Vlrich spricht.

Nun iß vnd trinck / vnd laß geschehen 330
Es kan jm Fegfewr nit anderst sein.

Der Pawr trinckt / vnd spricht.

Ey / ey / wie gar ein sawren wein
Den sewrstn den sie im keller hat
Mir armen Seel der karg vnflat
Hats geopffert auff den Altar 335
Sag mir wenn hab ich bûset gar
Das ich denn wirt gehn Hymel faren?

Herr Vlrich spricht.

Ja lieber kaum in hundert Jaren
Wann du hast dich versûndet weit
Mit dem Eyffern ein lange zeit 340
Es wer denn das du wûrst begabt
Durch fûrbit deins heiligen Abt
Das dein Seel wider kem zum Leyb
Jn die alt welt zu deinem Weyb.

Der Pawr hebt die hendt auff / vnd spricht.

O solt ich wider kummen auff erden 345
Wie wolt der frûmbst Mann ich werden
Wolt nit mchr Eyffcrn in meinem leben
Sonder wolts meim Weyb als nach gebē
Was sie nur wolt groß vnde klein
Das ich nit wider kem in die pein. 350

Der Abt kumbt / bringet das tolm tranck / vnnd spricht heimlich.

Herr Vlrich des schimpff ist genug
Seht gebt dem Pawrn wider ein trunck

Das er entschlaff / eh es thu tagen
Thut in sein grab jn wider tragen
355   Das er wider vom todt ersthe
Vnd heim zu Weyb vnd Kinden ghe.

Herr Vlrich gibt jm trincken / vnd spricht.

So trinck auch diesen süssen wein
Hat heut geopffert das Weybe dein.

Der Pawr trinckt / vnd spricht.

Ja werlich dieser schmeckt mir baß
360   Bey der mawr ligt das groß faß.

Der Pawr felt nider / Herr Vlrich tregt jn ab / vnd spricht.

Jtzt ist Heintz Düppel nit so schwer
Jst im Fegfewer worden lehr
Wann er hat schmale pfenbart gessen
Jch hab jmbs leichnam gnaw gemessen.

Der Abt kumbt vnd spricht.

365   Der Pawr ist im Fegfewr gelegen
Hat sein Eyffersucht auß müssn fegen
Vnd hat auch gentzlichen gelaubt
Er sey seines lebens beraubt
Jetzt thut er gleich wider erstehn
370   Wirt heim zu Weyb vnd Kinden gehn
Ehr vnd sein Weib sindt beydesander
Eins gleich so lappet als das ander

Der Pawr kumbt vnd spricht.

Ach mein Herr Dabt danck habet ir
Durch ewr Feistikeit so habt jr mir
375   Erworben wiederumb mein leben
Wie mir das hat anzeiget eben
Ein Seel vnden in dem Fegfewr.

Der Abt spricht.

Leb fort hin nicht so vngehewr
Mit deim Weyb mit der Eyffersucht
380   Weil sie selb helt Weybliche zucht.

Der Pawr beudt jhm thandt / S.
Herr da habt keinen zweyffel ahn

Der Abt spricht.

Nun thu hin heim zu Hause gahn
Jch wil hienein gehn zum frûambt
Das in der kirchē nichts wert versaumbt
Biß Suntag kum ins Kloster rein   385
Alda must du mein gast sein
Als denn must nach leng mir hersagen
Was sich im Fegfewr hat zu tragen.

Der Abt gehet ab.

So kummen sein zwen Nachtbawrn / Nickel Rubendunst
spricht.
Vns ist drauß gsagt vom Cuntz Rolandē
Heintz Dûppel sey vom todt erstanden   390
Wir sindt rein gschickt von seiner Frawē
Jns Kloster die warheyt zu schawen
Wie er in dem Kloster zu geh
Vnd sey frey lebendig als eh
Jch kan sein aber glauben nicht.   395

Eberlein Grôlzenbrey spricht.

Las mich triegn denn all mein gesicht
So steht Heintz Dûppel im Creutzgang
Ey wie sicht er so sawr vnd strang
Als ob er hab ein Kindt erbissen
Odr jm die Wôlff ein Kw zerrissen.   400

Nickel Rubendunst spricht.

Ja es ist warlich nur sein Seel
Jst herauff gfaren auß der Heel
Kum laß vns eilendt vor jm fliehen.

Sie zwen fliehen.

Heintz Dûppel schreidt.

Steht / steht / jr Nachtbawrn thut verziehē
Jch leb wider warhafftiglich   405
Steht / steht / jr dûrfft nit fûrchten mich.

Sie stehen. Eberlein Grölzenbrey spricht.

Ey lieber bist wider genesen
Wo ist die weil dein Seel gewesen
Jm Hymel oder in der Heel.

Heintz Düppel spricht.

410   Es ist gewest mein arme Seel
Ein monat lang in dem Fegfewr
Darinn gepeinigt vngehewr.

Nickel Rubendunst spricht.

Was hast im Fegfewer erlieden.

Heintz Düppel spricht.

Mancherley pein / doch vnterschieden
415   Man thet mich hart darinn peinigen
Mit vbel essen vnd hart liegen
Auch peinigtn mich darinn die Meuß
Die floch / vnd auch die hader leuß
Auch haut man mich vbel mit ruten
420   Das mir offt thet die kerben bluten
Auch stundt darinnen ein scheißkübel
Der stünck so leichnam hieren vbel
Auch war es drin gar stickfinster
Sach weder Sunn nach Stern glinster
425   Kein liecht man auch darinn anzündt.

Eberlein Grölzenbrey spricht.

Mein Heintz Düppel vmb welche sündt
Hat man mit ruten dich gehawen.

Heintz Düppel spricht.

Das ich het geyffert vmb mein Frawen
Das hat mein Seel so hart beschwert
430   Kein grösser Sünd kam nie auff erdt
Deñ Eyffern / drumb liebn nachtpawrn mein
Wölt vor dem eiffern gewarnet sein
Weil man es strafft so vngehewr
Mit ruten vndten im Fegfewr

Kumbt mit mir heim zum Weybe mein   435
Da wôl wir frisch vnd frôlich sein
Ein newe hochzeyt mit jr han
Jch wil werden ein ander Man
Das mir keyn nachrew drauß erwachs
Jn dem Fegfewr / wûnscht Hans Sachs.   440

Die Person inn das Spiel.

Der Abt von Certal	1
Herr Vlrich der Mûnch	2
Heintz Dûppel der Eyffert Pawr	3
Els scin Haußfraw ein Pewrin	4
Eberlein Grôltzenbrey ein Pawr	5
Nickel Rubendunst ein Pawr	6

Anno M. D. LII. Jar
Am Neundten Tag
Decembris.

4. Georg Rollenhagen

Spiel vom reichen Manne / vnd armen Lazaro (1590)

Rollenhagen (1542–1609) was a preacher and schoolmaster by profession—
for many years he was rector of the Magdeburg *Gymnasium*, which under his
direction became one of the most famous schools in North Germany—and
achieved fame as a writer of fable (cf. p. 125) and school drama. His *Spiel vom
reichen Manne / vnd armen Lazaro*, which went through four editions between
1590 and 1622, is a characteristic example of German Protestant school
drama, redolent of the biblicism of the age and written in order to implant
a sound moral lesson in the minds of the audience and the schoolboy actors,
while providing the latter with an opportunity to exercise their rhetorical
talents and putting before the spectators visible evidence of the 'gute sitten
vnd ein deutliche freudige sprach' which were being developed in the local
grammar school.

Offering, as it did, two sharply differentiated principal characters, a
certain amount of ready-made dialogue, and an unmistakably clear moral
message, St. Luke's account of the respective fates of Dives and Lazarus
(16: 19–31) had obvious attractions for the biblically minded dramatist and
had already inspired a number of school dramas in both Latin and German,
including versions by Hans Salat (1540), Georg Macropedius (1541),
Johannes Krüginger (1543), Jacob Funckelin (1550), Joachim Lonemann

(1564), and Georg Müntzer (1575). In an age in which plagiarism was an unquestioned fact of literary life, these playwrights naturally tended to draw on the efforts of their predecessors, and in the introduction to his play Rollenhagen tells us that his intention had simply been to 'renew' the version of Joachim Lonemann, now long out of print, and that in the process 'zum theil ein ander Werck draus worden ist'. No copy of Lonemann's play seems to have survived, but since no less than twenty scenes of Rollenhagen's version (including iii. 3, 5, 6, 7, 15, 16; iv. 4; v. 4) correspond closely to scenes in Macropedius's *Lazarus mendicus*, it is likely that Lonemann himself did little more than translate and 'renew' a Latin original. Rollenhagen's contribution consisted mainly in expanding his relatively modest model into a long five-act play of almost 4,000 lines and in creating some seventy-five new roles—a school with 1,600 pupils obviously needed a play with a correspondingly big cast!

The basic structure of the play is simple: Act I shows us Porphyrius the usurer at work; Act II introduces us to the world of poverty and shows how the deserving poor, like Lazarus, are neglected, while smooth-talking 'Böß Buben' enjoy the favour of the rich. In Act III the action proper begins with the rich Porphyrius spurning the poor Lazarus at his gate. In Act IV the death of the two principal characters occurs (surprisingly Rollenhagen does not show us Porphyrius's death agony, but simply informs us that he has died) and Act V shows us Lazarus and Porphyrius being treated according to their deserts in the life hereafter. This simple scheme is expanded by the introduction of a host of minor characters: beggars, mercenary soldiers, peasants, priests, doctors, servants, angels, and devils, and by an almost baroque love of spectacle which gains its most obvious expression in the ostentatious funeral procession of Porphyrius.

The play was probably staged in the town hall or on the market square. Scenery would be elementary: an archway to represent Porphyrius's gate, a raised dais for the festive gathering, a tower or balcony on the left which would serve as Heaven, and the entrance to Hell probably depicted in traditional fashion as the gaping jaws of a monster on the right. The basic message of the play on the necessity of performing the works of charity would be clear to all and in the context of Lutheran Magdeburg might seem to put an improper emphasis on works as a means to salvation ('Denn wer eim Armen gibt in Noth / Der kriegts widr mit Gewin von Gott', etc.). As a good Protestant, however, Rollenhagen is careful to remind the spectator of the importance of faith in Lazarus's death scene ('Ach Gott / mein sûnd / mein sûnd ist schwer / Dein Gnad allein erhelt mich HErr'), and characteristically Lazarus is saved not by his own merits, but by fiduciary faith and by the gracious non-imputation of his sins to him ('Denn du *gerecht geachtet* bist / Das dir mein Wort lieb gwesen ist.'). Even a polemical note creeps in: the rabbis who are more concerned with observing Mosaic law and with filling their bellies than with ministering to the poor and sick were probably intended to remind the audience of the alleged attitude of the Roman Catholic clergy.

Like many another dramatist Rollenhagen evidently found that wickedness was an easier and more rewarding theme for dramatic treatment than goodness, and at first sight it might appear as if his material and his treatment of it has involved the author in a rather unfortunate weighting of the dramatic interest away from the static and, to modern eyes at least, rather masochistic Lazarus (cf. III. 5) towards the more active Porphyrius. Certainly the latter engages our attention much more than the wretched Lazarus, with the result that at times the play is reminiscent of the *Everyman* theme with Porphyrius as Everyman. In spite of the praise of the patience of Lazarus under adversity, however, Rollenhagen's real purpose is not to encourage his respectable middle-class audience to emulate Lazarus and become poor and patient, but rather to exhort them to avoid the errors of Porphyrius. Lazarus in the last analysis is little more than a foil to his rich antagonist, and the concentration of the interest on Porphyrius is in fact a means by which the author—probably unintentionally—achieves his overriding dramatic aim.

Compared with the best creations of Hans Sachs and the Latin dramatists of the sixteenth century, even Porphyrius and the frequently not uninteresting minor characters scarcely represent an advance in characterization. Equally, Rollenhagen's handling of the dialogue is not conspicuous for its suppleness. It is, however, not so much on characterization and diction as on the skill with which the author captures and holds the audience's attention, while working with such a broad canvas, and on his evident ability to treat a serious subject in a serious, yet always lively manner, without descending into bathos or sententiousness, that the play's claim to represent one of the peaks of German vernacular drama in the sixteenth century must rest.

Our text is taken from the edition of 1591 printed in Eisleben by Urban Graubisch.

Actvs III. Scena III.

Porphyrius, Daemones, Lazarus, Byssinus, Euphraenon, Lampros.
Mnemon. Plusia.

Der Chorus oder die Spielleut empfahen den Reichen | sampt
Daemone, mit einem lieblichen Gesang.

Porphyrius.

So ist es recht mein lieber Freund |
   Drůmb ist es zeit | das wir jetzund
Nach diesm wol ebn ein ander Frewd
   Suchen | die ich bestelt hab heut.   10
Jn meinem Hauß | drůmb gehn wir nein |
   Das wir | wie allzeit | frŏlich sein.
Vnd nur zur Wollust vns ergebn |
   Denn mein hauß ist gweit zum wollebn.

Daemones.

Jn dem hast mich / mein lieber Freund /
   Wie ein gedingten Knecht all Stund.
Jch halt auch wol / die dort herkomn /
   Werdn sich in dem auch nicht verseumn.

20   *Porphyrius.*

Ja warlich / denn eben kommen hier /
   Wie ich seh / meine Brûder vier.
Wo mag der fûnffte bleiben doch /
   Vnd der ist auch der eltest noch?
Jedoch mus seinent halben nicht /
   Die Sache bleiben vnuerricht.
Wenn nur allein die andern Herrn /
   Die auch geladen / kommen wern.

Lazarus ad fratres.

30   O jr glûckselig reiche Leut /
   Jch bitt / denckt meiner in ewer Frewd.
Die Brosamen allein ich bitt /
   Die jr verwerffet / theilt mir mit.

Porphyrius.

Mein lieber Daemones wilkum /
   Vnd jr mein Brûder all herûmb.
Jr seid mir warlich liebe Gest /

Byssinus.

   Drûmb sein wir also willig gwest.

40   *Plusia ad singulos.*

Wilkom. *Singuli respondent,* Danck habt.

Plusia postremo.

Wilkom seid jr mir all Gotts sammn /

Mnemon.

Danck habt schwegrin in Gottes Namn.

Plusia.

Jr wolt mit dem Herrn gehn hinein /
Biß das die andern auch da sein.
Jch hoff / sie werden bald ankommn.
Wie ich von dem Diener vernommn.　　50

ingrediuntur.

Actvs III. Scena IIII.

Rabbi Iose. Rabbi Simon. Rabbi Salomon. Lazarus. Porphyrius.

Rabbi Iose

Wolan jr Rabbi alle beid /
So habt jr jetzt gehôrt die zeit.
Wie gern jetzund das gmein Volck doch /
Von sich weg thet / des Gsetzes Joch.
Das sie on Opffer nûchtern lebn /
Vnd vns zum dienst nichts dûrfftn gebn.　　60
Damit das best aus vnserm Ampt /
Vns wûrd entzogen allen sampt.
Allein / dweil denn die reichsten doch /
Jn dieser Stad / die Gwaltigsten auch
Vns halten hoch / vnd stets in Ehrn /
Vnd vnser Opffer teglich mehrn.
Schreckt vns nicht sehr der gmeine Man /
Wenn wir der Reichen Freundschafft han.
Derhalben / lieben Rabbi mein /
Rath ich / das wir auch willig sein /　　70
Zu jm zu gehn / wenn man vns bitt /
Ob schon der Pôbel lobet nit.

Rabbi Simon.

Das deucht mir auch gerathen sein /
Drûmb gehn wir stracks jetzund hinein /
Zu vnserm Freund Porphyrio /
Dieweil er vns hat gefordert nu.
Er ist doch reich / vnd hat viel Gut /
Gibt vns mehr / denn ein Armer thut.

80   *Rabbi Salomon.*

Jn dem halt ichs auch mit euch stets /
Denn darin folgt jr vnserm Gesetz.

Lazarus.

Ach lieben Herrn / seht jr doch an /
Mich armen vnd verlassen Man.
Ein selig Mensch ist / der versteht
Wie es eim armen Menschen geht.

Rabbi Simon.

Das ist fůrwar ein armer Man /

90   *Rabbi Salomon.*

Man seiner jetzt nicht warten kan.
Jch weiß gewiß / das wir zur stet /
Wol werden ankommen zu spet.

Lazarus.

Vbt doch mit mir Barmhertzigkeit /
Gott wirds vergeltn in Ewigkeit.

Porphyrius.

Ewr Ehrwirdn solln mir willkom sein /
Vnd jr auch lieben Herren mein.

100   *Rabbi Iose.*

Danck habet jr / mein gůnstigr Herr.

Porphyrius.

Jr seid gar langsam kommen her.
Drůmb bit ich jetzt euch nur zu Tisch /
Das Essen soll man bringen risch.

Rabbi Simon.

Mit vngewaschen Henden Herr?
Bhůt Gott Adonai dafůr.

Porphyrius.

110   Wolan / so wascht / wies euch gut deucht /
Sag du / das man dieweil anricht.

Actvs III. Scena V.

Lazarus.

O HERR mein Gott / was meinstu doch /
Das du mich lengr lesst leben noch?
Jch kan erwerben nicht mein Brot /
Bin kranck / vnd leid groß Hungerßnoth.
Noch ist kein Mensch der mich erkent /
All Man sich von meim klagen wend.
Fůr mir sein all Leut stum vnd blind /   120
Jr Ohren all verstopffet sind.
Der ein geht hin / der ander her /
Niemand ist der sich an mich kchr.
Jch bin veracht / vnd gar vernicht /
Als wer ich dein Geschöpffe nicht.
Als wer ich nicht dein Knecht / O HErr /
Ach HErr mein Gott / dich zu mir kehr.
Du bist mein Gott / ich harre dein /
Drůmb werd ich dir noch danckbar sein.
Das du HErr bist in dieser Noth /   130
Mein Angesichtes Hůlff vnd Gott.
Vnd weil kein Mensch sicht an mich armn /
Thun sich die Hund meiner erbarmn.
Die lecken mir die Schweeren mein /
Des ich dir Gott mus danckbar sein.

Actvs III. Scena VI.

Rabi Iose. Porphyrius. Sosia. Lazarus. Merimnus.

*Nach dem sie sich gewaschen / setzen sie sich zu Tisch / vnd der
Rabbi Jose segenet das Brot / auff diese weise:*

Gelobet seistu HERR mein Gott /   140
Kŏnig der Welt / der du das Brot /
Aus dem Erdreich herausser fůhrst /
Vnd vns damit reichlich ernehrst . . .

Porphyrius interrumpit preces:

Das Essen wil kalt werden nu mehr /
Drůmb last es bleiben lieber Herr.

Ein kurtz Benedict / vnd zu letzt /
Ein lang Gratias ist das best.
Drûmb greiffet zu / darûmb ich bitt /
150   Lasts euch schmecken / verseumpt euch nit.

Sosia.

Nu sitzen die Herren zu Tisch /
Vnd sein vielleicht zur Schûssel risch.
Allein Merimnus feilet noch /
Nu wolt ich warlich / das jn doch
Der Hunger plagt / wie mich bißweiln /
Was gilt / er wûrd zu Tisch wol eiln.
Sich da / er kômpt / nu mus ich gahn /
Das ich sag / das er kom heran.

160   *Lazarus ad Merimnum.*

Ach jr mein Herr / wer jr denn seid /
Erbarmt euch / ich groß Hunger leid.

Merimnus:

Was thut das Aß hie fûr der Thûr?
Pfuy weg / das dich der Hencker fûhr.

Actvs III. Scena VII.

Merimnus. Porphyrius. Rabbi Simon. Oeconomus.

Merimnus.

Jch grûß mein Herren all vmbher /

170   *Porphyrius.*

Ey Bruder / wo so langsam her?
Mein weiß ist / wer spat kômpt heran /
Der mus da vnten sitzen an.

Merimnus.

Nein warlich / diß ist vnten nicht /
Dieweils zur Schûssel ist gericht.

Porphyrius.

Wolan / du bist zu spat ankommn /
Leg fûr dich / thu dich nicht verseumn.

Merimnus.

Zu spat? hier ist doch alls genug /
Jch wil mein theil wol kriegen noch . . .

Porphyrius.

Das thu Bruder / es darff kein eil.
Vnd jr mein Herren vberall /
Seid doch frôlich zu diesem mahl.
Jr seid so still vnd trawrig gar /
Jch werd an euch keinr Frewd gewar.
Esst doch / vnd trinckt herûmb / last sehn /
Lasst doch das Gleßlein rûmmer gehn . . . 190

Actvs III. Scena XV.

Lazarus. Porphyrius. Byssinus. Oeconomus. Mastyx.

Lazarus.

O HErr / den Gott so miltiglich /
Mit so viel Gûttern / vnd reichlich /
Begabet hat fûr ander Leut /
Jch bitt durch Gotts Barmhertzigkeit.
Ewr Augen kert hier wenig her /
Erbarmt euch mein / drûmb bitt ich sehr.
Ewr Geld vnd Gut beger ich nicht / 200
Was euch kund schaden / ich nicht bitt.
Allein das jr verwerffet sonst /
Vnter den Tisch / gebt mir aus Gunst.
Denn ich leid Hunger vberaus /
Von ohnmacht ich verschmachten mus.
Lasst euch bewegen Herre mein /
Das wir all Menschen sterblich sein.
Das wir all eines Vaters Kind /
All eines Gottes Schôpffnis sind.
Will schweigen / das ewr Gûtigkeit / 210
Nicht werden lobn allein die Leut.
Sondern das daran selber Gott /
Ein lust vnd auch gefallen hat.
Auch werd jr des kein Schaden han /
Sondern viel mehr gewinnen dran.

Denn wer eim Armen gibt in Noth /
Der kriegts widr mit Gewin von Gott . . .
Derhalben Herr / bitt ich durch Gott /
Lasst mir werden ein Krůmlein Brot.

220   *Porphyrius.*

Was bleckt daraussen fůr der Thůr?
Hab ichs euch nicht gesagt zuuor.
Das jr kein Bettler lassen solt /
Fůr meinem Haus / wehr wer er wolt.
Niemand gedenck ich zu geben was /
Auch nicht / der sich heist Lazarus.

Byssinus, der ander Bruder.

Gib jm nur nichtes / rath auch ich /
Denn mehr hat man von jnen nicht /
230   Denn Stanck vnd Vnlust / wenn man wil
Mit Gesten frôlich sein bißweil.

Oeconomus.

Vnd ich / Mastyx / befehl hart dir /
Das du sie treibst mit Schlegn von hier.

Mastyx.

Jch habs gethan / vnd fůrnemlich /
Dem Lazaro gebn gute Streich.
Jedoch / dieweil er nicht kund gehn /
Fůr Kranckheit / erbarmt ich mich sein.
240   Vnd schlept jn an die ander seit
Des Hauses / da man nicht viel geht.

Porphirius.

Wer hat dir das befohlen dann /
Solstu nicht thun / was ich wolt han?
Geh hin / so er sich nicht weg macht /
So schlep jn / das jms Hertze kracht.
Kônn wir denn fůr dem Bôsewicht /
Ein Mahlzeit Brotes essen nicht.
Bin ich jm doch nichts schůldig zwar /
250   Oder wil er mich zwingen gar?

Es ist ein schand von dem Gesind /
    Das sie so vnuerschemet sind.
Wir aber wollen frôlich sein /
    Drûmb Syre heiß bald kommen rein
Die Spielleut jetzund allzumal /
    Das sie vns hier in diesem Saal /
Machen ein hûbschen schônen Gesang
    Das man vberall hôr den Klang.
Liebs Weib / mir vnd den Gesten alln /
    Tantz ein Galliart zu gefalln . . .   260

Actvs III. Scena XVI.

Lazarus. Mastyx.

Mastyx ad Lazarum. Finita chorea.

Wolauff / wolauff / du must dauon /
    Was murstu viel? Auff / sich mich an.
Auff Lazare / Wie / schleffstu noch?

Lazarus.

Laß mich mit frieden sterben doch /
Es wird der arme Lazarus /
    Euch bald nicht mehr machen verdruß.   270

Mastyx.

Bhût Gott / er stirbt vor Hunger nur /
    Ey das meim Herrn das Hellisch Fewr
Verbrenn in Ewigkeit hinein /
    Das er von all dem fressen sein /
Jm nicht ein Bißlein geben wil /
    Jch bin ein Knecht / hab selbst nicht viel.
Sonst geb ich jm / was ich vermôcht.

Angelus Raphael appropinquat Lazaro.

O weh / es kômpt mich an ein Furcht.   280
Es zittert mir Leib / Hend vnd Bein /
    Hilff Gott / was mag hier bey jm sein.
Er mag ligen / ich mus hin gahn /
    Vnd meinem Herrn es zeigen an . . .

Actvs IIII. Scena IIII.

Gabriel. Maleach. Ruach. Satan. Lazarus. Mors.

Gabriel.

Was hastu Satan hier verlorn?
Jch halt / du hast noch nie erfahrn /
290   Wies hab mit Lazaro ein gstalt /
Denn er ist nicht in deiner gewalt.
Wie sonst viel Leut in dieser Welt /
Wir sein von Gott darzu bestelt.
Das wir sein Seel entpfahen solln /
Drůmb magst dich wol von dannen trolln.

Satan.

Du schreckst mich auch noch nicht so bald.

Ad Lazarum.

Hôrstu / du bist in meiner gwalt /
300   Du bist ein Sůnder / hôrstus wol /
Drůmb bistu so der Schwåren voll
Vnd must von Hunger sterben doch /
Meinst das Gott deiner achtet noch?

Maleach.

War ist es / ein Sůnder ist er /
Aber Gott ist sein gnedigr Herr.

Lazarus.

Ach Gott / mein sůnd / mein sůnd ist schwer /
Dein Gnad allein erhelt mich HErr.

310   #### Satan.

Wie kan dir Gott sein genedig /
Gott vnd sein Gsetz ist wider dich.

Maleach.

Der Gnadenstuel bedeckt fůr jm /
All des Gesetzes Zorn vnd Grim.

Lazarus.

Der Sam des Weibes / HErr allein /
Machet mich durch sein Opffer rein.

Satan.

Du must gleichwol sterben doch / 320
Wenn du so sehr Gott trawest noch.

Maleach.

Der Leib stirbt / die Seel lebt doch /
Der Leib vom Tod auffstehet noch.

Lazarus.

HERR Gott nimm mich nur bald dahin /
Denn sterben ist mein bester Gwin.

Satan.

Du must gleichwol / hôrstu Gesell?
Mit mir hinunter in die Hell. 330

Sadiel.

Satan back dich / das hôrstu wol /
Hieruon dir doch nichts werden soll.

Satan.

Jch lauff fûr dir auch nicht so bald.

Sadiel.

So mustu gleichwol mit gewalt.

Mors.

Was / Habt jr noch nicht außgefecht?
Hart / hart / der Streit mus sein gelegt. 340
Satan / nim deiner ding in acht /
Mach dich heran / sey vnuerzagt.
Nur her Gesell / es ist dein zeit /
Nu streck dich / reck dich / ich nicht beit.

Lazarus.

Mein Seel O Gott /

Mors.

Must besser dran.

Lazarus.

350   Nim in dein Hend.

Mors.

Du must dauon.
Sich so mus den Leib tôdten ich /
Nu stirb / nu stirb / ich wûrge dich.

Emanuel.

Kom her / kom her / du liebe Seel /
Wir wollen nach Gottes Befehl /
Dich auffführen in Abrahams Schoß /
Du bist nu alles Elends loß.

360   *Satan ad mortuum Lazarum.*

Pfuy dich / du loser Betteler /
Meinst das ich mich an dich auch kehr?
Fahr hin / fahr hin / ich bger dein nicht /
Solch stinckend Schelm sein mir zu schlicht.
Jch weiß ein ander Wildbret gut /
Darauff hab ich ein guten Muth.
Der wird mir nicht / was gilts? entgehn /
Mein Gsellen werden wol drauff sehn . . .

Actvs V. Scena I.

370 *Hieher gehôrt das Geprenge mit der Leich / dauon zuuor geschrieben ist*
vnter den Personen. Man stellet aber diß also an / als wolte man die
Leich durch das Theatrum biß fûrs Thor hinaus tragen / vnd / wie im
Argument gemeldet wird / auff des reichen Mannes Schloß begraben. Der
gelegenheit nach kommen alle Personen von Theatro weg. Wil man auch
eine Leichpredigt halten / stehet zu eines jeden gefallen.
Folget die Leichpredigt.

Actvs V. Scena II.

Mammon. Porphyrius.

Mammon.

Wo ist denn mein gehorsams Kind? 380
  Wie kömpts? das ich dich hie so find?
Dein trewen dienst mein lieber Son /
  Den du mir hast von Kindauff gthan /
Den wil ich dir belohnen jetz /
  Mit Fewr / Schwefel / vnd grosser Hitz.

Porphyrius.

O weh / Ach Ach / O weh / Ach / Ach /

Mammon.

Ey lieber Sone thu gemach.

Porphyrius. 390

O weh.

Mammon.

  Ruff nicht so vngehewr /
Es ist gut Kurtzweil in dem Fewr /

Porphyrius.

O weh / o weh der grossen Noth.

Mammon.

Ey lieber Son / nim so für gut.
Es wird doch immer böser noch /
  Ey besser wolt ich sagen doch ... 400

Actvs V. Scena III.

Porphyrius.

Ach / Ach / das ich so gemartert bin?
  Ach / Wo soll ich mich wenden hin?
Hinauff? da sitzt der gestrenge Gott /
  Hinnab? da ist der Hellen Gloth.

Zur seiten? da ist der Teufel Schar /
Die haben mich vmbgeben gar.
Jn mir? da ist der Wurm / das Gwissen /
410   Der stirbt nicht / der hat mich zerrissn /
Der martert erst / vnd plaget mich /
Kein end der Qual / kein maß seh ich.
Was wil fûr Marter mir geschen /
Wenn der Sententz nu wird ergehn /
Wenn auch der Leib wird wider kommn /
Zu seiner Seel die von jm genommn?
Da wird erst recht / das grewlich Leidn
Mich martern / zetr / zu ewigen zeiten . . .
Jch kans albereit ertragen nicht /
420   Ach / Ach / wer ists? den ich dort sich?
Jn Abrahams Schoß? Lazarus /
Jst Lazarus in Abrahams Schoß?
Vnd ist so frewdig noch darzu /
Voll Trosts / Frewden / jmmer nu . . .
Das jm solche Frewd solt geschen /
Das hett ich mich nimmer versehn.
Den hielt ich fûr ein Fluch auff Erd /
Verhônt jn / acht jn nichtes werd.
Jagt / stieß jn / trieb jn allweg aus /
430   Ließ jn verschmachten fûr meim Hauß.
Was hilfft mich nu mein großes Gut /
Was hilfft mich auch mein Vbermuth?
Mein Reichthumb / vnd mein grosse pracht /
Habn mich in diese Qual gebracht.
Jn diese Qual / der Hellen Pein /
Daraus wird kein Erlôsung sein . . .

Actvs V. Scena IIII.

Porphyrius. Abraham. Mammon. Iehoua.

Porphyrius.

440   O Vater Abraham / ich bitt /
Erbarm dich mein / vnd dencke nicht
An meine vnthat / sondern sich
Wie grosse quale leide ich.

Der ich doch Vatr von deinem Stammn
  Gezeuget bin von heiligm Samn.
Drûmb bitt ich Vater / send hieher /
  Den frommen Lazarum / das er
Das eusserste des Fingers sein /
  Jns Wasser wenig tauch hinein.
Damit er meine Zunge kûhl /   450
  Denn ich groß Pein der Flammen fûhl.

Abraham.

Son / Son gedenck / gedencke Son /
  Das du dein gutes schon /
Von Gott im Leben hast empfangn /
  Vnd Lazaro ists vbel gangn /
Nu aber wird getrôstet er /
  Du wirst billich gepeinigt sehr /
Vnd vber das / alles fûrwar
  Jst zwischen vns / vnd euch so gar /   460
Ein grosse Klufft befestiget /
  Das / so einer im willen hett /
Von hin zu euch hinab zu fahrn /
  Kônd ers doch nicht es wer verlorn.
Auch kan von dannen nimmermehr /
  Einer zu vns hie fahren her.

Porphyrius.

So bitt ich dich doch Vater mein /
  Das du jn sendest / kan es sein /
Jn meines Vaters Haus hinnab /   470
  Denn ich fûnff Brûder da noch hab.
Das er jnen verkûndig dort /
  Was fûr Pein sey an diesem ort.
Das er sie warne bitt ich sehr /
  Das sie auch hie nicht kommen her.

Abraham.

Weistu nicht / das jn Gott hat gebn /
  Sein Wort darnach sie sollen lebn?
Sie haben Mosen / Gottes Wort /
  Vnd die Propheten / gliebts jn nort /   480

Laß sie die hören / wolln sie nicht /
Wie du verdammet sein / rath ich.

Porphyrius.

Ach Abraham / Ach Vater mein /
   Das wird bey jn nich hůlfflich sein.
Denn ich Gottes Wort auch habe gehört /
   Vnd mich aber leider dran nicht gekehrt
Weil sie auch / wie ich pflag / leben /
   Fůrcht ich / werden sie nicht drauff gebn.
490   Sondern / wenn einer von dem Tod
   Zu jnen gieng / hett es kein noth /
Sie wůrden Busse thun fůrwar.

Abraham.

Ey das geschicht / gleub / nimmerdar.
Denn werden sie Mosen nicht hörn /
   An die Propheten sich nicht kehrn /
So werden sie nichts geben drauff /
   Ob jemand stůnd vom Tode auff.
Weil du auch Gottes Wort veracht /
500   Mosen vnd die Prophetn verlacht /
Leidstu billich jetzt diese Pein.

Porphyrius.

Ach kan denn kein erbarmung sein
Bey dir / so kan ich Gott darůmb
   Ansprechen nicht / das ist kurtzůmb.
Er ist mein Feind / wie ichs befind /
   Denn Ers mit mir wol endern kůnd.
O wehe vnd Ach / O ewig wehe /
   Jch werd erlöst nimmermehr.

510 ### Mammon.

Ey ruff mich an / ich bin dein Gott /
   Jch wil dir helffen in der Noth.
Nach deinm verdienst wil ich dir gebn /
   Das Helsche Fewr fůrs ewig Lebn.

Iehoua.

Vnd Lazare mein lieber Son /
   Jetzund empfehestu den Lohn.
Denn du gerecht geachtet bist /
   Das dir mein Wort lieb gwesen ist.
Drůmb lebestu im Himmelreich /   520
   Mit allen Heiligen ewiglich.

Canunt Angeli.

IV·NARRATIVE PROSE

TRADITIONALLY almost all works of prose fiction published in German before 1600 tend to be described as *Volksbücher*. The term was coined by the Romantics and is even more misleading than its lyrical counterpart, *Volkslied*: not only were few *Volksbücher* written with the *Volk* in mind, but, since they were transmitted in printed rather than oral form, they were never subjected to the progressive modification (*Zersingen*) by which the *Volk* did in certain respects set its own seal on the *Volkslied*.

The concept that narrative prose was an acceptable alternative to epic verse was still relatively new in European literature, and not surprisingly, far from being native products, the earliest *Volksbücher* were in fact French romances, translated and adapted for the amusement of court circles under the auspices of two foreign princesses married to German husbands, Elisabeth von Nassau-Saarbrücken (d. 1456) and Eleonore von Vorder-Österreich (d. 1480). To the former we owe the traditional best sellers, *Herpin*, *Loher und Maller*, and *Hug Schapler* (tales of knightly adventure set in Carolingian and Capetian times, cf. p. 192), while Eleonore is chiefly remembered for *Pontus und Sidonia*, a tale of true love between an exiled and impecunious Spanish prince and the Princess of Brittany. There had been earlier attempts to write German prose fiction—Hermann von Fritslar had written legends of the saints in German as early as 1345 and a translation of the *Legenda aurea* appeared in 1362—but it was these degenerate *Ritterromane* which marked the beginning of a great era of translation and adaptation which, for all its derivative qualities, was to establish prose as the natural medium for fiction in German-speaking lands. Another princess, Mechthild von der Pfalz, following the French example, inspired the production of prose versions of native epics; Thüring von Ringoltingen published his rendering of the French fairy-tale romance, *Melusine*, in 1471; the following year saw the posthumous publication of Johann Hartlieb's *Buch von dem großen Alexander*, which drew on medieval Latin sources and, like *Melusine*, had originally been undertaken for the edification of a princely patron. Around 1472 also appeared the earliest prose version of a German courtly epic, *Wigoleysz vom Rade*, after Wirnt von Grafenberg's *Wigalois*. In 1483 the first printed edition of the translation of the ancient cycle of *exempla* known as *Die sieben weisen Meister* was published, a version of the Tristan legend followed in 1484, and a rendering of the Latin version of *Herzog Ernst* in 1493.

This remarkable activity in the translation and refurbishing of established models is paralleled by the work of a number of early humanists, notably Heinrich Schlüsselfelder, Niklas von Wyle, Heinrich Steinhöwel, and Albrecht von Eyb, who sought to make available in German the literature of the Italian Renaissance, especially Boccaccio. Their translations enjoyed a modest success, particularly their two renderings of the story of patient Griselda, but never achieved the sustained popularity of the romances and tended above all to be used as quarries for subject-matter rather than as stylistic models. This is a direct reflection of the unsophisticated taste of the age, whose sole interest lay in the story-line: characteristically, in the field of 'courtly' romance neither patrons nor printers showed much interest in what we would regard as the great works of medieval literature—neither the *Nibelungenlied* nor *Parzifal* was 'modernized', and it was on Eilhart von Oberge, not on Gottfried, that *Tristrant und Isalde* was based. The process of translation and adaptation represents an important historical development, but most of the works produced are almost entirely devoid of literary value: they address a courtly audience, but they are the equivalent of the Westerns, thrillers, and love-stories of our own day and their appeal is to the desire to be entertained and thrilled by deeds of high courage against heavy odds or moved by the spectacle of true love triumphing over adversity and years of enforced separation. These were, however, qualities which gave them perennial appeal (many remained popular until well into the eighteenth century) and made them a natural object for the process of democratization to which literature was inevitably subjected consequent on the invention of printing. The earliest *Volksbücher* were produced for the entertainment of aristocratic society and circulated in manuscripts on which the scribes and illuminators had lavished great care. In the closing decades of the fifteenth century they began to appear in de luxe printed editions which were richly illustrated with fine woodcuts and were clearly aimed at a wealthy upper-class public. With the gradual spread of literacy and the growth of a 'cheap market' in the sixteenth century, the outward physical appearance of the *Volksbücher* deteriorated until, shoddily printed on cheap paper and crudely illustrated from such blocks as the printer happened to possess, they became the genuinely popular fiction their Romantic name declares them to be.

The early sixteenth century continued to add to the stock of chivalric romances, notably *Die schön Magelone* (1527), *Fierabras* (1533), *Die vier Haimonskinder* (1535), and *Kaiser Oktavian* (1535), and characteristically Jörg Wickram's earliest ventures into narrative prose were very much in the style of these romances (*Ritter Galmy*, 1539; *Reinhart und Gabriotto*, 1551), but the latter represented only one of the prose traditions inherited from the previous century. Prose had hitherto been reserved largely for theoretical and devotional writing and prose *fiction* in the native tradition was generally confined to the *Schwank* or anecdote. The literary origin of the latter is to be sought in the collections of *exempla* or *Predigtmärlein*, the short and usually amusing stories which, like jokes in modern lectures, were used throughout the Middle Ages to add piquancy to sermons and to drive home the point the preacher was making by illustrating it with a realistic example. Although the underlying attitudes and the level of sophistication might differ, these anecdotes were not so very far removed from the short stories cultivated by the humanists both under the name of *facetiae* and in the form of the *novella*, which, though often far from moral, equally depended on brevity for their effect, turned on a *pointe*, and also commonly illustrated some general truth. The most important collection of *Predigtmärlein* was published by Johannes Pauli in 1522 under the title *Schimpf und Ernst* (cf. p. 228), and it was not until the appearance of Jörg Wickram's *Rollwagenbüchlein* (cf. p. 230) that, presumably under the influence of the *facetiae*, the German *Schwank* finally emancipated itself from the moral overtones associated with the *Predigtmärlein* and emerged as something intended strictly for amusement. The success of Wickram's little book ensured that it did not long stay free from competition, and the succeeding years brought forth a rash of *Schwankbücher* whose very titles, *Wegkürtzer, Rastbüchlein, Nachtbüchlein*, etc., not infrequently bear witness to the source of their inspiration.

It was, however, neither in the sustained narrative of the courtly romance nor in the genuine *Schwankbuch* that the sixteenth century was to make its distinctive contribution to German prose fiction. The celebrated accounts of the doings of Till Eulenspiegel (cf. p. 225) and Dr. Johann Faust (cf. p. 215) occupy a middle position between the two traditions, having a sustained biographical story-line, yet consisting largely of anecdotal material. Essentially, both works, although written in prose, look back to the 'wags' biographies' of the later Middle Ages which had recounted in doggerel verse the pranks of such popular heroes as Der Pfaffe Amis, Der Pfaffe von Kalemberg, Peter Lew, Neidhart Fuchs, etc. This primitive technique of grouping a number of anecdotes around some popular figure or collection of figures is characteristic of some of the most popular and successful publications of the century: *Der Finkenritter* (a sixteenth-century Münchhausen, 1560), *Historien von Claus Narren* (another Eulenspiegel, 1572), *Hans Clawerts werck-liche Historien* (yet another in the same vein, 1587), and finally the *Lalebuch* and the *Schiltbürgerbuch* of 1597-8 (cf. p. 232).

While the great mass of prose fiction in the sixteenth century thus tends to tread established paths, a number of remarkable experiments were none the less taking place. As early as 1509 an anonymous Augsburg merchant had experimented with the middle-class family chronicle in *Fortunatus*, a story of the rise and fall of a family in two generations, which in spite of its fairy-tale element (Fortunatus has a never empty purse and a magic cap which transports him wherever he wishes) represents a notable attempt to come to terms with social reality. Wickram was to continue this experiment in *Von Gûten vnd bôsen Nachbaurn* (cf. p. 200), while in his *Geschichtklitterung* (cf. p. 208) Johann Fischart was to put before his fellow-countrymen a totally new concept of the novel as a lin-guistic *tour de force*.

For such a young genre German sixteenth-century narrative prose exhibits a surprising range of subject-matter and style: it recounts high adventure and explores low life, it expresses pathos and sentimentality as well as humour and cruelty, it revels in robust obscenity and touches on the ultimate questions of the nature of man and God's purpose with him, and it can be long-winded and circumstantial, but also blunt and perplexingly subtle in its use of language. On the face of it then, one might have expected the sixteenth century to usher in a golden age of German prose fiction, yet this was not to be, and the sixteenth century falls into the pattern of false starts and thwarted beginnings which is charac-teristic of the whole of German cultural history. In part the explana-tion must lie in the fact of the Reformation which, by imposing narrow theological preoccupations on many of the best minds of the age, generally had a destructive effect on German culture with the notable exception of music. Few new *Volksbücher* appeared after 1535—these were now *pestiferi libri* which distracted man-kind from his real concerns—and while some of the experiments we have noted took place long after the Reformation, these tended to be overtaken by events and to fall a prey to the perennial German fascination with things foreign: a translation of the first books of the *Amadis* cycle which appeared in 1569 enjoyed an immediate success and established a pattern which was to be increasingly evident in the coming century: foreign models were to be imitated at the expense of the embryonic native tradition. Further, under the belated influence of the Renaissance as imported by Opitz, it was the lyric and not narrative prose, Ronsard not Rabelais, which the seventeenth century sought to cultivate most assiduously, so that on two distinct counts even the more remarkable narrative experiments in the sixteenth century were destined to remain isolated monuments rather than become the fountain-head of a grand tradition of prose fiction.

1. The 'novel'

(i) *Ein lieplichs lesen vnd ein warhafftige Hystorij wie einer (d' da hieß Hug schäpler vn wz metzgers gschlecht) ein gewaltiger küng zů Frankrich ward durch sein grose ritterliche manheit* (1500)

Hug Schapler (Hugh Capet) was adapted from the original French *chanson de geste* by Elisabeth von Nassau-Saarbrücken and like her other renderings of French originals (*Loher und Maller*; *Herpin*) was intended simply for the entertainment of the translator's own aristocratic circle, where the manuscript was probably read aloud on suitable occasions and circulated amongst the courtiers for private reading. The slightly modified printed version, edited by Konrad Haindorffer and printed by Grüninger of Strassburg in 1500, quickly established itself in the affections of a wider public, however, and remained popular until well into the next century. Heinz Kindermann classes *Hug Schapler* amongst the 'Volksbücher vom sterbenden Rittertum' and for the student of the sociology of taste the romance is indeed a remarkable document: the original product of a decaying knightly society in France (the *chanson* dates from the later fourteenth century) is transplanted across the Rhine and now in Germany similarly epitomizes the decay into which the ideals which had originally informed courtly society have fallen. As a product of the transitional period between medieval and modern times, the *Volksbuch*'s account of the rise of Hugh Capet (940–96) from low estate to the throne of France has often been adduced as evidence of the class war as the 'programmatische Erklärung des Machtanspruchs der bürgerlichen Klasse' (G. Schneider/E. Arndt), the hero in this analysis being regarded as the representative of the rising bourgeoisie who breaks into courtly society as the herald of the latter's final collapse before the onslaught of a more vigorous class. But in spite of his leadership of the good burghers of Paris against the rascally feudal princes, Hug Schapler cannot be fitted into Marxist categories quite so neatly. As the son of a prodigal noble and a butcher's daughter, Hug is distinctly uncourtly in origins and behaviour. For all his defence of the Queen of France, he is fundamentally nothing more than a swashbuckling bravo who owes allegiance to no ideal higher than the gratification of his own sexual appetites and his love of fighting. He is almost totally lacking in any moral sense. He cuts down those who get in his way without the slightest compunction. At times he shows a distinctly vindictive streak, at others he is basely calculating. Women are mere instruments of his pleasure and his 'Minnedienst' consists almost exclusively in the siring of illegitimate children—his ten bastards play quite an important role in the action. Yet if Hug is completely uncourtly, he equally cannot be considered as representing the middle-class ethic. He rejects the patient industry and commerce of his butcher-uncle in favour of a life of ostentation and adventure and characteristically, in most unbourgeois fashion, prefers random and illicit sex to the more stable relationship of marriage. Nor is there in him much trace of a middle-class sense of property or propriety. Hug thus stands between the classes without belonging to either, and far from acting as the vehicle for a system of class values he testifies rather to a certain lasciviousness of mind in the author and his public. Hug is not a brutal outsider compelling a shuddering but fascinated narrator to grudging admiration: the narrator's attitude is one of naïve approbation and even the more outrageous aspects of Hug's behaviour elicit no adverse comment. In this connection it is significant that there is in the *Volksbuch* no indication that the 'courtly' characters live by a code which is noticeably different from Hug's own attitude: the ladies of the court clearly weigh their virtue lightly, high-ranking princes readily poison and betray their liege lords, and for them, as for Hug, the only binding laws are those imposed by the limitations of their own power. The whole *Volksbuch* may thus be said to testify to the disappearance of the high Christian ideals which, in literature at least, had traditionally informed the knightly class. Obviously, it was not a mirror of chivalry nor yet a model of common or garden morality which the associates of Elisabeth von Nassau-Saarbrücken and the middle-class readers of the sixteenth century sought in the action-packed pages of *Hug Schapler*, and for noble and commoner alike Hug Schapler probably held the same sort of fascination as James Bond holds for many twentieth-century readers. Certainly, Hug's cathartic function is identical with that of Bond: he was a figure who dared to be what the readers would secretly have liked to be, a figure in whom their own suppressed libido could be liberated, in whom they could in imagination lead the life of a lady-killing he-man and emancipate themselves from the decent proprieties of normal civilized existence.

Our text is that of the edition of 1500, printed in Strassburg by Hans Grüninger.

Hie reit hug schapler gen Pariß zů sinem vettern Symon als er dan sin gůt verthon hett vnd wolt rath by im nemen.

Hug hat synen weg gen Pariß zů genůmen / als er vō snier můter wegen vil fründe do hett / vn̄ die was vō dannen geborn. So was sin vatter Gernier vß dem land lanoy bürtig vnd zů Pariß inn künig Ludwigs hoffe lôblicher gedechtnůß wolbekant / vn̄ des rath vn̄ liebster diener als vor gesagt ist. Der selbe ritter gewann eyn schône iunckfrow lieb die was zů Pariß eins metzlers dochter eyns richen mans als mocht in allem Franckrich sin. die ward im so gantz lieb als noch offt beschicht vnd nam sie zů der Ee. Vō den zweyē ward Hug geborē als hie nach geschribē stot. Hug reyt also lāg biß er kā gen pariß vn̄ fragt nach sins vetter Symontz huß der ein richer burger do selbs was. Do er dar für kam / do stůnd er vō synem pferd ab. so bald 10

er synen vettern gesach do zoch er synen hût ab vñ grůßte in
tugentlich. Lieber neue sprach Symon Jch sich wol das ir nit
halten üwers vatters stadt. dan wan er her zů mir kam in myn
huß / so hett er alwegē .x. oder zwôlff wol gerüster pferd vnnd
knecht die vff in wartent / vnd nympt mich frômbd an üch was
20 das bedütt. Lieber vetter sprach Hug Jch meyn ich hab im
genůg gethon. Myn vatter ist todt / got sy im barmhertzig ich
hab mich sither so herlich vnd so kôstlich gehalten dz ich das
myn vnd das sin als verthon hab vñ dennocht me darzů / dz
ich schuld hab gemacht dz ich nit im land bliben mag oder kan
vnd hab mût yergan einem fürstenn zů dienen / vnd bin darvmb
her geritten üch zů gesehē. Nun wolan lieber neue sprach Symō
sin vetter. Jr sint ein iung frisch mann vnd sollent by mir hie
bliben / so will ich üch lernen metzlen vnd üch wisen wie ir ein
ochsen vnd ein schwyn od' ander vyhe ab thůn sollen / vnd do
30 by ouch kouffmā schatz triben. vnd legen ir üch wol an alles
das ich hab mag üch nach mynē tod werden / wan ich kein
nehern erbē hab wā üch. Lieber vetter sprach hug Jch hab
wol ein and' besser meynūg vor mir. Metzlen od' kouffmanschatz zů triben hab ich keynen mût / od' ouch ochsen od'
schwyn ab zů thůn. Jch hab vil ein hübscher hantwerck
gelernet. Jch kan ein fürsten oder herrē wol gewapnen / die
glene ouch selber in der handt füren vnd mich dar mit be-
helffen. so hett ich gern ein yeglichen monat ein nüwes cleidt /
vnd hielt gern vier wind ein hasen zů fahen / vnd ein par falckē
40 zů beissen. vñ wer mir wol das ich dry pfyffer vnd luten
schlaher hett / das hort ich lieber dann ein ochsen oder ein kalp
blerren.

*Wie hug vnd sin vetter mit einander redten | vnd Symon der
ritter wer hugē gern wider ledig gewesen heymlich.*

Do der burger der ritter hort synen vettern also sprechē / alles
sin geblüt begūde im zů grüselen vnd gedacht wider fich selbs /
was saget diser iüngling Ya blibe er in mynem huse eī halb iar
er verthete mir alle myn barschafft. Jch soll anders vor handt
nemē vnd gieng stillschwigē in sin huß vñ holt dry hundert
50 güldin vñ gab sie hugen der was sin vast fro vñ dāckte sinem
vettern sere. Hug saß vff sin pferdt vnd schiede von Pariß. Er
reit solāg biß er kam in henegouw. do fande er in einer statt
genant Berge schôn geselschafft. Do was ein stechen vor der

ritterschafft vñ hetten ir hußfrowen mit innen dar gefûrt. Do
bleib hug so lang biß er sin gelt alles verthette / vnd gewan eins
ritters tochter so lieb in dem land zů henegow So das sie ward
von im eins kinds schwanger. Der ritter ir vatter ward des
gewar. vnd was gar ein grusamlicher man. vnd verhiesse Hug
müßte dar vmb sterben vmb solliche laster vñ schmacheit so
er an siner tochter begangen het. Eins mals kam hug in die 60
statt geritten do sin liebe in was. der ritter ward sin innen vñ
hielt vff hugē salb vierd. Do er wid' do innen ritē wolt kament
sie in an. Der ritter sprach also Hug du falscher bôßwicht du
hast mir myn kindt betrogē mit dinen falschen reden in schand
vnnd in laster bracht / des mûstu ouch hie sterben. Mit dem
schlûgen sie alle vier vff in Hug sach wol was sie willen hetten.
Er zuckt sin schwert vnd schlûg den ritter das er am sattel
hieng / vnd erschlûg im zwen knecht zů tod. der drit entreit im
zů der statt vnd schrei mort vnd hylff. Hug der sumpti sich nit
lang / er rant schnell von dannen zů eynem walde. wan er wüßte 70
wol wer er begriffen wordē / er keme sin ī groß lyden. Jn dem
wald verbarge er sich ein wyle vnd gedacht / Ach gott wye geet
es nun dinem liebē bůlen die vm̄ mynen willen vast bekümmert
ist. wer das volck in disem lande nit so stoltz vñ nydig / so môcht
ich mich nit von ir also gescheiden / Nun mûß es sin mit grossem
yamer . . .
   Hug schied von dannen vnd reyt da hyn in Brabannt / do
bleib er wol ein iar vnd hett gar eī frôlichs wesen mit den
iunckfrowen / dann sie waren im alle günstig. So was er ouch
alle zyt in frouwen dienst. Vnd saget die ware kronick das er 80
so lang in brabant vñ in henegow were vnd so vil kind dar in
hett dz ir wol .x. vff einem tag dar nach zů im gen Pariß kamēt /
als mā hyenach vernemē würt. Es ward an manchē enden vff
Hugē gesetzet vñ gewartet / dz er alles mit gewerter hand
enttranne. Dar nach eins mals füegte sich das Hug vff einen
sontag zů morgen eyns richen kouffmans dochter sinen bůlen
wolt gesehē do ander lüt in der kirchen waren.

Hie gieng hug schapler zů sinem bůlen do wartetent etlich
   gesellen vff in vñ hettent in gern zů tod geschlagen. aber er
   werte sich ir aller. 90

Der selbe kouffman wonet ī der statt zů Nyffel / vnd was vō
grosem geschlecht vñ hat sich darvff bestalt. Hug kam hynden

zů dem garten in vnd het synen harnsch an / er gieng zů sines
bůlen kammer / so bald im die thüre vff gieng / hettent sich wol
zwölff gesellē verborgen im huse die lieffent an in vnd schruwent
man solt in todt schlagen. Do diß Hug erhort / er gewann bald
sin schwert vñ stalte sich an eyn want vnd werte sich so lang
biß dz ir fünff todt vor im lagen. Die andern schlůgent vast
vmb in vnd vff in dz geschrey kam in die statt dz menglich
100 begund zů louffen. Do dz hug ersach er entlieff in allen in sin
herberg vnd saß vff sin pferdt vñ schied võ synem lieben bůlē.
Die vmb irē lieben bůlen heiß weynte / dan sie nit anders
meynte er möcht nit von innen kummen er müßte irent halbē
sterben. Dar nach reit er in hollant vñ fůr in frießlant vnd
sprach do zů im selbs. Ach herre gott wie bin ich so gar vnselig.
ein mā der bůlschafft übet der verthůt dz sin vnmessiglich vnd
waget sele vnd lyb zů dicker malen vnwißiglich. Aber iugent vñ
thorheit bringt mich darzů vnd schöne wiber / der diener ich
alle myn tag sin will. wer mich ouch dar vmb strafft ist wol in
110 bůlschaft groß thorheit. so ist ouch grosse freüd vnnd wollust
darin Vñ wer lust vñ freüd hat der ist rich genůg als mich
beduncket. Also reit Hug so lāg in frießlāt biß dz er in die
houbtstatt des landes genāt hütre kam / darin er des lands künig
genant hugen in sinem palast vand / dar in er gieng / vñ neygte
sich biß vff sin knüw vnd grůßte den künig gar höffelich. Also in
der künig an sach sin höffelich geberd vnd gůte gestalt / danckte
er im vnd fragte in võ wannen er were / vñ was er begert das er
ym das sagte . . .

Wie hug schappel vff dem palast redt von der künigin von der
120 *burger wegē wid' graff Sauari von Schampanien. &c.*

Also thet man meniglich still schwigen vff das man der burger
meynūg vñ willē in den sachen hören wolt. Hug hůb an
zereden. Jr herren sprach er vernement mich / hie ist Sauari
der graff von schampanien in disem palast vnd will vnser iunge
künigin zů eynem eelichē wyb habē wid' ir můter vnd ir selbs
willen. Aber vnser gůter rat will das nit verhengē noch folgē.
Fürwar herr Sauari / ir weren baß würdig das mā üch an einen
boum hanckt dan dz mā üch eī solliche edle künigī ze wib geb.
dā meniglich spricht Jr haben irem vatter dem edlen künig
130 Ludwigen vergeben / ir sint von dem geschlecht das wol

falscheit tribē kan. Dan von Gonnelin sint üwere besten fründ
vnnd üwer elter theten nye kein gůt. Vnd so wir nun d' sachē
vrteiler sint / so sprechen wir dz wir nit wőllen volgen üch die
schőne künigin zů geben / dan ir sint ir nit würdig / od' an
solliche ere ze kůmen. vn̄ wőllē üch ouch nit für ein herrē oder
künig vff nemē / dan ir haben als ein bőßwicht dem künig
vergebē. Darūb müssen ir üwern lon hützůtag enpfahē. Mit der
reden zoch er sin schwert vß vnd schlůg vff den grauen vnd
spielte im syn houbt biß vff die zene. Vnd růfft do kőnlich mon
yoie. dz ist dz geschrey zů Pariß / schlagen vff frummen burger   140
sprach Hug. Jch hab an dē recht schuldigen an gehaben. Do
ward in dem Palast nyemandt geschonet / er wer hertzog oder
graue.

Hie kummen der künigin burger vnd Hug schappel mit innen
vnd schlagen den grauen Sauari mit vil syner edlē todt / vn̄
kůpt der hertzog vonn Burgund / vnnd graff Friderich dar von.

Nuñ do die ritterschafft vn̄ burger sich also mit eynand' schlůgē in
dē macht sich der hertzog vō burgundiē. Vn̄ graff Friderich vnd'
dē volck hinweg mit grossē sorgē. Vn̄ also gieng Hug metzelen
vnder den edlen dz ir me dā hůdert todt blybē / die andern   150
entlieffē yeglicher zů syner herbergen so er best mocht / vn̄
sassent schnell vff ir pferd vnd rantent vß Pariß. Die künigin
was des gar fro vnd ouch ir dochter. Fürwar sprach die künigin
zů der dochter Der falsche graue mag üch nit werden / er ist
übel gestüret zů syner hochzyt die er meynt mit synem hochmůt
vnd gewalt zů volbringen. Der iung man hat im bald syn lon
geben. Jch gesach nye kein man so fast vmb sich schlahen.
werēt sie nit entrunen er het sie all erschlagē. Jst er ein edelman.
oder ein burger von diser statt. Da antwurt ir eī alter ritter wz
der künigin hoffmeyster genant Anssel. Gnedige frow / er ist ein   160
herr zů Genosse by burgel / ich kenn in wol er hat hüt vff dissen
tag manchem sin leben genūmē / er ist vō metzlers geschlecht
von siner můter / er hat gewenet er sy vnder den fleischbenckē.
Als nun das geschrei vergangen was / da nam die künigin ir
dochter mit der hant vnd fürte sie ī den palast zeschawē wie es
da gefaren were / mit ynnen giengent sechs ritter die in iren rat
gehortent . . .

Hie sint die von Pariß vßgezogen an iren vinde. vnd sint wider
hyndersich getriben biß in ir port | do bleib Hug schappel vff
170 *der brücken ston mit einer strit axst vnnd schlůg der vinde vil*
zetode vff der brücken die in nach geylet waren.

Vnns saget die hystory das die burger vast manliche warendt
vnd stritten so manlich das die vssern můstent hyndersich
wichen biß in der hertzog von Burgundien zů hilff kam / vnd
Hugwon von Frießlandt vnd der graff von der Felse die kament
so mit grossem volck das die vō Pariß mit gewalt getrungen
wurdent zů rücke vnd wart der Constabel ab gerannt vnd
wer ouch erschlagen worden wer im Hug schappel nit zehilff
kummē / der stund zů fůß ab vnnd hat syn schwert zů beidē
180 hendē gefaßt / er schlůg vnd stach vmb sich vnd macht bletz
recht als wie der wolff thůt vnder dē schaffen. Er kam zů dem
Constabel vñ was an dem dz er eym tütschē mā wolt haben
gesichert / an den kā hug vnd erschlůg in. sin roß nam er vnnd
halff dem Constabel dar vff des dancket er im flyssiglich. Zů
stundt kam der vssern mer dan sechs tusent vnd drungent die
von pariß mit gewalt zů der porten zů vñ erschlůgent ir me dan
zwey hůdert. Hug schappel stůd zů fůß an der porten vnd
schlůg vm̄ sich das wol .xiiii. todt vmb in lagen wen er draff
den schlůg er zů der erdē. Der graue von Sempe. der hertzog
190 von Berrey. vnd der graffe von blois kament vff die bruck vnd
woltē Hugen erschlagen haben vmb das er in so leid thette /
vnnd meyntent ouch domit die port zů gewynnē. Hug schappel
stundt vff der brucken vnd ward im ein gůt strit axst die im zů
gůtem staten kā. Der hertzog vō berry kam her dryngen vff hugen
vñ wolt in vō der brücken schlagen. Hug nam syn axst zů beiden
henden vnd schlůg in durch sin ysenhůt dz er todt nider viel.
Des erschrackent die andern vñ hieltent hynder sich. Hug lieff
als an die nechsten vñ wolt schlagē nach dē grafen Estempi vñ
velet sin vñ draff dz pferdt das es zů der erdē weich. Hug lieff
200 dar vnd fieng den grauen vnnd schleüffet in mit im zů der
porten yn. es wer den Schampaniern lieb oder leyt. Do schlos-
sent die von pariß yre port zů iren vindē vnd thetent in vil
schaden. Vnd in disem strit wurden der vssern wol .xxi. hundert
erschlagē. vnd der ynnern by den dry hundert erschlagen . . .

Hie wardt hertzog Hug die iunge Künigin vermahelt vnd im zů
der Ee geben | vnd wardt künig zů Franckrich | vnd was do
groß fest mit pfyffen | trumpten | vnd mit stechen vff der
hochzyt.

Die künigin sprach. Es ist mir lieb / ich will üch allen volgen
Vñ sie rüeffet Hugē dem hertzogen vonn Orliens vñ sprach 210
also lieplich Lieber hug / nement hie den soldt den ir verdienet habē / das ist myn liebe dochter wan alle menglich das geraten hatt üwer lyb vñ werck sint des wol würdig / getarff ichs
sagen / so habent ir sie ouch wol verdienet. Darūb wer wol thůt
dem würt ouch gůter lon Jst es nit in diser welt / so ist es aber
im ewigem leben. Hertzog hug sprach / genedige frow / dise
gab entpfahe ich gern dā solliche gab wer nit gůt ab zeschlagen.
Da wurden die zwei zesamē vermahelt in gegenwürtigkeit aller
der herschafft die vff dem palast warent. Das wardt zů hant
offenbar in der gantzen statt. Do erhůbe sich grosse freüd. 220
Hertzog hug frŏwte sich ouch syncs glücks als noch mancher
dette. Syne moge vnd fründ vnd syn zehē basthart die lobtent
des ouch got vñ sprachent heymlich vnder eynand'. wir sint zů
gůter stundē her in dis landt kummen / vnser vatter würt nun
ein künig in Franckrich / wir sollent des ouch genyessen. Also
ward Hugen (dem hertzog võ Orliens den mā vorhyn genennet her
hug schappler) die iunge küngin zů Fräckrich zů rechter Ee
vermahelt / das was in ouch beyder teyl wol zů willen. Da erhůb
sich vff dem sale ein pfiffen vñ trumpten das nyemandt den
andern gehŏren mocht. Do sach man die fürsten vnd herren 230
manig schŏn cleynot tragen / vnd die spilman herrlichen
begaben. Do warent so vil herren / geistlich vñ weltliche das on
zal was / dann man hett in allem franckrich vff lyb vnnd gůt
gebotten allen fürsten vñ herren das sie zů hoff kūmen solten.
Vñ ob yemant gegē der kron ychtz myßthon hette / der solt
ouch kūmen vnnd dem künig huldung thůn / man solt im
genediglich verzyhen. Vnd wer also keme / der solt zwen monat
trostung haben vñ frischt sich zů entschuldigen vor den gynnen
die von des künigs wegen darzů geordeniert warent. vñ wer das
nit thette / vnd beiten würde das mā in dar zů zwünge / dem 240
wolt man sin lehen andern geben vnd vß dem künigrich
vertriben / oder müst dar vmb sterben. Darnach gesach man vil
prelaten / hertzogen / marckgraffen Bischŏff vnd epte / vnd ouch

gûte ritter vnd knecht alle zů hoff kůmen / eyn teyl vmb freüd vñ kurtzwil willen. die andern vmb begerung gûte fründ zů hoffe sůchen / vñ vm̄ gnad zů erwerben die denn wider die künigin gewesen warent vnd sich zů entschuldigen wie sie mochten.

(ii) Jörg Wickram: *Von Gûten vnd bôsen Nachbaurn* (1556)

Von Gûten vnd bôsen Nachbaurn is the first genuinely middle-class novel in German literature. There are earlier claimants to the title, notably the *Volksbuch Fortunatus* (1509) and certain of Wickram's own previous novels (*Der Jungen Knaben Spiegel* (1554); *Der Goldfaden* (1557, but written earlier)), but although these works show marked middle-class influence in their bold assertion that native intelligence, industry, and integrity are more important than inherited social position and traditional privilege, they also reveal a sense of insecurity in their preoccupation with the need to compete with the nobility on the latter's terms and characteristically they accept absorption into the aristocracy as the natural goal of the bourgeois meritocracy. In *Von Gûten vnd bôsen Nachbaurn*, by contrast, the nobility is totally excluded. The middle-class author (Wickram (1505–c. 1560) was the illegitimate son of a prosperous Colmar burgher; he practised the trade of goldsmith before holding office in the administration of his native city and subsequently became town clerk of Burckheim/Alsace) no longer looks nervously over his shoulder at the upper classes, but with admirable self-confidence portrays the world of the commercial middle class as being sufficient unto itself and unambiguously proclaims the rightness and soundness of the middle-class ethic.

The novel takes us through three generations of a prosperous merchant family. In order to escape from a quarrelsome neighbour Robertus moves his home and his business from Antwerp to Lisbon, where his family is able to live in close and mutually beneficial amity with their new neighbours, much of the subsequent action being designed to show how 'one hand washes the other'. Robertus's only daughter, Cassandra, marries the Spanish merchant Richardus, whom they had met on the voyage to Portugal and whom they nurse back to health when he falls sick. Subsequently when Richardus is attacked by robbers, he is saved by the intervention of a certain Lazarus, who becomes a close friend of the family and later accompanies Richardus on a trading journey, during which he is abducted and sold as a galley slave, but is rescued in the nick of time þy Richardus. Latterly, Richardus's daughter, Amelia, marries Lazarus's son (also called Lazarus), after the latter has spent his 'Wanderjahre' abroad and, amongst other things, has survived an attempt on his life by a robber-innkeeper in Venice.

Other 'sagas' of this kind, from *Fortunatus* to the family chronicles of Mann and Galsworthy, have tended to social criticism or cultural and moral pessimism, but Wickram's merchants are paragons of goodness and moral rectitude: their fortunes move in a steadily ascending line and are troubled only by minor vicissitudes, which in the end usually turn out to be blessings in disguise and serve to add interest to the novel by contrasting the safe stronghold of orderly bourgeois existence with the dangers and chaos lying in wait for the unwary in the wide and wicked world outside.

Within the ethical limits of their class, Wickram's burghers are internationalists free from any taint of national or racial prejudice, at home everywhere where they can pursue their business interests without let or hindrance. Commercial activity is their one real purpose in life: the world of art and culture exists for them only in so far as it has applicability within this overriding preoccupation, and characteristically love—in which Wickram shows considerable interest, using monologues, letters, and dreams in anticipation of the seventeenth-century practice to give us insight into states of mind—serves as a cement to strengthen business relationships, material interests and emotional inclination going hand in hand. The characterization is generally weak: there is no noticeable difference in character between any of the merchants; but Wickram is not attempting to introduce us to interesting or remarkable individuals, and the characters really only have significance as vehicles for his own middle-class ethic. Wickram is above all a pedagogue, and aesthetic considerations are subordinate to his didactic aim: the inculcation of certain standards of behaviour in his readers by presenting them with an idealized picture of middle-class values in operation. Civil and domestic peace, industry, moderation, practically conditioned respect for the rights of one's fellow men, charity to those less fortunate than oneself, a harmonious family life, and friendship based on mutual respect and mutual advantage: these are the characteristic virtues of Wickram's merchants, and these same virtues he commends to the reader as a guarantee of prosperity both in this world and in the world to come.

While Wickram's didacticism thus stamps him as a child of his age, in certain other important respects he is notably different from his contemporaries. Wickram alone in the prose fiction of the sixteenth century makes any attempt to come to terms with the world of middle-class reality; he alone produces a novel which on the one hand is possessed of a recognizable unity of interest and does not degenerate into anecdote, and on the other is neither an allegory nor a fairy-tale writ large. Wickram's interest in psychological states is equally unique, as is his conscious attempt, in the speech of his burghers and in his nature descriptions (cf. p. 206), to write in a dignified, 'poetic' style. These dignified and poetic passages today often strike an almost ludicrously forced and clumsy note, but nevertheless they represent the first intimations in German fiction that prose can be something more than a simple listing of actions, events, and ideas, and as such they are not lacking in historical interest, even though they did not evoke any immediate response in other German writers.

Our text is taken from the edition printed by Knobloch in Strassburg in 1557.

(a) Robertus der alt Kauffman vnnd Richart mit einander in
einen schônen garten spatzieren gond | Richardus mitt gantz
weiten vmbschweiffenden worten kumpt an den alten | Zů
letst bit er vm̄ Cassandra zům weib.

Dje lustigest zeit so im jar sein mag / was yetzund vorhanden /
dann die fruchtbaren beum mitt jrer edlen vn̄ wolschmackenden
blůst fiengend an haraus zů prossen / Das erdtreich erzeigt sich
auch mit wunsamen vnd schônen blůmlin / von allen farben /
vn̄ mancherley art gestaltet / So hort man die vôgel allenthalben
10 vff den zweigē mit lieblichem gesang zů samen stimmen / gleich
als wañ sie vmb ein kleinat kempfften / vnnd einer vber den
anderen vermeint zů steigen / vnd mit gesang obzůligen /
Dauon es dann sehr lustig inn dem feld zů spatzieren was. Diss
bewegt Robertum den altē herren das er zů Richarden dem
jungē kauffherren gieng / vnd jn bat / er wolt mit jm hinaus in
den garten spatzieren gohn / des dann Richardus gantz willig
was. Also zugent sie miteinander hinaus / sunder alle diener
vnnd geselschafft / retten von maniger hand kauffmanschafft
vnd gewerbshåndlē. Zu letst fieng Richardus an vnd sagt /
20 Mein hertz aller liebster herr Roberte / Jch soll vn̄ můs euch
billich einen vatter vnd meinen aller besten freunt bekennen /
dann ich nit wissen mag / das mir von meinen fründen allen /
die wenigst freundtschafft widerfaren sey / so ihr mir bewisen
hand / dann ich zů vorderst Gott die ehr geben will / Dieweil
ich waiß sunder sein hilff vnd ewere vilfaltigen vnd bewisenen
gůtthaten / Wer mir nit wol müglich gewesen / lebendig von
dem schiff zů kummen / Darzů habend jhr mich erst als wir
zů land kummen sind / in ewerem haus mit den allerbesten
wartungen zů meinen krefften bracht / das alles mir nit müg-
30 lichen zůuergleichen ist / ob ich eüch schon als mein gůt / vnd
was ich vermag / dar für geben solt / Vnd mich darzů für einen
leibeigenen knecht willig in ewer dienst ergeb / môchte es
dannnoch nimmermer vergolten sein. Darumb mein aller liebster herr vnd vatter / bitt ich euch jr wôllen mir zůuerston
geben / wardurch ich doch solche vberschwenckliche gůtthat
vergeltē mag / damit ich nit als ein vndanckbarer gast geachtet
werdē môcht / Dann es sagen die altē / das kein grôsser laster /
weder vndanckbarkeit môge funden werden. Darauff antwurt
Robertus / Holtseliger lieber Richarde / es ist noch nit an dem /

das wir von einander schaiden / noch vnser fründtschafft 40
zertrennen wöllend / Dieweil du wider zů deiner gesuntheit vnd
krefften kummen bist / wend wir erst ein fröliche zeit miteinander
haben / will vns anderst der almechtig ein semlichs
günnen. So dirs gefalt / magstu dein handel gleich so wol bey
mir fůren / als wann du in Hispanien werest / ich will dir ein
eygen Contor vnd gewelb ihngeben / darum soll dich niemant
nit hinderen / vnd bleib so lang bey mir / als dir mein haußhaltung
vnd kost gefallen thůt. Mir hat Got der Herr zů wasser
vnnd land vil glücks verleihen / auch seer gros gůt bescheret /
das will ich mit lieben vnd gůten fründen brauchen / so lang 50
ich leb / Dann es sol das gůt nit mein / sunder ich will sein herr
sein / niemant hatt mir darein zůredē. Jch hab doch nit mer
dann ein einige tochter / bin auch sunst keiner kinder mer
warten / sie würt dannocht nach meinem absterben gůts genůg
findē. Daruff sagt herr Richart / Herr jr habt fürwar ein schöne
tochter / der ewig Got geb euch genad das jr sie nach ewerem
wolgefallen verheuraten / O wie ein sáliger jüngling ist der /
welchem ein semliche schöne braut an seine arm kumen sol /
Jch sag bei meiner selen / wañ mir ein solche junckfraw in
Portugal zů einer Ehegemaheln zůston möcht / wolt ich all 60
mein hab vnd gůt in Hispanien zů barem gelt machen / vnd in
Portugal ziehen mitt allem sam. Robertus der alt kauffherr /
het mit gantzem fleiß auff des jungen wort acht genumen / er
ward gantz kurtz mit jm zů rath / vñ sagt / O mein liebster
Richarde / wañ ich gedencken möcht / dz dir in diser sachē
ernst were / oder das du ein ehrliche liebe zů meiner tochter
trůgest / du soltest in kurtzer zeit ein freuntliche antwort von
mir empfahen. Ach herr vnnd vatter / sagt Reichart / wie wolt
ich doch ewiglichen ein solchen bedrug gegen Gott verantwortē
/ wañ ich dem / der mir souil gůtthat erzeigt / solt ein 70
bedrug vnnd die vnwarheit anzeigen / Jch sag also / wann ich so
gůt binn / das jhr mich für ein tochterman haben wöllend / so
stand ich hie vnd bit euch durch Gottes willen vmb ewer
dochter / alles das / so einem ehren mañ zůston mag / will ich
mich allzeit befleissen / vnd darneben ewer dochter schon vnd
ehrlich halten / wie dañ einem ehrlichē mañ gebůrt / Darzů
steth mein hertz vnd gemůt gántzlich bey euch zů bleiben
vñ zů wonen / dañ mir vátterliche trew von euch bewisen. Dar
auff antwort Robertus / Dieweil es dann / mein aller liebster

80 Richarde / die meinung hat / so sey dir auff meinem theil mein
dochter zůgesagt / Mir aber wil dannocht gebůren / die můter
vnd die dochter darunder anzůsůchen / damit harnach kein
verwiss dar aus eruolgen thůe / so wolt ich auch (sie die dochter)
nit gern zwingen / das sie wider jren willē einem jüngling oder
witwer solt vermehlet werden / zů welchem sie keinen willen
het / Wiewol etliche vnd vil våtter vnd můtern der neigung
sind / jhre kinder etwan von grosses gůts wegen an ein ort wider
vnnd vber ihren willen zůstossen / da sie weder gunst / liebe
noch willē hin haben / was aber zů zeiten aus solcher vermåh-
90 lung gůts erwachset / sicht man leider zů vil wol / ja das offt
die alten ihr hånd ob den kôpffen zůsamen schlagen můssen /
Dann es nit sehr lang vnd noch in frischer gedechtnus ist /
das ein gůter Edelman seiner tôchteren eine versorgen / vñ
einem alten Edelman (der jr gar zů wider was) gebē wolt / Sie
aber erfůr die sach / wolt der hochzeit nit warten / Nam jres
vatters karchknecht zůr Ee / vnd souil sie mocht raum vnnd
blatz haben / packt sie jrer kleider zů samen / vnd fůr mit jm
daruon / habē beid lang mit einander gehauset / vil schôner
vnd lieber kinder sidhar gezeuget. Darumb lieber Richhart /
100 sag ich das / damit mein tochter nit vbernacht vrsach hett mit
mir zů zürnen / wann ihr etwan ein wentzig miteinander
stôssig würden / vnd sie sagen môcht / ich het sie gezwungen
einen man zů nemen / so mir (vnd nit jhr) gefallē het. Daruff
sagt Richart / Von gantzem grund meins hertzē / solt mirs leid
sein / Es wer gleich ewer tochter oder ein andere / solt ich deren
wider jren willen vermåhelt werden / Was lieber stund würdē
wir doch bey einander habē? Als sie nůn mit disen vñ deren-
gleichē reden jr zeit vertriben / bis das es vmb den ymbis war /
da zugen sie mit einand' zů haus gantz frôlich / dañ sie wol
110 vermůten kunden / das die sach einen fürgang haben würd . . .

(b) Ein reicher goldtschmidt / der sein handel mit berlin vnd
  kostlichem edlem gestein fůret / kumpt Reicharten zů hilff /
  dann jm die vier gar vberlegen waren / Die beyden Riffiener
  bleiben todt.

Avff disen nachtimbis / was auch bey gedachter geselschafft
gewesen ein junger mañ ein goldschmit / welcher einen schweren
vnnd grossen handel fůrt mit edlem gestein / vñ den aller

kostlichsten Orientischen berlin / Darumb er dañ gar wol
bekant was vnder den kaufleuten / so aus ferren landen waren /
der sass nit gar weit von herr Roberten haus / darumb dann 120
beyde gůten herren / Reichart vnnd der goldtschmidt / eins
wegs heim giengen / sie hetten beydsamen jre jungen mit
zweyen windtliechtern bey jhn / daruor die erbar geselschafft /
nit zů schwert kummen kunden. Also schlichen sie so lang
hinach / biss der goldtschmidt vrlaub von herr Reicharten
nam / vñ schlos sein haus vff / gieng mit seinen jungen hinein.
Bald waren die schålck alle vier mit gewerter hand ob dem
gůten jungen herren / des er gar kein flucht wußt. Auff dlest /
riss er sich mit gantzem gwalt von jhn aus / er wücht seiner
pomerantzen eine / warff damit den einen Riffiener an sein 130
schlaff / das er todt nider zů der erden sanck. Reichart schreye
sie an / vñ sagt / Jhr verzweifleten bőßwicht / was ansprach habt
jr an mich vnschuldigen / es ist mir doch keiner vnder euch
allen bekant. Nůn waren sie noch so nahend bey des golt-
schmits haus / das er alle wort von Reicharten vernemē mocht /
so erkant er jhn auch an seiner red / Er hies eylents ein wint-
liecht oder zwei anzündē / nam sein gůt schwert von der wand /
damit zů seinem haus hinaus / vñ sprach herr Reicharten
mannlichen zů vnd sagt / Lieber herr / sind manlich / vnd
vnerschrocken / ich will vff dise nacht / mein leib vnd leben bey 140
euch lassen / wir beid wend diser dreyer schålck wol mechtig
sein / Von disen trostlichen worten / die drey grossen schrecken
empfiengen / Richart der hett erst noch mer mannes můt
vberkumē / zucket die ander kugel / vnd fasset einen solchen
starcken wurff / das den andren Riffiener sein pantzer gar nit
gehelffen mocht / sunder můst den tod an der pomerantzen
fressen / wie dann sein gesel an der anderē gethon het. Da diss
die zwen gewar wurden / vnderstůnden sie die flucht zů gebē /
Der goltschmit aber eylet hinach / vñ in der flucht wundet er
Richarten find gar hart. Also haben sie die Riffiener vff der 150
gassen ligen lassen / welchen das blůt zům mund / ohren / vñ
nasen außlieff. Der goldschmit ist mit herr Reicharten zů haus
gangen / haben gar manigerley von diser sachen / wohar das
kumen mőcht / berhatschlaget / aber den rechten zweck nicht
treffen kündē / Also miteinander der sachen eins worden / das
sie den künfftigē morgen in alle balbierer / vnd scherheuser gon
wolten / vñ erforschen / was sie inn der nacht für wunder leut

verbunden hetten. Zů letst name der goltschmit vrlop / vnd
gieng mit seinem diener zů haus. Es was aber der alt herr vñ
160 fraw schon zů beth gangen / wußtē gar nichts vmb die sachen /
desgleichen auch die jung fraw / dann sie versahend sich nit /
das Reichart so zeitlich zů haus keme / vnd was gar niemants
mer / so auff jn wartet vorhanden / wann das gesind im haus.
Also gieng Reichart auch zůbeth / befalh dem hausgesind fewr
vnd liecht / zůuerwarē. Er sagt seiner Cassandra auch gar nicht
von dem lerman / damit er sie nit angsthafft machet / vnd
erschreckte. Des nachts gedacht er gar manigerley / vnnd sun-
derlich an den goldschmit / der jm so trostlich zůgesprungen
was / besan sich offt womit er jm doch semliche gůtthat
170 mōcht vergeltē / vnd nam jm entlich für / dieweil jm Gott sein
leben günnet / das er jn für einen brůder vnd freundt / ansprechen wolt.

(c) *Wie morgens frů zů schiff geblasen ward / dauon Amelia*
    grossen schmertzen empfieng / vnd iren jüngling Lasarum
    klaget / vnd dabey beschalte.

Dje nacht was yetzund durch Auroram die morgen rōte gar
veriagt / vnd hinder die hohen gipffel der bergen getriben /
Phebus hette seine vier schnellen pferd inn sein wagen gesetzt /
kame mit grossen frewden mit glantzender sunnen daher ge-
180 faren / die sůssen vnnd kůlen windlin mit jrem sanfften wehen /
daher bliesen / dauon alle gewechs quickung namen / Die
vōgel auff den zweigen mit jren sůßklingenden stimmen / den
tag mit frōlichem gesang empfiengen. Der Patron des schieffs
erfrewet sich auch nit wenig ab semlichem gůten wind / vnd
wetter / Er schicket eylends sein trometter in die statt / vmbzůblasen / dann er gleich willens was von land zůsåglen / Also
versamleten sich alle die so willens hetten zůfaren / mit grossen
freudē / bey dem schiff / allein Lasarus der jüngling in grossem
trawren stůnd / dann jm nit weil werden mocht / sein aller-
190 liebste Amelia zůgesegnen. Er genadet seiner můter / dañ er nit
meinet das sie an das port zů dem schiff gehn würd. Es hette
aber Cassandra vnd Lucia am abent zůuor ein pack vnd
anschlag miteinander getroffen / das sie sampt jrer tochter
Amelien / Reicharten vnd den jüngling Lasarum zům schiff
beleiten wolten. Cassandra kam sampt jrer tochter gegangen /

in das haus Lasari / Da aber waren Richardus vnd Lasarus
aller ding schon beraidt. Aber es gefiel Richarten sonderlichen
das der jüngling zůuor / vnd ehe er von land schied / dem alten
Roberto genaden solte / desgleichen der altē můter / die sich
dañ der welt gantz entschlagen hetten / jres betagten alters 200
halben / sie beliben eintzig in jrem gemach / dariñ wurden sie
mit speiss vnnd dranck / auch ander wartung wol versorget /
von Cassandra / vnd Amelia jrer tochter. Also gieng Reich-
hardus mit dem jüngling zů jn / Da warend sie eben erst
auffgestanden. Reichardus zeigt jhn an / wie er yetzund willens
were / sampt dem jüngling Lasaro in Brabant zů schiffen /
weren derhalben kumen / jnen beiden zůgenaden. Es wußten
auch die alten zůuor allen anschlag / auch von der eheberedung
zwischen Amelien vnnd dem jüngling. Der alt Robertus souil
jhm müglich vnd die zeit ertragen mocht / vnderwis er den 210
jüngling / gab jm ein gůte letze / sein darbey vnnd seiner lehr
zů gedencken. Nit weniger het sich die gůt alt můter mit
Lasaro früntlich geletzet / vnd gewünschet das jhm vil glücks
auff seiner raiss widerfaren / vnd jm Got ein selige vnd frőliche
haimfart verleihen wolt / damit sie jn mit frewdē wider sehen
mőchten. Also giengend sie sambt dem alten Lasaro / den
beiden weiben vnd junckfrawē zů dem schiff / das was schon
aller ding bereit zůfaren. Lasarus genadet seinem vatter vñ
seiner lieben můter / sein hertz aber was jm so gros das er
Amelia seine libeste junckfraw nit gesegnen kund / sunder 220
befalhe das seiner můter / der junckfrawen ein brieff zů antwurten / darinn er sie zům allerfreuntlichsten gesegnet. Des
aber die junckfraw nit kleinen vnmůt empfieng / ward auch
gåntzlich in heimlichen zorn gegen Lasaro entrüstet / wiewol
sie nicht d'gleichen thet / biss sie wider haim inn jhr gemach
kam. Also fůr das schiff mit vffgerichtem ságel vnd gůtem glück-
seligem wind daruon. Sie stůndē an dem port ein gůte zeit / dem
nach sahen / biss das sie es gar aus jrem gesicht verloren. Demnach sind sie wider zů haus gangen. Amelia die junckfraw ist
in jhr gemach gangen / jhren jüngling schwerlich beklagt / vmb 230
das er on gnadet von jr weg gefaren ist. Sie hůb an auff nachuolgende meinung mit jr selb zůreden / O Amelia / sagt sie /
wo hast du dein hertz vnd vertrawen hiengesetzet / wie hast
du dein hertzliche vnd stete lieb so gar vbel angelegt / auff
einen sand vnnd schmeltzend eyss hastu gebawen / Ey du

vnuerstandner jüngling / wie hastu an deinem hertzen haben môgen / also von mir sunder alles vrlop hinweg zû schaidē / binn
ich doch die / so dir nachgeuolget ist biss an das port des Mers /
vnd hast mir nit mit einem früntlichen wort genaden môgen /
240 Wolan ich wais mich inn keinen weg an dir zûrechen / dañ das
ich dich aus meinem hertzen setzen vnnd ausschliessen will /
dañ das zûsagen vnser baider âlteren / mag mich noch gar
nichts an disem ort binden / dieweil d' handschlag noch nit
geschehen ist / Far nur hin Lasare / du vnbedachter jüngling /
mein stete trew vnd lieb wil ich einem bekantern vnd ver-
stendigern jüngling behalten dañ du bist / mich aber rewet all
mein tag / dz ich mich deines abscheids halben / so jâmerlich
gehebt hab wolan / hin ist hin / ich kan vnd mags nit wider
bringen.

(iii) Johann Fischart: *Affentheurliche Naupengeheurliche Geschichtklitterung* (1575/90)

The *Geschichtklitterung* (1575, revised 1582 and 1590), the largest and most
important work of the Strassburg lawyer-poet, Johann Fischart (1547–90),
is an adaptation of François Rabelais's *Gargantua* (1534). Fischart did not
possess a particularly inventive mind, and almost all his writings are translations and adaptations of other men's work, but it is not accidental that it
should be precisely Rabelais who provided the inspiration for the novel for
which Fischart is mainly remembered. As the foremost literary spokesman
of the German Protestant bourgeoisie in the later sixteenth century—he was
brought up a Lutheran, but was subsequently converted to Calvinism and
in a number of his writings (*Binenkorb Deß Heyl. Römischen Imenschwarms*,
1579; *Vierhörniges Jesuiterhütlein*, 1580) launched a series of bitterly savage
attacks on the Roman Church—Fischart lacks Rabelais's scepticism and has
a tendency to moralize; in other respects, however, especially in his highly
developed sense of humour and his distinctly satirical bent, in his love of the
monstrous and the grotesque, and in his inventive approach to language, he
has obvious affinities with his model. The outlines of Rabelais's story are
faithfully retained: the birth and education of the giant, Gargantua, the war
between Grandgosier and Picrochole, and the foundation of the monastery
of Thélème. As a translation Fischart's rendering is inferior to Urquhart's
English version (1653) (cf. the way Fischart often loses the flavour of the
grotesque names in our passage (*b*)), and although Fischart frequently
follows his model almost literally, he also feels free to modify and expand
his source as fancy takes him, with the result that his version is almost three
times as long as the original. For both authors the satirical elements—the
castigation of scholasticism and monasticism, the mockery of human folly in
all its aspects, and the literary burlesquing of the chivalric novel—are important, but for Fischart as for Rabelais the main purpose of the work is

simply to amuse the reader. Humour was not, of course, something new in German prose fiction; what is new is the sustained and sophisticated nature of the humour: Rabelaisian touches are very common, but it is not from these, nor from jokes in the tradition of the *Schwankbücher*, but from Fischart's use of language that the essential humour derives.

As a writer Fischart is possessed of a certain Janus-like quality. On the one hand, in his revival of religious polemicism and in his rhymed satires, he looks back to the early sixteenth century; on the other hand, his emancipation of literature in the *Geschichtklitterung* from didacticism and polemicism and his—by no means unscholarly—preoccupation with words and linguistic effects look forward to the seventeenth century and more modern times. For the English reader the *Geschichtklitterung* is at times more reminiscent of *Finnegan's Wake* than of *Gargantua*, for like Joyce, Fischart is fascinated by the sounds and associations of words. Unlike his contemporaries and immediate successors Fischart is not very much interested in the actual story he is telling: in his case the normal role of narrative and language is reversed, the former serving merely as an excuse for the latter, which is endowed with an almost magical, independent life of its own and sweeps the reader along with cascades of puns, proverbs, quotations, allusions, and synonyms which seem calculated to overwhelm rather than to enlighten. The expansion of the French model is not so much due to the insertion of new material as to Fischart's intoxication with words: as Wolfgang Stammler remarks, 'where Rabelais has a word, Fischart composes a list; where Rabelais composes a list, Fischart compiles a catalogue'. Like Rabelais, Fischart loves to construct words and names for things and people, punning on them, distorting them, allowing his imagination free rein to call up and mix associations and allusions in order to achieve grotesque effects. The title of the novel, for instance, associates 'abentheurlich' with 'Affe', 'Naupe' (= 'whim', 'difficulty') with 'geheurlich' (= 'gentle', 'safe'), and 'klittern' (= 'scribble', 'botch') with 'Geschichte' to produce three 'new' words.

The result is not easy to read—often it becomes downright unintelligible—and for modern taste at least the sustained nature of the effects and the monstrous lists of synonyms can rapidly become tedious. Not surprisingly, for all its undoubted linguistic virtuosity and its unique verbal agility—indeed, precisely because of these qualities—Fischart's masterpiece did not long survive him as a work of living literature. Nor did it exert any immediately discernible influence on succeeding generations of writers, although the fantastic allusiveness and suppleness of Fischart's style remained a striking monument to the potentialities dormant in the German language.

Passage (*a*) retells the famous incident in Chapter 17 of *Gargantua* (Fischart's ch. 19), in which Gargantua's mare destroys a forest with a swish ⌣ her tail, but embellishes the story in entirely characteristic fashion. Passage (*b*) (Rabelais ch. 26, Fischart ch. 29) deals with the outbreak of the war between Grandgosier, Gargantua's father, and Picrochole, King of Lerné. Rabelais's satire on the quarrel between his own father and Gaucher de Sainte-Marthe, Seigneur de Lerné, in respect of fishing and navigation rights on the Loire is, of course, lost on a German audience, but the satire on the folly of war remains: the conflict originates in the refusal of the

baker-subjects of Picrochole to sell their wares to the servants of Grandgosier,
since they regard them as being too coarse and vulgar to appreciate such
fine cakes.
The extracts are taken from the edition published in Strassburg in 1590.

(a) *Wie Gargantua gen Pariß geschickt ist worden | vnd wie
das vngläublichgroß Elendeiß oder Vrthier | welches jhn trug |
die Roßbrämen vnd Kühmucken im Beaucerland straffet vnd
erschlug.*

Also reyseten sie jren weiten weg ... Biß sie vber Orleans kamen:
Allda was ein weiter breiter Wald / in die lång auff treissig fünff
Meilen / vnd inn der breite sibenzehen / drunder vñ drüber
vngeferlich: Derselbige war grausam fruchtbar / vnnd voll von
Brämen oder Kühfligen / also daß es für die arme Thier / Esel
10 vnnd Pferd / die da durchzogen / ein rechte Rauberei vnnd
Mörderei war: ... Aber vnsers Gurgelstrossa Lastmaul rach
allen vnbill / jm vnnd seins gleichen Geschlecht bewisen / sehr
redlich an jhnen / vnd dasselbige mit eim solchen Duck / dessen
sie sich am minsten versehen hetten.
    Dann alsbald sie inn den Forst kamen / vnnd jm die Roß-
bremen ein Schlacht lifferten / vnd dapfer den Sturm anlieffen /
zog er seinen Schwantz von Leder / scharmützelt mit jhnen /
schnitzelt vnnd schneitzet jhnen so gewaltig / daß er den
gantzen Wald / alle Bäum / Stock vnd Stauden / das hoch vnd
20 nider gehöltz / das baw vñ daubholtz / alle hursten / vom
nidersten Liebstöckel an biß zum Cederbaum hinauff / vnd
vberall den Forst niderschlug / zerschmiß / zerriß / zerbiß / zer-
stieß / von oben an biß vnten / zur seiten / die quäre / vber-
zwerch / da vnnd dort / disseit vnd dort seit / vber vnd vber /
dorthinauß / da hinein / in die lång vnd inn die breit / vnd
in summa schmettert das Holtz hernider / wie ein Mäder das
Häu: Also daß es forthin da weder Holtz noch Roßmucken
hat / sonder die gantze gegene ist seidher zu einer feinē ebene
worden / wie die Lunenburger Heyd / da diß gehörnecht
30 VrChammel hernachgehends auch einen solchen Scharmützel
hat gehalten. Dañ im gedachten Wurtzeldelber Land / wurden
abermal viel Legionen Tobbrämen vertrieben / das vernamen
die Wendischen / vnd Sorbischen Crabrowespen / berufften sie
wider die Herulisch fliegend Herd der ScharpSchröter / also
zogen sie vber Mör mit der Spanischen Flut der Mosquiten vnd

Zeunganischer Zigeiner /vñ Meylåndischen grünen Canthar-
kåfern / kamen an vmb Holm / Bommeln vnd Bråmen (die
noch den Namen daruon haben) verderbten den Teuffel mit
einander / biß ein alte Wurtzeldelberin den Raht gab / mit jrs
gleichen sie zuvertreiben / wie die Scorpion bôß mit bôsem / 40
nemlich mit Rauch vō Bruñ vnd Hundsbråmen / von der
Titanischen Himmelstûrmer Blut (dann dise Wolckentreñliche
Gigfitzen waren auch nur Wespen) von Brombeerhecken vnd
Brembûschen: das that man / brants alles auff sechtzig meiln
auff: biß auch die alten andechtigen Weiblein jhre Wehrebenische vnd Segamenisch Wûrtzwisch von Donnerwurtz mûßten
herfûr suchen vnd verbrennen / die sie von vilen Jaren auff
den Tag vnser Liebenfrawen Himmelfahrt fûr Gespenst vnnd
Vngewitter geweicht vnnd gesammelt hatten: da wich das
Geschmeiß / vnd traff eben den Gargantua / so auff ein Hoch- 50
zeit reyßt / mit seim Vlckthier / auff gedachter Heid an / da
waren sie empfangē wie gehôrt: wiewol Lazius nichts daruon
hat gehôrt: Als nun vorgemelt Bremenschlacht Gargantua sah /
het er seine hertzliche freud darab / vnd ohn ferner rhûmen /
sprach er zu seinem Volck auff desselben Landssprach / O wie
Beau ce, das ist / wie ein schôner Besen fûr die bôsen beissige
Bremen? Daher wûrd darnach das Land allzeit Beauce oder
Bôßausse genant . . .

(b) *Wie das Landvolck vmb Lerne auß geheiß ihres Kônigs*
    Picrocholi vnuersehen die Hirten vnd Bangart des Grand- 60
    gusiers vberfulen / weil sie jnen die Krapffen stulen.

SObald die Kåßflademer wider heim gehn Lerne kamen / fûg-
ten sie sich / eh sie etwas asen oder trancken / zu dem Capitolio
oder der gemeinen Laub vnd hallen vberm dē statthor vnnd
trugen daselbs jhr klag fûr bey dem Kônig Picrocholo / dem
Herrn der Bittergallier / vnd Gallenkoderer / dem dritten dises
Namens / zeigten da jhr zerrissene Fanen vnd Paner der Plagē /
so vber die Kårch gespant warē / die Filtzhût vol beulen / die
Nestel daran verloren / die Juppen vñ Blatrôck besudelt
vnnd zerrissen / jhre Notelbauntzen und Kåßkrapffen verloren / 70
vñ fûrnemlich den Saur im Arß gefehrlich verwundt auff der
seiten / da die Scherer den Strel ins haar hinstecken: vnd sagten darbey / das diser vberfall alleine von deß Grandgoschiers

vō Großkål Hirten / Bangarten / Wingartsknechten vnd Nußschwingern bey dem grossen furweg jenseit Sewiler / geschehen
sey. Welcher alsbald ers hôrt / ward er gleich vnsinnig / Gallen-
bitterig zornig / vnd ohn weiteren bedacht oder nachfrag wie
oder warumb / ließ er gleich durch sein Land die acht vnnd
aberacht / Bañ vñ aberbann / lermen in allen Gassen vmb-
80 schlagen vnd außschreien / mandiren vñ Remandirē / dz ein
jeder bei leibs straff / so lieb jm die Weinstraß ist / sich vm̄
Mittag zeit in der Rûstung vff dē grossen Platz di S. Marco vor
dē Schloß zum Musterplan finden lasse. Vñ sein ernstlich vorhaben noch ernster zumachē / ließ er selbs vor jm her vmb die
Statt die Spil gehen / Trometē vñ Hôrpauckelen: vñ zwischen
der weil dz man dē Jmbiß zubereitet / dz Feld geschütz vff
der Achß herfûr zihen / seinē Haubt vñ Blutfanen vnd Oriflant
fligen / dz Zeughauß / wie dz Rômisch Capitoli zum vnfriden auffthun / Harnisch / Halßkrågē / Ringkrågē / Kraut
90 vñ Lot / Schrôt / Zûndstrick / Puluerfleschē / Faustkolbē / kurtz
vnd lang wehren / Schlachtschwerter / Partesanen / Schûrtzer /
Lemeisen / Handrohr / Handgeschûtz / Hacken / Bûchssen /
Toppelhacken auff Bôcken / Zielrohr / Schlencken / Werffzeug /
Hagelgeschûtz / Ladstecken / Sturmkrûg außtheilen: Auch den
Spissern / Trossern / Vorreutern / vnd Botten pferd darfûhren
vnd geben / jhre Kûriß mit gantzen Parschen / wolbedeckt stålen
Glider / vnd verdeckt Hengst / Hauptharnisch die wol schliessen
vnd visieren / gute ståhlin Krågen / Armzeug / Rucken vnnd
Krebs / Schûrtz / Kniebuckel / Roßstirnen / knopff / stålen
100 Puckelbantzer / vnd was darzu gehôrig.

Zwischen dem essen bestellt er die Aempter / die hohen
gefell vnd Commissionē / die musterung / die ober vnnd unter-
wachten / Hut / Statthalten / Starten / forderst vñ hinderst
vnterhalten / Schilt vnd Scharwachten / das Lehengelt / die
Vbersold / Toppelsold / den Bestallbrieff / Articulbrieff /
Kammerwågen / den verlornen Hauffen / den Rennfan / die
angehenckt Flûgel / die Zugordnung / die Glider: ernant die
Malstatt / Pherien vnnd Feldzeichen / den Feldmarschalck /
Cardinal Obersten / vnnd wa er etwann nicht zugegen wer /
110 sein Lochotenent / die Vnterhauptleut / Fenderich / Rittmei-
ster / Quartiermeister / Wachtmeister / Profosen / Feldweibel /
Fûrer / Rottmeister / Hurnweibel / Steckenknecht / Brand-
meister. Zum abentheurwertigen Vorzug aber erkant er mit

dem Schützenfanen den Herrn Trapelum vom Wetterhan: der führet sechzehen tausent / vierzehen Hackenschützen / sampt treissig tausenten vnnd eilff Läuffern vnnd Waghälsen.

Zur Artilleri ward bestallt der groß Schilttrager Truckedillon / darunter neun hundert vierzehen grosse Feldstuck vnnd Maurbrecher waren / Scharffmetzen / Basiliscen / Nachtgallen / Singerin / Virteilbüchs / Passevolanten / Spirolen / Cartaunen / Notschlangen / Schlauckenschlangen / halb Schlangen / Falckenetlin / on die Mörthier / Böler / Narren / Orgeln / Nachbüchssen / das Geschreigeschütz / Kamerbüchssen / Scharffentinlin / die zwölff Botten. Welche samptlich mit aller darzu gehöriger Munitionzeug wol versehen waren / als mit Zünd vnd Werckpuluer / Ansetzkolben / Zündruten / Raumern / Wischern / Ladschauffeln / Feurkugeln / Bechringen / allerhand Sturmfewrwercken / Mörseln / Sturmleitern / Feurleitern / Feldbären / Zügkriegen / Spritzen / Legeisen / Hebtremeln / Walhöltzern / Hebzeug / Geyßfüssen / Winden / Spannern / Schiffbrucken / Rüstwägen / Schleppkarren / Roßpfelen / Schlachtmessern / Lanten / Lunten / Feldfleschen / Brechwinden / Getterschrauben / Fewerpfannen / Multer / Reyß vnnd Roßbaren / Rantzwegen / Deichsselwegen / Zeugwagen / Bruckwagen / Arckelleiwagen / Schmidtwagen / Kugelwagen / Bleiwagen / Stemeisenwagen / Senfftwagen / Schantzzeug / Handwaffen / Gießlöffel / Spießeisen / Geschifft vñ vngeschifft Spieß / Fürsetzzeug / Eselzeug / Stoltzbcum / Straubhöltzer / Feldmülen / Zugmülen / Handmülen / Treibmülen / Zielscheiter / Lannegel / Brechmeyssel / Lanseyler / Lanstangen / Zeltbäum / Zeltnägel / Lanbäum / Kipffblöck / Tragkörb &c. Zusampt jhren Feldzeugmeistern / Schantzmeistern / Zeugwarten / Wagenburgmeistern / Puluerhütern / Zeugdienern / Schnellern / Schützen-Pferden / Schantzgräbern.

Der hinderharrenwertig Nachzug ward bestimpt dem Hörtzogen von Rackedennarren: Jnn mitteler Feldschlachtordnung ließ sich der König sampt seinen Landfürsten selber finden / mit Keihel / Wecken vnd Monordnungen / von siben tausent Janitscharen / grad gerechnet / vmbgeben. Also kurtz vberschlagen vnd gerüstet / ehe sie sich in den Anzug begaben / oder den Feind anwendeten vnnd ersuchten / schickten sie mit dem Hauptmann Eugulewind von Klatterbuß / drey hundert leichte Pferd das Land zuberennen / ob jrgends ein verborgener

Hinderhalt versteckt lige. Aber nach dem sie es fleissig erspehet /
befunden sie die gantze Landschafft daselbs herumb gantz still
vnnd sicher / ohn einige auffwickelung / vergaderung oder
widerstand. Welches so bald es dem Kõnig Picrocholo verkund-
schafft worden / befahl er das alle Fånlin zu gleich streng fort-
zuziehen sich nicht saumeten. Darauff fulen sie mit gewalt ein /
160 zertheileten sich auff beide seit / streiffeten ferr vnnd weit /
verderbten / jagten / blånderten / raubten / garteten / brand-
schatzten alles was sie ankamen / ohn einige ansehung der
Person / wer arm oder reich: Kirchen oder Klõster / Witwen
oder Weisen: war alles preiß / triben hinweg Ochssen vnd
Kûh / Lemmer vnd Hemmel: Geiß vnd Bõck / Han vnd
Hennen / Henn vnnd Hûnlin / Antrach vnd Enten / Ganß vnnd
Ganser / Moren vnd Såu / kein Vogel war inn seim Nest
sicher / namen die Taubhåuser auß / frasen das Nest mit dem
Vogel / liessen den Wein außlauffen / schossen / warffen vnd
170 schlugen alle Nuß herab / machtē inn eim augenblick den
Herbst ein / namen die zåun hinweg / als ob sie auff Moscouitisch fûr Polotzko schantzkõrb tragen wolten / knipfften vnd
kuppelten Mågd vnd Knecht / Jungfrauen vnnd Junge Knaben
zusamen / vnd tribens vor jhnen her / stûrmeten die Binenkõrb:
wiewol mit gefahr / dann sie mußten das Visier fûrthun:
schmissen die schõnsten õpffel / Biren / Kûtten vnnd Nespeln
von båumen herab / ja hiewen die fruchtbarn Beum vmb / wie
der Fucker zu Bredau / stiessen alle thûren auff vnd liessen kein
Nagel inn der Wand? Ach es war ein jåmerliche vngestalte
180 vnordnung / als ob sie vmb den lõffel renten / welcher jhn am
ersten der Braut bring. Vnd da fanden sie keinen widerstand /
Juncker Frech mut saß im Sattel / vnd Jungfraw Reutrut
dahinden: Wa sie hinkamen ergab sich ein jeder auff gnad /
bittend zu dem freundlichsten mit jhnen zufahren / auß
betrachtung daß sie allzeit gute liebe Nachbauren gewesen
weren / Vnnd jhnen nie nichts vnbilles oder gewalts zugefûgt
hetten / Gott werds gewiß nicht vngestraffet lassen / wa sie vber
die Schnur hawen. Ja ja liebe Nußheintzen / hett ich seidher
gelt zuzehlen / sprachen sie / biß ewer straff kommet / Botz
190 todenbaum / wir wõllen euch die Kåßkrapffen gesegnen / daß
euch alle Plag vnd Beulen schend: biß Gott selbst kompt / haben
wir Vogel vnd Nest weg geraumt.

(iv) *Historia von D. Johañ Fausten* (1587)

The *Historia von D. Johañ Fausten / dem weitbeschreyten Zauberer vnnd Schwartz-künstler* . . . written by an unnamed author and published by the Frankfurt bookseller Johann Spies in 1587 is the most significant literary product of German Protestantism in the sixteenth century. Judged purely on its own merits it is crude in technique, episodic in form, and heavily didactic in purpose, yet it gave literary currency to a theme which was to be a perennial source of inspiration for European writers and musicians: Marlowe, Lessing, Goethe, Chamisso, Byron, Grabbe, Heine, Lenau, Valéry, Thomas Mann, D. L. Sayers, Berlioz, Gounod, and Wagner, writing in their various media, are all indebted to the *Volksbuch* of 1587.

Spies's anonymous author fashions his book from a series of established legends and anecdotes associated with the academic vagabond and necromancer, Dr. Georg Faustus. The latter's origins and identity are obscure, but on the basis of such contemporary evidence as has survived, it seems probable that Faustus (he is also referred to as Sabellicus (latinized form of Zabel) and presumably 'Faustus' (Lat. = 'happy') is an assumed name) was born at Knittlingen in Baden-Württemberg in 1480. His name is early associated with Heidelberg (subsequently, under the influence of the Reformation, with Wittenberg), but it is uncertain where he studied—if at all—and he was almost certainly not entitled to the magisterial and doctoral titles to which he laid claim. Equally, he does not seem ever to have had an official position as a university teacher, but apparently belonged to the academic *demi-monde* of the age, an object of both scorn and fear to his more orthodox contemporaries. A man of unsavoury moral character—he fled from Kreuznach in 1507 (?) in order to escape a charge of pederasty and was expelled from Ingolstadt in 1528 on unknown grounds—he apparently lived by his wits, drifting from one town to the next and trading on the superstition of the age by his professed skill in necromancy and astrology, telling fortunes, casting horoscopes, and giving advice to wealthy clients (the Bishop of Bamberg consulted him on one occasion, as did Philip von Hutten before leading an expedition to South America). He is reported to have died about 1540 in Staufen (Breisgau), and almost immediately it was rumoured that the Devil had killed him in order to claim his soul.

For no very obvious reason the author of the *Volksbuch* divides his story into three parts. The first deals with Faust's origins, his life as a student, his conjuration of spirits, and his pact with the Devil, who supplies him with information about Hell and the way things are ordered there. The second part continues the account of the Devil's instruction of Faust in astronomical and meteorological matters; Faust descends into Hell and explores the heavens, before embarking on a 'grand tour' of Europe and the Near East. In the third part Faust visits the courts of several princes, plays a variety of tricks on bishops, knights, and peasants, conjures the shade of Helen of Troy and has a child by her, and finally, the twenty-four years of his pact having passed, is killed by the Devil.

The story of the historical Faust is thus developed in a number of different directions. The status of Faust as a practitioner of the occult arts enables the learned author to include much material connected with witchcraft and demonology and, since Faust is a seeker after truth, he also takes the opportunity to introduce a number of scientific speculations, mostly connected with meteorology. Similarly, Faust's 'grand tour' enables him to put his geographical knowledge to good use. On occasion, too, the Protestant author engages in polemical attacks on the Roman Catholic Church: Mephostophiles appears as a monk and insists that Faust remain celibate, and when Faust is in Rome even he is appalled by the immorality of the Pope. Elsewhere the author almost seems to lose sight of his serious moral purpose and amuses his readers by recounting numerous *Schwänke* in which a distinctly waggish Faust plays pranks on the people with whom he comes into contact.

Like other popular figures from Till Eulenspiegel to Winston Churchill, the historical Faust was subject to the process of 'anecdotal accretion', i.e. once his reputation as a wag and necromancer was established in popular mythology, anecdotes originally connected with other men began to be associated with him. Thus the dragon-drawn chariot with which Faust explores the heavens is a modification of the vehicle allegedly first used by Alexander the Great, while Faust's conjuration of Helen of Troy goes back to an incident associated with the activities of Trithemius Abbot of Sponheim at the court of Maximilian I, which has been given literary currency by Hans Sachs in a poem of 1564. Even the central idea of the pact with the Devil was not specifically Faustian, but had been connected originally with Theophilus, the medieval cleric who sought the aid of the Devil to recover his lost position of honour at his bishop's court, but experienced a change of heart and was saved from damnation by the Virgin. In much the same way the *Schwank* in which Faust swallows the horse and cart of a peasant who refuses to get out of his way was originally associated with a magician called Wildfeuer. Most of these accretions are probably the result of the working of the popular mind rather than of a conscious act on the part of the author; the latter did not, however, scruple to borrow other men's work where it suited his purpose and, in the fashion of his times, simply took over from Sebastian Münster's *Cosmographia* descriptions of the various towns Faust visited.

But the *Faustbuch* is much more than an omnium gatherum of odd scraps of scientific information, religious polemicism, and the pranks of a sort of academic Eulenspiegel, with whom Faust has an undeniable kinship in his waggishness and in his alienation from society. The author occasionally gets carried away by his story-telling and momentarily forgets his moral purpose, but he is above all concerned to advance a Christian theory of knowledge and to warn his readers against trying to emulate Faust. It is obviously unfair to read the *Faustbuch* with literary hindsight, but one cannot help feeling that his moral concerns have blinded the author to the tremendous possibilities dormant in his material: he is clearly unaware of the poetry inherent in the Helen episode and similarly has no sense of the starkly tragic nature of Faust's fate. In many respects, too, the book is an obscurantist and anti-intellectual document, and it is easy to see it as evidence of the blighting of the human spirit by an intolerant and narrow religious orthodoxy. Fundamentally the author denies the individual's right to pursue truth uninhibitedly: he is a prisoner of the religious outlook of his age and, following the venerable distinction between black and white magic, he indicates permissible areas of intellectual speculation by anxiously labelling those favoured by Faust as being 'off limits'. The pursuit of knowledge, he suggests, should never be an end in itself; indeed, in some matters ignorance is infinitely preferable to knowledge, and a man may pay too high a price for what he learns. Faust is such a man. Like his descendant in Goethe's drama, he has exhausted all natural means of acquiring knowledge and in his pact with the Devil he trades his soul for the knowledge he could not gain by any other means. As a child of the Enlightenment, Goethe could see in the urge to strive after knowledge even at the price of eternal damnation something great and noble, an expression of that quality which distinguished man from the beasts—hence the ultimate salvation of his hero in spite of the latter's crimes. The stern Protestant author of the *Volksbuch* is a stranger to such humane optimism, however, and for him Faust's desire 'alle Gründ am Himmel vnd auff Erden zu erforschen' is a sign of his 'Fürwitz / Freyheit vnd Leichtfertigkeit', an example of that impious and frivolous curiosity which impels a man to investigate those things which a wise Godhead has seen fit to hide from him. The modern reader may find such a view of the world and the attendant belief in the physical existence of the Devil quaintly naïve; Goethe's sophisticated demons, who, for all their negation, ultimately work for good, are certainly more congenial than the full-blooded Devil of 1 Peter 5: 8 who speaks from the *Volksbuch*. Yet in the last analysis the *Faustbuch* may well be nearer the mood and insights of our own age than Goethe's masterpiece, and behind all the quaint demonology and blatant obscurantism the message of the book is frighteningly modern. The author is simply saying that, emancipated from a controlling morality which can give ethical direction to scientific discovery, the indiscriminate pursuit of the power which knowledge confers is ultimately an evil and self-destructive thing. And in the middle of the twentieth century it would be a very foolish reader who would seek to disagree with such a claim.

Our text is taken from the edition of 1587, published by Johann Spies of Frankfurt.

(a) D. Faustus låst jhm das Blut herauß in einen Tiegel / setzt es auff warme Kolen / vnd schreibt / wie hernach folgen wirdt.

JCh Johannes Faustus D. bekenne mit meiner eygen Handt offentlich / zu einer Bestettigung / vnnd in Krafft diß Brieffs / Nach dem ich mir fürgenommen die Elementa zu speculieren / vnd aber auß den Gaaben / so mir von oben herab bescheret / vnd gnedig mitgetheilt worden / solche Geschicklitkeit in meinem Kopff nicht befinde / vnnd solches von den Menschen nicht erlehrnen mag / So hab ich gegenwertigē gesandtem 10 Geist / der sich Mephostophiles uennet / ein Diener des

Hellischen Printzen in Orient / mich vntergeben / auch
denselbigen / mich solches zuberichten vñ zu lehren / mir
erwehlet / der sich auch gegen mir versprochen / in allem
vnderthenig vnnd gehorsam zuseyn. Dagegen aber ich mich
hinwider gegen jhme verspriche vnd verlobe / daß so 24.
Jahr / von Dato biß Brieffs an / herumb vnd fürvber gelauffen / er mit
mir nach seiner Art vnd weiß / seines Gefallens / zuschalten /
walten / regieren / führen / gut macht haben solle / mit allē /
O HERR es sey Leib / Seel / Fleisch / Blut vnd gut / vnd das in sein
Gott
behůt. Ewigkeit. Hierauff absage ich allen denen / so da leben /
allem Hiṁlischen Heer / vnd allen Menschen / vnd das muß
seyn. Zu festem Vrkundt vnnd mehrer Bekråfftigung / hab
ich disen Receß eigner Hand geschrieben / vnderschrieben /
vnd mit meinē hiefůr getrucktem eygen Blut / meines Sinns /
Kopffs / Gedancken vnnd Willen / verknůpfft / versiegelt vnd
bezeuget / &c.

Subscriptio,

30
Johann Faustus / der Er-
fahrne der Elementen / vñ
der Geistlichen Doctor.

(b) *Von Dienstbarkeit deß Geistes / gegen D. Fausto.*

ALs D. Faustus solchen Grewel dem bösen Geist mit seinem
eignen Blut vñ Handschrifft geleistet / ist gewißlich zuver-
muhten / daß auch Gott vnd alles Himmlisches Heer von jhme
gewiechen. Jn dem hat er nun sein Thun angerichtet / nit wie
ein rechter Gottseliger Haußvatter / sonder wie der Teuffel /
wie Christus der HERR von jhme sagt / der ein solche Behausung vnd Tabernacul hat / wo er in einem Menschen wohnet /
40 Der Teuffel hat bey jhme einforiert / vnd gewohnet / wie auch
zwar nach dem Sprichwort D. Faustus den Teuffel zu Gast geladen hat.
D. Fausti   D. Faustus hat seines froṁen Vettern Behausung jnnen / wie
famulus ers dann jme auch im Testament vermacht hatte / bey jhme
hett er tåglich ein jungen Schůler zum famulo, einen verwegnen
Lecker / Christoph Wagner genannt / dem gefiele dieses Spiel
auch wol / deßgleichen jne sein Herr tröstete / er wolte einen
hocherfahrnen vnd geschickten Mann auß jhme machen /
vnndt wie die Jugendt vorhin mehr zum bösen / denn zum

guten geneiget / also war diesem auch. So hat D. Faustus / wie oben gesagt / niemands in seinem Hauß / als seinen famulum, vnd seinen bösen Geist Mephostophilem, der jmmerdar in gestallt eines Mönchs vor jhme wandelte / den beschwur er in sein Schreibstüblein / welches er jederzeit verschlossen hatte.

Sein Nahrung vnd Prouiandt hatt D. Faustus vberflüssig / wann er einen guten Wein wolte haben / bracht jme der Geist solchen auß den Kellern / wo er wolte / wie er sich dann selbst einmal hören lassen / er thete seinem Herrn dem Churfürsten / auch dem Hertzogen auß Bäyrn / vnd dem Bischoffen von Saltzburg / viel Leyds in den Kellern / So hatte er täglich gekochte Speiß / dann er kundte ein solche zauberische Kunst / daß so bald er das Fenster auffthete / vnd nennet einen Vogel / den er gern wolt / der floge jhme zum Fenster hinein. Deß-gleichen brachte jhme sein Geist von allen vmbligenden Herr-schafften / von Fürsten oder Graffen Höfen / die beste gekochte Speiß / alles gantz Fürstlich / Er vñ sein Jung giengen stattlich gekleydet / welches Gewand darzu jhme sein Geist zu Nachts / zu Nürmberg / Augspurg oder Franckfurt einkauffen oder steh-len muste / dieweil die Krämer deß Nachtes nicht pflegen im Kram zusitzen / So müssen sich auch die Gerber vnnd Schuster also leiden.

Der Teuffel tregt D. Fausto zu.

Jn Summa / es war alles gestolne vnd entlehnete Wahr / vnnd war also ein gar erbare / ja Gottlose Behausung vnd Narung / Wie Christus der HERR durch Johannem / den Teuffel auch einen Dieb vnd Mörder nennet / der er auch ist.

Noch hat jme der Teuffel versprochen / er wölle jme Wochent-lich 25. Kronen geben / thut das Jahr 1300. Kronen / das ward sein Jars Bestallung.

(c) *FOLGET NUN DER ANDER THEIL dieser Histo-rien / von Fausti Abenthewren vnd andern Fragen.*

DOct. Faustus / als er von Gottseligen Fragen vom Geist keine Antwort mehr bekommen kondte / mußt ers auch ein gut Werck seyn lassen / Fienge demnach an Calender zu machē / ward also derselben zeit ein guter Astronomus oder Astrologus, gelehrt vnd Erfahren / von seinem Geist in der Sternkunst / vnd Practicken schreiben / wie männiglichen wol bewust / daß alles / was er geschrieben / vnter den Mathematicis das Lob

D. Faustus ein Astro-logus vnd Calender-macher

darvon gebracht. So stimpten auch seine Practicken / die er
Fůrsten vnnd grossen Herren dedicierte / vbereyn / Denn er
90 richtet sich nach seines Geistes Weissagungen vnnd Deutungen
zukůnfftiger ding vnd Fåll / welche sich auch also erzeigten. So
lobte man auch seine Calender vñ Allmanach vor andern /
denn er setzte nichts in Calender / es war jhm also / als wann er
setzte Nebel / Windt / Schnee / Feucht / Warm / Donner /
Hagel / &c. hat sichs also verloffen. Es waren seine Calender
nit / als etlicher Vnerfahrnen Astrologen / so im Winter Kalt
vnnd Gefroren / oder Schnee / vñ im Sommer in den Hunds-
tagen / Warm / Doñer oder Vngewitter setzen. Er machte auch
in seinen Practicken Zeit vnd Stunde / wann das Kůnfftiges ge-
100 schehen solt / warnete ein jede Herrschafft besonder / als die
jetzt mit Theuwrung / die ander mit Krieg / die dritte mit
Sterben / vnnd also forthan / solte angegriffen werden . . .

Rom. (d) Fůrters kam er gen Rom / welche ligt bey einem Fluß
Tyberis genannt / so mitten durch die Statt fleußt / vnd jenseyt
der rechten Seyten / begreifft die Statt siebē Berg vmb sich / hat
eilff Pforten vnd Thor / Vaticanum, ein Berg / darauff S. Peters
Můnster oder Thuɱ ist. Dabey ligt deß Bapsts pallast / welcher
herrlich mit einem schônen Lustgarten vmbfangen / dabey die
Kirchen Lateranensis, dariñen allerley Heylthuɱs / vnd die
110 Apostolische Kirch genannt wirt / welche auch gewiß eine
kôstliche vnnd berůhmte Kirchen in der Welt ist. Deßgleichen
sahe er viel Heydnische verworffene Tempel. Jtem / viel Seulen /
Steigbogen / &c. welches alles zu erzehlen zu lang were / also
daß D. Faustus sein Lust vnnd kurtzweil dran sahe. Er kam
auch vnsichtbar fůr des Bapsts Pallast / da sahe er viel Diener
vnd Hoffschrantzē / vnd was Richten vnd Kosten man dem
Bapst aufftruge / vñ so vberflůssig / daß D. Faustus darnach zu
seinem Geist sagte: Pfuy / waruɱ hat mich der Teuffel nicht
auch zu einem Bapst gemacht. Doct. Faustus sahe auch darin-
120 nen alle seines gleichē / als vbermut / stoltz / Hochmut / Ver-
messenheit / fressen / sauffen / Hurerey / Ehebruch / vnnd alles
Gottloses Wesen deß Bapsts vnd seines Geschmeiß / also / daß
er hernach weiters sagte: Jch meynt / ich were ein Schwein
oder Saw deß Teuffels / aber er muß mich långer ziehen. Diese
Schwein zu Rom sind gemåstet / vñ alle zeitig zu Bratē
vnd zu Kochen. Vnd dieweil er viel von Rom gehôrt / ist

er mit seiner Zauberey drey tag vnnd Nacht / vnsichtbar / in
deß Bapsts Pallast blieben / vnnd hat der gute Herr Faustus
seythero nicht viel Guts gessen / noch getruncken. Stunde also
vor dem Bapst vnsichtbar einmal / wañ der Bapst essen wolt / so 130
macht er ein Creutz vor sich / so offt es dann geschahe / bließ
D. Faustus jhm in das Angesicht. Einmal lachte D. Faustus /
daß mans im gantzen Saal hôrete / dann weynete er / als wenn
es jm ernst were / vnd wusten die Auffwarter nit was das were.
Der Bapst beredet das Gesinde / es were ein verdampte Seele /
vnd bete vmb Ablaß / Darauff jhr auch der Bapst Busse auff-
erlegte. Doct. Faustus lachte darob / vnd gefiel jm solche Verblendung wol. Als aber die letzte Richten vnd kosten auff deß
Bapsts Tisch kamen / vñ jn / D. Faustum / hungert / hub er /
Faustus / seine Hand auff / als bald flogen jm Richten vñ Kostē / 140
mit samt der Schûssel in die hand / vnd verschwand also
damit / sampt seinem Geist / auff einen Berg zu Rom / Capito-
lium genañt / asse also mit Lust. Er schickte auch seinen Geist
wider dahin / der must jm nur den besten Wein von deß Bapsts
Tisch bringen / samt den silbern Bechern vnd Kanten. Da nun
der Bapst solchs alles gesehē / was jm geraubt wordē / hat er in
derselbigē Nacht mit allē Glockē zusammen leutē lassen.
Auch Meß vñ fûrbit fûr die verstorbene Seel lassen halten / vñ
auff solchen Zorn deß Bapsts / den Faustum / oder verstorbenen
Seel in das Fegfeuwer condemniert vnd verdampt. D. Faustus 150
aber hette ein gut fegen mit deß Bapstes Kosten vnd Tranck.
Solchs Silbergeschirr hat man nach seinem Abschiedt hinder
jhm gefunden. Als es nun mit Mittnacht ward / vnd Faustus
sich von solcher speiß gesättigt hatt / ist er mit seinem Geist
widerumb in die Hôhe auffgeflogen / vnd gen Meyland in Meylandt.
Italiam kom̄en / welches jn ein gesunde Wohnung dauchte /
dann es ist da kein anzeigung der hitze / auch sind da frische
Wasser / vnd 7. gar schône See . . .

(e) D. Faustus betreugt einen Roßtäuscher.

GLeicher weiß thete er einem Roßteuscher auff einem Jahr- 160
marckt / dann er richtet jhme selbsten ein schôn herrlich Pferd
zu / mit demselben ritte er auff einen Jahrmarckt / Pfeiffering
genannt / vnnd hatt viel Kauffer darumben / letzlich wirdt ers
vmb 40. Fl. loß / vnd sagte dem Roßtäuscher zuvor / er solte jhn

vber kein Tråncke reiten. Der Roßtåuscher wolte sehē / was
er doch mit meynete / ritte in ein Schwemme / da verschwand
das Pferd / vnd saß er auff einē Bûndel Stro / daß er schier
ertrunckē were. Der Kauffer wuste noch wol wo sein ver-
kauffer zur Herberg lage / gieng zornig dahin / fand D. Faustū
170 auff einem Betth ligen / schlaffendt vnnd schnarchend / der
Roßtåuscher name jhne beym Fuß / wolt jn herab ziehen / da
gieng jhme der Fuß aussem Arß / vnnd fiel der Roßtåuscher
mit in die Stuben nider. Da fienge Doctor Faustus an Mordio
zuschreyen / dem Roßtåuscher war angst / gab die Flucht / vnd
machte sich auß dem Staub / vermeinte nicht anderst / als
hette er jhme den Fuß auß dem Arß gerissen / also kam D.
Faustus wider zu Gelt.

(f) *Am weissen Soñtag von der bezauberten Helena.*

AM weissen Soñtag kamen offtgemeldte Studentē vnversehēs
180 wider in D. Fausti behausung zū Nachtessen / brachten jhr
Essen vnd Tranck mit sich / welche angeneme Gåst waren.
Als nu der Wein eingienge / wurde am Tisch von schônē
Weibsbildern geredt / da einer vnder jnen anfieng / daß er kein
Weibsbildt lieber sehen wolte / dañ die schône Helenā auß
Græcia, derowegen die schône Statt Trodantt grund gangen
were / Sie mûste schôn gewest seyn / dieweil sie jrem Mann
geraubet wordē / vnd entgegen solche Empôrung enēs zuia
were. D. Faustus antwurt / dieweil jhr dann so begirig seidt /
die schône gestalt der Kônigin Helenæ, Menelai Haußfraw /
190 oder Tochter Tyndari vñ Lædæ, Castoris vñ Pollucis Schwester
(welche die schônste in Græcia gewesen seyn solle) zusehen /
wil ich euch dieselbige fûrstellen / damit jhr Persônlich jhren
Geist in form vñ gestalt / wie sie im Leben gewesen / sehen
sollet / dergleichen ich auch Keyser Carolo Quinto auff sein
begerē / mit fûrstellung Keysers Alexandri Magni vnd seiner
Gemåhlin / willfahrt habe. Darauff verbote D. Faustus / daß
keiner nichts reden solte / noch vom Tisch auffstehen / oder sie
zuempfahen anmassen / vñ gehet zur Stuben hinauß. Als er
wider hinein gehet / folgete jm die Kônigin Helena auff dē Fuß
200 nach / so wunder schôn / daß die Studenten nit wusten / ob sie
bey jhnen selbsten weren oder nit / so verwirrt vnd innbrûnstig
waren sie. Diese Helena erschiene in einem kôstlichen schwar-

tzen Purpurkleid / jr Haar hatt sie herab hangen / dz schõn /
herrlich als Goldfarb schiene / auch so lang / daß es jr biß in die
Kniebiegen hinab gienge / mit schõnen Kollschwartzen Augen /
ein lieblich Angesicht / mit einem runden Kõpfflein / jre
Lefftzen rot wie Kirschen / mit einẽ kleinen Mûndlein / einen
Halß wie ein weisser Schwan / rote Bâcklin wie ein Rõßlin / ein
vberauß schõn gleissend Angesicht / ein lânglichte auffgerichte
gerade Person. Jn summa / es war an jr kein vntâdlin zufinden / 210
sie sahe sich allenthalben in der Stuben vmb / mit gar frechem
vnd bûbischem Gesicht / daß die Studenten gegen jr in Liebe
entzûndet waren / weil sie es aber fûr einen Geist achteten /
vergienge jhnen solche Brunst leichtlich / vnd gienge also
Helena mit D. Fausto widerumb zur Stuben hinauß. Als die
Studenten solches alles gesehen / baten sie D. Faustum / er solte
jhnen so viel zugefallen thun / vnnd Morgen widerumb fûrstellen / so wolten sie einen Mahler mit sich bringen / der solte
sie abconterfeyten / Welches jhnen aber D. Faustus abschlug /
vnd sagte / daß er jhren Geist nicht allezeit erwecken kõnnte. 220
Er wolte jhnen aber ein Conterfey darvon zukommen lassen /
welches sie die Studenten abreissen mõchten lassen / welches
dañ auch geschahe / vnd die Maler hernacher weit hin vnd
wider schickten / dann es war ein sehr herrlich gestalt eins
Weibsbilds. Wer aber solches Gemâld dem Fausto abgerissen /
hat man nicht erfahren kõnnen. Die Studentẽ aber / als sie zu
Betth kommen / haben sie vor der Gestalt vnd Form / so sie
sichtbarlich geschen / nicht schlaffen kõnnen / hierauß dañ
zusehen ist / daß der Teuffel offt die Menschen in Lieb entzûndt
vnd verblendt / daß man ins Huren Leben gerâth / vñ hernacher 230
nit leichtlich widerumb herauß zubringen ist.

(g) Von der Helena auß Griechenland / so dem Fausto Beywoh-
nung gethan in seinem letzten Jahre.

DArmit nun der elende Faustus seines Fleisches Lûsten genug-
sam raum gebe / fâllt jm zu Mitternacht / als er erwachte / in
seinem 23. verloffenẽ Jar / die Helena aus Grecia / so er vormals
den Studenten am Weissen Soñtag erweckt hatt / in Siñ /
Derhalben er Morgens seinen Geist anmanet / er solte jm die
Helenam darstellen / die seine Concubina seyn mõchte / welches
auch geschahe / vnd diese Helena war ebenmâssiger Gestalt / 240

wie er sie den Studenten erweckt hatt / mit lieblichem vnnd
holdseligem Anblicken. Als nun Doct. Faustus solches
sahe / hat sie jhm sein Hertz dermassen gefangē / daß er mit jhr
anhube zu Bulen / vnd fůr sein Schlaffweib bey sich behielt / die
er so lieb gewañ / daß er schier kein Augenblick von jr seyn
koñte / Ward also in dem letzten jar Schwangers Leibs von
jme / gebar jm einen Son / dessen sich Faustus hefftig frewete /
vnd jhn Iustum Faustum nennete. Diß Kind erzehlt D. Fausto
vil zukůnfftige ding / so in allen Låndern solten geschehen. Als
250 er aber hernach vmb sein Leben kame / verschwanden zugleich
mit jm Mutter vnd Kindt. ...

(h) Es geschahe aber zwischen zwölff vnd ein Vhr in der
Nacht / daß gegen dem Hauß her ein grosser vngestůmmer
Wind gienge / so das Hauß an allen orten vmbgabe / als ob es
alles zu grunde gehen / vnnd das Hauß zu Boden reissen wolte /
darob die Studenten vermeynten zuverzagen / sprangen auß
dem Bett / vñ huben an einander zu trösten / wolten auß der
Kammer nicht / Der Wiert lieff auß seinem in ein ander Hauß.
Die Studenten lagen nahendt bey der Stuben / da D. Faustus
260 jnnen war / sie hörten ein greuwliches Pfeiffen vnnd Zischen /
als ob das Hauß voller Schlangen / Natern vnnd anderer schåd-
licher Wůrme were / in dem gehet D. Fausti thůr vff in der
Stuben / der hub an vmb Hůlff vnnd Mordio zuschreyen / aber
kaum mit halber Stimm / bald hernach hört man jn nicht
mehr. Als es nun Tag ward / vnd die Studenten die gantze
Nacht nicht geschlaffen hattē / sind sie in die Stuben gegangen /
darinnen D. Faustus gewesen war / sie sahē aber keinen Faustum
mehr / vnd nichts / dañ die Stuben voller Bluts gesprützet / Das
Hirn klebte an der Wandt / weil jn der Teuffel von einer Wandt
270 zur andern geschlagen hatte. Es lagen auch seine Augen vnd
etliche Zåen allda / ein greulich vñ erschrecklich Spectackel.
Da huben die Studenten an jn zubeklagen vnd zubeweynen /
vñ suchten jn allenthalben / Letzlich aber funden sie seinē Leib
heraussen bey dem Mist ligen / welcher greuwlich anzusehen
war / dann jhme der Kopff vnnd alle Glieder schlotterten . . .

(i) Also endet sich die gantze warhafftige Historia vnd Zåuberey
Doctor Fausti / darauß jeder Christ zu lernen / sonderlich aber
die eines hoffertigen / stoltzen / fůrwitzigen vnd trotzigen Sinnes
vnnd Kopffs sind / GOtt zu förchten / Zauberey / Beschwerung

vnnd andere Teuffelswercks zu fliehen / so Gott ernstlich ver- 280
bottē hat / vñ den Teuffel nit zu Gast zu laden / noch jm raum
zu gebē / wie Faustus gethan hat. Dann vns hie ein erschrecklich Exempel seiner Verschreibung vnnd Ends fůrgebildet ist /
desselben můssig zu gehen / vnnd Gott allein zu lieben / vnnd
fůr Augen zu haben / alleine anzubeten / zu dienen vnd zu
lieben / von gantzem Hertzen vnd gantzer Seelen / vnd von
allen Kråfften / vnd dagegen dem Teuffel vnnd allem seinem
Anhang abzusagen / vñ mit Christo endtlich ewig selig zu
werden. Amen / Amen / Das wůndsche ich einem jeden von
grunde meines Hertzen / AMEN. 290

I Pet. V.

Seyt nůchtern vnd wachet / dann ewer Widersacher der
Teuffel geht vmbher wie ein brůllender Lôwe / vnd suchet
welchen er verschlinge / dem widerstehet fest im Glauben.

2. The *Schwank*

(i) *Ein kurtzweilig lesen von Dyl Vlenspiegel* (1515)

Ein kurtzweilig lesen von Dyl Vlenspiegel, which appeared anonymously in 1515
in Strassburg and almost certainly draws on older sources now lost, sets out
to give an account of the life and doings of the celebrated Low German
wag and trickster who reputedly died at Mölln in Holstein about 1350. In
spite of the biographical framework, the book, like almost all the genuinely popular prose fiction of the century, is little more than a collection of
Schwänke, many of which had appeared originally in other versions in earlier
anthologies (*Ropuos franches, Pfaffe von Kalemberg,* Poggio's *facetiae,* etc.), and
which are now attributed to Ulenspiegel, either as a deliberate act of book-
making on the part of the author, or by the less conscious process of 'anecdotal accretion', to which all wags and 'originals' are exposed.

Perhaps because he is a peasant's son, Vlenspiegel's pranks have not infrequently been seen rather fancifully as constituting the anecdotal revenge
which the rural population takes on the rest of society for all the humiliation
and mockery to which they were subjected in the literature of the fifteenth
and sixteenth centuries. In spite of his origins, however, Ulenspiegel in fact
belongs to no social class: he is a completely asocial vagabond who wanders
about the Empire living by his wits at the expense of prince and peasant
alike, a victim of the arrogance, greed, and dishonesty of his more settled
fellows and in return exacting a merciless vengeance on both innocent and
guilty. Not that he can be seen simply as a victim of society, however: in the
context of his age he is the personification of the waggery and trickery of the
'fahrendes Volk', the gypsies, wandering scholars, mercenary soldiers, and

'verkrachte Existenzen' of all kinds who constituted a serious social problem and, living outside normal society, were regarded with fascinated anxiety by the settled bourgeoisie. Ulenspiegel views the whole of contemporary society in a negative light and applies his not inconsiderable intelligence to negative and antisocial ends. In this sense he becomes the representative of a cleverness that is ultimately foolish: as the High German version of his name suggests, he holds up a mirror to wisdom and inverts it, and thus in some respects anticipates the more genuine examples of foolish wisdom which the sixteenth century was later to bring forth in the exploits of the Schiltbürger, for instance (cf. p. 232). The equation 'Eulenspiegel' = 'Owl-Glass' may, however, be folk-etymology: 'ulen' in Low German means 'to clean' and 'spegel' means 'rear', 'backside', so that the name may originally simply have anticipated the snooks which Ulenspiegel cocks at the whole of contemporary society from the King of Denmark to the local baker. Occasionally Ulenspiegel's exploits have a satirical point, reminiscent of the picaresque novel, in the mockery of the dishonesty and hypocrisy of some of his victims; in the overwhelming majority of cases, however, the anecdotes are clearly intended simply to amuse and the *Volksbuch* is conspicuously lacking in the didacticism which is so characteristic of literature in the early sixteenth century. The humour is generally unsophisticated and often more than a little crude, proceeding either from a curiously naïve and uninhibited coarseness, usually of an excretory nature, or from Dyl's standard device of taking metaphors and commands literally (passage (a) unites both the coarseness and the literal-mindedness of Dyl). Even when seen in the context of a 'Rabelaisian' century, this coarseness undoubtedly constitutes a barrier for the modern reader. Historically, however, it was not the least of the factors which made the book a best seller which passed through innumerable editions, adaptations, and translations. And even in the more refined atmosphere of the twentieth century, it is difficult not to be captivated by the robust vigour of the hero, or to laugh at the sheer exuberance of such pranks as that recorded in passage (b).

Our text is that published by Johannes Grüninger of Strassburg in 1515.

(a) *Die .XII. history sagt wie vlēspiegel ein meßner ward in einem dorff zů Budensteten | vñ wie der pfarrer in die kirchen schiß | das Vlenspiegel ein bierthunnē da mit gewann.*

Als nun Vlēspiegel in dē dorff eī meßner wz da kūt er nit singē als dā eim sigristē zů gehŏrt. Als nun d' pfaff bereit wz mit eim krutster. Da stůd d' pfaff eīs mals vor dē altar | vnd tet sich an vnd wolt meß halten. Da stund Vlenspiegel hinder im vnnd richtet im sein alb zů recht | da ließ der pfaff ein grossen furtz dz es vber die kirchē erhalt. Da sprach Vlenspiegel herr wie
10 dem | opffern ir das vnserm herren für weyrauch hie vor dem altar | der pfaff sprach. Was fragstu dar nach ist doch die kirch

mein / ich hab die macht wol / das ich mŏcht mitten in die
kirchen scheissen. Vlenspiegel sprach / das gelt euch vnd mir
ein thuñ bierß / ob ir das thŭn. Ja sprach er es gilt wol / vnd
sie wetteten miteinander / vnd der pfaff sprach. Meinstu nit das
ich so frisch sei / vnnd korte sich vmb / vnnd schis einen grossen
hauffen in dye kirchen / vnd sprach. Sich her Custor / ich hab
die thunn bierß gewunnen. Vlenspiegel sprach. Nein herr wir
wŏllen vor messen / ob es mitten in der kirchen sei / als ir dañ
sagten. Also maß es Vlenspiegel / da felet es weit der mitten   20
in der kirchen. Also gewan vlenspiegel die thunnen bierß. Da
ward die kellerin aber zornig vnd sprach. J wŏllen des schalck-
hafftigen knechts nit mŭssig gon / biß das er euch in alle schand
bringt.

*(b) Die XVII histori sagt wie Vlenspiegel alle krancken in
einem spital vff einē tag on artznei gesund macht.*

Vf ein zeit kam Vlenspigel gen Nürnberg / vñ schlŭg groß
brieff an die kirch thūē / vñ an dz rathuß vñ gab sich vß für ein
gŭtē artzet zŭ aller kranckßeit vñ da was ein grosse zal krancker
menschē in dē nüwen spital Da selbst da das hochwirdig heilig   30
sper Cristi mit anderen mercklichē stückē rastē ist Vñ d' selbē
kranckē mēschē d' wer d' spitel meister eins teils gern ledigig
gewesen Vñ het in gesuntheit wol gegund. Also gieng er hin
zŭ Vlēspiegel dē artzet / vnd fragt in nach laut seiner brieff
die er an geschlagē het / ob er dē kranckē also ßelſſen kunt es
solt im wol gelont werdē vlēspiegel d' sprach er wolt in seiner
kräckē vil gerad machē wā er wolt zwei hund' guldē anlegē /
vñ im die zŭ sagē wolt / der spitelmeister sagt im dz gelt zŭ / so
fer er dē kräckē hülff. Also verwilliget sich Vlēspiegel wa er die
kräckē nit grad macht so solt er im nit eī pfennig gebē dz ge-   40
fiel dē spitelmeister wol vñ gab im .xx guldī daruff. Also giēg
vlēspiegel in spital vñ nā zwē knecht mit im / vñ fragt die kräckē /
eī ietlichē wz im gebrest / vñ zŭ letsch wā er vō eim kräcken
gieng so beschwur er in vñ sprach wz ich dir offenbarē wurt das
soltu bei dir heimlich bleibē lassen vō nieman offenbarē das
sagtē dan die siechē vlēspiegel bei grossem glouben zŭ daruff
sagt er dā eim ietlichē bsund' / sol ich nū vch kräcken zŭ gesuntheit helffen vnd vff die füß bringen das ist mir vnmiglich ich
v'bren dā euwer einen zŭ puluer / vnd gib dz den and'n in dē

50 leib zetrincken / dz můß ich thůn. Darumb welcher d' krenckst
vnder euch allen ist vnd nit gō mag / dē wil ich zů puluer ver-
brennē / vff dz ich dē andern helffen mõg damit / euch all
vffzebringē / so würde ich den spytalmeister nemē / vñ in d'
thür des spitals stō vñ mit luter stym rüffen / welcher da nit
kranck ist / d' kū heruß / dz verschlaff du nit. So sprach er zů
ieglichē alleī dañ d' letst můß die ürten bezalen. Solcher sag
nam yeglicher acht / vñ vff den gemeltē tag yltē sie sich mit
kēncken vñ lammē beinē / als keiner d' letst wolt sein. Da nū
Vlenspiegel nach seinē anlaß růffte / da begundē sie von stat
60 lauffen / etlich die in .x. iarē nit vō bet kumen warn vñ da d'
spital nun gantz ler wz / da begert er seines lons von dem spittelmeister / vñ sagt er müst an ein and' end ylens / da gab er im
das gelt zů grossem danck / da reit er hin weg. Aber in dreien
tagen / da kamen die krerckē all herwider vñ beclagten sich
irer kranckheit. Da fragt der spittelmeister. Wie gat das zu /
ich hett in doch den grossen meister zů bracht / der in doch
geholffen het / das sie all selber dauon gangen waren. Da sagten
sie dem spitalmeister / wie dz er in getrouwt het. Welcher der
letste wer zů der thür hinuß wen er der zeit růfft den wolt er
70 verbrennen zů puluer. Da mercket der spitalmeister das es
Vlenspiegels betrug wase Aber er was hinweg vnd er kund im
nüt angewinnen. Also bliben die krancken wider im spital wie
vor / vnd was das gelt verlorn.

(ii) Johannes Pauli: *Schimpf vnd Ernst* (1522)

Johannes Pauli (*c.* 1450–*c.* 1530) belongs to the Alemannic tradition which
had brought forth Sebastian Brant, Geiler von Kaisersberg, and Thomas
Murner. He was a member of the Franciscan order, which had traditionally
cultivated the popular sermon, and as a popular preacher himself it was
perhaps not surprising that he should see in the collection of some 693
preachers' examples, fables, and parables which he published in 1522 under
the title *Schimpf vnd Ernst* a didactic vehicle intended for the betterment and
edification of his readers, for whose benefit he loves to expound the moral
application in a lengthy and—to modern taste—sometimes rather tedious
fashion. As the title suggests, the collection is a *pot-pourri* of stories grave and
gay, although in view of the evident didactic intention, one cannot help
feeling that the *Schimpf* is rather nearer to *Ernst* than the contrasting sub-
titles might lead us to believe. For his day Pauli writes a surprisingly light
German style in which the influence of the oral tradition is evident and tells
his anecdotes with admirable directness and economy. It was, however, as
a storehouse of subject-matter that *Schimpf vnd Ernst* achieved lasting im-

portance, and until well into the following century the anecdotes it contained continued to be plundered, refurbished, and adapted by generations of German writers.

Our text is taken from the edition printed in Strassburg in 1533 by Bartholomeus Grüninger.

Von schimpff das ix.

Wjr leesen von dreiē hanē die zů nacht kreiten. Da die fraw bei dem ehebrecher lag vnd die kellerin in dem hauß die verstůnd der vogel gesang. Der ein han kreiet die erst nacht. Mein fraw ist dem herren vntrew. Das sprach die kellerin zů der frawen. Die fraw sorach / der han můß sterbē vnd der han ward gebraten. Der ander han sang die ander nacht / als die kellerin das außlegt / da sie gefragt ward / da sagt sie / der han het gekreiet. Mein gesel ist gestorben vmb der warheit willē. Die fraw sprach der sol aüch sterben / vnd der ward auch gebraten. Da 10 die fraw bei dem bůlen lag / da kreit der drit Han / als es die kellerin vßlegt. *Audi, uide, tace, si uis uiuere in pace.* Sihe vnd hŏr vñ schweig / wilt du leben inn dem frid.

Von schimpff das xxv.

Nit weit von der Narren kappen / was ein bawr / der hat ein garten / da kam ein haß yn / d' thet jhm vil schaden / als der narr meint. Da bestalt er einen edelman der solt den haßen vertreiben vnd fahen / der edelmank am reiten / vnd bracht fünff oder sechs hund mit jhm / vñ iagt den hasen inn dem garten mit einem grossen geschrey. Der haß entgieng jhnen / er 20 wüscht durch den zaun hinauß / vñ ward jm nit. Diser reüter mit den hunden / thet dem bauren vil me schaden in einer stund / dañ jm der haß in zehen jarē het gethon / noch so wolt sich d' baur rechen an dem haßen / vnd ward jhm dannocht nit. Also sein vil neydiger menschen / die nit wŏllē ablassen vnd verzeihen / sie wŏllen sich rechen / vnnd greiffen Gott in seinen gewalt / dem da zů gehŏrt zů rechen / vnd wann sie es lang machen / so thůnd sie jnen selbs den grŏsten schaden / vnd gaht jhnen als dem Aman / der Mardocheo ein galgen ließ machen / vnd ward er daran gehenckt. Also aüch / es grebt 30 einer eim ein grůben / vnd felt er selber darein / vnd wañ sie schon dem weltlichen richter entlauffen / der sie nit straffet / so mŏgen sie doch dem gewalt gottes nit entlauffen / der sie straffen

würt / das sie jhm in seinen gewalt gegriffen haben / Psal.
Mihi vineictam &c.

Von ernst das cxxi.

Man lißt vō einem edelmā / der was ein ampt man / ein richter
inn einer statt / der niemans übersach / vnnd was nach Gottes
grechtigkeit hiesch / dem gieng er nach. Vnd vff ein zeit ward
40 er kranck / da er also an dem bet lag da hort er ein dochter
ein iunckfraw schreien. Er fragt seinen diener einen / d' da für
gieng warumb die dochter also geschrwē het / er wolt es wissen.
Der knecht sprach / euwer vetter / euwers brůders sůn hat mit
jhr geschimpfft &c. Der edelman verstůd es wol / vnd nam ein
brotmesser / vnd legt es vnder das küssin / vff ein mal erblickt
er in / da er für die kamer anhin gieng / er rüffet im vnd hieß
jhn zů jhm komen / vnd er kam zů jm / vnd er truckt jn an sein
brust stach im das messer zů dem rucken hinin in das hertz / vnd
stach jn zů tod / vnd stieß in vō im / vnd hieß in vergraben.
50 Vnd sin siechtagen namen zů / drumb begert er zů beichten /
vnd das Sacraments. Der priester kam vnd hort jhn beicht / der
edelman beichtet mit grosser andacht / er gedacht aber des
todsschlags nit. Der priester saget / ob er den todschlag den er
gethon het nit auch beichtē wolt. Der edelmā sprach ich hab
es für kein sünd / was sol ich daran bichtē. Der priester sprach /
so wil ich euch das Sacrament nit geben. Der edelman sprach /
ich habs nit von neid gethon / mir ist nie kein knab lieber
gewesen dañ der allein / ich hab es in strafs weiß gethon. Der
priester wolt im das Sacrament nit geben / vnd trůgs wider
60 hinweg / vnd da er zů der thür kam / da růfft jhm der edelman
wider vnnd sprach / herr sehen mir inn den mund / da lag im
das Sacrament vff der zungen vnd sprach / den jhr mir nit
haben wóllen geben / der hat sich mir selber geben. Darinn
mag man auch erkennen wie Gott in gerechten richtern ein
wolgefallē hat / vnd sie lieb hat.

(iii) Jörg Wickram: *Das Rollwagenbůchlin* (1555)

Pauli's anecdotes were a didactic means to a moral end; the importance of
Wickram's *Rollwagenbůchlin* of 1555 lies in its emancipation of the *Schwank*
from didacticism. As the title suggests, the stories were intended simply as
light entertainment to beguile the tedium of contemporary travel and, in
spite of the *Vlenspiegel-Volksbuch* and the verse *Schwänke* of Hans Sachs, this

view of literature as entertainment was still sufficiently novel to ensure for Wickram's collection of jokes a startling success which naturally led to the appearance of numerous imitations. Wickram's stories are brief almost to a fault and are told with evident good humour in a German which in its straightforward simplicity is in striking contrast to the often involved style and somewhat pretentious diction of his other prose works (cf. p. 200). Some of the anecdotes have dated badly and to modern taste are not only crude, but pointless; in the main, however, they are as effective as ever, revealing a sharp eye for the incongruities and absurdities of human behaviour and making few demands on the reader other than a readiness to be amused.

Our text is taken from the edition of 1555, which appeared without imprint.

Von einem der Håring feil hat.

Ein junger Kauffman fůrt Håring auß Brabant in dz Oberlandt / wie er aber seiner schätz nit wol warname oder die Håring sunst überfůrt wurden / oder villicht mer acht hette zů schönen frauwen / dañ zů seinem handel / kan ich nit wissen ja in suma das er ein merckliche summa gelt auff die selbig reyß verlorn hett / also das er schier nit wider heim zů hauß dorfft kummen / vnnd also in einem grossen traurē vñ vnmůt zoch er zů fůß über feld heimwertz / vnnd auff der straß traff er vngeferd ein gar übelgemacht vnnd vngestalt Crucefix an / stůnd also ein 10 wenig still den Herrgott an zů schauwen sein ellend vñ verlust zů betrachten / zůletst spricht er auß einfalt oder auß grossem vnmůt den er hette / ach du lieber Herrgott wañ du auch Håring hettest feyl gehapt so küntestu nicht wol übeler sehen.

Von einem einfaltigen Bauren.

Ein einfaltiger Baur kame in ein kirchen vnd alß er das bild Christi darinn geschnitzlet fande / mit vil blůtstropffen übermalt alß ob er gegeiselt wåre / vnnd er ein groß mittleiden mit vnserm Herrgott hette / bettet er ein vatter vnser vñ sprach zů letst / Ach lieber Herrgott laß dirs ein witzgůg sein / vnnd kum 20 nit mer vnder die schnöden bösen Juden.

Von einem der ein fürsprechen vber listet / vnd hett jn der fürsprech das selbs gelert.

Ejner ward vor dem gericht vmb ein sach angesprochen / des er sich wol versach / er wurde on gelt nicht daruon komen / das klagt er einem fürsprechē / oder redner / der sprach zů jm: Jch will dir zůsagen auß der sach zů helffen vnnd on allen kosten

vnd schaden daruon bringē / so ferne du mir wilt vier gulden
zů lon für mein arbeit gebē. Diser war zů friden vnd versprach
30 jm die vier gulden / so verne er jm auß der sach hulffe zů geben.
Also gab er jm den radt wañ er mit jm für das gericht keme so
solt er kein ander antwort geben / God geb was man jn fragt
oder schalt dañ das einig wort / blee. Do sie nun für das gericht
kamen / vnnd vil auff diesen geklagt ward / kunt man kein
ander wort auß jm bringen dañ blee. Also lachten die Herrn
vnd sagten zů seinem fürsprechen: Was wŏlt jr vō seinet wegē
antwortē? Sprach der fürsprech / ich kā nichts für jn reden dann
er ist ein Narr vñ kan mich auch nichts berichten das ich reden
sol / es ist nichts mit jm anzůfahen / er sol billich für ein Narren
40 gehalten vnd ledig gelassen werden. Also wurden die Herrn
zů rath vñ liessen jn ledig / darnach hiesch jm der fürsprech die
vier gulden. Do sprach diser blee. Der fürsprech sprach / du
wirst mir das nit abblehen ich will mein gelt haben / vnnd bot
jm für das gericht. Vñ als sie beide vor dem gericht stunden /
sagt diser alweg blee. Do sprachen die Herrn zum fürsprechē /
Was macht jr mit dē Narren / wist ir nit dz er nit reden kan?
Also můst der redner das wort Blee für seine vier guldē zůlon
han / vñ traff vntrew jren eygen Herrn.

(iv) Das Lalebuch (1597)

The *Lalebuch*, the account of the *Wunderseltzame / Abentheurliche / vnerhörte /
vnd bißher vnbeschriebene Geschichten vnd Thaten der Lalen zu Laleburg* appeared
anonymously in 1597 and was almost immediately superseded by a pirated and somewhat extended version in which the name of Laleburg
was changed to Schilda, the Lalebürger correspondingly becoming Schiltbürger, a name under which they were to enjoy perennial popularity down
to the children's programmes on German television. The theme of the
Lalebuch, the mockery of a given group of people who are particularized
either in terms of their occupation or in terms of the place they live, is a very
ancient one: the Abdera of ancient Greece is the best-known example—
largely, at least for German readers, because of Wieland's treatment of it in
Die Abderiten. As in most popular fiction in the sixteenth century, the
approach is essentially episodic, although like the author of *Vlenspiegel* the
author gives his *Schwanksammlung* a superficial 'biographical' framework by
offering us a chronicle of the fortunes of his collective hero from the founding
of their community until it is ultimately destroyed and dispersed as the
result of a fire. The Lalen were originally very wise and assumed foolishness
simply as a device to protect themselves from being constantly called on to
act as advisers in foreign lands. In time, however, the assumed role becomes
reality, and the Lalebürger come to constitute a community of fools whose

foolishness ultimately destroys the body politic it was intended to preserve. (The fire is started by the Lalen themselves in order to kill a cat they mistakenly believe to be a fierce carnivore.) The viewpoint of Ulenspiegel is thus reversed: Ulenspiegel is an amoral wag, the intelligent outsider who exploits his intelligence in order to live off his settled and slower-witted fellows. The Lalen are, by contrast, the slow-witted and settled community whose foolishness exposes them to every smart alec who happens along (such a one sells them the cat), but whose foolishness is a misconceived device calculated to achieve a moral aim—the peaceful preservation of the society in which they live. Inevitably the Lalen thus achieve a serious, at times almost tragic, quality which the resilient Ulenspiegel lacks. The satirical elements too are more pronounced than in the *Vlenspiegel-Volksbuch* and, since the keynote of the *Lalebuch* is collective responsibility (they never tire of holding meetings and conducting public inquiries), the satire often assumes political overtones.

The purpose of the politically oriented satire in the *Lalebuch* has variously been interpreted by Marxist critics as an expression of frustrated impotence on the part of the author, who thus protests against the territorial princes who have allegedly robbed municipal governments of political power and left them with only empty democratic forms. Liberal critics, on the other hand, have seen in the absurdity of the Lalen a serious warning of the dangers inherent in any democratic community. It is, however, questionable whether the author is quite such a good democrat as such interpretations assume him to be: he obviously has experience of the workings of committees and councils and goes out of his way to mock the long-windedness of his democrats (cf. passage (*a*)), their desire to have meals at the public expense, etc., and a considerable portion of his book is devoted to the way the democrats of Laleburg elect the most unsuitable person to the highest office (the local swineherd becomes *Schultheiß* and several stories play on his ludicrously inflated sense of his own dignity). Yet it is probably a mistake to see the Lalen primarily in political terms. In the first place, for all its chronicle framework, the *Lalebuch* is essentially a collection of anecdotes, many of which were in common currency long before 1597 and have continued to enjoy popularity down to our own day (the present writer first met the story told in passage (*b*) in the guise of two Lancashire tacklers—traditionally held to be especially stupid—who chalked a cross on the floor of their boat to mark a spot where the fish seemed to bite particularly well!), and there can be little doubt that contemporary readers were delighted with the book simply because it brought together a variety of amusing tales rather than because they saw in it a political allegory. Further, in so far as the author is concerned to advance a 'moral', his stated aim is to exemplify the rather obvious platitudes that habit is second nature, that even the greatest gift will be lost unless practised frequently, that too much intelligence and too little intelligence can be equally harmful, and that the too rigorous application of the cleverest idea can constitute an act of folly— whether it be the misapplication of the 'scientific method' in passage (*a*) or the Lalebürgers' original stratagem of assuming foolishness as a means of self-defence.

In spite of its late appearance, in content and form, in its rather flat-footed didacticism and its unsophisticated humour, the *Lalebuch* is a true child of the sixteenth century.

Our text is taken from the edition of 1597, which appeared under a fictitious imprint.

(a) *Wie die Lalen rhatschlugen | das Liecht in jhr Rhathauß zu tragen.*

Als nun der bestim̄ete Rhats Tag kommen | erschienen die Lalen fleissig | also daß keiner außblieb | dann es jhnen allen gegolten | vnd setzten sich. Es hat aber jeder ein angezůndtē Liechtspan mit sich gebracht | vn̄ denselbē | nach dem sie nider gesessen | auff sein Hut gesteckt | damit sie in dem finstern Rhathauß einandern sehen | vnd der Schultheß einem jeden in der vmbfrag kônte seinen Namen vnd Titul geben. Da nu die
10 gemeine vmbfrag gethan wurde | wessen man sich in fůrgefal-lenem handel zu verhalten | fielen viel widerwertige meinungen: wie gemeinlich in zweyffeligen Håndeln pflegt zugeschehen.

Vnd als es sich schier ansehen ließ | als wôlte das mehrste werden | daß man den gantzē Baw wider auff den bodē ab brechen | auff ein newes auffführen | vnd besser sorge haben solte: trat einer | welcher wie er zuvor vnter allen der aller weyseste gewesen | also wolt er jetzund als der aller thorech-tigste sich erzeigen | herfůr | vn̄ sprach: Er habe in wårender seiner Weißheit | eh er sich derselbē verziegen | offtmaln gehôrt |
20 daß man durch Exempel vnd Beyspiel vil lehren | lehrnen vnd ergreiffen kônne. Daher dann der Aesopus seine Lehren durch Fabeln | in gestalt kurtzer Historiē | fůr Augē stellen wôllen. Solchem nach | wolle er auch ein Geschicht erzellen | so sich mit seiner liebē Großmutter Großvatters Bruders Sons Frawen begeben vnd zugetragen habe.

Meiner Großmuter Großvatters Bruders Sohn | Vtis ge-heissen | hôret auff ein zeit von einem | daß er sagt: Ey wie sind die Rephůner so gut. Hastu dan̄ geessē | sprach meiner Großmuter Großvatters Bruders Sohn | dz du es so wol weist?
30 Nein | sagt der ander: aber es hat mirs einer vor fůnfftzig jarē gesagt | deßn Großmutter Großvatter sie inn seiner Jugend hat sehen von einem Edelman̄ essen. Auß anlaß solcher rede | stieß meiner Großmuter Großvatters Bruders Sohn ein Kindbettern gelust an | daß er gern etwas gutes essen môchte | sagt deßhalben zu seinem Weybe | Vdena geheissen | sie solte jhm Kůchlin

bachen: dann Rephûner kont er nicht haben / so wuste er
bessers nicht / als Kûchlin. Sie aber / als deren was das Butter-
hâfelin vermôgens were besser als jhme bewust gewesen /
entschuldiget sich: sie kônne jhm auß mangel des Butters /
Anckens oder Schmaltzes (wie du wilt) auff diß mal keine 40
Kûchlin bachen / bate jhn derowegen biß auff ein andere zeit
der Kûchlin halb geduld zuhaben. Aber meiner Großmuter
Großvatters Bruders Son hatte hiemit keine Kûchlin geessen /
vnd seinen Gelust nicht gebûsset / wolte sich mit so schlechtem /
magerem / dûrren / trockenem / vngesaltzenē vnd vngeschmal-
tzenem bescheid / nit also schlechtlich abweysen lassen / sprach
derowegen nachmaln: Wie die sach jmmer beschaffen were /
das Anckenhâfelin belangend / so solte sie sehen / daß sie jhm
Kûchlin bachete: vnd hette sie nit Butter oder schmaltz / so
solte sie es mit wasser versuchen. Es thuts nit / mein Vtis / 50
sprach die Fraw Vdena: ich selbst wollte sonst so lang nit ohne
Kûchlin geblieben sein / weil ich mich das Wasser nicht hette
bedauren lassen. Du weist es nit / sprach meiner Großmuter
Großvatters Bruders Sohn / weil du es niemaln versuchet hast.
Versuche es erstlich: vnd so es nicht wil gerhaten / magst du
als dañ wol sprechen / es thue es nicht.

Mit einē wort zusagen / wolte meiner Großmuter Großvatters
Sons Fraw ruhe haben vñ zu friedē sein / so muste sie dem Mañ
seines begerens halben willfahren: rhûret derowegen einen
Kûchlin teyg an / gantz dûnn / als ob sie wôlte Streublin ba- 60
chen / setzt ein Pfannen mit Wasser vbers Fewer / vnd mit dem
Teyg dareyn. Mit nichten aber wolt es sich schicken / es wolt
sich eben gar nicht zusamen wallen / daß Kûchlin darauß wurden / dieweil der Teyg im Wasser zerflosse / vnnd ein Muß oder
Brey darauß wurde: darab die Fraw zornig / der Mañ aber leidig ward. Dann sie sahe / daß die Arbeit / Holtz vnnd Mâl /
deß Wasserbutters vngeachtet / verlorē were: so stunde meiner
Großmuter Großvatters seligen Bruders Son darbey / hielt einen
Teller dar / vñ wolte das erstgebachene Kûchlin also warm auß
der Pfannen geessen haben / ward aber betrogen. Botz kramet 70
schem dich / sprach meiner Großmutter Großvatters bruders
Sohns Fraw / guck / habe ich dir nit gesagt / es thue es nicht?
Allzeit wilt du recht haben / vnd weist doch nit ein dinglin
darumb / wie man Kûchlin bachen soll. Schweyg mein Vdena /
sprach meiner Großmuter Großvatters Bruders Sohn / lasse

dichs nicht gerewen / daß du es versuchet hast. Man versucht
ein ding in so vil wege / biß es zu letzt gerahten muß. Jst es
schon dißmals nicht gerhaten / so gerhatets etwan ein ander
mal. Es were ja ein feine nutzliche kunst gewesen / wañ es
80 vngefehr gerhaten wer. Jch mein wol ja / sagt meiner Großmuter Großvatters Bruders Sons Fraw: ich wolt selbs alle tag
Kûchlin geessen habē. Daß ich aber / sprach der obgemelt Lale /
dise Geschicht auff vnser vorhaben ziehe: Wer weist / ob dz
Liecht vñ der tag sich nit in einē Sack tragen liesse / gleich wie
das Wasser in einem Eymer getragen wirt. Vnser keiner hats
jemaln versucht: darum̄ wa es euch gefelt / so wôlln wir dran
stehen. Gerhatet es / so haben wir allzeit vm̄ so vil zum besten /
vñ werden als erfindere diser kunst grosses Lob damit erjagen.
Gehts aber nit ab / so ist es doch zu vnserm vorhaben der
90 Narrey halben gantz dienstlich vnd bequem.

Diser Rhat gefiel allen Lalen solcher massen / dz sie beschlossen / solchem in aller eyle nachzukom̄en. Kamen derowegen
nach mittag / da die Sonne am besten geschienen / bey dem
Eyd gemahnet alle fûr das neuwe Rhathauß / jeder mit einem
Geschirre / damit er vermeint den Tag zufassen vnd hineyn
zutragen. Etliche brachten auch mit sich / Bickel / Schauffeln /
Kârste / Gabeln vñ and's / auff ein fûrsorg / damit ja gar kein
fehler begangen wurde.

So bald nun die glockē eins geschlagen / da solte einer sein
100 wunder gesehen haben / wie sie alle angefangen haben zu
arbeitten. Etliche hatten lange Secke / liessen die Soñe dreyn
scheynē biß auff den boden / knûfften jn dann eylends zu /
vnnd lieffen damit ins Hauß / den Tag außzuschûtten. Ja sie
beredeten sich selberst / sie trûgē an den Secken vil schwerer /
als zuvor da sie lâhr gewesen. Andre theten eben deßgleichen /
mit anderen verdecketen Gefessen / als Hâfen / Kesseln / Zu-
bern / vnd was dergleichen ist. Einer lude den Tag eyn mit
einer Strogabeln in ein Korb / der ander mit einer Schauffeln:
etliche gruben jn auß der Erden herfûr. Eines Lalen soll sonder-
110 lich nicht vergessen werden / welcher vermeint den Tag mit
einer Maußfallen zufangen / vnd also mit gewalt zu bezwingen /
vnd ins Hause zubringen. Dz ichs kurtz mache: jeder hielte
sich da / wie sein nârrischer Kopff es jhme an vnnd eyngab.

Solches trieben sie denselben gantzen tag / weil die Sonne
geschienen / mit solchem eyfer vnnd ernst / daß sie alle darob

ermüdeten / vnd von hitze schier verlechten vnnd erlagen. Aber
sie richteten mit solcher arbeit eben so wenig auß / als vor
zeiten die vngehewren Riesen / da sie viel grosse Berge zuhauffe
trugen / vnd den Hiṁel zustürmen vermeinten. Darumb sie
dann letztlich sprachen: Nun were es doch ein feyne Kunst 120
gewesen / wans gerahten were. Also zogen sie ab / vnd hatten
dennoch diß gewonnen / daß sie dorfften auffs gmeine Gut hin
zum Weyn gehn / vnnd sich wider erquicken vnd erlaben.

(b) *Die Laleburger verbergen jhr Glocken in den See.*

Avff ein zeit als Kriegs geschrey eynfiele / forchten die Lalen
jhrer Haab vnd Gütern sehr / daß jhnen die von den Feinden
nicht geraubt vnd hinweg geführt wurdē: sonderlich aber war
jnen angst für ein Glocken / welche auff jrem Rhathauß hienge /
gedachten man wurd jn dieselb hinweg neṁen / vñ Büchsen
darauß giessen. Also warden sie nach langem rhatschlag eins / 130
dieselb biß zu ende deß Kriegs in dē See zuversencken / vnd sie
alsdañ / wañ der Krieg fürüber / vnnd der Feynd hinweg were /
widerumb herauß zuziehen / vnnd wider auffzuhencken: tragen
sie derowegen in ein Schiff / vnd führens auff den See.
   Als sie aber die Glocke wöllen hinein werffen / sagt einer vngefehr: Wie wöllen wir aber dz ort wider finden / da wir sie auß-
geworffen habē / wañ wir sie gern wider hetten? Da lasse dir /
sprach der Schultheß / kein graw Har im &c. wachsen: gieng
damit hinzu / vnd mit einem messer schneid er eine kerff in dem
schiff an daß ort / da sie die hinauß geworffen / sprechende: 140
Hie bey diesem schnitt wöllen wir sie wider finden. Ward also
die Glocke hinauß geworffen / vñ versenckt. Nach dem aber
der Krieg auß war / fuhren sie wid' vff den see / jr Glockē
zu holē / vñ fandē den kerffschnit an dem Schiffe wol / aber
die Glock konten sie daruṁ nicht finden / noch den ort im
Wasser / da sie solche hineyn gesenckt. Manglen sie also noch
heut diß tages jhrer guten Glocken.

V · THE LYRIC

THE literary Renaissance, which in other European lands produced such an outburst of lyric poetry, largely by-passed Germany, and the German lyric in the sixteenth century tends to be a degenerate descendant of an outworn tradition rather than the expression of a new feeling for life or literature. Yet, for all its degeneracy, the lyric in Germany is perhaps truer to its name than the sophisticated products of a Tasso or a Ronsard in that it was still intended to be sung. The music was what mattered, so that the learned Georg Forster could state openly in his introduction to his *Frische Teutsche Liedlein* of 1539—the biggest anthology of lyrics the century produced—that his purpose had been to publish the melodies rather than the lyrics, and that he had felt himself at liberty to modify and adapt received texts in the interest of the total musical effect.

The German lyric in the sixteenth century falls into three main types: the *Meistergesang*, the folk-song, and the hymn. Both the *Meistergesang* and the folk-song look back to the classical poetry of the Middle High German period for their inspiration. The former was the product of the curious socio-literary phenomenon known as the *Singschulen,* or the lodges of 'Master-singers' who derived ultimately from the medieval lay brotherhoods devoted to the cultivation of choral church music and who sought to apply to the business of poetry a hierarchical structure which was taken over from the trade guilds to which the Singers belonged, the 'school' constituting a sort of literary Rotary Club. The Master-singers' approach to their poetry was above all a formal one governed by a body of complicated prosodic rules which they claimed to derive from the great medieval masters (Walther, Frauenlob, Reinmar, etc.). Excellence lay in the past, in the *Töne* (the metrical and strophic forms) established by the twelve original masters, and although by the mid-fifteenth century the prohibition of new *Töne* was superseded by the demand that a master must have invented a *Ton* of his own, poetry was a matter of knowing and applying the precepts of the *Tabulatur* or rule-book. The esoteric nature of the schools was emphasized by the fact that, originally at least, the poems produced by members were not to be published: they were for private consumption only, being written for the competitions in which they were sung unaccompanied before the members of the school, who appointed judges from amongst their number. In its basic structure the *Meistergesang* retained the tripartite form of the Middle High German lyric: a poem was made up of three stanzas (or occasionally a multiple of three). Each stanza consisted of an *Aufgesang* of two *Stollen*, which had the same metrical structure and were sung to the same melody, and an *Abgesang* of different structure and sung to a different tune, but which in the closing lines returned to the same strophic form as the *Stollen*. In the school the songs were usually on a serious, preferably religious, subject, but as well as this serious *Wettsingen*, the schools also held sessions known as *Zechsingen* in the local hostelries, in which a somewhat more earthy tone prevailed.

By contrast with the pedantic exclusiveness and complicated prosody of the *Meistergesang*, the folk-song, as befits a popular genre, was possessed of a certain naïve spontaneity and basic simplicity. Sentences tend to be short, verse and sense to coincide, and assonance and rhyme are equally acceptable. The metrical structure is relatively uncomplicated for the most part: rhyming couplets, usually of three or four stresses, or lines rhyming alternately are the rule, while rhymeless lines (*Waisen*) facilitate improvisation. Metrical irregularities are common, but in the context of songs intended to be sung are not so disturbing as they would be in poems intended for reading or recitation. The Romantic fiction that the folk-song was a spontaneous product of the *Volksseele* has long been exploded: often the 'reiter gut' or the 'gut gesell' who composed it 'signed' his work by mentioning himself, even if not by name, in the last stanza. The oral tradition, depending as it did on the melody rather than the sense, inevitably led to a progressive distortion (*Zersingen*) of the original texts, however, and thus enabled the *Volk* in an indirect way to set its seal on them, so that Georg Forster's cavalier approach to his texts was not quite so inappropriate as might appear at first sight. The other traditional fiction associated with the folk-song, that it flourished in the sixteenth century as never before, is based on the fact that it was only now, with the development of the printing industry, that anthologies began to appear in large numbers, so that often the oldest known version of a given song dates from the sixteenth century. The song itself is often considerably older, of course; indeed, many of the songs clearly derive directly from the *Minnesang*, so that a large measure of their historical interest lies in their function as purveyors of *gesunkenes Kulturgut*, in their vulgarization of the classic themes of the medieval lyric. Drinking songs, ballads, and songs commemorating historical events notwithstanding, the folk-song's principal concern is with love, and many of the stock situations of the *Minnesang* recur: the lovers still part at dawn on hearing the warning cry of the watchman, the *merkaere* still survives in the malicious, gossiping *klaffer*, and not infrequently the lady is unmoved by the lover's song and rejects him for another. The stock medieval types have been demoted socially: the aristocratic knight is now a journeyman, a peasant lad, or a student, and the noble lady has reverted to a 'feins brauns megtlein', but the same tendency to stock epithets is very evident: flowers are usually red, valleys deep, mountains high, lips red, and eyes clear. Stock formulas also occur frequently, especially in the *Natureingänge* ('Gar schön blüt uns der meye', 'Entlaubet ist der Waldt', etc.) and in the standard conclusion, where the lover shrugs off his—usually unhappy—relationship with his lady and sets off on his travels ('So gesegne dich got, mein feines lieb, iez far ich ins elend', 'Alde, ich far dohin', etc.).

But perhaps the most characteristic feature of these songs— a reflection no doubt of the manner of their transmission—lies in what Herder in another context describes as 'Sprünge und Würfe', in their lack of a strictly coherent or organic structure. One stanza, one sentence even, does not necessarily follow on from or have any obvious relationship with its predecessor, and it is frequently left to the reader to establish for himself what the connection really is. Often there probably never was a logical connection; outright contradictions are not unknown, and the song frequently consists of two or more stanzas which originally belonged to different poems but which, because they used the same metre, dealt with the same sort of topic, and could be sung to the same tune, have been brought together more or less fortuitously. This points to what is probably the most important single fact about these songs, namely that their appeal is above all to the *Gemüt*—to the sentiment rather than to the intellect. They do not express the personal outlook, joy, or anguish of the writer, but set out to evoke the generality of the emotion, and it was precisely this irrationality and the capacity to reflect mood rather than thought or event that conferred on them a popularity which has survived into the age of radio and gramophone.

In the midst of the anthologies of folk-songs, the publication of Jacob Regnart's *Kurtzweilige Teutsche Lieder, nach Art der Neapolitanischen oder Welschen Villanellen* in 1576 strikes a somewhat discordant note: the very title seems to announce the arrival of those foreign influences which were finally to bring the German lyric into line with that of Italy and France. Significantly, Regnart was of Dutch origin, and it was via Holland that the Renaissance was to be imported into Germany in the next century. The sorrows of love are still the principal theme of Regnart's *Gesellschaftslieder* (so called because of their popularity amongst fashionable society), but in the intellectual manner in which this theme is treated the poems are far removed from the emotive atmosphere of the folk-song. As the title suggests, Regnart uses Italian verse forms, especially the tercet, and it is in their concern with form, in the careful logic of their argument, in their preference for dialectics rather than *Stimmung*, in their love of antithesis, word-play, and also in a certain coquettishness, that Regnart's songs may be regarded as the precursors of a type of poetry which was to come to full fruition in the next century in the writings of Opitz and his successors.

Interesting and remarkable as Regnart's experiments undoubtedly were, it was not in his pre-baroque verses, but in the Protestant hymn that the German lyric was to find its most important expression in the sixteenth century. The hymns of Luther and his imitators have a twofold importance: they are often remarkable literary products in their own right, but they also constituted a formidable ideological weapon which—often subliminally—carried the evangelical teaching into the hearts and minds of men, and probably did more to establish the new faith there than many a more pretentious piece of writing. As the learned Jesuit Conzenius remarked: 'Luther's songs have killed more souls than all his books and sermons.'

There were, of course, hymns in German long before Luther's day, but the Protestant Reformation gave a heightened importance and status to the hymn as such, and in this field as in so many others even spurred the Roman Church to emulate the Protestant example. Luther was possessed of an instinctive feeling for poetry and considerable musical talents (traditionally he is held to have composed the tunes for many of his hymns), and with the example of his beloved Psalter before him it was inevitable that he should regard the hymn with special favour. As early as 1523 he was calling on German poets to supply religious songs which would provide an alternative to the 'fleischliche Gesänge und Buhllieder' of the day and at the same time correct the often unacceptable theology of the older Catholic hymns. Further, the very nature of the Protestant service, with its emphasis on corporate worship rather than priestly action, was calculated to give the singing of hymns by the congregation a very special role in the life of the Church. Until they established themselves, the hymns continued to be sung by the choir only, but it is not accidental that the Germans describe Luther's hymns as 'Gemeindelieder'. Even where they draw on personal experience, they are clearly designed as community songs: the characteristic pronoun form in them is the first person plural, and their strength lies precisely in their capacity to express communal religious experience.

At first Luther's call to the German poets to write hymns fell on deaf ears and as so often he was compelled to set the example others might follow. In 1524, as a result of his collaboration with the professional musician Johann Walther, there appeared two collections of hymns, the *Achtliederbuch*, containing four hymns by Luther, and the *Geystliches gesangk Büchleyn*, in which twenty-four of the thirty-two hymns were again from Luther's pen. Over the years these were added to, so that the *Geystliche Lieder* of 1545 contained no less than a hundred and five hymns, of which Luther had written thirty-six. Altogether some forty-one hymns are attributed to him. Without exception they are designed expressly as vehicles for the evangelical teaching: occasionally they are no more than rather clumsy versified expositions of Lutheran doctrines, but in the best examples Luther shows a surprising range of tone, and his hymns have seldom been surpassed—no matter whether he sets out to express naïve wonder at the mystery of Christmas, as in the children's carol *Vom himel hoch da kom ich her*, or to capture in verse the stalwart manly strength and Christian confidence which are at the heart of his faith, as in the famous paraphrase of Psalm 46, *Ein feste burg ist unser Gott*. For preference Luther tends to adapt the text of the Psalms (12, 67, 124, etc.) or the Bible (Luke 2, Rev. 12), but not uncommonly he translates traditional Latin hymns or refurbishes older translations (*Veni sancte spiritus, In media vita in morte sumus*), and very occasionally adapts secular folk-songs to his religious purpose. Equally, we find a number of original compositions, like the fine ballad on the death of the first Protestant martyrs in Brussels in 1523, or the celebrated *Erhalt uns, Herr, bey deinem Wort*. Luther's intention was to write religious folk-songs and accordingly he was concerned, as in his translation of the New Testament, to write real German: new-fangled courtly expressions were to be avoided, 'Text und Noten, Akzent, Weisen und Gebärden müssen aus rechter Muttersprachen und Stimme kommen'. As folk-songs, the hymns are characterized by a simplicity of diction which not infrequently confers on them a uniquely rugged quality: monosyllables predominate, the thoughts are brief and clear, and although he not infrequently simply alternates stressed and unstressed syllables, normally the verses follow the natural rhythm of German speech. Even more important than Luther's individual achievement as a poet-musician, however, is the fact that his outwardly modest stock of hymns acted as a model for other writers, and thus inaugurated that characteristic alliance between the Lutheran Church and choral music which was ultimately to culminate in the cantatas and oratorios of Bach and Händel.

1. Secular poems

(i) *Von einem Einsidel vnd seinem hônigkrug*

Von einem Einsidel vnd seinem hônigkrug is a characteristic example of the *Meistergesang*, written in the later part of the century by an unknown author for the edification of his fellow *Meistersinger*. For all its poetic pretensions, it is little more than an exercise in prosody, a rendering of a suitably moral story into rhymed verse which, in spite of the metrical structure, remains essentially prosaic. The subject-matter is not taken from religious history, but from the secular bible of the age, the collection of ancient oriental fables and anecdotes entitled *Buch der Beispiele der alten Weisen*, usually known in English as the *Fables of Bidpai*. While our story is thus of great antiquity and perennial popularity, it was not the hermit who was destined finally to establish it in Europe, but his latter-day descendant, the milkmaid immortalized by La Fontaine in *La Laitière et le Pot au Lait*.

Our text is somewhat unusual in that it was one of the few *Meisterlieder* to appear in print, being published by Friedrich Gutknecht of Nürnberg about 1580. It was written, as the title-page tells us, 'im Speten thon'. This 'Ton' may be characterized as follows. Lines vary in length; those with eight or nine syllables have four stresses and end in a masculine rhyme, those with eleven syllables have five stresses and end in a feminine rhyme. The *Aufgesang* is made up of two *Stollen* of four lines rhyming 4a, 4a, 4a, 5b+, 4c, 4c, 4c, 5b+ (+ = feminine rhyme). The *Abgesang* of seven lines rhymes 5d+, 5d+, 5e+, 4f, 4f, 4f, 5e+, the last four lines having the same metre and rhyming scheme as the *Stollen*.

Von einem Einsidel vnd seinem hônigkrug

Jm Buch der alten Weisen las / ich wie das ein Einsidel was /
der inn eim finstern holtze sas / vñ samlet das wild hônig in
dem Waldt.
Als er des vil gesamlet het / inn ein jrden Krug er das thet /
vnd hienge jn vber sein beth / vnd frewet sich des Hônigs manichfalde.
Eins mals erwachet er nach miternachte / vnd in den hertzen
sein also gedachte / mein Hônig das gûlt mir fûnff gûlden geren /
darumb kaufft ich der schaff fûnff par / die trûgen Lemer / alle   10
Jar / ehe siben jar verlûffen zwar / wurden jr sechs hundert vñ
viertzig weren.

2

Also nem ich in Reichthumb auff / der schaff ich den eins teils
verkauff / vnd richt mich nach der Welte lauff / kauff Ecker
heuser felder vnd die wisen.
Vnd ein ehrlich Haußhalten treib / nem mir darnach ein

schônes Weib / die gebirt mir auß jrem leib / ein schônen Son
das môcht ich wol geniessen.

Das ich nach meinem todt lies einen Samen / dardurch
20 außpraitet wûrd mein gschlecht vñ namen / daruon nach folget
mir groß lob vñ ehre / nach dem gedacht er widerumb / vnd
wûr mein Sun bôß tholl vñ thuṁ / schalckhaftig lesterlich
vnfruṁ / vñ wolt nit folgen meiner weissen lehre.

3

So wolt ich jn zûchtigen fein / darmit zucket er den stecken
sein / zu zeygen jm selber allein / wie hart er wolt dem Sun sein
haut ergerben.

Die krucken er gar hoch auff zug / vñ nider auff das bethe
schlug / vñ draf ob jm den hônig krug / das er zerstûcket sich zu
kleinen scherben.

30 Das Hônig auff jn in das bethe runne / als er von dem anschlag
nit mer gewunne / denn das er sich sampt dem bethgwandt
muß waschen. also auff schlegt jm mancher man / jm hertzen
sein ein gûldē kron / on allen grund auff eitel wan / nach
kurtzer zeit ligt all sein freud im aschen.

(ii) *Danheuser*

The received version of the Tannhäuser legend, as represented by our folk-
ballad of about 1530, draws on much older traditions and represents the
somewhat uneasy fusion of three distinct themes: (1) a basic pre-Christian,
Celtic story of adventures in the Otherworld inside a hollow hill, which—in
what is probably already a later addition to the original story—is ruled over
by a fay queen who suborns mortals to go and live with her; (2) a standard
medieval story of a 'great penitent' (cf. Gregorius, Theophilus, Robert the
Devil) who, having covered himself with terrible sins, in this case impurity
and apostasy, could still by faith and penance receive the grace of God;
(3) a swingeing attack on the person of Pope Urban IV (1261–4), whose
gratuitous cruelty and contumely towards the penitent Tannhäuser are
rebuked by the introduction of the not uncommon legend of the miraculous
blossoming of the staff.

It is uncertain exactly why Tannhäuser was chosen to figure in this context, yet the choice is by no means an inappropriate one. Very little is known
about the historical Tannhäuser (*c.* 1205–*c.* 1270), beyond that he achieved
a certain fame, together with Neidhart von Reuental, as an exponent of
'höfische Dorfpoesie', but tradition has it that he led a somewhat immoral,
picaresque type of existence, before repudiating the errors of his wild youth,
and it has even been suggested that he may have participated in the quarrels
of the Hohenstauffen with the papacy—and with Urban IV. However that
may be, legend early seized upon his name and associated it with a sojourn
in the realm of the Goddess of Love, partly because he was said to have

spent some time in Cyprus, the legendary birth-place of Venus, where he may have been wrecked in the course of a voyage to the Holy Land.

In adapting a pious legend for polemical purposes, the anonymous author of our poem has been compelled to do serious violence to the original and change it from a tale of redemption to a tale of apparent damnation: in order to drive home the enormity of the Pope's attitude, God is not allowed to intervene effectively until Tannhäuser is safely back in the *Venusberg*—to the peril of his immortal soul. It should, however, be pointed out that the return to the magic mountain was also a common element of the Celtic tradition, and that both the Dutch and the Low German versions seem to envisage the possibility of redemption even after the return, as indeed our version almost does in stanza 23. The conflict between the original tale of redemption and the damnation necessitated by the anti-papal polemic has not, in fact, been completely resolved. The central episode of the blossoming staff clearly implies redemption, and stanza 23 tells us that it is God who is sending Tannhäuser back to the mountain, and we can scarcely assume that, even in an age which inclined to a mechanistic view of the sacraments, God was held to have willed the damnation of a penitent sinner. Yet such lines as 'O Got von hymel sey dir klagt Muß jch nun von dir scheyden' and 'ewigklich on ende'—assuming that they do have precise meaning and are not used simply to fill in the stanza—seem to mean that, even if Tannhäuser is not damned, he will have to pass the rest of eternity in a sort of erotic limbo.

Problems and inconsistencies of this kind are an inevitable consequence of the genesis of the work and the manner of its transmission, and although they may exercise the modern reader, they do not seem to have worried the contemporary public unduly: our ballad enjoyed great popularity and earned itself a place in many anthologies, as well as being republished frequently in broadsheet form.

Our text is that published by Kunegund Hergotin of Nürnberg about 1530. As a relatively late version, it shows a number of corrupt readings, and at times a metrical roughness, which are probably a reflection of the oral tradition from which the poem derives.

Nun wil jch aber heben an   1
Von dem Danheuser zů singen
Vnd was er hat wunders gethan
Mit seyner fraw Venußinne.

Danheuser was ein Ritter gůt   2
Wann er wolt wunder schawen
Er wolt in fraw Venus berg
Zů andern schônen frawen.

Herr Danheuser jr seyt mir lieb   3
Daran solt jr mir gedencken
Jr habt mir eynen ayd geschworn
Jr wôlt von mir nicht wencken.

4   Fraw Venus das enhab jch nit
     Jch wil das widersprechen
     Vnd redt das yemand mer dann jr
     Got helff mirs an jm rechen.

5   Herr Danheuser wie redt jr nun
     Jr solt bey mir beleyben
     Jch wil euch meyn gespilen geben
     Zů eynem ståten weybe.

6   Vnd nem jch nun ein ander weyb
     Jch hab in meynen sinnen
     So můst jch in der hellen glůt
     Auch ewigklichen prinnen.

7   Jr sagt mir vil von der hellen glůt
     Vnd habt es doch nie empfunden
     Gedenckt an meynen roten mund
     Der lachet zů allen stunden.

8   Was hilfft mich ewer roter mund
     Er ist mir gar vnmere
     Nun gebt mir vrlaub Frewlein zart
     Durch aller frawen ehre.

9   Herr Danheuser wŏlt jr vrlaub han
     Jch will euch keynen geben
     Nun bleybet Edler Danheuser
     Vnd fristet ewer leben.

10   Mein leben das ist worden kranck
     Jch mag nicht lenger bleyben
     Nun gebt mir vrlaub frewlein zart
     Von ewrem stoltzen leybe.

11   Herr Danheuser nicht redet also
     Jr thůt euch nicht wol besinnen
     So gehen wir in ein kåmmerlein
     Vnd spilen der edlen minne.

12   Gebrauch jch nun ein frembdes weib
     Mich dunckt in meynem sinne
     Fraw Venus edle Frawe zart
     Jr seyt ein Teuffelinne.

Herr Danheuser was redt jr nun   13
Das jr mich gynnet schelten
Nun solt jr lenger herinnen seyn
Jr mûstet des offt entgelten.

Fraw Venus vnd das wil jch nit   14
Jch mag nit lenger bleyben
O Jesu Christ von hymelreych
Nun hilff mir von den weyben.

Herr Danheuser jr solt vrlaub han   15
Meyn lob das solt jr preysen
Wo jr da in dem land vmb fart
Nembt vrlaub von dem greysen.

Do schied er wider auß dem berg   16
Jn jamer vnd in rewen
Jch wil gen Rom wol in die Stat
Auff eynes Bapstes trawen.

Nun far jch frôlich auff die ban   17
Got mûß seyn ymmer walten
Zû eynem Bapst der heist Vrban
Ob er mich môcht behalten.

Ach Bapst lieber herre meyn   18
Jch klag euch meyne sünde
Die jch mein tag begangen hab
Als ich euchs wil verkûnden.

Jch bin gewesen auch ein jar   19
Bey Venus eyner Frawen
So wolt jch beicht vnd bûß empfahen
Ob jch môcht Got anschawen.

Der Bapst het ein steblin in der hand   20
Das was doch also dûrre
Als wenig als es grûnen mag
Kumbstu zû Gottes hulde.

Nun solt jch leben nur ein jar   21
Ein jar auff diser erden
So wolt jch beicht vnd bûß empfahen
Vnd Gottes trost erwerben.

22   Da zoch er wider auß der Stat
           Jn jamer vnd in leyden
           O Got von hymel sey dir klagt
           Můß jch nun von dir scheyden.

23   Er zoch da wider in den berg
           Vnd ewigklich on ende
           Jch wil zů Venus meyner frawen zart
           Wo mich Got wil hin sende.

24   Seyt Got wilkum̃en Danheuser
           Jch hab ewer lang emporen
           Seyt Got wilkumen mein lieber herr
           Zů eynem bůlen außerkoren.

25   Das weret biß an den dritten tag
           Der stab hůb an zů grůnen
           Der Bapst schickt auß in alle land
           Wo Danheuser wer hin kummen.

26   Do was er wider in den berg
           Vnd het seyn lieb außerkoren
           Des můß der vierdte Bapst Vrban
           Auch ewigklich seyn verloren.

                              Gedruckt zů Nůrnberg durch
                              Kunegund Hergotin.

(iii) *Ejn meidlein zu dem brunnen gieng*

Ejn meidlein zu dem brunnen gieng, like the next three poems also, is taken from
Georg Forster's anthology of lyrics and music generally known as *Frische
Teutsche Liedlein*. Each of the five parts of the anthology has a different title:
the first and fourth of our poems are taken from the *Discantus Des andern
theyls | viler kurtz-weyliger frischer Teutscher Liedlein* (Nürnberg, Johann vom
Berg, 1559), the second and the third from *Der dritte teyl | schöner | lieblicher |
alter | vnd newer Teutscher Liedlein (Tenor)* (no imprint, 1559). Forster (c. 1500–
68) was a friend of Luther and Melanchthon and at Luther's request set the
Psalms to music, but it is for his collection of folk-songs that he is chiefly
remembered. As a musician of some standing, Forster is above all interested
in the tunes to which his folk-song texts were sung: in the introduction to his
first volume he states that his main reason for going into print is to save
traditional melodies from oblivion and to serve 'die edel Music' which, with
Luther, he regards as the noblest and most innocent of all pastimes. For him
textual clarity and correctness were secondary considerations: his anthology
appeared 'nicht der Text, sonder der Composition halben' and he simply

shrugs off textual problems as being of no real significance, admitting that he has supplied texts where none existed and provided new ones where the received texts 'fast ser vngereumbt gewest'. Since Forster clearly was no philologist, this has probably often added to the difficulties the modern reader experiences when reading his anthology, especially as the texts, even before Forster's intervention, had often suffered from the accretion of stock formulas and the general process of 'Zersingen'.

Ejn meidlein zu dem brunnen gieng consists of two stanzas of contrasting mood and content. In the first stanza we have a wooing scene with a well forming the traditional background; the second stanza strikes a coarser, more humorous note with a girl rejecting the advances of the lads of the village, while the latter mockingly adopt the traditional attitude of 'Let her go, let her tarry'. This suggests an unmotivated juxtaposition of the opening strophe of a romantic ballad and a strophe from a *Tanzlied* in the tradition of *Dorf-poesie* first popularized by Neidhart von Reuental, but, particularly in the light of the introduction of the 'pantoffel' (see note), the second stanza can be seen as explaining the consequences of what we have heard in the first one, the poem thus constituting a meaningful whole, in spite of the break in mood and the possibility that we may in fact be dealing with stanzas which originally belonged to different poems.

Ludo. Senfl.

EJn meidlein zu dem brunnen gieng / vnd das was seuberlichen / begegnet jhm ein stoltzer knab / der grůsset sie hertziglichen sie setzt das krieglein neben sich / vnd fraget wer er were / er kůsts an jren roten mundt / jr seid mir nit on mere / tret here / 5
tret here tret here tret here tret here.

Das meitlein tregt pantoffel an / dar in thuts einher schnappen / wer jr nicht recht zusprechen kan / dem schneid sie bald in kappen / kein zucht daran wirt nie gespart / kan eynem hôfflich zwagen / spricht sie wôl nicht mer vnser sein / sie hab ein andern 10
knaben / lat traben / lat traben lat traben lat traben lat traben.

(iv) *Wol auff gut gsel von hiñen*

Wol auff gut gsel von hiñen is a good example of the inconsequent nature of the folk-song and its tendency to bring together disparate elements. It starts out with a familiar *Wanderzeile* (i.e. one which occurs in other poems: 'Wolauff gut gesel von hinnen, meins bleibens ist nimmer hie', etc.). This is not developed in the first stanza as a journeyman's song which might suitably be sung as he set out on his wanderings, however, but as an invitation on the part of an amorous lady to the 'gut gsel' to elope with her. Stanza two intro-duces a motif closely related to that of 'der untreue Knabe': the young man she addresses, and who has apparently enjoyed her love, explains with the verbosity of a guilty conscience why he cannot go with her. How the scholar-secretary and the lady came to know each other is not explained, although largely because he addresses her as 'zart fraw' one gains the impression that she may be his employer's wife; certainly he would not address a low-born woman in these terms. What is clear, however, is that while the scholar was happy to enjoy their relationship during the summer, he cannot afford to have dependents, and in face of the chill winds of autumn, when a wandering scholar needs to look for a warm billet for the winter, this relationship and the impossible romantic suggestion of the 'zart fraw' are an embarrassment to him, and he declines her offer. The third stanza does not really belong to this poem at all: it is a well-known *Wanderstrophe* which sings the sorrows of parting and has been grafted on to the story of seduction and betrayal hinted at in the first two stanzas, with which it is quite out of keeping.

Joa. Leonhar. de Langenaw.

WOl auff gut gsel von hiñen / schlag vm̄ vñ weit hindan / laß sagen was man wólle / ich wil dich gātz einig han / wil stet bey dir bleiben / schaff deinem hertzen rw / von dir wil ich nit
5 weichē / wer wil vns schaidē thū?

Zart fraw ich bin ein schuler / darzu noch vnbekand / von rechter art ein buler / vnd lern eß mit der hand / kan wol schreyben vnd lesen / ghórt einem buler zu / der herbst ist abgelesen / so han wir beyd kein rw.

10 Jch scheid mich mit dem leybe / laß jhr das hertze mein / dem aller schónsten weybe / das auff der erdt mag gsein / ach wehe du bitters scheyden / wer hat dich mich erdacht / hast mir mein freudt genommen / mein hertz in trawren bracht.

(v) *Jch hórt ein frewlein klagen*

Jch hórt ein frewlein klagen is chiefly remarkable for its preservation of the *Tagelied* convention of the medieval lyric in the second and third stanzas: the lovers enjoy their brief tryst, thanks to the generosity of the watchman, whose cry at the approach of dawn is the cue for the regrets of the lady that her lover must depart. The *Tagelied* is, however, sandwiched between two stanzas whose relationship to it is, to say the least, problematical. Stanza one begins with a standard folk-song opening: 'Jch hórt . . .', but the singer's report of what he heard seems to be somewhat confused: 'klagen' and 'verzagen' (= 'to lose heart in a struggle') suggest the anxiety and weakness of a girl falling in love in spite of herself and hardly seem to be in keeping with the undeniable note of triumph in the crafty boast of the lady who tells us that her beloved lies on her breasts. If we disregard this apparent inconsistency, take 'er ligt an meinen brüsten' literally, and ignore the consequent improbability of the remark, a connection of sorts can be established. The first three stanzas can then be understood as referring to a single incident: the poet overhears the lady thinking aloud as she lies in bed with her lover. Precisely because 'er ligt an meinen brûsten' is such an odd remark, however, it is likely that it should be understood metaphorically: the *Ambraser Liederbuch*, which omits stanza four and reprints a modified text, has 'er ligt in meinem hertzen', and 'er ligt an meinen brûsten' probably means that she has a locket with a picture of her beloved. 'Mit listen' in this reading would then indicate her satisfaction at having, in a manner of speaking, outwitted those who would keep the lovers apart. Stanzas two and three would then have to be seen either as a flash-back, with the lady recalling the night of love, or as the description of the subsequent consummation of the wish implicit in stanza one. The connection of the *Tagelied* to stanza four is equally contrived. The lady's regrets that her lover must leave her are made to merge with a well-worn theme of the folk-song, a general complaint on the sorrows of parting, expressed here in a number of *Wanderzeilen* ('ach scheiden ymer scheyden / wer hat dich doch erdacht', etc.), and the poem ends bathetically and—in view of the fact that this is a *dawn* song—inappropriately in the hackneyed folk-song formula 'alde zu guter nacht'.

As in the case of the two previous songs, we are thus presented in *Jch hôrt ein frewlein klagen* with an example of thematic accretion, rather than with a strictly homogeneous poem.

G. Oth.

JCh hôrt ein frewlein klagen / fûrwar ein weyblich bildt / Jr hertz wolt jr verzagen / gegen eim jûnglich mildt / Das frewlein sprach mit listen / das frewlein sprach mit listen / er ligt an meinen brûsten / der aller liebste mein / der aller liebste mein. 5

Die zwey die theten rasten / nicht gar ein halbe stund / der Wechter auff den kasten / den hellen tag verkund / sein hôrnlein thet er schellen / sein hôrnlein thet er schellen / frewlein weckt ewren gsellein / denn es ist an der zeit / denn es ist an der zeit. 10

Warum solt ich auff wecken / den aller liebsten mein / ich forcht ich môcht erschrecken / das junge hertze sein / er ist meins hertzen gselle / er ist meins hertzen gselle / es mûhe recht wer es wôlle / wie gern ich bey jm bin / wie gern ich bey jm bin.

Wir zwey mûssen vns scheyden / gegen helle liechte tag / ach 15 scheiden ymer scheyden / wer hat dich doch erdacht / muß ich mich von dir scheidē / muß ich mich von dir scheidē / gschicht meim hertzē groß leide / alde zu guter nacht / alde zu guter nacht.

(vi) *Dje weiber mit den flôhen*

It was a standard article of faith amongst sixteenth-century men that women had a special attraction for fleas, a phenomenon they usually explained in grossly obscene terms, and the lubricity inherent in the theme of *Dje weiber mit den flôhen* naturally ensured it great popularity. Our text, which is taken from the second part of *Frische Teutsche Liedlein*, is an abbreviated version of a much longer song (reprinted R. von Liliencron, *Deutsches Leben im Volkslied um 1530* (Berlin and Stuttgart, 1884), p. 154) and treats a theme of great antiquity which can be traced back to Ofilius Serganius' *De pulice*—commonly attributed to Ovid. It had latterly appeared in the work of such different writers as Heinrich Bebel and the author of Neidhart Fuchs and was, before the end of the century, to be immortalized by Fischart (cf. p. 121). Our song not only casts light on the broad and uninhibited humour of the sixteenth century, but also reflects on social fact: the low standard of personal hygiene meant that vermin was common, and it was not unusual for aristocratic ladies to have a special *Flohpelz*, a small piece of fur with which, even in company, she could fish under her clothes for fleas. The catch was then shaken out on to the floor.

Niclas Piltz.

DJe weiber mit den flôhen haben ein stetten krieg / sie geben
gern außlehen / vñ das mans all erschlůg / vnd ließ jr kein
entrinnen / das wer der weiber rach / so hettens frid beym
5 spinnen / vnd in der kůchen gemach / so hettens frid beym
rocken vnd in der kuchē gmach.

Der krieg bebt an am morgen / vñ werd biß in die nacht / die
weiber thund nit borgen / vnd heben an ein schlacht / vnd so
die schlacht facht ane / werffens von jn dz gwand / in streit sie
10 nacket stonen / weil sie zu fechten handt / im streit sie nacket
ston / weil sie zu fechten hondt.

(vii) *Den liebsten Bulen den ich hab*

Den liebsten Bulen den ich hab exploits the traditional conceit of seeing the barrel-clad juice of the grape as a mistress in order tacitly to contrast the fidelity of the wine with the inconstancy of womankind. The present setting is highly sophisticated, but, as will have been noted from the other songs reprinted here, the folk-song in the sixteenth century is not always quite so simple as we tend to assume, and even stripped down to its basic metrical and strophic pattern the poem is really quite complicated. It consists of two seven-line stanzas with rhyming scheme ababcdc, efefghh, the 'Waise' of the second stanza rhyming internally. The lines are of seven or eight syllables;

those with seven syllables have three stresses and end in a feminine rhyme, those with eight syllables have four stresses and end in a masculine rhyme. The text is taken from Antonio Scandelli's *Nawe vnd lustige Weltliche Liedlein*, printed in Dresden in 1578 by Gimel Bergen.

DEn liebsten Bulen / den liebsten Bulen den ich hab / der leit beim Wird / der leit beim Wird im keller / der leit beim Wird im keller / Er hat ein hôltzens / er hat ein hôltzens rôcklein an / er heist der Muscateller / er heist der Muscateller / Er hat mich nechten truncken gemacht / vnd frôlich heut / vnd frôlich 5 heut den gantzen tag / Gott geb jhm heint ein gute nacht / Gott geb jhm heint ein gute nacht / Gott geb jhm heint ein gute nacht / ein gute nacht.

Von diesem bulen / von diesem Bulen den ich mein / wil ich dir bald / wil ich dir bald eins bringen / wil ich dir bald eins bringen / 10 Es ist der aller / es ist der aller beste Wein / macht mich lustig zu singen / macht mich lustig zu singen / Frischt mir das blut / vnd gibt freien muth / als durch sein krafft als / durch sein krafft vnd eigenschafft / Nu grûs dich Gott mein rebensafft / Nu grûs dich Gott mein reben safft / nu grûs dich Gott mein reben safft 15 / mein reben safft.

(viii) Jacobus Regnart: *Venus du vnd dein kind*

The verse form introduced in *Venus du vnd dein kind*, a stanza of three rhyming couplets of three stresses per line, remained popular for almost a century. Regnart was a musician and intended his poem to be sung, but in his case the text has emancipated itself from the simple evocative function it possessed in the folk-song, and its purpose is no longer simply to strike a number of emotive chords. Attention is concentrated on one single idea and the new sensitivity to language and form manifests itself in the strict regard for metre and rhyme, in the predilection for puns and antitheses and in the careful development of the subject throughout the poem, culminating in the neat finality with which '*Wie* ich wol hab erfaren . . .' becomes '*Das* hab ich als erfaren . . .' in the last stanza. The poet's approach is an intellectual one designed to appeal to the reason rather than the *Gemüt*; the poem advances a definite argument and each stanza is used to establish a definite point in which very little is left to the imagination. Not only is the structure of the poem characterized by a rational, dialectical approach, but the actual content is informed by a belief in the ultimate supremacy of the human will and the human reason over the undoubted powers and dangers of love, about which the author warns us. Venus is not, as in *Danheuser*, a dark daemonic force; she is an intellectualized allegory whose blindness illustrates the

blindness of men in love. Love is not experienced as something incomprehensible, a sort of natural disaster which overcomes a man, but as something
which can be observed with clinical detachment and from which a man can,
by an act of will, emancipate himself. The effects of love, as experience shows,
are on the whole unpleasant—a state of affairs expressed in the characteristic
antithesis 'ein freud allein / vil tausent pein; ein freundlichs schertzen / vil
tausent schmertzen'. The unpleasant nature of love having thus been established, the author draws his strictly rational conclusions: '*Drumb* rath ich
jederman . . .', a piece of advice which is underlined by the summary:
'*Dann* nichts ist zuerjagen . . .' The premiss has been established, the logical
conclusion drawn, and the reader convinced. The poem is, of course, written
very much tongue in cheek, and this is probably the most significant thing
about it; in spite of all the empirical argument, Regnart is not writing about
experience or recording real emotions or even giving a serious warning to
his readers to avoid emotional entanglements, he is playing a sophisticated
literary game in which the conceits and conventions and the virtuosity with
which they are handled are of paramount importance.

The text is taken from *Der erste Theyl / Schöner kurtzweiliger Teutscher
Lieder zu dreyen Stimmen / nach art der Neapolitanen oder Welschen Villanellen . . .
Discantus*, printed in Nürnberg in 1578 by Katharina Gerlach and the heirs
of Johann vom Berg.

Jacobus Regnart. Discantus.

VEnus du vnd dein kind / seid alle beide blind / vnd pflegt auch
zu verblenden / wer sich zu euch thut wenden / wie ich wol hab
erfaren / in meinen jungen jaren.

5   Amor du Kindlein bloß /
   Wem dein vergifftes Gschoß /
   Das hertz ein mal berůret /
   Der wird als bald verfůret /
   Wie ich wol hab erfaren / &c.

10   Fůr nur ein freud allein /
   Gibstu vil tausent pein /
   Fůr nur ein freundlichs schertzen /
   Gibstu vil tausent schmertzen /
   Wie ich wol hab erfaren / &c.

15   Drumb rath ich jederman /
   Von lieb bald abzustahn /
   Dann nichts ist zuerjagen /
   Jn lieb / dann weh vnd klagen /
   Das hab ich als erfaren /
20   Jn meinen jungen jaren.

2. Hymns

(i) *Ein feste burg ist vnser Gott*

Ein feste burg ist vnser Gott, which uses a variant of a strophe form which Luther seems to have borrowed from the *Meistergesang*, is in many ways Luther's most characteristic and successful hymn, in terms of both popularity and sheer linguistic power. It has dated less than many of the others, has been translated into a variety of languages (Carlyle's *A safe stronghold our God is still* is the most famous English version), and with its strong rhythm and rugged monosyllabic strength is an ideal expression of the pugnacity and confidence of the Reformed Faith. But while it has commonly, and rightly, been described as a 'battle hymn' or the 'Marseillaise of the sixteenth century', and has even been interpreted as a rallying call in the face of the threatened Turkish invasion of 1529–30, it is also a very conscious expression of a number of central Lutheran doctrines. Psalm 46 is the immediate point of departure, but the hymn is redolent of Luther's belief in the exposed nature of the Christian community, his conviction that the community—and the individual believer—can achieve nothing by their own efforts and his confidence that those who turn to God in fiduciary faith will never ultimately be confounded.

The text, like that of all the hymns reproduced here, is taken from the edition of the *Geistliche Lieder* printed in Leipzig by Valentin Bapst in 1545.

Der XLVI. Psalm.
Deus noster refugium et virtus &c.
D. Mart. Luther.

Ein feste burg ist vnser Gott, ein gute wehr vnd waffen, Er hilfft vns frey aus aller not, die vns itzt hat betroffen, Der alt böse 5 feind, mit ernst ers itzt meint, gros macht vñ vil list, sein grausam rüstung ist, auff erd ist nicht seins gleichen.

Mit vnser macht ist nichts gethan / wir sind gar bald verloren / Es streit für vns der rechte man / den Gott hat selbs erkoren / Fragstu wer der ist? er heisst Jhesus Christ / der HERR Zebaoth / 10 vnd ist kein ander Gott / das felt mus er behalten.

Vnd wenn die welt vol Teuffel wer / vnd wolt vns gar verschlingen / So fürchten wir vns nicht so sehr / es sol vns doch gelingen / Der Fürst dieser welt / wie sawr er sich stelt / thut er vns doch nicht / das macht / er ist gericht / ein wörtlin kan jn fellen. 15

Das wort sie söllen lassen stan / vnd kein danck dazu haben / Er ist bey vns wol auff dem plan / mit seinem Geist vnd gaben / Nemen sie den leib / gut / ehr / kind vnd weib / las faren dahin / sie habens kein gewin / das Reich mus vns doch bleiben.

(ii) *Aus tieffer not schrey ich zu dir*

Aus tieffer not schrey ich zu dir of 1524 is another paraphrase of one of the
Psalms (130) and is remarkable for its doctrinal content and forits introduction of a seven-line strophe of four stresses per line with a final unrhymed
line which achieved such currency that it is sometimes referred to as the
'Reformationsstrophe'. Whereas Luther had needed to modify Ps. 46 considerably in order to make it a vehicle for his own theology, Ps. 130 already
expressed sentiments dear to his heart: the Psalmist's cry 'If thou, Lord,
shouldst mark iniquities, O Lord, who shall stand?' is central to Luther's
whole outlook, as is the answer the Psalmist supplies, 'But there is forgiveness in thee . . . I wait upon the Lord, my soul doth wait and in his word I
hope.' Luther thus only needed to expand what was already present in the
Psalm in order to expound his own characteristic doctrines—the valueless-
ness of good works ('Es ist doch vnser thun vmb sunst . . .'), the impossibility
of self-justification ('Fûr dir niemand sich rhûmen kan . . .'), and the necessity of damnation unless saved by grace freely bestowed ('Bey dir gilt nichts
denn gnad . . .', 'Ob bey vns ist der sunden viel . . .'). Similarly, the last
three stanzas are developed into a statement of the doctrine of justification
by fiduciary faith.

Der CXXX. Psalm |
De profundis clamaui ad te Domine.
D. Mart. Luther.

Aus tieffer not schrey ich zu dir, HERR Got erhôr mein ruffen,
5 Dein gnedig ohren ker zu mir, vnd meiner bit sie ôffen, Denn
so du wilt das sehen an, was sund vnd vn recht ist gethan, wer
kan Herr fûr dir bleiben?

Bey dir gilt nichts denn gnad vnd gunst / die sunde zuuergeben /
Es ist doch vnser thun vmb sunst / auch in dem besten leben /
10 Fûr dir niemand sich rhûmen kan / des mus sich fûrchten
jederman / vñ deiner gnaden leben.

Darumb auff Gott wil hoffen ich / auff mein verdienst nicht
bawē / Auff jn mein hertz sol lassen sich / vnd seiner gûte trawē /
Die mir zusagt sein werdes wort / das ist mein trost vñ trewer
15 hort / des wil ich allzeit harren.

Vnd ob es werd bis in die nacht / vnd wider an den morgen /
Doch sol mein hertz an Gottes macht / verzweiueln nicht / noch
sorgē / So thu Jsrael rechter art / der aus dem Geist erzeuget
ward / vnd seines Gotts erharre.

20 Ob bey vns ist der sunden viel / bey Gott ist viel mehr gnaden /
Sein hand zu helffen hat kein ziel / wie gros auch sey der

schaden / Er ist allein der gute hirt / der Jsrael erlôsen wird /
aus seinen sunden allen.

(iii) *Nu freud euch liebē Christē gmein*

Nu freud euch liebē Christē gmein is one of Luther's earliest hymns and, perhaps
for that reason, starts off with what seems like a paraphrase of his famous
justification of the hymn, as quoted by Berger, 'denn Gott hat unser Herz
und Mut fröhlich gemacht durch seinen lieben Sohn, welchen er für uns
gegeben hat zur Erlösung von Sünden, Tod und Teufel; wer solches mit
Ernst glaubet, der kanns nicht lassen, der muß fröhlich und mit Lust davon
singen und sagen . . .' The hymn is largely autobiographical in content,
reflecting Luther's despair as a young priest and the solution he found to
that despair in the doctrine of Justification by Faith. This is not to say, however, as some critics have argued, that the plural forms of the first stanza are in
conflict with the first person singular of the succeeding ones—Luther clearly
regards his own experiences as a typical and necessary step in the development of the true believer: until a man has known the fear consequent on the
recognition of his own incapacity to do good and has found a solution to that
fear in faith in Christ, he cannot be a true Christian. The passages in direct
speech are in keeping with the ballad-like tone of the whole poem, but
whether they in fact constitute 'dramatische Vorgänge von erschütternder
Gewalt', as Berger would have us believe, or strike an almost disturbingly
naïve note, is a matter for individual judgement.

Ein dancklied / fûr die hôchsten wolthaten / so vns Gott in
Christo erzeigt hat.
D. Mart. Luther.

Nu freud euch liebē Cristē gmein, vñ lasst vns frôlich springen,
Das wir getrost vñ all in ein, mit lust vñ liebe singen, was Gott   5
an vns gewendet hat, vñ seine susse wunderthat, gar thewr hat
ers erworben.

Dem Teuffel ich gefangen lag / im tod war ich verloren / Mein
sund mich quelet nacht vnd tag / darin ich war geboren / Jch
fiel auch imer tieffer drein / es war kein guts am lebē mein / die   10
sund hat mich besessen.

Mein gute werck die golten nicht / Es war mit jn verdorben /
Der frey will hasset Gotts gericht / er war zum gut erstorben /
Die angst mich zu verzweiueln treib / das nichts deñ sterben bey
mir bleib / zur hellen must ich sincken.   15

Da jamerts Gott in ewigkeit / mein elend vbermassen / Er dacht
an sein barmhertzigkeit / er wolt mir helffen lassen / Er wand

zu mir das Vater hertz / es war bey jm fûrwar kein schertz / er
lies sein bestes kosten.

20 Er sprach zu seinem lieben Son / die zeit ist hie zurbarmen / Far
hin meins hertzens werde kron / vnd sey das heil dem armen /
Vnd hilff jm aus der sunden not / erwûrg fûr jn den bittern tod /
vnd las jn mit dir leben.

Der Son dem Vater ghorsam ward / er kam zu mir auff erden / Von
25 einer Jungfraw rein vnd zart / er solt mein bruder werden / Gar
heimlich furt er sein gewalt / er gieng in meiner armen gsalt /
den Teuffel wolt er fangen.

Er sprach zu mir halt dich an mich / es sol dir itzt gelingen / Jch
geb mich selber gantz fûr dich / da wil ich fûr dich ringen /
30 Denn ich bin dein / vnd du bist mein / vnd wo ich bleib / da
soltu sein / vns sol der feind nicht scheiden.

Vergiessen wird er mir mein blut / dazu mein leben rauben /
das leid ich alles dir zu gut / das halt mit festem glauben / Den
tod verschlingt das leben mein / mein vnschuld tregt die sunde
35 dein / da bistu selig worden.

Gen himel zu dem Vater mein / far ich von diesem leben / Da
wil ich sein der meister dein / den geist wil ich dir geben / Der
dich in trûbnis trôsten sol / vnd leren mich erkennen wol / vnd
in der warheit leiten.

40 Was ich gethan hab vnd gelert / das soltu thun vnd leren /
Damit das reich Gotts werd gemehrt / zu lob vnd seinen ehren /
Vnd hût dich fûr der menschen gsatz / dauon verdirbt der edle
schatz / das las ich dir zu letze.

AMEN.

(iv) *Es ist das heil vns komen her*

Es ist das heil vns komen her, written by the Lutheran preacher, Paul Speratus
(1484–1551), is not untypical of the versifications of Lutheran doctrine
which often passed for hymns in the early years of the Reformation, and in
their day apparently enjoyed considerable popularity. It reads almost like
a textbook summary of the main tenets of the evangelical faith: salvation is
given 'von gnad vn̄ lautter gûte', good works are of no avail, the commandments are designed to show man's incapacity to do good, man is justified
through fiduciary faith, but faith will be active in works, etc. Quite apart
from odd infelicities, such as the syntax of stanza two or the inclusion of the
Lord's Prayer in an already lengthy hymn, the dogmatic element, when

pronounced in such unmistakable tones, produces the effect of a sermon in verse—and a rather long-winded sermon at that. The Lutheran Church was never averse to long hymns (it is no accident that Lutherans sit to sing and stand to pray!), but even for Lutheran taste the present example proved to be too much of a good thing, and it tended to be sung in shortened versions— the last two stanzas, for instance, were often sung independently. Today it is little more than a historical curiosity.

Ein geistlich lied | Pauli Sperati | Wie wir für Gott gerecht werden &c.

Es ist das heil vns komen her, von gnad vñ lautter gůte, Die werck die helffē nimermehr, sie můgē nicht behůten, Der glaub siht Ihesum Christū an, der hat gnug fůr vns all gethan, er ist 5 der mittler wordē.

Was Gott im Gsetz geboten hat / da man es nicht kund halten / Erhub sich zorn vnd grosse not / fůr Gott so manigfalte / Vom fleisch wolt nicht heraus der geist / vom Gsetz erfordert allermeist / es war mit vns verloren. 10

Es war ein falscher wahn dabey / Gott het sein Gsetz drumb geben / Als ob wir mōchtē selber frey / nach seinem willen leben / So ist es nur ein spiegel zart / der vns zeigt an die sundig art / in vnserm fleisch verborgen.

Nicht můglich war die selbig art / aus eigen krefften lassen / 15 Wiewol es offt versuchet ward / doch mehrt sich sund on masse / Denn gleisners werck Gott hoch verdampt / vñ jedem fleisch der sunde schand / allzeit ward angeboren.

Noch must das Gsetz erfüllet sein / sonst wern wir alle verdorben / Darumb schickt Gott sein Son herein / der selber mensch 20 ist worden / Das gantz Gesetz hat er erfůlt / damit seins vaters zorn gestilt / der vber vns gieng alle.

Vnd wenn es nu erfüllet ist / durch den / der es kund halten / So lerne jtzt ein fromer Christ / des glaubens recht gestalte / Nicht mehr / denn lieber HERRE mein / dein tod wird mir das 25 lebē sein / du hast fůr mich bezalet.

Daran ich keinen zweiuel trag / dein wort kan nicht betriegen / Nu sagstu das kein mensch verzag / das wirstu nimer liegen / Wer gleubt an mich vnd wird getaufft / dem selben ist der himel erkaufft / das er nicht werd verloren. 30

Er ist gerecht für Gott allein / der disen glauben fasset / Der
glaub gibt aus von jm den schein / so er die werck nicht lasset /
Mit Gott der glaub ist wol daran / dem nechsten wird die lieb
guts thun / bistu aus Gott geboren.

35 Es wird die sund durchs Gsetz erkand / vnd schlecht das
gwissen nider / Das Euangelj kômpt zu hand / vnd sterckt den
sunder wider / Es spricht / nur kreuch zum creutz herzu / im
gsetz ist weder rast noch rhu / mit allen seinen wercken.

Die werck die komen gwislich her / aus einem rechten glaubē /
40 Wenn das nicht rechter glaube wer / wolst jn der werck
berauben / Doch macht allein der glaub gerecht / die werck die
seind des nechsten knecht / dabey wirn glauben mercken.

Die hoffnung wart der rechten zeit / was Gottes wort zusagen /
Weñ das geschehen sol zu freud / setzt Gott kein gwisse tagen /
45 Er weis wol wens am besten ist / vnd braucht an vns kein arge
list / das soln wir jm vertrawen.

Ob sichs anlies / als wôlt er nicht / las dich es nicht erschrecken /
Deñ wo er ist am besten mit / da wil ers nicht entdecken / Sein
wort las dir gewisser sein / vnd ob dein hertz sprech lauter
50 nein / so las doch dir nicht grawen.

Sey lob vnd ehr / mit hohem preis / vmb dieser gutthat willen /
Gott Vater / Son / heiligem geist / der wôll mit gnad erfûllen /
Was er in vns angfangen hat / zu ehren seiner maiestat / das
Heilig werd sein name.

55 Sein reich zukom / sein will auff erd / gscheh wie im himels
throne / Das teglich brod ja heut vns werd / wôll vnser schuld
verschonen / als wir auch vnsern schuldigern thun / las vns
nicht in versuchung stan / lôs vns vom vbel / Amen.

NOTES

I · THE REFORMATION

1. Luther as an old man recalls the outbreak of the Reformation.

Wider Hans Worst (1541)

1 **Prediger Münch:** i.e. a member of the Dominican order, founded as a preaching order by St. Dominic in 1216. Traditionally the Dominicans were the rivals of the Augustinian order, to which Luther belonged.

2 **Detzel:** Tetzel (as a Saxon Luther voices the initial 't') had been sentenced to be tied in a sack and drowned in the river Inn as an adulterer, but the sentence—the usual one for adulterers at this time—had been commuted to life imprisonment at the intercession of Frederick the Wise of Saxony. Archbishop Albrecht of Mainz had then secured his release from prison.

4 **zur erseuffen:** misprint for 'zu erseuffen'.

10 **allhie:** i.e. in Wittenberg.

11 **newlich aus der Esse komen:** 'newly forged'. Luther had taken his doctorate in 1512.

14 **Jütterbock vnd Zerbest:** Jüterbog and Zerbst, towns just outside electoral Saxony. Elector Frederick the Wise had refused to allow indulgences to be sold in his domains—not because he objected to indulgences as such, but because Tetzel's activities might reduce the appeal of the indulgence attaching to his own collection of relics housed in the Allerheiligenkirche in Wittenberg, where the penitent could on All Saints' Day obtain something like 127,799 years' remission of purgatory. Part of the money which this indulgence brought to Wittenberg was devoted to the upkeep of the University. The fact that Luther chose to launch his protest on the eve of All Saints' Day (31 Oct.) suggests that it was not only the excesses of Tetzel and his kind against whom his attack was directed. Exactly a year earlier, and again in the previous February, he had preached against indulgences and thereby incurred the displeasure of the Elector. The statement that no one knew what indulgences were is thus not strictly true, except in the sense that the doctrine attaching to indulgence had never been authoritatively defined by the Church. As early as Clement VI (1343) the Church had taught that it possessed a 'treasury' of merit acquired by Christ and the saints and martyrs and could 'apply' these merits for the benefit of the faithful. It was usually emphasized by responsible theologians that this process was dependent on true contrition on the part of the person concerned, i.e. it was assumed that the sin had been duly regretted and forgiven in the sacrament of penance. But although the sin was forgiven, the punishment due to sin must be

undergone either here on earth or in purgatory, and indulgence constituted a means whereby, in return for a 'good work' (pilgrimage, alms-giving, etc.), the Church applied its treasure of merits on behalf of the sinner and thus freed him of the punishment due to his sin. In the late Middle Ages increasing emphasis was placed on alms-giving, so much so that 'letters of indulgence' were offered 'for sale' by papal commissioners from time to time in order to raise money. The letter could then be presented to one's confessor during the sacrament of penance. Inevitably this commutation of the third part of the sacrament (satisfaction) to a financial contribution led to a prostitution of the sacrament itself, and as such had often been attacked by orthodox theologians. Pope Pius V formally and finally prohibited in 1567 the abuses complained of.

18 **weder Ablas lôsen**: 'than buying indulgence'.

20 **sein Stifft**: i.e. the Allerheiligenkirche and the collection of relics.

23 **grewlich schreckliche Artickel**: The claims attributed to Tetzel here— and at the time hotly contested by him—were quoted and condemned point by point in the 75th, 79th, 77th, 27th, 33rd, and 35th of Luther's ninety-five theses, a fact which points to their probable historicity and also accounts for their widespread dissemination amongst Protestant polemicists.

30 **das Rote Ablas Creutz**: Indulgences were usually sold in church under a red cross from which hung the papal banner.

45 **kauffet / (ich solt sagen / lôset)**: A quite characteristic trick of Luther's polemical style was to introduce a deliberate 'Freudian slip' in order to be able to make a point and then correct himself (cf. 'Drecketen', below).

45 **vnd verkaufft auch künfftige Sünde**: 'and he also sold forgiveness of future sins'. Theologically this was an important point. If future sin was forgiven, contrition and confession, the necessary preconditions for the satisfaction—for which the purchase of indulgence was a substitute—could not take place. To claim that future sin or the penalty due to it could be forgiven through indulgence thus rendered the whole sacrament of penance superfluous.

48 **Da gieng ein Büchlin aus**: The book referred to was the *Instructio summaria pro subcommissariis* which was issued by Albrecht of Mainz for the guidance of indulgence sellers and followed the standard pattern of providing instruction on the nature of indulgence, tariffs to be charged, etc.

51 **Da kams erfûr**: 'And then it came out'.

55 **drey Bisschoff**: Berthold died in 1504, Jacob in 1508, and Uriel in 1514. Naturally the expenses involved in this rapid succession of bishops strained the finances of even such a rich see as Mainz.

58 **das Pallium zu keuffen**: There is a degree of uncertainty about the amount Albrecht had to pay. The figure most commonly quoted is 14,000 ducats for the pallium plus 10,000 ducats for the dispensation in respect of the plurality of the benefices he enjoyed (Archbishop of Magdeburg, Administrator of Halberstadt, and now Archbishop of Mainz). In order to meet the financial demands made on him Albrecht had to take up a loan

of 29,000 gulden from the Fuggers (the 'Focker'—Luther uses a CG form—the great Augsburg banking-house referred to in the next paragraph). At the suggestion of the Curia, Albrecht agreed to accept responsibility for the sale in Germany of the indulgence proclaimed by Leo X in order to finance the building of St. Peter's: half the proceeds were to be sent to Rome, half were to be retained by Albrecht to pay his debt to the Fuggers. A representative of the Fuggers travelled with Tetzel in order to look after his employers' interests.

66 **begonst:** old sing. pret. indic. of 'beginnen'.

68 **die hand mit im Sode:** i.e. 'a finger in the pie too'.

70 **giengen . . . hinan mit freuden:** 'set to work gleefully'.

73 **brieff mit den Propositionibus:** i.e. with the ninety-five theses. Contrary to his usual custom Luther carefully preserved a copy of this letter (W.A. Br. I, 110) as evidence of his observation of the legalities. Partly on the basis of this letter, partly because Luther himself never claims to have nailed his theses to the Wittenberg church door (the first mention of this action occurs in Melanchthon's preface to the second volume of Luther's Latin works, not published until after Luther's death), a number of modern scholars have claimed that the *Thesenanschlag* is a legend and regard the sending of this letter as the action which sparked off the Reformation. The strict legality of Luther's actions would thus emphasize his unwillingness to come into conflict with the Church. Even if Luther did nail up the theses, however, it was not an action which possessed the revolutionary significance subsequent generations have tended to attribute to it. Church doors served as noticeboards, and in pinning up his theses Luther would simply be indicating in the traditional manner that he was prepared to dispute with other scholars on the validity of the views advanced.

78 **mir ward kein antwort:** Albrecht submitted the letter and the theses to the theologians of Mainz University for an opinion and also sent a copy to Rome. Hieronymus Schulz, Bishop of Brandenburg and *inspector ordinarius* for Wittenberg, apparently took no action. The views attributed to him by Luther here were in fact expressed with regard to the *Resolutions* on the theses, which Luther wrote and sent to him in February 1518.

85 **wider des Detzels Artickel:** Luther probably means 'against those things, listed above, which Tetzel preached'. In view of the challenging of the historicity of the *Thesenanschlag* by Roman theologians, it is, however, interesting to note that they argue that theses 92 and 93 do not date from October 1517, but were later added to the original ninety-three theses and are in fact a reply to the theses published by Tetzel and Wimpina late in 1517. The ambiguity of Luther's words here could lend support to their view.

86 **im gedrückten:** 'in print', i.e. in the printed versions of the theses.

90 **der Katzen die Schellen anbinden:** 'to bell the cat', a characteristically popular image.

91 **Ketzer meister / Prediger Ordens:** The Holy Inquisition was vested in the Dominicans.

94 **eingetrieben:** 'cowed'. Legend has it that Tetzel used to cause fires to be lit in the market places of the towns where he preached in order to remind his congregations of the fate awaiting those who opposed the Pope and his indulgence.

97 **vnd das lied wolte meiner stimme zu hoch werden:** i.e. 'the situation was getting beyond my control'.

101 **mit seinem vnzeitigen Bann:** The citation of 7 Aug. 1518 had allowed Luther some sixty days in which to come to Rome to answer the charges of heresy. The condemnation of Luther as a heretic was contained in a letter to Cajetan, the Papal Legate, ordering him to arrest Luther. This letter was dated 23 Aug. 1518, some six weeks before Luther's period of grace had elapsed.

101 **Doctor Saw:** i.e. Johann Eck, professor of theology at Ingolstadt. Eck was probably the most able exponent of the Roman position in Germany in the early years of the Reformation and one of the earliest to appreciate that Luther's protest against indulgences raised the whole question of papal authority, hence the virulence of Luther's attacks on him (he frequently ran Eck's doctoral title together with his name and called him simply 'Dreck').

102 **da jderman wolt Ritter an mir werden . . .:** 'since everyone wanted to win his spurs on me, whoever could wield a pen wrote and cried out against me.'

106 **gewapent:** = 'gewapnet'.

106 **Drecketen:** another deliberate slip, 'Dekreten'; 'excretals'.

108 **Resolution:** i.e. the *resolutiones disputationum de indulgentiarum virtute* which Luther sent early in 1518 to Schulz of Brandenburg and, via his ecclesiastical superior, Johann von Staupitz, to the Pope together with a quite humble letter.

111 **Meintz vnd Heintz:** i.e. Albrecht of Mainz and Heinrich of Braunschweig, against whom the pamphlet is directed.

113 **Questores:** i.e. those charged with preaching the indulgence.

113 **die Seelen nicht aus dem Fegfewr mit Ablas lôsen kûndten:** Luther probably refers to an article of canon law which, on the basis of a ruling of Clement VI, declares that indulgence preachers may be suspended for abusing their office and lists amongst the abuses the suggestion that indulgence can be bought for the dead.

115 **Jch muste das schaff sein:** The reference is to one of Aesop's fables (which Luther regarded highly and subsequently translated) in which a wolf picked a quarrel with a lamb by complaining that the lamb, drinking downstream from him, had muddied the water he was drinking.

116 **.16. tage verdampt:** see note above. Luther seems to be confused: the order for his arrest was *issued* sixteen days after the citation to Rome.

121 **Doctor Staupitz:** Staupitz was vicar of the Saxon province of the Augustinian order and an old friend and spiritual adviser of Luther.

124 **gen Augsburg zum Cardinal:** Since he had been ordered to arrest Luther, Cajetan (cf. p. 138) was making a very considerable concession in seeing him. As the papacy wished to sway the forthcoming imperial election, however, it was forced to pay attention to the wishes of Frederick the Wise, who was one of the most influential electors. The discussion with Cajetan only served to illuminate how deep the division was between Luther and the Church on the question of the nature of the sacraments and the authority of the Pope. The curious compromise Luther mentions here was subsequently negotiated with Karl von Miltitz, a Saxon curial official, but proved to be short-lived.

127 **Concilio:** the general council of the Church.

131 **widernander:** NHG 'wider einander'.

133 **dazu nichts zu leren hetten / wenn vnser Bůcher thetten:** 'would have nothing to teach, if our books did not exist'.

138 **Sie důrffens:** 'sie důrffen es'. The 'es' is a genitive governed by 'schuld'.

2. Luther explains the issues at stake in the indulgence controversy

Eyn Sermon von dem Ablaß vnnd gnade (1518)

3 **Magister Sentē:** Peter Lombard (*c.* 1100–60), an Italian theologian who taught theology at Paris. His *Sententiarum libri* exercised great influence on Catholic doctrine.

4 **S. Thomas:** Aquinas, probably the greatest theologian of the Middle Ages and the normative authority for the modern Roman Catholic Church.

6 **adder:** NHG 'oder'.

7 **gegrundet erfunden wirt in der heyligenn schrifft:** The exclusive authority of the Scriptures was one of the main tenets of the Reformation, and the early Church Fathers, to whom Luther refers subsequently, were only important in so far as they confirmed the testimony of the Bible. Luther's insistence on the authority of the Scriptures did not, however, except in rare cases, degenerate into scriptural dogmatism, and in this connection it is interesting to note that although he recognized secret confession to be non-scriptural, he was prepared to retain it on pastoral grounds.

9 **nach yrher weyß reden:** 'argue from their point of view'.

10 **Czum andernñ:** This paragraph touches on the central point at issue in the indulgence controversy, which in simplified terms constituted a dispute about the efficacy of 'works' as opposed to 'faith'. The vendors of indulgence inevitably laid emphasis on the 'work' of—financial—satisfaction, while for Luther—and for many an orthodox Roman theologian—the 'faith', the contrite state of mind of the sinner, was of prime importance. Thus thesis 35 rejected the view that repentence was not necessary to achieve a state of grace, thesis 36 claimed that every truly contrite Christian had free remission

of sins without letters of indulgence, and thesis 40 rejected indulgences as being inimical to true repentance.

11 **sunderū:** misprint for 'sunderñ'.

14 **almuße:** 'alms-giving'.

21 **vor die sund schuldig czuthun adder auffgeseczt:** 'which one is obliged to do for one's sins or has imposed on one (by one's confessor)'. Luther was concerned that the Pope's power to remit punishment should be restricted to the ecclesiastical penalties instituted by the Church itself. The 5th thesis had asserted that 'the Pope cannot and does not desire to remit penalties, except such as are imposed at his own discretion or by canon law', while the 34th was even more specific in its claim that 'indulgences relate only to the penalties of sacramental satisfaction decreed by a mere man' (cf. *Czum Sibenden*). Theses 41–5 correspondingly emphasized that it was more important to perform the works of charity than to buy indulgences (cf. *Czum Neunden*; Secheczehendē).

26 **Ab der ablas auch etwas mehr hynnehme:** NHG '*Ob* der Ablaß'.

30 **auff das mal:** 'for the time being', 'on this occasion'.

32 **fodere/vonn dem sunder. Dañ allein . . . :** The punctuation is deceptive: 'Demands no penalty or satisfaction of the sinner, save his heartfelt and true repentance.'

36 **Dañ ßo spricht er durch Ezechie:** Ezek. 18: 21; 23: 14f.

37 **Man sich der sunder:** misprint for 'Wan sich der sunder . . .'

39 **Maria Magda:** Luke 7: 36ff.; Mark 14: 3ff.

39 **den gichtpruchtigē:** 'the man sick of the palsy'; Mark 2: 1–12; Matt. 9: 1–8.

39 **Die eebrecherynne:** 'the woman taken in adultery'; John 8: 3ff.

40 **Uñd mocht woll:** The subject 'ich' has been omitted.

41 **Unangesehen das eczlich doctores ßo gedaucht haben:** 'Despite the fact that it has seemed so to some theologians.'

44 **ym .88. p̄s.:** Psalm 89: 30ff.

49 **Czum Achten:** 'Eighthly. Therefore one cannot give this postulated penalty (which indulgence allegedly removes) any name, nor does anyone know what it is, since it is not this punishment (of *Czum Sibenden*) and is not the above-mentioned good works.'

53 **Czum Neunden:** Luther had expressed much the same ideas as in this paragraph in the first four and last two of his theses. He denies that the 'poenitentia' of which Christ speaks in Matt. 4: 17 (the Authorized Version renders the Greek which the Vulgate translates as *poenitentiam agite* by 'repent', Luther by 'Tut Buße') refers to the sacrament of penance, but equally denies that it can be restricted to mean only 'inner penance'; rather is it a 'hatred for oneself' which will last until the sinner enters heaven (4th thesis), so that the whole life of the faithful will be one long penance (1st thesis), the mark of the Christian being that he joyfully shares in the suffer-

ings of his Master (94th thesis) and expects to 'enter heaven through suffering rather than easy peace' (95th thesis).

54 **auß ercleret:** 'declared'.

58 **nach mag werden:** NHG 'noch kann werden'.

59 **die man billich solt erwellē dann vorlassen:** 'which one should [more] fittingly choose [to suffer] than [seek to] avoid'.

61 **Medicatiuas Satisfactorias:** 'reformative and retributive punishment'.

63 **sulchs vnnd des gleychen plauderey:** 'this and such similar talk'.

67 **Das ist nichts geredt:** 'It is nonsense to say'.

70 **Antwort ich das / das keyn grundt hab:** The *virgula* is used to separate the homonyms: 'I reply that there is no foundation for that.'

72 **.S. Paul sagt:** 1 Cor. 10: 13.

77 **Czum eylfften:** 'My eleventh point: even if the penalty laid down in canon law were still to obtain, that seven years' penance should be imposed for every mortal sin, nevertheless Christendom . . .' Several editions have 'gingen', which would make 'puß' in the first instance the plural of a strong feminine noun.

80 **dañ sye eynem yglichen czu tragē warē:** 'than [that] they were to be borne by everyone', i.e. 'than anyone could bear'.

81 **nu sye iczt nicht seyn:** 'now they [i.e. the penalties prescribed by canon law] are no longer applied'.

88 **Czum Dreyczehendē:** After his pastoral concern that the penalties should not exceed the penitent's capacity to bear them—repeated once more in the last sentence of this paragraph—Luther asserts the central doctrine of his faith: the forgiveness of sins is the result of a free act of grace on God's part, and any attempt on the part of the sinner to justify himself by his own actions is vain, foolish, and impertinent.

91 **dā hynfurder woll leben:** 'than that he should henceforth lead a good life'.

95 **kecklich vben in guten wercken:** In spite of his assertion of the primacy of faith over works, Luther nowhere rejects good works as such; he simply maintains that they do not enable the doer to merit salvation. Luther is concerned with the inner spiritual attitude, the ethical intention rather than its result: the good man will produce good works, but it is the good man who does the good works, not the good works which make the good man, and in contrast to the Aristotelian view that 'law-givers make men good by habituation' in Luther's view good works are the result, not the cause, of a man's goodness. (Cf. *Von der Freiheit eines Christenmenschen*, below p. 24.) Similarly the protest against indulgences was conditioned by the fact that their purchase tended to be motivated by attrition (sorrow for sin on account of the punishment due to it) rather than contrition (sorrow for sin because it is an offence against God).

96 **vnleydlich seyn:** 'be free from pain or trouble'.

98 **yr vnuolkōmen:** NHG 'ihre Unvollkommenheit'.

105 **Czum Secheczehendē:** This paragraph is a partial paraphrase of the 43rd thesis: 'Christians should be taught that it is better to give to the poor or lend to the needy than to buy indulgences.'

109 **ader ist nichts nach gelassen:** i.e. if indulgences have any meaning at all, they must mean that one is excused the performance of certain good works.

112 **widder sanct Peters gebewde noch ablas angesehen:** 'regardless of the building of St. Peter's or indulgence'.

115 **das ob gottwil nymer gescheen sall:** Matt. 26: 11.

116 **tzu den kirchen / altarn / schmuck / kelich:** 'decorations for the churches, chalices for the altars'.

118 **Dañ aller erst:** 'Only then'.

120 **sant Paul spricht:** 1 Tim. 5: 8.

122 **vñ halts dafur frey:** 'and you may be certain of this'.

124 **Szo sprichstu. Szo . . .;** 'If [now] you say, "Then I will never again buy indulgence," my reply is . . .'

128 **gang du fur dich:** 'you look to yourself'.

129 **Czum Sibenczehenden:** Cf. thesis 47, 'Christians should be taught that the purchase of indulgences is voluntary and not prescribed', and thesis 40, 'True penitence seeks and loves punishment . . .'

132 **außczug des gehorsams:** 'exception, excuse from obedience'.

134 **and:** misprint for 'vnd'.

135 **die do nachgelassen:** 'which are remitted [by the indulgence]'.

136 **Czum Achtczehendē:** In fact theses 27 and 28 suggest fairly strongly that he did not accept such a view. Cf. *Wider Hans Worst*, p. 9.

149 **im kasten:** i.e. it affects their takings.

150 **sintemal das nit thun / dañ eczlich finster ghyrne:** 'since no one does this, but a few obscurantists'.

153 **sundern in yhren lochereten vnd czurissen opinien vill nah vorwesen:** 'but almost come to grief in the rags and tatters of their opinions'; 'locheret' = 'full of holes'.

155 **vnuorhort vñ vnuberwundē:** 'untried and unconvicted'.

3. Luther expounds the doctrine of Justification by Faith

Von der freyheyt eynes Christen menschen (1520)

3 **vnd wie es gethan sey vmb die freyheit:** 'and of what nature that freedom is'.

10 **Diße tzwen beschluß sein klerlich:** 'These two propositions are clearly [the same as are found in] . . .'

10 **Paulus i. Cor . xij.:** in fact, in 1 Cor. 9: 19.

11 **eins ydermā:** 'of everyone'.

12 **Ro .xiij.:** verse 8.

15 **Gal .iiij.:** verse 4.

16 **vnd'thā:** printer's abbreviation for 'vnderthan'.

18 **tzuuornemen:** here 'to understand'.

23 **die do stracks widernander sein:** 'things that are flatly contradictory'.

27 **was dartzu gehore das ein frum / . . .:** Other editions have an 'er' after 'das', which makes the sentence more readily intelligible.

36 **Dißer ding reichet keynes biß an die selen:** 'None of these things affects (lit. "reaches to") the soul.' All that Luther is concerned to do here and in the next paragraph is to emphasize the *spiritual* nature of religion. While this may be a commonplace for us, it was not so obvious in the context of an age in which instituted religion had increasingly become a matter of ritual, observances, and 'good works'.

44 **das der selen bringe / vnd gebe . . .:** The *virgula* should be ignored.

47 **Auch durch solch weßen keyn ander volck / dann eyttel gleißner werden:** 'By such means nothing is achieved except [the creation of] a race of arrant hypocrites.'

56 **Johan . xi.:** verse 25.

57 **Jtem . xvij.:** or rather, 14: 6.

58 **Jtem Math . iiij.:** verse 4.

61 **on des wort gottes:** 'except the word of God'. The 'des' is a misprint for 'das'.

69 **Es ist nit anders / dann die predigt von Christo . . .:** 'It is nothing else than the message proclaimed by Christ as contained in the gospels, which should be—and indeed is—done in such a way that . . .'

75 **der spruch Osee:** Hos. 13: 9.

81 **So sollen dir vmb desselben glaubēs willen . . .:** 'Then for the sake of this same faith all your sins will be forgiven, all your evil overcome, and you will be righteous, true, serene, holy, and all commandments will be fulfilled, [and you will be] free of all things.'

85 **Ro . i.:** verse 17.

86 **Ro . x.:** verse 4.

89 **wol in sich bildeten:** 'should impress it on their hearts and minds'.

91 **Joan . vi.:** verse 29.

98 **Mar. vlt.:** 'vltimo', i.e. Mark 16: 16.

101 **Czum achten . . . neunden:** The view which sees a meaningful whole in the dialectical tension between the Old and the New Testaments is characteristic for Luther's approach to the Bible. It is, however, difficult to agree with Luther's contention that the Commandments are a device by which men

are made to realize their own incapacity to do good. Apart from the ease with which it can be reduced to absurdity ('Thou shalt not take the name of the Lord thy God in vain' means 'Thou canst not help cursing and swearing'!), such a view makes the God of the Old Testament a particularly unpleasant kind of sadist, and can only be understood in the light of the morbid scrupulosity and pathological sense of his own sinfulness which tormented Luther as a young man.

112 **lernen was man thun sol:** here, 'teach . . .'

128 **vnd tzu nicht worden:** 'and become as nothing'.

131 **wilt du alle gebot erfullen deiner boßen begirde / vnd sund loß werden:** In spite of the *virgula*, the pause should be after 'erfullen' rather than after 'begirde'.

135 **Dann das dir vnmuglich ist mit allen wercken der gebot . . .:** 'For that which is impossible for you with all the works of the Commandments, of which there are many, but which can help you none, becomes simple and easy for you to do through faith.'

139 **Also geben die tzusagung gottes:** 'tzusagung' is here a strong fem. plural noun. 'Thus the promises of God give what the Commandments require and fulfil what the Commandments demand.'

152 **Johan . i.:** verse 12.

154 **Czū . xij.:** Echoes of the Song of Songs and of bride mysticism in this passage have occasionally caused *Von der Freiheit* to be regarded as a mystical work. In fact, the union with Christ here is an intellectual image rather than an emotional reality and there is no trace of that merging of the personality of the believer with the Godhead which is central to the *unio mystica*: the persons of Christ and the sinful believer remain distinct and their relationship is not so much communion as community of goods, the sinner's dowry of sin being swallowed up in the excellence of Christ, in which through faith the sinner shares.

157 **wie sant Paul sagt:** Eph. 5: 30.

158 **beyd' gutter fal / vnfal:** 'the possessions of them both, good fortune, bad fortune . . .' One would expect a *virgula* after 'gutter'.

160 **Chr̄i.:** abbreviation for 'Christo'.

160 **So hat Christus alle guter . . .:** 'Since [or "if"] Christ has all virtues and blessedness, these [now] become the property of the soul; since the soul has all vices and sins, these become the property of Christ.'

164 **vnuberwĭtlich:** NHG 'unüberwindlich'.

166 **dz ist / d' glaub:** We should expect the *virgula* to come *after* 'd' glaub'.

175 **dz die sund sie vordāme / dā sie ligē nun auf Christo:** Luther uses 'die sund' first as singular and then as plural: 'that sin should damn it [i.e. the soul], for they [i.e. the soul's sins] now rest on Christ.'

178 **i. Cor . xv.:** verse 57.

182 **Czum neuntzehenden:** The emphasis on the need to continue to perform good works, however paradoxical, was clearly justified in the light of the antinomian consequences which were often drawn from the doctrine of Justification by Faith and the associated doctrine of Predestination. It is, of course, one of the great paradoxes of the Reformation that the theology of Luther and Calvin replaced 'works' by 'faith' and yet, since works came to be regarded as signs of probable justification, produced amongst its adherents an attitude which led to the establishment of a positive cult of work and commercial and industrial activity.

185 **iha yr schedlich ist:** 'indeed, which [i.e. the law and its works] is harmful to it [i.e. the freedom and justice of the inner man], if . . .'

196 **Daher heisset der Apostel primitias spiritus:** Other editions have an 'es' after 'heisset', which gives a more intelligible sentence. The reference is to Rom. 8: 23.

199 **gleich / wo er frey ist / darff er nichts thun . . .:** 'which is like saying "Where he is free, he need do nothing, but where he is a servant, he must do all kinds of things" '.

204 **on das der selb glaub vnd gnugde muß ymmer tzunemen biß in yhenes leben:** 'except that this same faith and sufficiency must always increase until the next life'.

218 **vnd legt sich mit lust an seinen halß . . . :** 'and joyfully takes it by the throat to subdue and control it'.

220 **Ro . vij.:** verse 22.

225 **Gal . v.:** verse 24.

229 **der alleyn ist / vnd sein muß die frümigkeyt vor got:** 'which is and must be the only thing [which counts as] holiness in the sight of God'.

237 **muß vil gutter werck darober vben / das:** 'must do many good works to the end that . . .', i.e. 'in order that'.

241 **welchs willen:** 'whose will'.

242 **Darauß dann eyn yglicher kan selbs nemen die maß . . . :** 'Thus everyone can then assess and understand the manner and extent to which he should mortify his flesh.'

249 **tzu weylen tzu brechen die kopff̄ / vnd vorterbē yr leyb daruber:** Although it is technically possible to see 'kopff' and 'leyb' here as subjects of the two clauses, they are probably to be seen as objects, 'they' (i.e. those who think to be justified by their works) being the subject of both clauses.

260 **Gleich wie Christus sagt.:** The full stop has the force of a modern colon. In spite of the reference to Matt. 7: 18, Luther's argument here is somewhat reminiscent of the old problem of the chicken and the egg!

266 **wid':** NHG 'weder'.

277 **auß lautterer freyheyt vmbsunst thut / als was er thut / nichts damit gesucht . . . :** 'does everything that he does entirely voluntarily and without reward and seeks nothing by these (actions) for his own profit or salvation';

'seines nutzs' is a genitive dependent on 'nichts', 'gesucht' is read as a perfective form.

287 **Wie der weyße man sagt:** Ecclesiasticus 10: 12; 'weyße' here = 'weise'.

288 **Also leret auch Christus:** Matt. 12: 33.

299 **Math .vij.:** verse 20.

311 **Nichts anders ym furbilde:** 'Have no thought of anything, but what . . .'

313 **als sant Paulus leret die Galatas:** Gal. 5: 6.

320 **Johan . i.:** verse 51.

326 **tzuuorsten:** NHG 'zu verstehen'.

4. Luther explains his approach to the task of translating the Bible

Ein Sendbrieff | von Dolmetschen | vnd Fürbitte der Heiligen (1530)

3 **sondern solum:** A nice touch; having roundly abused his opponents as donkeys, he suggests now by a concrete example that their Latin is inadequate.

10 **M. Philips:** i.e. Magister Philip Melanchthon, Professor of Greek at Wittenberg. Aurogallus (Goldhahn) was Professor of Hebrew. Together with Johann Bugenhagen and Justus Jonas, these two scholars were Luther's principal collaborators.

17 **wir haben müst schwitzen:** NHG 'wir haben schwitzen müssen'.

21 **da wil niemand an:** 'nobody is ready to turn to and do *that* work'.

21 **Es ist bey der welt kein danck zu verdienen:** a variation on the common proverb that 'Undank ist der Welt Lohn'.

24 **des Teuffels namen:** an abbreviated form of the phrase 'in des Teuffels namen'.

30 **wie die kue ein new thor:** a characteristically popular image.

31 **das gleichwol die meinung des Texts jnn sich hat:** a slightly elliptical sentence: 'that the sense of the text nevertheless contains "sola"'.

35 **dolmetschen:** In the sixteenth century, 'dolmetschen' could mean either 'translate' or 'interpret'; today it can only be used in the latter sense.

36 **weñ sich ein rede begibt:** 'when there is talk of . . .'

47 **deste völliger vnd deutlicher sey:** In a way, therefore, Luther is admitting that he has in fact strengthened St. Paul's antithesis and that, as his examples show, the 'allein' is not absolutely necessary. But if the premiss is somewhat shaky, one must still recognize the validity of the conclusions drawn from it. In this respect one is reminded of the conclusions which Herder drew from reading Ossian—conclusions which represent a literary counterpart to Luther's relativist approach to language.

60 **Ex abundantia cordis os loquitur:** Matt. 12: 34. The Authorized Version has: 'Out of the abundance of the heart the mouth speaketh.'

76 **Matthei xxvj.:** verse 8. Both here and in Mark 14: 4 the Authorized Version has: 'To what purpose is this waste?'

78 **buchstabilist:** a word of Luther's coining to describe someone who translates too literally, 'literalist'.

93 **bessern rat damit zu schaffen:** 'to put it to better use'.

94 **da der Engel Mariam grûsset:** Luke 1: 28, 'Hail thou that art highly favoured.'

99 **was gesagt sey / vol gnaden?:** 'what "vol gnaden" might mean'.

117 **sie dûrffen fur mein dolmetschen nicht antwort geben . . .:** 'they are not required to accept responsibility for my translation or to hold themselves accountable for it.'

129 **wo etwa an einem wort gelegen ist / hab ichs . . .:** 'where a word was of particular importance, I have rendered it literally.'

131 **Johan .vj.:** verse 27, 'For him hath God the Father sealed.'

133 **gezeichent:** 'marked by means of a sign'.

136 **die tollen heiligen:** Luther seems to have in mind the false saints of 2 Cor. 11: 13. The reference is to the edition of a translation of the prophets produced by the Anabaptists Hans Denck and Ludwig Hätzer which was published in Worms in 1527.

139 **rotten geist:** 'a person who loves creating divisions and factions', 'sectarian'. The word was a favourite of Luther's.

142 **fast nach gangen ist:** 'came very close to'.

6. The reaction to Luther

(i) Hieronymus Emser rejects the doctrine of the Priesthood of All Believers and Luther's view of the papacy

Wid' das vnchristenliche buch Martini Luters Augustiners / an den Tewtschen Adel außgangen (1521)

2 **da durch sie sich her beschûtzt:** misprint for 'bisher beschûtzt'.

6 **obangeregt:** NHG 'oben angeregt', 'touched on above'.

11 **Eneidos .vi.:** line 549. The image of the triple wall is one of the few classical allusions to be found in Luther.

14 **Esaie lxij.:** verse 6. By contrasting the image Luther borrows from a 'heathen poet' with one taken from the Scriptures, Emser scores a neat point, especially in view of the emphasis Luther puts on the Bible. Characteristically, however, Emser will subsequently draw to a considerable extent on Church Fathers such as Augustine, Gregory, Cyprian, and Alexandrinus.

21 **Das sie aber tzimlicher weiß reformirt werden:** a concession such as nearly all the defenders of the Old Faith were ready to make. The issue at stake was no longer—indeed never had been—just one of reforming abuses, however.

26 **eyn feyn coment oder gleyssen:** 'a fine lie or specious deception'.

35 **secundum cōmunem vsum . . . :** 'according to the common usage of all Germans'.

38 **von der kirchen yren enthalt . . . entbinden haben:** 'who have their living from the Church and have to order matters concerning the Church, have to bid and forbid, bind and loose.' The last words refer to Matt. 16: 19.

43 **fallaciam equiuocationis:** 'fallacy of equivocation'. This is, however, tautological in English, since equivocation is in the technical sense itself a fallacy consisting in the use of a word in different senses at different stages of the argument.

51 **vnd tzwischen dißen beiden stenden . . . :** 'and [which] [i.e. canon and imperial law] have put between these two estates various ordinances and laws . . .'

58 **vnd der heylig Matheus betzeuget eiusdem xiij.:** 'and [as] St. Matthew testifies in ch. 13 [verse 11] of his gospel'.

66 **die prister tzu beten . . . tzu arbeiten:** This was a venerable triad which remained a standard element of social theory until well into the eighteenth century and was often used as a caption for popular prints depicting the three estates.

70 **eynen auß dem hauffen nheme / die . . . :** In using the plural of the relative pronoun Luther is thinking of the individuals in the crowd. The 'Samlung' referred to is the community of Christian believers. Cf. below, 'samlung desselben', where it refers to the congregation of the bishop.

77 **beyder seyt:** 'on both counts'.

86 **bis auff dise stund:** Significantly, Luther does not discuss the doctrine of Apostolic Succession in his argument that all Christians are in fact priests or even refer to the coming of the Holy Ghost on the first Whitsun.

93 **seins gefallens:** 'according to his own desires, as it pleased him'.

93 **wurd sie mehr synn kriegen / dann hydra heupter hat:** In raising the question of authority, Emser puts his finger on the central weakness (and strength!) of the Lutheran position. Contrary to what is often suggested, the Roman Church was not 'against the Bible', but merely against 'the fundamental fallacy of individual interpretation'. Luther was rapidly to discover that almost any given text could be interpreted in a variety of ways, and in the light of the development Emser here predicts was forced to become the 'Pope at Wittenberg' and to impose his own view on his followers as the only valid one.

95 **das aber Luter die tzu Rom so vor vngelert halt macht alleyn . . . :** Modern punctuation would demand a comma after 'halt'.

98 **vnnd mogen ouch keinen buchstaben auffbringen . . . :** 'and can point to no single letter [in the Scriptures] to prove that it is the Pope's prerogative to interpret Scripture.'

101 **Sie haben ynen die gewalt selbs genomen:** 'They have arrogated this power to themselves'; 'ynen' is an old form of the reflexive pronoun.

104 **der das tzil der alten Christenlichen lerer nicht vberschreit:** 'who does not go beyond the limit set by the old Christian teachers'.

106 **epl'a:** abbreviation for 'epistola'.

108 **vorborgen haben wollen:** The auxiliary is omitted.

112 **li. iij. cap. ci.:** 'Book III, ch. 101'.

114 **aus eim einigē gold / einer . . . macht:** 'from a single piece of gold one man makes . . .'

120 **sie werde dan vō der Christenlichen kirchen vor gut erkent:** 'unless it be recognized and accepted as good by the Christian Church'.

129 **alien:** misprint for 'alein'. The reference is to Matt. 16: 19.

136 **vnd hor niemant der das anfecht:** 'and I hear [of] no one who challenges this'.

141 **Jst doch ein Esel ouch from:** 'from' can mean 'quiet', 'tame', as well as 'pious'.

146 **Malachie. ij:** verse 7.

147 **dan er ist ein engel der spitz des herrē:** 'for he is an angel [i.e. a messenger], the spokesman of the Lord'. The use of 'spitz' is unusual here and suggests 'that which goes before'.

152 **so darff man . . . in bapst nicht sonder gleuben:** 'one need not believe in the Pope in particular', i.e. in isolation from the rest of the Church.

154 **quia vbi totū ibi etiā pars est:** 'because where the whole is, there the part is also'.

158 **die den hals dar uber abgefallen sint:** 'who have fallen and broken their necks in the process'.

172 **weychvild:** for more usual 'weichfeld', 'weichbild', the area in which municipal laws are valid. Here the laws themselves, 'by-laws'. We should expect a full stop after 'tzu setzē'.

175 **dñs:** abbreviation for 'dominus'.

176 **di.:** abbreviation for 'distinctio'.

177 **actuū quinto:** Acts 5 (in fact 15: 6).

186 **pharisey:** for more usual 'Pharisäer'.

196 **ab auctoritate negatiue:** 'from negative authority', i.e. since we are *not* told that St. Peter *did* call the council.

197 **vnd ym fal ob das gleich Jacobus:** 'and even if it were the case that James . . .'

205 **conciliabulum:** 'a hole-in-the-corner gathering'.

205 **Gerson:** Jean Charlier (b. at Gerson; 1362–1428), known as 'the most Christian doctor', one of the greatest of the late medieval theologians. He was the moving spirit at the Council of Constance, which was much concerned to re-establish Church unity and papal authority after the Great Schism.

216 **von iuget:** misprint for 'von iugēt'.

(ii) Albrecht Dürer bewails the alleged death of Luther

Tagebuch der Reise in die Niederlande (1521)

2 **geng Antorff:** Dürer stayed in Antwerp for the greater part of his time in the Netherlands.

2 **so verrätherlich gefangen hett:** Largely thanks to the influence of Frederick the Wise, Luther, although a condemned heretic, was invited to defend himself before the Imperial Diet at Worms in 1521. The safe conduct guaranteed to Luther by the Emperor was faithfully observed, but the Diet, in the famous Edict of Worms (26 May 1521), put Luther under the ban of the Empire, i.e. the secular arm confirmed the findings of the ecclesiastical courts and the excommunicated monk was outlawed: all loyal subjects of the Emperor were forbidden to give him food, lodging, or assistance of any kind, but were called upon to arrest him and hand him over to the imperial authorities. By the same edict, it was made an offence to publish, sell, read, or possess his writings, and a system of ecclesiastical censorship was instituted for all books and pamphlets, no matter what their subject-matter might be. Luther's safe conduct covered the journey back to Wittenberg, but before leaving Worms he was informed of a plan to rescue him from any possible danger by 'abducting' him and bringing him to a place of safety—the example of the Czech heretic, John Huss, who in spite of a safe conduct had been burnt at the stake by the Council of Constance some hundred years previously, did not inspire confidence. The plan for Luther's abduction emanated ultimately from Frederick the Wise, who, although not a Lutheran in the normal sense, was rather proud of the shining light of his new university at Wittenberg and for political reasons was unwilling to have his subject sentenced by a 'foreign' authority. Since he did not wish to be seen openly to defy the imperial edict, Frederick left the details of the plan to his advisers, in order to be able to claim honestly that he did not know where Luther was. Luther left Worms on 26 Apr., and on 2 May, shortly after Möhra in the Thuringian Forest, his coach was surrounded by horsemen and conducted to the Wartburg, not far from Eisenach. Not unnaturally, the news of Luther's 'abduction' caused consternation amongst those of his admirers who had no inkling that it was organized for his protection. Luther remained safely at the Wartburg, busily occupied with the translation of the New Testament, until 1522, when the deterioration of conditions in Wittenberg, largely because of the activities of radical Protestant preachers who were advocating the abolition of Church ceremonial and a return to the material simplicity and communism of primitive Christianity, forced him to return home.

3 **Dann do in des kaisers Carols herolt mit dem kaÿserlichen glait war zu geben, dem ward vertrauet:** 'For when the Emperor Charles's herald with the imperial safe conduct was added to his party, Luther's safety was entrusted to him.' The Imperial Herald (not Charles's personal herald), Kaspar Sturm, was responsible for ensuring that the safe conduct was observed, but Dürer apparently thinks he has abandoned Luther to his fate. Actually, Luther sent Sturm back from Friedberg, with a message to the Diet to the effect that he would gladly obey the Diet in all temporal matters, but that he could not compromise on a matter of conscience. Dürer was well acquainted with Sturm, having sketched his portrait the previous year.

9 **nachfolger Christj:** Rupprich suggests that Dürer is probably thinking of the famous contemporary pamphlet *Doctor Martin Luthers Passion*, which parodies the Biblical account of the sufferings of Christ and sees Luther as a latter-day Christ destined to die as a result of the machinations of the priests at Worms, as Christ died because of the intrigues of the priests at Jerusalem. There is, however, no evidence that Dürer knew this pamphlet.

14 **beschwerung der menschlichen gesecz:** The idea that the papacy had imposed human institutions on God's Church is standard to all reformed thinking and had been proclaimed by Luther especially in *An den Christlichen Adel* and *De captivitate babylonica ecclesiae*. The emphasis Dürer lays in this passage on the economic greed of the late medieval Church is quite typical for many nationalistically minded converts to Protestantism, and no doubt has special significance for Dürer who, as a son of commercial Nürnberg, was very careful in money matters, and even recorded in his diary the tips he gave to servants.

14 **und auch darumb, das wir unsers bluth und schweiß also beraubt . . . :** 'and so that we may be thus robbed and plundered of our sweat and blood', i.e. the papists have killed him so that they may continue to exploit the faithful.

21 **vätter:** i.e. Church Fathers.

so er das heilig evangelium furth: 'when he expounds the Holy Gospel'.

26 **nit zuverbrennen:** Dürer is probably thinking of the burning of Luther's books in Cologne and Louvain after the publication of the bull of excommunication in 1520, and the controversy this aroused.

26 **es wer dann . . . opinionen:** literally, 'Unless . . .', i.e. 'It would be more fitting to burn his opponents, who have always fought against evangelical truth, together with their opinions.' Dürer may well be thinking of Luther's burning of the bull of excommunication and the books of canon law on 10 Oct. 1520.

29 **aber doch, das man wieder neuer luterische bücher truck hett:** In spite of the odd syntax the meaning is clearly 'and, by contrast, have new Lutheran books printed'.

34 **gott geistig:** 'possessed of the spirit of God'. 'ihn' here = 'God'.

35 **O Erasme Roteradame:** Dürer met the great Dutch humanist (cf. p. 3) through his contacts with the Nürnberg humanist Willibald Pirckheimer and portrayed him several times. The appeal to him was perhaps natural in view of the popular misconceptions about his attitude to Church reform. Largely because of his outspoken criticism of the papacy and ecclesiastical abuses in his writings, Erasmus was commonly regarded as a precursor and ally of Luther. In fact, the apparent similarity of their attitudes is highly misleading. Both Erasmus and Luther were from the first aware that they differed radically on important theological issues, and it was only Erasmus's pusillanimity and unwillingness to commit himself irrevocably which prevented these differences from gaining immediate expression. Dürer's appeal to Erasmus to grasp the martyr's crown rests on a fundamental misunderstanding of his character: Erasmus naturally tended to compromise and, as he said himself, in any dangerous situation would 'play the part of Peter'. Eventually, but only as a result of prolonged promptings on the part of his Roman Catholic friends, Erasmus in 1525 joined in the controversy and, in Luther's own phrase, 'took him by the throat' by attacking Luther's doctrine that man did not have free will—which, behind all the incidental concern with abuses, faith, etc., was the fundamental issue which divided the Protestants from the defenders of the Old Faith.

38 **ritter Christj:** The image derives ultimately from Eph. 6: 10 ff., but Dürer is probably thinking of the title of Erasmus's book *Enchiridion militis christiani* (*The hand-book [or sword] of the Christian soldier*). It is sometimes held that the knight in Dürer's famous engraving *Ritter, Tod und Teufel* is a representation of Erasmus's Christian soldier.

40 **meniken:** 'mannikin', Dutch for 'Männchen'.

44 **nit wider dich mügen:** Matt. 16: 18. Dürer seems to have omitted the main verb; Luther has 'vnd die Pforten der Hellen sollen sie nicht vberweldigen'.

45 **gleich förmig:** 'similar'.

49 **auß dem kelch trinckest:** Matt. 26: 42; Mark 14: 36.

51 **weißlich:** 'wisely', i.e. with the appropriate fear of God.

52 **Davidt:** I have been unable to trace the alleged reference; Dürer is probably thinking of such passages as 2 Sam. 7: 5 ff.

54 **Dann gott gestehet beÿ der heÿligen christlichen kirchen . . . :** 'For God stands by the holy Christian Church, as indeed he is also among the Roman party according to his divine will.' These much debated lines represent, as Rupprich points out, no more than a general statement that God is ready to help men of all parties who sincerely believe in him.

(iii) Thomas Murner mocks Luther's view of the sacraments

Von dem grossen Lutherischen Narren wie in doctor Murner beschworen hat (1522)

2 **Das ich mein tag hab ein genumen:** 'That I have taken possession of all my days', i.e. 'that my days are over'.

9 **So ich mich nun entsetz darab:** 'So that I am afraid of it now.' A new sentence now begins.

20 **v'lot:** printer's abbreviation for 'verlot' = NHG 'verläßt'.

22 **alles sandt:** 'everything'.

30 **So sei meins trosts der anefang:** 'Let it be the beginning of my help that you do not delay long now', i.e.: 'Take the advice I am about to give without arguing about it.'

33 **Es kumpt dir wol ia folgstu mir:** 'If you follow me, all will be well with you.'

34 **Du hast ein widerwertigkeit . . .:** 'You have stirred up strife in Christendom.'

43 **Zům dritten lůg . . .:** 'Thirdly, look to it and choose for yourself (i.e. take) the sacrament and sacred oil.'

45 **in krafft der dreier ding:** 'fortified by these three things'.

54 **Ja dir gethon hast gar verzigen:** 'Indeed, that you have even forgiven those trespasses I committed against you.'

56 **Thů ich vff diser erden nit:** Murner cheats a little here. Luther's dissatisfaction with the sacrament of penance lay in the fact that, since absolution was dependent on confession, it was directed towards the forgiveness of individual sins, but did nothing to alter man's sinful nature. Further, his unease in the matter of the sacrament had little to do with the doctrine of the Priesthood of All Believers; nor was it true to suggest that Luther was opposed to confession as such. He asserted that the confession of sins was 'necessary and ordained of God', and saw in aural confession 'a unique source of help for the uneasy conscience', although, in keeping with the doctrine of the Priesthood of All Believers, he maintained that all Christians had the right to hear confession and absolve the penitent.

63 **Doch wil ich got . . .:** The next four lines offer a fair paraphrase of the Lutheran doctrine that the sins of the sinner who comes to God in fiduciary faith will not be imputed to him.

70 **Dan ich haltz nur für ein testament:** In *De captivitate* Luther had rejected the Roman doctrine that in the mass the sacrifice of Christ was re-enacted and offered to God. This, he suggested, constituted an idolatrous denial of the 'one, true, and sufficient' nature of Christ's original sacrifice on the Cross. Like most Protestants after him, Luther retained from the Roman mass only the communion service as a sacrament and saw it as a testament or legacy of Christ to be divided amongst his followers after his death.

74 **Jetz diser zeit:** 'At this present time'.

78 **vmb vndumb:** misprint for 'vmb vnd vmb' = 'everywhere'.

86 **ia vnd nein:** 'yes or no'.

87 **zů dem dot:** 'at your death'.

90 **So wil ich lůgen das ichs thů Darin:** 'I will see to it that I do that in which . . .'

93 **Als von cristo selbs erstifft:** 'All [of which] was instituted by Christ himself.' This was precisely the point at issue in the question of extreme unction. As Luther had pointed out, while the anointing of the sick was referred to in Mark 6: 13 and James 5: 14, such anointment was in Biblical times not seen as a last rite, but as a cure. Nor was the cure instituted by Christ. On both counts Murner is somewhat wide of the mark.

100 **Keiben:** 'corpses', but with pejorative overtones, 'carrion'.

106 **rief:** NHG 'rufe'.

108 **Es wil doch an ein scheiden gan:** 'The hour of departure draws near.'

112 **Jch halt nichtz druff vnd wil ir nit:** 'I don't hold with those you have enumerated above and don't want [anything to do with] them.'

114 **Sie ist ein mensch als andre sint:** Although Luther did not deny that saints *might* intercede for us, he was opposed to praying for their intercession as resting on the idea that they had acquired special merit before God—a thing which in Luther's view was impossible because of the inherently sinful nature of *all* men and their actions. We should no more call on saints to intercede for us, he suggests, than we should call on our fellow Christians to do so.

115 **frint:** NHG 'Freund'.

116 **Als andere heiligen alle sant:** 'Like all the other saints'.

118 **Jch ken kein heiligen me dan got:** Luther would certainly have subscribed to this view, which could in fact be seen as the central idea of his theology. It seems curiously inappropriate that Murner should have put such a sentiment, with its obvious reminiscence of Luke 18: 19, into the mouth of a man he meant to attack.

120 **Nim her mein seel:** NHG 'Nimm, Herr, meine Seele.'

125 **kein andere freit:** NHG 'Keine andere Freude.'

129 **Als ins scheißhuß:** NHG 'Ins Scheißhaus also . . .!'

133 **Dem nie kein boßheit vber bleib:** 'For whom no evil was too much'.

(iv) Thomas Müntzer castigates Luther as a cowardly braggart and a lackey of the princes

Hoch verursachte Schutzrede | vnd Antwwort | wider das Gaistloße Sanfft | lebende fleysch zů Wittenberg . . . (1524)

1 **Der arme schmeichler:** i.e. Luther. Elsewhere Müntzer calls him 'Vater Leisetritt', 'Doctor Lügner', or simply 'Der neue Papst'. Luther had cited the example of Christ in order to demand respect for instituted authority and to condemn civil commotion; Müntzer, however, interprets 1 Tim. 1: 9 ff. as an injunction to apply the rigour of the law to all evil-doers. The sword of justice, he says, is given to the whole community, not to the individual ruler, and rulers who do wrong should be punished. Luther's citation of Christ is thus a cowardly evasion of his Christian responsibility.

3 **sôllen getrost vndter die diebe vñ Rauber streichen:** 'should without hesitation smite the thieves and robbers'. In the treatise *Von kauffs handel vnd wucher* (1524) Luther had suggested that, while footpads and highwaymen were simply 'expropriating the expropriators' in their attacks on merchants, the princes had a duty to keep the roads safe for good and bad men alike, and should punish highway robbery.

4 **Jm selbigen:** i.e. in the same book.

5 **Heerholt:** 'a master's man', 'someone unduly subservient to his master'. Presumably Müntzer intends a pun on 'Herold'.

7 **welches doch got nit auff seine maynung befolhen:** 'which God did not intend in his Commandments'.

11 **Esaie. v.:** verse 8.

13 **es dienet aber jn nit:** 'but this does not apply to them', i.e. the princes.

16 **Michee. iij. ca.:** verse 2; ca. = 'caput'.

16 **So er sich dann vergreifft:** The 'er' is the poor peasant.

20 **So ich das sage / mûß ich auffrûrisch sein / wolhyn:** 'If I say that, it is I who am a revolutionary.' 'Wolhyn' is a synonym of 'wolan' and has emphatic force when placed at the beginning or end of a main clause following a conditional.

22 **wiltu dich mit der jrrenden welt heüchlen zû flicken:** 'do you want to cover up your nakedness with the hypocrisy of the erring world?' 'Zuflicken' means to 'clothe' or 'dress'.

23 **Luce. ix.:** Müntzer is probably thinking of verse 25.

26 **darumb hast du sye wol zûschelten:** 'therefore you do well to abuse them'. The reference is again to *Von kauffs handel vnd wucher* as well as to Luther's anti-monastic writings.

28 **Daß du aber den pawrn setigst:** 'In order to satisfy the peasants.' The views quoted here constitute the burden of the opening paragraphs of the *Brief an die Fürsten zu Sachsen.*

29 **zû scheytern gen:** 'die', 'perish'.

30 **gloß vber das newlichiste Kayserlich Mandat:** The full title of Luther's work was *Zway keyserliche vneynige vnd wydderwertige gepott den Luther betreffend,* which appeared in 1524.

31 **Du sichst sye auch an vor Kauff lewth:** 'You regard them as merchants also', i.e. in the concluding paragraphs of *Von kauffs handel,* where Luther quotes Isa. 1:23 in support of his thesis that the princes are the associates of the merchants, who are in his eyes all thieves.

32 **bey der nasen rucken:** 'tweak their noses', i.e. 'abuse', 'take to task'.

34 **was lassen sye abgen? an jren zynsen vnd schynderey &c?:** 'What do they give up out of their taxes and extortion?'

35 **kanstu sy wol wider mûts machen:** 'you can easily put them in a good frame of mind again'! 'Mûtes machen' is an abbreviated form of 'gûtes mûtes machen'.

39 **nun die noet heer geet**: 'now that the hour of danger has come'.

40 **du meynst aber es sey gůt worden / so du einen grossen namen vberkoṁen hast**: 'you think things have turned out well, since you have made a great name for yourself.'

41 **vnd kummest ane ende**: 'and can't stop talking about'.

42 **zů Leiptzgk**: i.e. at the Leipzig disputation with Eck in 1519. The accusation of cowardice goes back to Müntzer's *Protestation odder empietung* of 1524, where he had offered to listen to anyone disagreeing with him 'fur einer ungefherlichen gemeine'. Luther seizes on this in the *Brief an die Fürsten zu Sachsen* and boasts that in Leipzig *he* had defended *his* views 'fur der allergeferlichsten gemeyne'. Müntzer now seeks in his turn to show that Luther was a coward, and that his claim was exaggerated—which indeed it was, although it is true that the climate at Leipzig was unfavourable to Luther, the presiding prince, Duke George of Saxony, being a convinced opponent of religious innovation. The wreaths of carnations to which Müntzer refers were in fact a posy which Luther carried to one of the debates. While at Leipzig Luther stayed with his publisher and printer, Melchior Lother, who also kept an inn.

43 **dye leüte blindt machen**: 'to blind people', i.e. 'put something over on them'.

46 **zů Augspurg**: i.e. at the Diet in 1518 to meet the Papal Legate, Cardinal Cajetan.

47 **Stupicianum / Oraculum**: 'the Staupitzian oracle'. Johann von Staupitz was Vicar-General of the German congregation of the Augustinian Eremites—to which Luther belonged—from 1503 until 1520. For a number of years he was Luther's immediate superior, confessor, and teacher in Erfurt. He accompanied Luther to Augsburg, but thereafter increasingly regarded him as a heretic. He ended his days as abbot of St. Peter in Salzburg in 1524.

51 **Doch er forchtet sich iṁ bůchlein vom auffrhůr**: The 'er' is Luther, not the Devil! Müntzer recalls how Luther says in *Eyn trew vermanung zu allen christen sich zu vorhuten vor aufrur vnd emporung* of 1522 that he is amazed at the mischievousness of the Devil who has sought to undermine the reformed teaching by causing prophecies to circulate against it and its founder.

53 **vō den newen Propheten**: The word 'prophet' is used in a wide sense here and is applied to those who 'spoke with tongues' and derived their authority from personal revelation rather than from the Scriptures. For Luther this type of independence from the received word was anathema and 'prophet' for him rapidly became a term of abuse in the sense of Jer. 23: 11 ff.

54 **Johannis.viij.c.**: verse 13 (c = 'caput').

56 **j. Corint.xiiij.**: verses 3 ff.

59 **so du dich iṁ Münch kalbe des ambts eüßserst**: The reference is to *Deuttung der zwo grewlichen Figuren Bapstesels zu Rom vnd Munchkalbs zu freyberg in Meyssen funden* of 1523 in which Melanchthon interprets the allegorical meaning of a donkey-like creature allegedly found in the Tiber, and Luther

interprets the significance of a misshapen calf born in Freiberg. Luther
opens his remarks by denying that he is a prophet and says that he can only
give a very general interpretation.

61 **ynß maul geschlagen:** Actually the image used in the *Brief an die Fürsten zu
Sachsen* was of—metaphorically—hitting Murner on the nose!

63 **die gůten brůder:** Müntzer is probably thinking of Marcus Stübner
and Michael (Martin?) Keller, the two more sophisticated of the Zwickau
Prophets. Both were men of some academic standing, who together with
Niklas Storch and Marcus Thomä were largely responsible for the civil and
religious disturbances in Wittenberg which compelled Luther to return
from the Wartburg in 1522. The meeting with Stübner and Keller ended
in a quarrel, and Luther saw to it that they were not allowed to stay in
Wittenberg. Luther's subsequent meeting with Storch had similar results,
however, and Müntzer may be thinking of this as well.

66 **Matthei. xviij.:** verse 10.

69 **danck hab:** 'credit is due to . . .'

71 **Beheymische geschenk:** 'Bohemian presents', i.e. secularized Church
lands after the fashion of the Hussites in Bohemia.

75 **Du darffst warlich dir nit zů schreiben . . . wilder tück vnnd lyste:**
Müntzer is probably thinking of the passage in the *Brief an die Fürsten zu
Sachsen* where Luther speaks of the 'wilde / seltzame tück vnd list' that the
imperial authorities had deployed against him at Worms and asserts that
he would have gone there, even if as many devils had lain in wait for him as
there were tiles on the roofs of the houses.

78 **Du liessest dich durch deinen rath gefangen nemen / vñ stellest
dich gar vnleydlich:** Note the dramatic change from the preterite to the
historic present. The charge that Luther arranged his 'capture' in order to
make sure of his own safety is, of course, untrue. Cf. p. 276.

82 **hafen oder topff:** 'Topf' is the CG form, 'Hafen' the UG form. It was
thanks to Luther that 'Topf' became standard.

83 **Hierem. j.:** verse 13.

84 **Ezechielis. xxiij.:** Müntzer is thinking of Ezekiel 24: 3 ff., but the homely—
and in view of the title of the pamphlet not inappropriate—image of Luther
stewing in his own juice is unbiblical.

86 **deinen milch meülern:** 'for your milksop followers'.

(v) Huldrych Zwingli deprecates Luther's boastfulness and intemperance and rejects his teaching on the sacraments
*Das dise wort Jesu Christi | Das ist min lychnam der für úch hinggeben
wirt | ewigklich den alten eynigen sinn haben werdēd* (1527)

1 **Jch verschon din hie:** He has been rebuking Luther for boasting of his
achievements.

13 **wie der schmåchlich Antichrist hin wurd genoṁen:** The clause is elliptical; we must read the 'wie' as suggesting 'and the depth of this fear is shown by the fact that the shameful Antichrist went unchallenged [lit. was tolerated]'.

17 **do es nieman waagen dorfft:** The 'es' must be understood as referring back to the idea contained in 'stalltist dich dem fyend engegen'. 'Dürfen' here = 'dare'.

18 **nutzlich gschirr:** 2 Tim. 2: 21.

21 **so wilt du es nit erkennen:** 'though you refuse to recognize it'.

23 **din eygen bůch:** i.e. *Daß diese Worte Christi (Das ist mein Leib, etc.) noch fest stehen widder die Schwermgeister.* Since his experiences with the Zwickau Prophets in 1522, Luther was apt to classify all his non-Catholic opponents as 'enthusiasts'. The interpretation of the text 'This is my body' (Matt. 26: 26; Mark 14: 22) as meaning 'This represents my body', which was suggested by Zwingli (following Cornelis Hoen), seemed to Luther to constitute an assault on the authority of the Scriptures and to throw open the gate to all the errors he had sought to overcome in his dealings with the Prophets and Andreas Carlstadt, sometime Dean of the Wittenberg theology faculty, who had equally 'perverted' the 'evident' meaning of the same text. At the Marburg Colloquy of 1529 Luther is reported to have chalked 'Hoc est corpus meum' on the table before him and refused to contemplate any modification of the literal meaning of the text.

26 **wo ye gheiner jm selbs so gar engangen sye:** 'if anyone has ever gone astray and lost control of himself so completely.'

28 **Vñ solt man das in eynen geyst kõnnen rechnen?:** The meaning is not clear—'Should one regard it as being consonant with a great spirit?' (?)

30 **Saul was zum ersten milt:** 1 Sam. 12 ff.

32 **nam jṁ vnerbere ding für:** Saul is the subject here. Like most sixteenth-century writers Zwingli often uses the old form of the reflexive, which in oblique cases was identical with the personal pronoun.

33 **geschickt:** here, 'called by God to His service'.

39 **eigenlicher:** 'in greater detail'.

40 **sam du die ban des Euangelij allein gerütet habist:** 'as though you alone had prepared the way of the Gospel.'

43 **du habist dann deß selben widruṁ vergessen:** 'unless it be that you have forgotten it again.'

44 **Du hast dem Fegfhür allweg ... etwas zůgegeben:** The mature Luther does not seem to have been particularly interested in purgatory. It is, however, true that in his early writings Luther assumes its existence: the ninety-five theses, for instance, do not challenge the fact of purgatory, but merely claim that the Pope cannot release souls from punishment there.

52 **fürbitt der såliḡe die im hiṁel sind:** While the Swiss reformers rejected both the invocation of the saints in heaven and the possibility of their inter-

cession on our behalf, Luther, as so often, occupied a rather indistinct position between this view and the traditional Roman teaching that the believer might pray to a saint to intercede on his behalf and that the saint could in fact do so. The Roman doctrine, Luther maintained, had no scriptural basis and, like indulgence, depended ultimately on a 'debit and credit' view of justification by which the saint transferred his credit to the account of the believer, thus obscuring the fact that God bestowed His grace solely according to His own omnipotent will. Luther (who, incidentally, interpreted *communio sanctorum* as meaning the communion of all Christians *on earth*) was, however, prepared to concede that the angels and saints in heaven might, like our brethren on earth, pray to God to give us His grace.

54 **nun einē mitler**: '*only* one mediator'.

55 **in dem span der Bilderen**: The quarrel referred to is that with the Zwickau Prophets and Carlstadt, whom Zwingli followed in the question of the ecclesiastical use of pictures. I have been unable to trace the actual words Zwingli quotes here, but they seem to be a paraphrase of the sentiments expressed by Luther in *Widder die hymelischen propheten von den bildern vnd Sacrament* of 1525.

60 **1. Corinth. 8**: verse 4.

64 **Matth. 22**: verses 37 ff.

75 **Spricht yeman**: Luther does precisely that in *Wider die himmlischen Propheten*.

77 **so ligt nit daran**: 'it does not matter whether . . .'

82 **zucht empieten**: 'offer discipline, service to'.

85 **dañ lassend wir sy ston: gebend wir . . .**: This is a new sentence. The colon, as so often in the sixteenth century, has the force of a modern comma.

90 **Dise ort**: i.e. the points on which Luther is in error.

95 **so verr jm also wer**: 'in so far as this is in fact the case'.

96 **Aiax oder Diomedes**: Ajax and Diomedes in the *Iliad* were great warriors, Nestor, Ulysses, and Menelaus less so, being greater in the council-chamber than on the battlefield. The classical allusion is typical for the humanistically minded Zwingli.

97 **das klein glid**: Jas. 3: 5. 'The tongue is a little member, and boasteth great things.'

99 **Demosthenes** (384–322 B.C.) and Cicero (106–43 B.C.) were the two great orators of classical antiquity. St. Paul, as the Apostle of the Gentiles, was also reputed to have great oratorical powers.

100 **aber es ist vns allweg zebesinnen.**: Unlike many full stops in this passage, the one after 'zebesinnen' does not approximate to a modern comma, but has the force of a colon.

109 **ob jm also sye**: 'whether this is so'.

112 **Luter / Trûb / oder vnsauber**: Zwingli takes up an established pun of the sixteenth century, Luther = 'Luter' = 'pure'.

113 **Pflegel Gottes worts:** The image of the flail, chaff, and ox seems to be a confused reminiscence of such texts as Jer. 23: 28 and 1 Cor. 9: 9 ff.

114 **denn vallt von etlicher:** i.e. 'etlicher leer'.

116 **Dine bede bûcher:** In fact *Widder die hymelischen propheten von den bildern vnd Sacrament* was only one book, although it did fall into two distinct parts.

120 **der fygenboum:** highly charged image. Cf. Matt. 21: 19.

122 **dine eygne wort setzen:** The quotation is from the tract *Daß diese Worte Christi . . . noch fest stehen.* See *Weimarer kritische Gesamtausgabe,* 33: 70, 30 ff.

131 **der arm Tüffel:** The rebuke is a fair one—Luther's pamphlet is full of references to the Devil. In a very real sense Luther gave the Devil a new lease of life by seeing his hand in every contretemps, a point of view which led him into numerous theological difficulties of the kind Zwingli mentions here.

132 **wie in minem huß der Nieman:** The personification of Nobody (Nemo, Utis, Niemand) and, to a lesser extent, Somebody, was a standard joke of the age. It gained literary expression in the comedy *Somebody and Nobody* in both English and German, and Nobody was frequently represented with a padlock on his lips (because he could not speak against his accusers) amongst the broken dishes, spilt milk, etc., for which servants commonly claimed him to be responsible.

132 **wond:** NHG 'wähnte'.

148 **min gnâdige frow Stultitia:** A reference to Erasmus's *Praise of Folly* (*Laus stultitiae*) of 1509, in which Dame Folly defends herself against her detractors and claims to hold sway over all men.

154 **Die da erkennend . . . ins menschē mund essen:** 'Those who recognize that there can be no eating of the body of Christ except in the spiritual sense which can everywhere be sustained in the light of the clear meaning of the Scriptures, or those who wish to eat him physically and extend his body, against the whole force of his own word, to the Godhead and want to eat him completely in the mouth of a man.'

176 **der lychnam zů der vrstende erhalten:** The 'lychnam' here probably refers to the body of the participants in the Sacrament, rather than to the body of Christ.

179 **Vnd do du jm die büchs vmbkartest:** 'And when you upset his collecting-box.' Zwingli is thinking of the box in which receipts from the sale of indulgences were placed.

188 **alle die den Herren Christum Jesum . . . doch ouch nun bedütlich werden / essind:** 'all those who confess the Lord Jesus Christ to be their saviour hereby give thanks for the death which he suffered for us and eat together that true sign through which Paul teaches us to become one body and bread, yet even here only symbolically'. The reference is to 1 Cor. 10: 16 f.

195 **so verr malzeichen zů gůtem genom̄en wirt:** 'in so far as "mark" is understood in a good sense'. Zwingli is anticipating possible negative overtones by association with 'Kainsmal' or the 'mark of Cain'.

200 **dann du hast gelert das es ein brot sye:** In the sense that the bread remained bread, but was fused with the substance of Christ just as iron was 'fused' with fire when heated. Zwingli is here making no more than a debating point, since he ignores Luther's teaching that Christ was really present in the elements.

212 **Warumb legst du nun . . . das du redest?:** 'Why do you impose on us what you have done or censure us now [for saying] what you yourself say?'

7. The Peasants' War

(i) The peasants state their aims

Dye Grundtlichen Vnd rechten haupt Artickel / aller Baurschafft vnnd Hyndersessen der Gaistlichen vñ Weltlichen oberkayten / von wôlchen sy sich beschwert vermainen (1525)

2 **Der erst Artickel:** The democratic principle is not entirely unknown in the Christian tradition, but the peasants' demand for the right to appoint their own priest is almost certainly a child of Luther's teachings on the Priesthood of All Believers, which saw priestly authority as being delegated by the members of the Christian community—who were in fact all priests, but did not necessarily exercise priestly functions. In *An den christlichen Adel* Luther actually uses the image of ten king's sons appointing one of their number to rule for them to illustrate the difference between 'priest' and 'layman'. The affirmation of Justification by Faith and the rather pathetic appeals to the Scriptures—which Luther in the *Ermahnung zum Frieden* (cf. p. 70) rejects out of hand—equally bear witness to the ultimately Lutheran inspiration of the articles. Luther was prepared to allow the first article to stand, suggesting that whoever paid the priest should have the right to appoint him.

9 **dañ vns den waren glaubē stetz verkündigen:** From the sense one must understand 'nichts dann'—'teach us nothing but the true faith'.

10 **geyt vns ain vrsach:** 'if there is a reason for us . . .'

10 **got vnd sein gnad:** misprint for 'got vmb sein gnad'.

19 **Der ander artickel:** Luther rejects this article as 'eytel raub vnd offentliche strauch dieberey', since he regards the tithes as something which belonged to the landlord by natural law. Traditionally the 'large tithe' was a share, usually a tenth, of the fruits of the field, while the 'small tithe' was in respect of livestock. As the article indicates, tithes on future crops were occasionally mortgaged in order to raise money in times of great need.

21 **als erfüldt:** NHG 'also erfüllt'.

25 **disen zehat / vnser kirch Brôpst:** The word order is difficult; 'vnser kirch Brôpst' is the subject, 'Sollen einsemlen' the verb, and 'disen zehat' the object of this clause.

32 **Raysen:** here, 'to participate in a military expedition'.

33 **Darmit man kain landts steüer . . . oder welttlich:** This long sentence can be divided into four parts, the first ending at 'überschuß außrichten', the second at 'nit entgeltñ', the third at 'zeyt ablassen', and the fourth at 'oder welttlich', where, in spite of the absence of punctuation, a new sentence begins.

33 **dürff auff den armen anlegen:** A. Götze and L. E. Schmitt in their edition of our text (Halle, 1953) read this phrase as 'dürff auff den armen man legen'. The original does make sense, however: 'anlegen' = NHG 'auferlegen'.

35 **Auch ob sach were:** 'Further, if it were the case that . . .'

36 **die selbigē so darumb zů zaigen / in der gestalt haben von aynem gantzen dorff der sol es nit entgeltñ:** 'those who can show with reference to the tithe ['darumb'], so to have bought it from the whole village, he [change to a singular subject] shall not be forced to give it back.'

39 **nach gestalt vñ sach:** This should probably read 'nach gestalt der sach', as suggested by Götze and Schmitt.

40 **ablassen:** From the sense, we must read 'ablösen', 'to buy back'.

44 **Nachmalen ablesen:** 'Subsequently remit' ('ablesen' is read as 'ablassen'), i.e. after they have paid the parson, the balance can be held over and an appropriate reduction made in the next tithe.

46 **oder welttlich den klaynen zehat wöllen wir:** One would expect a full stop after 'welttlich'.

51 **Der drit artickel:** In spite of the affirmation of secular authority, this is by far the most far-reaching demand made by the peasants. Not surprisingly, Luther with his transcendental view of religion protested vehemently at this attempt to 'make Christian freedom a thing of the flesh'. This, he declares, 'ist stracks widder das Euangelion . . . Es will dieser artickel alle menschen gleich machen / vnd aus dem geystlichen reich Christi eyn welltlich reich machen.'

53 **aigen leüt:** 'serfs'.

53 **wölch zů erbarmen ist:** Götze and Schmitt amend 'wölch' to 'wölchs'.

56 **Darnmb erfindt sich mit der geschryfft:** 'Darnmb' is a misprint for 'Darumb'—'Therefore it is in keeping with the Scriptures . . .'

58 **Lernet vnß Gott nit . . . zů ainer letz:** The punctuation in this sentence —which should be read as a rhetorical question—is misleading; 'Does not God teach us to live in His commandments and not in the free lustfulness of the flesh, but to love God, to recognize Him as our Lord in our neighbours . . .?' The syntax now becomes difficult, and Götze and Schmitt insert 'thon' after 'alles das'. If the later part of the sentence is to make complete sense, we must also assume that the scribe or printer has omitted after 'hetten' the words 'das vns die Leute thon sollen'—the reference is to Luke 6: 31. The parting gift referred to in the next clause is Christ's commandment at the Last Supper, 'That ye love one another' (John 13: 34 f.).

63 **darumb sollen wir . . . oberkait:** We must assume a break after 'leben'. Götze and Schmitt read this as a continuation of the preceding sentence inserting a question-mark after 'seyen' and omitting the second 'nit'. There seems to be no compelling reason to accept this reading, since the sentence makes complete sense as it stands: 'Therefore we should live according to His command, and this command does not teach and instruct us to be disobedient ("korsam" = "gehorsam") to those in authority, and not only to those in authority . . .'

68 **geren gehorsam sein:** 'geren' = 'gern'. There is a break in the sentence after 'sein'.

69 **jr wedendt:** misprint for 'jr werdendt'.

70 **oder vns jm Euangeli des berichten dz wirß seyen:** 'or show us on the basis of the Scriptures that we are serfs (lit. "it")'.

72 **Der Viert Artickel:** In keeping with his distinction between godly and worldly things, Luther denied that he was competent to judge the last eight articles and suggested that they be referred to lawyers for a decision.

77 **Auch in etlichen ortern . . . dem nechsten ist:** Ellipsis, a misprint, and the absence of punctuation make this a difficult sentence. 'Wil vns dz vnser' should read 'wir vns dz vnser', and we must assume a break after 'still-schweigen', the 'das' serving the same function as 'was' in modern German. 'Also in many places the landlord keeps game to our despite and great loss, and we must allow the brute beasts to eat uselessly and destructively our crops which God let grow for the benefit of mankind, and we dare not raise our voices in protest against this . . .'

85 **mit gnûgsamer schriff:** misprint for 'schrifft', i.e. 'documents', 'deeds'.

86 **das man das wasser vnwyssenlych also erkaufft hette:** Götze and Schmitt would have us read 'in wyssenlych' instead of 'vnwyssenlych', and following them Walter Zöllner (*Zur Geschichte des großen deutschen Bauern-krieges*, Berlin, 1961) translates the passage 'daß er das Wasser mit Wissen und Willen der Bauern gekauft hat'. The original can still be read meaning-fully, however, as 'that he bought the water without knowing [that it was not in fact the vendor's to sell]'. On the whole Götze/Schmitt's reading makes better sense.

92 **beholtzung:** One would expect simply 'holtzung'; 'beholtzung' would suggest 'afforestation'.

94 **vmb zway geldt kauffen:** 'pay double the money for it'. In a modern text a new sentence would now begin: 'In the matter of woods and forests, it is our opinion . . .'

98 **aim yetlichē sein noturfft jnß hauß zù brēen vm̄ sunst lassen nemen:** 'for anyone to be allowed to take for nothing the wood he needs to heat his house'.

102 **mit den selbigen:** i.e. with those who bought the wood honestly.

104 **auß jnen selbs:** 'arbitrarily'.

109 **der dyenst halben:** i.e. the feudal services peasants were obliged to perform for their landlords.

116 **dz wir hinfüro vns ain herschafft nit weyter wôlle lassen beschwerē:** 'that we will accept no further burdens from any lord, but the peasant shall hold the land on the terms on which it is rented to him according to the agreement between him and the lord.'

121 **rüeblich:** 'without let or hindrance'.

123 **für ander:** i.e. other services.

125 **dyen:** misprint for 'dynen'.

125 **deñ thûn:** Götze and Schmitt print this as 'denst thûn', 'denst' being a misprint for 'dienst'. The present writer is, however, tempted to read it as an article used as a demonstrative. This would not, however, affect the meaning.

127 **vñ der vil. so gûter jnnen haben:** 'as are many of those who have smallholdings'.

129 **das jr darauff einbiessen vñ verderben:** 'lose all their money on them and are ruined'.

129 **das die herschafft dieselbigen gûter / Erberleüe besichtigen lassen:** 'let the landlords have these same estates surveyed by honourable men'. 'Erberleüe' is a misprint for 'Erberleüt'.

135 **so man stetz new satzung macht . . . gestalt der sach:** 'that new statutes [i.e. Roman law] are constantly being introduced and that we are not punished according to the nature of the case.'

139 **darnach die sach gehandelt ist:** 'according to the nature of the case'.

142 **haben jnen zûgeaignet / wisen:** The *virgula* has the force of a colon here.

143 **zû geherendt:** NHG 'zugehören'.

145 **Es sey dann sach:** 'Unless it be the case that . . .'

150 **todt fall:** 'death duties'.

154 **vñ von den:** The 'den' refers to the peasants' goods and chattels. For 'besitzen' Götze and Schmitt read 'beschitzen', which clearly is the only possible reading.

155 **geschunden vnnd geschaben:** a standard doublet, 'robbed (lit. "flayed") and bled us white (lit. "scraped")'.

155 **vnd wañ sy wenig fûg . . . diß gar genomen:** 'and if they had had the slightest claim in law, they would have taken the whole of it [i.e. the property]'.

157 **sunder sol gantz absein:** 'but shall be null and void'.

160 **Zûm zwelften . . . erklert:** a rather confused and repetitive sentence. 'It is our decision and conclusive opinion that if one or more of the articles set forth here were contrary to the word of God—which we do not think them to be—if they were shown on the basis of God's word to be improper,

we would not insist on them, if it were shown to us on the evidence of the Scriptures.' 'Grnndt' is a misprint for 'grundt'. Götze and Schmitt would have us read 'wol (instead of "wo") man vns mit dem wort Gots für vnzimlich anzaigen'—'let it be shown to us . . .'—which gives a much clearer sentence.

(ii) Luther changes sides

(a) *Ermanunge zum fride auff die zwelff artikel der Bawrschafft ynn Schwaben* (1525)
(b) *Wider die mordischen vñ Reubischen Rotten der Bawren* (1525)

(a)

7 **Dazu ym welltlichen regiment nicht mehr thut / denn das yhr schindet vnd schatzt / ewern pracht vnd hohmut zu furen:** 'Also in your temporal government you do nothing else but extort and tax in order to lead a life of luxury and arrogance.'

15 **Psalm. 104:** in fact, 107: 40.

22 **Die zeychen am hymel:** The sixteenth century in general exhibited a marked interest in unusual phenomena, comets, misbirths, and the like, which were always interpreted as signs of the wrath to come. The mood of apocalyptic expectation in the years immediately preceding 1524 was heightened by the publication of numerous pamphlets and broadsides in which such portents were described.

24 **Es ist schon des zorns eyn gros teyl angegangen:** 'A great part of His wrath has already been vented [lit. 'begun'], in that God . . .'

25 **viel falscher lerer vnd propheten:** i.e. the radical Protestant sectarians, such as the Zwickau Prophets (cf. p. 52). The reasoning behind this sentence casts a particularly interesting light on Luther's view of God.

28 **Das ander stuck . . .:** 'The rest [of God's wrath] is also upon us, namely that the peasants are mustering . . .'

37 **vnweise:** Luther coins a negative form of 'weise' to match the situation envisaged. He may also intend to play on 'unweise' = 'foolish'.

41 **Es sind nicht bawren:** The declaration that the peasants were the avenging ministers of God makes Luther's subsequent condemnation of them as limbs of Satan appear in a doubly unfortunate light.

44 **die Luterische lere auszurotten:** This is the crux of the matter for Luther. In spite of his mention of the extortions of the princes, he is not so much concerned with social injustice as with the religious affiliations of the princes.

45 **wenn yhr ewr eygen prophetē weret gewesen:** 'if you had prophesied your own doom'.

48 **vnd ist eyn solcher ernst worden:** 'and it became so serious that . . .'

(*b*)

6 **Gebt dem Kayser:** Luke 20: 25.

7 **Roma. xiij:** verse 2.

14 **die nicht jr seyndt:** 'which are not theirs' (lit. 'of them').

27 **zerschmeyssen:** 'smite'; the normal form is 'zuschmeißen'.

35 **nemen ayd vnd hulde:** 'take an oath and covenant'.

43 **vñ will dye grundsuppe rûren vnd den boden gar außstossen:** 'and wants to stir up the dregs [of hell] and knock the bottom out [of the barrel].' The idiom 'Dem Faß den Boden ausstoßen' suggests the wrecking of an already precarious situation. If the Devil felt that the Day of Judgement were at hand, he would naturally want to do his worst while he still had the chance.

45 **Aber die ôberkayt so Christlich ist:** 'But the government which is Christian'. He has just said that even unchristian (i.e. non-Lutheran) governments have the right and duty to put down the rebels.

46 **keynen schein wider sie haben:** 'have not the semblance of a case against it [i.e. 'die ôberkayt']'.

51 **Denn wir fechtenn:** Eph. 6: 12.

52 **die geystlichen bôßwicht in der lufft:** Eph. 2: 2.

56 **sol man sich . . . zû recht vnd gleichem erbieten:** 'one must in addition offer the mad peasants a just and honourable settlement, even though they do not deserve it.'

61 **Roma. am xiij:** verse 4.

65 **es sey durch mord oder blûtuergiessen:** 'either on account of a murder [which has been committed] or blood shed'.

74 **weyl sie ein ader regen kan:** 'as long as it can move a limb' (lit. 'sinew').

75 **vrtayl:** Other editions have 'vorteil', which clearly makes better sense.

76 **vnrecht sachen:** 'an unjust cause'.

89 **vnnd werd erfunden im gehorsam deynes befelhs vnnd meines ampts:** 'and will be found obedient to your command and my office'.

100 **da Got fur sey:** 'which God forbid!' Although the punctuation does not indicate it, the remark is in parenthesis.

101 **ob er villeicht zum vorlauff des Jungstê tags . . . hauffen werffen:** 'whether perhaps, as a prelude to the Day of Judgement, which cannot be far off, He wishes to use the Devil to destroy all [civil] order and instituted authority and reduce the world to utter and complete chaos.'

104 **sterben doch sicher:** 'die secure [in the knowledge they are serving God]'.

107 **dz ein Fürst den himel mit blûtuergiessen verdienenen kan:** A particularly unfortunate 'Freudian' slip, which was to be seized upon by all Luther's opponents—believers could not merit heaven by their good works,

but princes could apparently earn ('verdienenen' is a misprint for 'verdienen')
a place in heaven by butchering their subjects!

112 **bleybstu drûber tod:** 'if you die while doing so'.

115 **den en:** misprint for 'deinen'.

115 **zurretten:** contraction of 'zuerretten'.

122 **der denck das vntreglich ist auffrûr:** 'let him consider that civil commotion is intolerable'.

123 **alle stunde:** 'at any moment'.

8. The sectarian legacy of the Reformation

(i) Balthasar Hubmaier preaches Anabaptism

Ain Suṁ ains gantzen Christenlichen lebens (1525)

3 **Enderend oder besserend ewer leben / vnd glaubend dem Euangelio:**
Mark 1: 15. The precise meaning of the original Greek (= 'do penance',
'repent', 'change') was a source of great controversy in the sixteenth century.
Both Luther and Hubmaier see it as referring to the inner life rather than
to the sacrament.

14 **der mensch / so do war in die morder eingefallen:** 'the man who had
fallen among thieves'. The reference is to the parable of the Good Samaritan
(Luke 10: 30–7) which, like the parable of the Prodigal Son, was ideally
suited to illustrate the common Protestant doctrine that justification was a
free gift of God, given without regard for the merits of the justified and to be
obtained by faith alone.

19 **wunden / Wein / er gibt . . . .:** The *virgula* in Hubmaier's usage can
perform the same function as both the modern colon and the full stop,
as well as the comma. T. Bergsten and G. Westin in their edition of Hubmaier's *Schriften* (Gütersloh, 1962) reprint the phrase as: 'wunden. Wein: er
gibt . . .'

35 **Nun die leeren all . . . seind sy ain bûchstab vnd tôdtendt:** 'Now all
those teachings which show the sickness or point to the doctor are, before
they are believed, a letter and kill, but in faith the spirit of God gives them
life.' The reference is to 2 Cor. 3: 6. For all their biblicism the Anabaptists
had a rather ambivalent attitude to the Scriptures and often adduced such
texts as this in order to exalt direct revelation and the 'inner light' over the
evident meaning of a given text.

39 **frücht bingen:** misprint for 'frücht bringen'.

40 **auff d' hochzeit:** John 2: 1–11.

40 **rock Joañis:** Matt. 3: 4; Mark 1: 6.

45 **Also bekennt Paulus offentlich:** Gal. 2: 20.

47 **vnd ausserhalb deß Christi:** 'and outside that of Christ', i.e. except for
what he is and does in Christ.

60 **schlichten vnd richten:** two near synonyms. 'Schlichten' basically means 'to make something smooth', 'richten' 'to make something straight'.

68 **mit der entpfahung deß wassers:** 'by receiving baptism'.

72 **Matth. 18.:** verse 15 ff. The whole of the preceding paragraph is characteristic of the role which the Anabaptists ascribed to baptism as a sign of church membership and to the community as a normative and disciplinary body.

75 **noch mag auß ym selbs kayn gůte frucht bringen:** a reminiscence of Matt. 7: 17; Luke 6: 43. Cf. Luther's use of the image, p. 24.

81 **dañ es ist als nun ain krafft:** 'for everything is now one single power', i.e. everything is brought into the single focus of God.

82 **auß dem allē eruolget:** A new sentence begins here: 'From all this it follows logically . . .'

85 **gibt sich deßselben schuldig:** 'declares himself to be guilty of this', i.e. that he is a sinner.

93 **darmit im nit beschehe wie Petro:** Mark 14: 66 ff.

94 **spricht Christus:** John 15: 5.

97 **macht groß:** 'magnifies', Lat. 'magnificere'.

103 **Die welt will nit ain übelthåtterin seyn:** 'The [children of the] world will not accept that they are evil-doers, but seek to be pious and justified by their own works.'

107 **Hie springt herfür der alt Adam:** 'Here the old Adam leaps up.'

112 **da solle das flaysch getödt werden / vnd wil aber es nun leben . . .:** 'then let the flesh be mortified, even though it now wishes to live and govern according to its own desires.'

124 **Math. 26:** in fact 24: 31 ff.

128 **welcher ye die welt also ynbrünstigklich geliebt hat:** John 3: 16.

136 **saget wol:** 'blessed [it]', Lat. 'benedicere'.

136 **Nement vnd essend:** Matt. 26: 26; Mark 14: 22.

144 **Als offt wir das brot mit aynander brechen . . .:** Westin and Bergsten print 'als' with a small letter and regard it as introducing a dependent clause: '. . . instituted by Christ as a memorial and remembrance, so that, as often as we break the bread together and divide it and eat it, we should be mindful of his body which was broken for us on the Cross and distributed to all those who eat and enjoy it in faith.' Cf. Zwingli's view of the sacrament, p. 62.

148 **da greyfft man augenscheynlich:** 'then one understands what is obvious' (lit. 'obviously').

153 **der rayff vor dem wirtzhauß:** A hoop from a barrel served the same purpose before German inns as a bush did before English ones.

157 **1 Corinth. 11. cap.:** verse 26.

165 **blitz:** here 'light'.

170 **ain bern mose:** Westin and Bergsten correct this to 'ain bern mess'—'a bear's mass', i.e. something unseemly. Hubmaier uses the expression elsewhere, and although not explicitly stated, the reference is probably to the Roman doctrine of the sacrificial nature of the mass, according to which the sacrifice of Christ at Calvary was re-enacted in the 'offering' of the elements. The Protestants denied this, of course, maintaining that Christ's death was 'one sacrifice for sins, for ever' and holding that the Roman doctrine constituted an idolatrous and impious denial of the efficacy of Christ's original sacrifice.

189 **die Axt ist an die wurtzel:** Matt. 3: 10; Luke 3: 9.

190 **ist nichts verhanden:** 'there is no help for it, but that . . .'

193 **dañ Christus sagt:** Matt. 10: 32; Luke 12: 8. 'Heytter' here means 'clear'.

197 **fürchtent nit die:** Matt. 10: 28.

200 **wer oren hab:** Matt. 11: 15.

201 **über die / stillschweiger:** The punctuation here is misleading. The *virgula* should be ignored.

204 **Sambstag nach Petri vnd Pauli:** 1 July.

(ii) Sebastian Franck condemns a literal approach to the Bible, rejects all institutionalized religion, and preaches the Church Spiritual

Paradoxa (1534)

11 **Vnd das haben allweg die weysesten vnd frümbsten der welt gethan:** 'And this [namely that God's messengers have perished as knaves and heretics] has always been the doing of the wisest and most pious [children] of the world.' The whole paragraph plays on the irreconcilable hostility between the Gospel and the world, in which fair is foul and foul is fair— so much so that in the world God is regarded as the Devil and the Devil as God.

15 **Es můß der teuffel vnd nit Got seyn:** Franck is quoting the view of the children of this world.

16 **Auß mit disem feindtseligen Got:** 'Away with this hostile God.'

18 **vnd ein yeden sich seiner selbst verzeihen heißt:** 'and commands everyone to deny himself'. The reference is to texts such as Matt. 10: 39 and 16: 24–5.

28 **Joh. am 12.14.16:** verses 31, 30, and 11 respectively.

28 **2. Corinth. am 4.:** verse 4.

30 **spricht sie:** i.e. the world.

31 **Luc. 11. Matt. 12. Joh. 8.:** verses 15, 24, and 44–59 respectively.

33 **Psal. 14.:** verse 1.

37 **nit bey jr fehet noch stat hat:** 'does not establish itself [lit. 'take hold']
or have any place in the world'.

39 **dañ sie lassen jnen diß nicht eingehen:** Franck changes the subject from
singular to plural. He began by talking about the world, now he is thinking
of the children of the world. The 'diß' refers to 'die Schrift' = 'Gottes
wort'; 'jnen' would appear as 'sich' in a modern text.

40 **sind vil anders gesinnet / Ja stracks des widerspils:** literally 'they
are very much otherwise-minded, indeed of entirely the opposite persua-
sion', i.e. 'their minds are closed, indeed, diametrically opposed to it'.

41 **diß bůch:** Franck means the Bible, not his own book.

41 **mit siben Sigeln:** Rev. 5: 1.

42 **vorhin:** i.e. before they can understand it.

47 **Wie Christus deutlich sagt:** Matt. 13: 11 ff.

49 **Pythagoras:** The teachings of Pythagoras, a Greek philosopher of the
sixth century B.C., combined a strong mathematical interest with a highly
developed ethical outlook. In the sixteenth century Pythagoras was commonly regarded as a poet and magician and—erroneously—as the author
of the *Cabbala*. Franck seems to be thinking of him in this last capacity.

51 **in der Schůl:** i.e. a secret.

52 **Matth. 12:** in fact 13: 11.

52 **Joh. 12:** verse 40.

54 **sew vnd hund:** Matt. 7: 6.

62 **tödtender Bůchstab:** 2 Cor. 3: 6. Almost all sectarians interpret St. Paul's
words as meaning that the 'inner voice' must quicken the objective revelation of the Scriptures, and that without the former the latter is meaningless.
(Cf. Hubmaier's use of the text, p. 79.)

65 **2. Cor. 3.:** verses 7 ff.

66 **Mosi nit vnder die augen mochten sehen:** 'could not steadfastly behold
the face of Moses'.

71 **Joh. 7.:** verse 17.

76 **den selbigē:** i.e. 'den Bůchstaben', not 'den geyst'!

76 **für sein Apollinē:** Apollo was, amongst other things, the god of prophecy.
The oracle at Delphi was under his guidance.

77 **ein krip Christi:** 'a crib of Christ', i.e. something which shields Christ and
hides him from us.

84 **Es ist nit zůsagen ... verstehet:** 'There is no telling, if one understands
the Scriptures according to the dead letter, what doors one opens . . .'

87 **Ouidium de Arte amandi:** Ovid's notorious textbook on the Art of Love.

90 **Die hend abhawen ... hundertfeltig wider nemen:** Whatever one may
think of Franck's religious views, one cannot help sympathizing with his
complaint at the literal-mindedness of many of his contemporaries who, as
the examples he cites show, often carried the biblicism they had learnt from

Luther to absurd lengths, refusing to wear shoes on the basis of Matt. 10: 10, for instance, and preaching only from rooftops on the basis of Matt. 10: 27. Franck lists the principal texts whose metaphors are capable of producing such bizarre results when applied literally, Matt. 18: 8–9; 26: 26–7; John 3: 3; Matt. 26: 61; 16: 18; John 3: 15, etc.

95 **Wie der prophet Hiere.:** Jer. 48: 10.

104 **Auß disem folgt . . . der geister:** Syntactically, this is a rather confused sentence. 'From this it follows that the letter and grammatical meaning of the Scripture cannot also be the touchstone and balance by which the spirits [of those who claim to be Christians] are judged, but that the spirit, meaning, interpretation, and understanding of it [the Scripture] alone is [like] God's word, and is the test to be applied to the spirits'; i.e. men cannot be judged by whether they conform to the letter of the Scriptures, but by whether they conform to their spirit. Equally God's word cannot be approached in terms of its literal meaning, but only in terms of its spiritual meaning.

109 **Silenus Alcibiadis:** The reference is to the *Adagia* of Erasmus, where the term is interpreted as a synonym for deceptiveness. A 'silenus' was a statuette, ugly in appearance, which could be opened to reveal the figure of a handsome god concealed within, and Erasmus recalls that in Plato's *Symposium* Alcibiades likens Socrates to a 'silenus' because his ugliness concealed a beautiful mind. In the course of his remarks, Erasmus goes into detail on the deceptiveness of the Scriptures, contrasting the often unchaste and absurd 'fable' with the divine wisdom it conceals.

113 **wie er da laut:** NHG 'wie er da lautet'.

115 **Gal. 5.:** verses 19 ff.

123 **Matt. 13.:** verses 24 ff.

125 **Luce 21.:** verses 5 ff.

127 **eyn sondere Sect / tauff . . .:** The reference is, of course, to the Anabaptists.

133 **oder hauffen spreüe:** This is in apposition to 'einem vnkrauttige acker', not to 'eynn kleines überigs heuflin waytzen'.

134 **das er dan vmb Gottes willen leydenn soll / biß man jhn nimmer leyden will:** 'which he shall suffer for God's sake, until they will no longer allow him to stay'. The reference is to Matt. 10: 14 ff.

137 **er darff jhm nit erst . . .:** The 'er' refers to 'eyn yeder'.

141 **wie jhr vil teglich:** 'as many of them [i.e. the sectarians] do every day'.

145 **Matth. 16.:** verse 18. The interpretation given to this text by Franck is a highly original one! It is, however, by no means untypical of the freedom of interpretation amongst the sectarians.

145 **Vnd was eüsserlich . . . Euangelium ist:** This inordinately long sentence can be broken at 'biß ans ende'. The first part is still dependent on 'dieweyl ich weyß'. 'And that the Holy Ghost has not neglected His own, but has used and restored inwardly in spirit and in truth that which externally has

been lost and abused—and is still being lost—in the matter of the keys, sacraments, etc., and in the midst of Babylon has baptized and taught His own . . .'

153 **Dieweyl die Kirch** . . .: It would be difficult to find a more succinct statement of the spiritualist position than that contained in this sentence.

154 **fingerzeyge Sect**: 'a sect which can be pointed out with the finger', i.e. which exists physically.

164 **ausser deren keinn heil**: The 'deren' refers to 'versamlung vnd gemeyn'. Franck is here misapplying the venerable tag: *Extra ecclesiam nulla est salus*.

166 **bin / ich**: One would expect the *virgula* to come after 'ich'.

174 **die Schaff von Bôcken**: Matt. 25: 32.

177 **Joan. 13.**: verse 35.

180 **welche sein**: 'those that [are] his'.

180 **2. Timoth. 2.**: verse 19.

183 **d' mich darfür acht**: 'who regards me as such [i.e. as his brother]'.

184 **odder wie Petrus / auß erfarung sagt**: The *virgula* should be ignored. The reference is to such texts as 1 Pet. 2: 17, 1 Pet. 3: 11.

187 **widder den Heiligen geyst**: This was the unforgivable sin, Matt. 12:31–2.

189 **dem Herrn felt**: We should expect 'der dem Herrn felt', 'who falls in the Lord'.

192 **Roma. 2. 14.**: verses 1 ff. and 3 f. respectively.

II · MORAL SATIRE

1. Standard themes: Folly, Vulgarity, and the Devil

(i) Sebastian Brant: *Das Narren schyff* (1494)

(a) *Von vnnutzē buchern*

Although Brant on occasion speaks of himself as 'der narr sebastianus brandt', the suggestion that he is thinking of himself in his attack on the false scholar who collects books but does not read them is almost certainly mistaken. The art of printing was already some fifty years old, but books were still expensive and were often prized as articles of *virtù* and Brant is probably attacking a contemporary fad. The books collected by the bibliophile in the engraving are, Brant suggests, doubly useless: their owner does not use or understand them, but even if he did, they would not communicate to him anything really worth knowing: true wisdom is not to be culled from learned tomes, but lies in the knowledge of God and His purpose with man.

1 **vordantz**: In the sixteenth century, as today, it was considered a great honour on formal occasions to lead off the dance. The image of the dance is no more than a convenient metaphor here, however, although Brant does elsewhere (ch. 62) refer to his collection of fools as a 'narrendantz'.

6 **Das hat worlich eyn sundren gryff:** 'There is indeed a special reason
for this.' Ulrich Gaier has suggested that the special significance here
attributed to the foolish man who possesses books, but does not read them,
lies in his intended function as a warning to the purchasers of Brant's own
book—unlike this particular fool, they should read and profit from the book
they have bought.

10 **verstand:** present tense!—a common Alemannic form.

12 **Das ich jnn wil der fliegen weren:** 'that I will strive to keep the flies off
them'—a proverbial and ironic way of saying he puts them to no use.

13 **von künsten reden:** 'discuss learned things'.

17 **Ptolomeus:** Ptolemy the Great (285–246 B.C.), King of Egypt, built one
of the great libraries of antiquity at Alexandria.

17 **bstelt:** here 'arranged', 'took steps to ensure that'.

20 **das recht gesatz:** 'the true Law', i.e. the Christian faith, of which Ptolemy,
for all his books, had no knowledge.

24 **brechen myn synn:** 'cudgel my brains'.

27 **Jch mag doch sunst wol sin eyn here:** The title 'here' was not only
applied to those of noble rank and wealth, but was also conferred on
scholars who held a doctorate. Our bibliophile is prepared to forgo the
latter, since he can claim the title on the grounds of his social position.

28 **Vnd lonen eym der für mich ler:** 'ler' here suggests 'learn' rather than
'teach'. The reference may be to some academic abuse of the times, conceivably the hiring of substitute candidates for disputations, etc.

31 **So kan ich jta sprechen jo:** 'I can say "ita" for "yes".'

32 **Des tütschen orden bin ich fro:** 'I am glad when things are done and
said in German [rather than Latin].' 'Orde' originally meant a community
of people who lived by set rules, and then came to mean the rules themselves.
'Orde' was often used to convey the idea of a group of people devoted to
some more or less reprehensible idea ('der bûler, säufer orden', etc.).

35 **gouch:** 'cuckoo'. The word is rich in pejorative associations in the sixteenth
century and ranges in meaning from 'simpleton' to 'scoundrel', and is
frequently applied to those guilty of sexual immorality.

38 **eins mullers thier:** i.e. a donkey.

(b) Von narrechtez anslag

The preamble and the woodcut are inspired by the words of Christ: 'For
which of you, intending to build a tower, sitteth not down first and counteth
the cost, whether he have sufficient to finish it? Lest haply, after he have
laid the foundations, and is not able to finish it, all that behold it begin to
mock him' (Luke 16: 28–30).

4 **narrechtez:** misprint for 'narrechtem'.

11 **Nabuchodnosor:** The reference is to Daniel 4: 30 ff., where Nebuchad-
nezzar boasts of his achievements in building Babylon, but is interrupted

by a voice from Heaven which announces the loss of his kingdom, 'and he was driven from men, and did eat grass as oxen, and his body was wet with the dew of Heaven.'

16 **Das er jm feld bleib / wie eyn kû:** proverbial for 'to leave something unfinished'.

17 **Nemroth:** Brant associates Gen. 10: 10 and 11: 9, and concludes that Nimrod was responsible for the building of the Tower of Babel. Being built after the Flood, 'lest we be scattered abroad on the face of the whole earth', the tower is in Brant's view an example of the presumptuous folly of mankind, who refuse to take God into account.

18 **für wassers klüfft:** Following Zarncke's note, Bobertag suggests 'Zerklüftung, Zerstörung durch das Wasser', but Grimm does record later examples of 'Wasserkluft' as a compound meaning 'huge expanse of water', and both the Latin and Low German translators seem to have understood the term in this sense.

22 **Lucullus:** Roman general (c. 117–56 B.C.) who was renowned for his lavish banquets and the construction of the famous *horti Luculliani*, to which Brant is probably referring here.

23 **das in nit ruw:** NHG 'daß es ihn nicht reut'.

28 **der soll sin selbst bewerung han:** 'he should be sure in his own mind'.

31 **gluck:** here, 'mishap', 'misfortune'. 'Gluck' is any unforeseen change of fortune.

33 **weger:** comparative of 'wege' (MHG 'wæge') = 'advantageous'.

36 **Labyrinthus by dem Nyl:** The labyrinth referred to is that built by Amenemhet III about 2200 B.C. at Medinet el Fajum as a palace and said to contain 3,000 rooms.

38 **Keyn buw mag lang vff erd hye syn:** The platitudinous quality of the last four lines is exceptional even for Brant.

(*c*) *Von dantzen*

Traditionally moralists have objected to dancing as an immodest spectacle and as an invitation to sexual immorality. For the Middle Ages, however, scriptural evidence corroborated empirical fact: on the basis of Exod. 23: 19, it was commonly held that the first dance was executed by the Israelites around the golden calf (hence the latter's inclusion in the woodcut) and that dancing was a favourite device of the Devil by which he turned men from the service of God. Further, in the fifteenth and sixteenth centuries the frequently obscene nature of the accompanying songs and the somewhat boisterous nature of the dances themselves inevitably made dancing a target for the moralist, and even led to the introduction of by-laws in a number of towns in an attempt to control the worst excesses.

2 **yenierdar:** misprint for 'yemerdar'.

5 **Jch hieltt nah**: 'I almost considered them . . .', i.e. 'I nearly made a mistake by considering them merely as fools, when in reality they are something worse—sinners.'

7 **toub**: here 'mad', 'senseless'.

12 **das es der tüfel hat vff bracht**: 'that the devil invented it'.

18 **für louff der vnlutterkeyt**: 'a source of impurity, lewdness'.

24 **kilchwih / erste meß**: festivities celebrating the consecration of a church, the first mass said in the church, or their anniversaries.

25 **Do dantzen pfaffen / mynch**: It was counted a mortal sin for anyone in orders to take part in a dance. In the woodcut the man on the left who is in the act of lifting his partner's skirt appears to be wearing a cowl.

26 **Die kutt můß sich do hynden reyen**: 'The cowl must line up behind', i.e. 'the clergy must join in too'.

27 **vnd würfft vmbher eyn**: 'and throws one [i.e. his partner] about'.

30 **bas dann essen fygē**: 'better than eating figs'. Because of their sweetness figs were, in an age which knew neither sugar-cane nor sugar-beet, a great delicacy.

31 **Kůntz mit Måtzen**: common peasant names—Kunz = Konrad, Mätzen = Mechthild.

33 **des kouffes eys**: 'to strike a bargain'. 'Eys' is an Alemannic form of 'eins'.

34 **wie man eyn bock geb vmb eyn geiß**: 'give tit for tat'. 'Bock' and 'Geiß' were often used together to indicate a pair, but the choice of these animals with their notorious sexual appetite is particularly appropriate here.

(d) võ abgang des gloubē.

In spite of his rather wooden pedantry in many chapters of the *Narrenschiff*, Brant could achieve a surprising emotional intensity when the issues involved affected him directly. To a deeply pious and conservative-minded man the political situation in 1494 was profoundly disturbing and in the present chapter he reviews the sad decay into which Christendom has fallen, with the Turks pressing on the eastern frontiers of the Empire, the religious unity of Europe torn by heretical movements, and the authority of the Emperor a pale shadow of its former self in a context where political initiative was increasingly becoming the prerogative of the individual territorial princes. Rather surprisingly Brant eschews any reference to ecclesiastical abuses save in the most innocuously general terms, and sees the problems of his age as being above all political ones, believing that if the authority of the Emperor can be restored, the ecclesiastical abuses he complains of in other chapters will be capable of a rapid cure. His analysis is probably not very far from the truth, but in the light of subsequent history and the role of the territorial princes during the Reformation his appeals to the secular and ecclesiastical rulers to forsake their petty ambitions and advantages and unite in the defence of Christendom against her internal and external enemies gains an unexpected, added pathos.

8 **wer wunder nit:** 'it would not be surprising'.

17 **die kåtzer hert:** presumably the Hussites.

18 **den halb zerrissen:** i.e. 'den krysten glouben', to which the 'den' of line 21 and the 'der' of line 22 also refer.

19 **Machamet:** Mohammed, i.e. the Turks.

21 **sym:** contracted form of 'synem'.

27 **On das:** 'Apart from the fact that'.

29 **Zwey keyserthům:** i.e. Constantinople (1453) and Trebizond (1461).

33 **lyt:** NHG 'liegt'.

35 **Do man hielt Patriarchen stadt:** 'Where one kept patriarchal state', i.e. which were the seat of a patriarch.

39 **Es würt bald an das houbt ouch gon:** 'It will soon reach [i.e. affect] the head', i.e. Rome itself.

43 **eyn gmeyner rott:** 'a common council', i.e. the Senate.

44 **noch hochfart staltt:** 'strove after vainglorious things'.

51 **Bist funffzehen hundert jor gesyn:** Traditionally, by regarding the Byzantine and the Holy Roman empires as the successors of imperial Rome, an unbroken line of succession was held to lead from Julius Caesar to the latest Holy Roman Emperor.

52 **vnd von:** Zarncke regards the 'vnd von' as being synonymous with the 'ab' of 'abgenommen', which it thus serves to strengthen.

57 **Do mit du sygest:** 'Sygest' is here present subjunctive of 'sein', not the present indicative of 'siegen'!

58 **Den dunkt nit / das er ettwas hab . . .:** An impersonal construction—literally, 'He who does not get it [break it off] from the Roman Empire, considers himself to have nothing', i.e. princes consider themselves to be cheated, if they do not take part in the carving up of the Holy Roman Empire.

64 **Vil stett sich brocht hant jnn gewer:** 'Many towns have taken up arms.' Zarncke suggests that Brant is thinking particularly of Bruges and Vienna.

66 **Eyn yeder fürst / der ganß bricht ab . . .:** 'Every prince attacks the goose so that he can have a feather from it'—essentially the same idea as that just expressed. It has been suggested that the goose is here intended as an ironic reference to the imperial eagle. While this would fit the sense, it is unlikely that Brant would thus mock the symbol of his political ideals. He is merely using a proverbial image for 'to get one's share of what is going'.

68 **Durch gott:** 'For God's sake.'

70 **joch:** an intensifying particle common in Alemannic.

74 **zerteilt von eyn:** 'split up', 'divided against itself'.

84 **die stůdt:** 'stud-farm'. 'Bissen' is here present, not preterite. The image of horses biting each other's tails is proverbial for discord.

87 **Cerastes**: a monstrous snake, variously reputed to have two or four horns.

87 **Basylist**: 'basilisk', a monstrous reptile hatched by a snake from a cock's egg.

89 **Der gyfft dar schmeycht**: 'Who with false, deceitful flattery offers poison.' The basic meaning of 'schmeichen' is 'to make supple by oiling'.

94 **zwor**: not concessive, but emphatic here—'You have in very truth . . .'

94 **eyn künig milt**: i.e. Maximilian I (1493–1519). Because of his knightly ambitions he was often described as 'der letzte Ritter'. The rulers of the Holy Roman Empire were held to be King (of the Romans) by virtue of their election by the Electoral College, made up of the seven 'Kurfürsten', and Emperor by virtue of their anointing by the Pope. Maximilian was elected in 1486, but was not anointed until 1493.

96 **Der zwyngen tůg all land gemeyn**: 'Who is [would be] capable of conquering all common land [i.e. all that should belong to Christendom], if only you are willing to help him.'

101 **die heilig erd**: presumably the Kingdom of Jerusalem. The crusading ideal was still very much in the air in Brant's time. Both Maximilian and Charles VIII of France toyed with the idea of leading a European crusade, and as late as 1536 Charles V seriously suggested to his rival Francis I of France that they should sink their differences and unite in such an enterprise.

105 **Dann kleynes heres / walttet gott**: 'For God looks after little armies.'

112 **Truw / frid / vnd lieb sich bruchen důt**: 'And use (or exercise) fidelity, peace, and charity'. 'Truw', 'frid', and 'lieb' are genitives dependent on 'sich bruchen'.

117 **flißt schloffes sich**: NHG 'sich des Schlafs befleißigt', i.e. 'sleeps'.

123 **die axt stat an dem boum**: Matt. 3: 10.

127 **aller sorgen keyn**: i.e. no fear at all.

133 **noch üwerm stadt**: 'by virtue of your position in life'.

135 **Das jr sônt**: NHG 'daß ihr sollt'.

136 **Nit lont / das es an uch er sitz**: 'Do not let things go wrong through your fault.'

139 **die Sunn / vnd mon**: i.e. the Emperor and the Pope.

142 **jch man noch manchen dran**: Brant was as good as his word and produced a number of broadsheets which set forth his political views and appealed for public support.

(ii) Thomas Murner: *Doctor murners narrē beschwerůg* (1512)

(*a*) *Ein wechsen naß machen.*

Murner opens his review of human follies with the same woodcut Brant had used to illustrate his first chapter (cf. p. 95), and, apparently under the impression that Brant had meant to satirize himself in the figure of the foolish bibliophile, applies it to himself also. Presumably because the figure in the engraving had a rather well-developed nose, Murner in typically idiosyncratic, whimsical fashion takes this as his point of departure and mocks the false scholars who are prepared to mould and distort the Scriptures to their own purposes, as though they were a nose of wax to be pushed and pulled into any desired shape. The element of self-satire—Murner includes himself amongst the false scholars in quite unambiguous fashion— is retained throughout the chapter, but Murner's real purpose is to launch a swingeing attack on the laziness and hypocrisy of the contemporary clergy, his self-identification with the latter enabling him to attack their failings all the more savagely.

In spite of odd infelicities, Murner's language is much more supple than Brant's and the verses flow more easily. Equally, as a popular preacher, Murner avoids the pedantic quotation of rather fusty Biblical and historical examples and authorities, citing for preference proverbs and concrete, familiar things from his own and the reader's immediate experience. Compared with the general atmosphere of book-learning which pervades the *Narrenschiff*, Murner's work seems immediate and close to everyday life, and while Brant is concerned to maintain his donnish dignity and treat his subject with befitting seriousness, Murner rather delights in playing to the gallery and raising a laugh by cheeky—and not always altogether appropriate—humour: 'We still have St. Peter's keys, but God has changed the lock', etc.

3 **Das macht das ich beschweren kan:** Just as Brant had the allegory of the ship to give his review some sort of formal unity, Murner uses the device of conjuring: as the learned doctor, he is going to exorcize the follies of his fellow men, a procedure which naturally enables him to review them.

7 **Dz ich meī ort nit het versessen:** 'That I (almost) did not take my place'.

14 **beneuenut:** 'welcome'.

15 **in eygner hut:** 'in the flesh' (lit. 'skin').

16 **meister der geschrifft:** in the sense of the academic title 'Magister'. The idea of being master of the Scriptures is developed more fully below.

17 **sele antrifft:** 'concern souls'.

19 **Vnd wissent nit was die rûben gelten:** 'And do not know the price of turnips'—proverbial for complete ignorance.

25 **Als weñ du küwtest bonenstro:** 'As though chewing bean-straw'— proverbial for something distasteful.

28 **Wir seindt die ersten vndern gelerten Die bösen valschen vnd verkerten:** The association of 'gelert' and 'verkert' was traditional.

31 **So wir weit louffen irr dar neben:** 'But we ourselves run far astray from it.'

34 **were.:** The full stop, like the only other one in the chapter ('Wir solten die vnwysen leren.', below), is misleading—the sentence ends at the end of the next line.

37 **Das wir dich leren vnd dir roten:** 'That which we teach and advise you.'

41 **Das wir dir geben . . . vnd vnser nit vergessen:** 'That we should give you an understanding of your salvation and not forget ourselves [in the process].'

45 **Vnd lauffent wir den affen steg:** 'And we ourselves take the path of folly': 'affe' here means 'fool'.

49 **Nach dem ein yeder opffer gyt:** 'According to the amount of each person's financial contribution.' Both moderate reformists, like Murner or Erasmus, and the radical Protestant reformers were united in their condemnation of the commercialization of late medieval religion.

52 **sant peters schlüssel:** Matt. 16: 19, one of the principal texts on which the case for the supremacy of the Roman Church rested. Murner was subsequently to use this text most effectively in his quarrel with Luther.

56 **Got můß vns yetz barmhertzig syn:** Murner parodies the vulgarization of the Vicarship of the Pope and Roman clergy.

58 **Gůtter ding můß mit vns lachen:** 'He must laugh cheerfully with us.'

61 **Vff erden vnd in hymels thron:** another reference to Matt. 16: 19.

62 **ein eben man:** 'an amenable fellow'.

63 **schribs nit an:** 'did not book it up', 'put it on the account'.

64 **geschwister kindt:** 'cousins'.

67 **Als das wir wendt ist mit jm schlecht:** 'Everything we want is easy with Him', i.e. 'O.K. by Him'.

69 **Do ich vormals herr thoman was:** i.e. before he had a doctorate to give him authority. Murner is here punning on his name 'Thoman/dummen'.

72 **Dañ ich das selb geschriben fandt:** 'Than I found written', i.e. in the Scriptures and the Church Fathers, so that he was preaching something he had invented.

77 **Vnd lerne das:** here, 'And teach that'.

82 **deller schlecken:** 'lick plates'; idiomatically this can mean 'to curry favour'; it might possibly also be intended to indicate that he is concerned to fill his belly rather than preach the Gospel.

83 **Vil lassen in der feder stecken:** 'Leave much unsaid', i.e. in his desire to curry favour.

84 **Wañ dich der dodt würt strecken baß:** 'When Death will stretch you better.' The reference is to the current practice of torturing prisoners on the rack in order to secure a confession.

88 **Zů des rechten hirten st:** misprint for 'stall'.

89 **So bringen wirs den wölffen all:** 'But we bring it to [all] the wolves.' It is also possible that Murner was now thinking of 'Das irrendt schäflin' in the plural, and that the 's' is an enclitic form of the plural pronoun: 'We bring them all to the wolves.'

91 **durß:** misprint for 'druß'.

93 **das er auch selber solt Darzů lůgen offt vnd dick:** 'that he constantly keep an eye on it himself'.

98 **ein zytiger reg:** 'rain in due season' (Deut. 11: 14), i.e. 'it was an appropriate moment'.

99 **Die zecken mir ouch ab zůlesen:** 'To get rid of the ticks that infest me', i.e. 'To make a confession of my own faults'!

(*b*) *Zu dantz stellen*: 'To invite to dance', 'Come dancing!' The preamble to the attack on dancing is clearly imitated from Brant, but Murner turns Brant's generalized remarks on dancing into a specific reference to the woodcut (in the edition of 1512 he reproduces the one from the *Narrenschiff*) by the introduction of 'also' in the second line. As in *Ein wechsen naß machen*, Murner stays much more closely to the reality of everyday life than Brant had done and, equally typically, is prepared to join in the dance himself.

3 **Lieffens:** The 's' is an enclitic form of 'sie'.

5 **Rat du wañ wurdens wider kummen:** The implied answer is, of course, never, since they will all have been consigned to hell.

7 **wotl:** misprint for 'wolt'.

12 **Pfeyff vff:** the instruction to the piper to begin playing. In our edition Brant's woodcut has been replaced by a picture of two girls talking to a fool, while a piper plays on his pipe behind them.

12 **dranraran** (Dran, ran, ran): the name of the dance. That this was also the traditional cry of German 'Landsknechte' when storming an obstacle probably provides an indication of the nature of this particular dance.

13 **Elßlin / gretdlin:** common names for girls—'Betty', 'Maggie'.

14 **Die nit hübsch seindt:** here, 'gay', as opposed to 'frum' = 'pious', 'well behaved'.

16 **hôrt nit an den reyen:** 'should not be at the dance'.

18 **So hat die erberkeit ein endt:** borrowed almost literally from Brant's line 20.

19 **Das kritzen krammen in der hendt:** Both words mean 'to scratch'. This is something rather stronger than 'palm-paddling', however; the scratching of the palm constituted an invitation to sexual intercourse.

21 **grieß:** NHG 'Grüße'.

22 **Als ich verstandt:** 'As I understand it'. 'Verstanden' = 'verstehen' is not uncommon in Alemannic.

24 **Nun die den knaben stüren kan:** '*Only* the one who can swing [lit. "support"] her partner'.

30 **sich hoch ynher bricht:** 'leaps up high'.

31 **Das man ir weiß nit wo hin sicht:** 'So that you can see I don't know how far up her skirt.'

34 **Der schåffer von der nüwen statt:** the name of a contemporary dance which involved embracing and kissing.

38 **frauwen huß:** 'brothel'.

42 **du vil böses lied:** Having punningly personified the dance, Murner now addresses the lyrics which were sung while dancing. The song is 'böse', because it was obscene.

43 **mied:** NHG 'müde'.

47 **vor dem thor:** i.e. in their immediate neighbourhood.

49 **versient:** NHG 'versühnt'.

60 **Da wirt üch dañ dar nach ir ringen:** 'Then you will get what you are striving for.'

69 **herfür bracht:** 'brought to the fore'; a reference to the previous injunction 'Die nit hübsch seindt laß da hinden'.

71 **Vnd mit maria dantzen schon:** a reference to the old legend of a virtuous maid who scorned earthly dances and was rewarded by being invited to dance with the Virgin.

(iii) Kaspar Scheidt: *Grobianus. Von groben sitten / vnd vnhöflichen / geberden* (1551)

9 **Erstlich soll dir zun ohren gehn:** 'The first piece of instruction I would have you hear is . . .'

18 **am kalten ston:** 'stand about in the cold'.

25 **mach dein fadenrecht für dich:** 'do as it suits you'. 'Recht' is an adverb, not the second half of a compound noun.

38 **Man möcht dirs sonst zur hoffart wenden:** 'People could otherwise interpret it as undue pride on your part.'

41 **maußbild:** misprint for 'manßbild'.

43 **hoffzucht:** 'behaviour such as would be suitable for courtly society'.

52 **Dang har:** misprint for 'Lang har'.

53 **hettens ehr:** The 's' is an enclitic form of the third person plural of the personal pronoun.

67 **Was hast an meinen zeenen feel?:** 'What do you find wrong with my teeth?'

(iv) Andreas Musculus: *Vom zuluderten / zucht vnd Ehrerwegnen pludrichten Hosenteuffel* (1555)

1 **die dritte sünde:** Altogether Musculus lists some eight sins in which the new fashion involves men, and devotes a chapter to each. The long first sentence can be divided into three parts, the first ending in 'von jugent auff' and the second in 'zu gangen were'. The 'zulumbt' of the title (NHG

'zerlumpt') refers to the slashes in the garment, which Musculus scornfully dismisses as 'ragged'.

25 **ziegenbeltz**: The reference is to Gen. 3: 21, but neither the Authorized Version nor Luther's translation contains any reference to *goats'* skins.

34 **zuflambten**: NHG 'zerflammt'. There is no English equivalent for this word, which can occasionally mean 'tattered' but was used also to describe the effect of the brightly coloured lining or undergarment showing through the slashed tunic.

45 **Wenden**: 'Wends', the Slav people who originally peopled the lands east of the Saale and were subjugated by the Germans in the course of the Middle Ages. A small enclave of Wends still survives in Lusatia.

55 **in jrem Frawenzimmer**: 'amongst the women of their household'.

55 **das michs nit anders ansicht / als**: 'that it seems to me [not otherwise than] that . . .'

56 **vnd sich an die stadt allenthalben eingesatzt**: 'and has taken its place everywhere'.

63 **Venus berg**: the hollow mountain where Venus kept court.

65 **Erbar / Ersam / vnd Ernfeste**: These were polite adjectives, used in spoken and written forms of address.

74 **pfuē dich an**: 'cry "Pfui" at you'.

78 **Legion**: Mark 5: 9.

88 **Meerwundern**: 'sea monsters'. Interest in freaks and unusual phenomena was widespread in the sixteenth century and exhibitions of freaks and prints representing them were very popular.

2. The fable and the animal epic

(i) Hans Sachs: *Die drey Hannen* (1557)

5 **vbert maß**: contracted form of 'vber die maß'.

14 **Verporgen halff jr Bulerey**: 'aided and abetted her lewdness secretly'.

27 **Drey guter Hannen vberauß**: NHG 'drei überaus gute Hähne'. The genitive after numerals and adjectives of quantity is still common in ENHG.

35 **sie fragen was**: 'she asked'.

38 **hinn**: abbreviation for 'hinnen', 'here, in this place'.

45 **Euch vor der Bulerey zu schewen**: 'To make you afraid of committing adultery'.

65 **Sein Gsell gar on vnschuld verdorben**: 'on vnschuld' does not make sense here. In spite of the need for the extra syllable, we must understand 'on schuld'.

69 **Jn zoren**: NHG 'in Zorn'.

70 **diesem Han gescheid:** NHG 'diesem gescheiten Hahn'.

95 **weil ich mag:** 'as long as I can'.

96 **zessen:** contraction of 'zu essen'.

(ii) Johann Fischart: *Flôh Haz | Weiber Traz* (1573/7)

6 **Wann man zwo arbait ainsmals thut:** 'When one does two jobs at the same time.'

15 **Notstall:** a special stall in a forge used by blacksmiths to control unruly horses.

28 **Die nie kain Wasser betrubt hâtten:** a typical example of Fischart's ability to exploit a figure of speech for humorous effect. 'Kein Wasser trüben' is idiomatic for 'to be completely inoffensive'.

30 **Der Hochpliz vnd der Wollenschreter:** The humorous—and often obscene—names of the fleas are a feature of the work: 'Hochpliz' = 'High-jumper' (MHG 'blitzen' = 'hop'), 'Wollenschreter' = 'Wool-bug'; cf. 'Hundshummel' = 'Dog-bee', 'Schlizscheu' = 'Slit-fright', 'Supfloch' = 'Sip-hole', 'Schratter' = 'Imp', 'PfezsieLind' = 'Tweak-her-gently'.

43 **Die losung war jr nicht dermasen ... baide bain:** 'The price [she has been haggling with a customer] was not so important for her that she could stop herself from reaching between her legs.'

58 **ir hart mas:** 'attacked her fiercely'.

59 **Fuhr sie hinein:** 'She reached under her skirt.'

65 **Da dacht ich an den Traculam:** The Transylvanian Count Dracula, immortalized for English readers by Bram Stoker and for cinema-goers by Bela Lugosi, was a human vampire who drank his victims' blood.

69 **da hastu gute weil:** 'there is a good opportunity for you'.

77 **Vnd hub sich schnell auf hinden:** 'And quickly lifted up her skirt at the back.'

78 **jren:** NHG 'ihr'; a common Alemannic form.

79 **Jch markt den bossen:** NHG 'ich merkte den Possen', i.e. 'noticed the catch', 'saw what she was up to'.

(iii) Georg Rollenhagen: *Froschmeuseler* (1595)

(*a*)

1 **Darauff wird Vlysses gewahr:** The passage occurs early in the book, before the Homeric element has been overlaid by other themes.

2 **Das deins Geschlechts einer da war:** Actually the sorceress Circe had changed Ulysses' men into swine (*Odyssey*, Bk. X), but Rollenhagen suggests that the spy Ulysses had sent out was changed into a mouse.

7 **Circes ruth:** Rollenhagen attributes to Circe's wand the magical powers which in Homer are reserved for Circe's potions and ointments.

8   **was jhm dauchte lieb vnd gut.**: Rollenhagen follows standard sixteenth-century practice in using full stops with the force of modern commas.

14 **wie sehr sie auch verborgen waren**: 'kuntschafft' is treated as the plural of a strong feminine noun.

19 **nach so vielen Kriegs jahren**: The Trojan War lasted for ten years, Ulysses' voyage home a further ten.

23 **der Katzen orden**: For a note on 'orde' see p. 299.

28 **ohne ziel**: 'without limit, restriction'.

30 **Eim jedem seine weiß gefelt**: 'Everyone is pleased with his own way of life.'

34 **Bey allen Menschen hôren / riechen**: i.e. in his capacity as a spy.

47 **Da rhůmt man jhn ein hand voll ehr . . .**: 'One speaks glowingly to them about a scrap of honour, a paltry sum of money, and other things.'

51 **Das sie auff solch stelhôltzlein mausen**: The man-mouse humorously sees things in 'mouse terms', calling ships mousetraps and likening quests for fame and honour to the thieving proclivities of mice ('mausen' = 'to steal'). 'Mausen' can also mean 'to sit still for a long time', 'to be cooped up', and this would also fit the sense admirably.

60 **Jch hett fůr Circe wol genesen**: 'Circe would not have done me any harm.'

(b)

1   **Es gschach im Herbst**: Like most of the stories brought together in *Froschmeuseler*, the fable is not an invention of Rollenhagen. It is taken over from the popular cycle of oriental anecdotes known as the *Buch der Beispiele der alten Weisen* or, in English, as the *Fables of Bidpai*. Here, however, it did not have political overtones, but reflected simply on the dangerous futility of attempting to instruct those who were unwilling to be instructed.

44 **Vnd rieff jhnen noch zu viel mehr**: 'And called to them all the more.'

56 **Das guter Rath findt selten stath**: 'That good advice is seldom followed.'

58 **Es stehe darauff gut / Ehr vnd leben**: 'Although goods, honour, and life itself are at stake.'

59 **Herr Omnis**: i.e. the common man. The term, with its contemptuous overtones, was popularized by Luther.

62 **in solchem fall**: 'In such a case' i.e. the case just narrated.

III · DIALOGUE AND DRAMA

1. Ulrich von Hutten: *Die Anschawenden* (1519)

Die Anschawenden: The title is taken over from the sub-title of Lucian's dialogue *Charon*, and Hutten uses the same basic situation as Lucian, who envisaged Charon, from a vantage-point high above earth, being given instruction on the ways and foolishness of mankind by Hermes. In Hutten's dialogue it is Sol, the Sun-God, who gives instruction to his son Phaeton from his chariot in the sky.

6 **von grossen dingen sich zů beraten:** The Diet of Augsburg took place in the later part of 1518. Hutten was present in the retinue of Albrecht of Brandenburg, Archbishop of Mainz. Surprisingly, in spite of his anti-papal attitude, Hutten did not scruple to take service with the German Primate— perhaps because he regarded Albrecht as a good German, perhaps for less worthy reasons—nor did Albrecht, initially at least, apparently have any qualms about employing him. An even more striking paradox is that, superficially, Hutten and the papacy pursued the same policy at the Diet and sought to revive the crusading zeal of the members, Hutten hoping that a crusade against the Turks would prove a means of cementing national unity, while the Pope seems to have been more interested in persuading the Estates to grant a tax which allegedly was to be devoted to such a crusade. Both Hutten and the Papal Legate failed to move the Estates with their oratory, however, and no crusade was organized. Luther was also in Augsburg shortly after the close of the Diet to meet the Papal Legate, Cardinal Cajetan, who was charged with persuading him to recant (cf. p. 265), but the only practical result of their meeting was to reveal the gulf which separated them. It is characteristic of Hutten's attitude to the Reformation, in which he saw as yet only a 'monkish squabble', that, although he stayed on in Augsburg for treatment of the syphilitic complaint which troubled him in his later years, he made no attempt to meet Luther and does not mention him in the dialogue.

8 **den båpstlichen Legaten:** Thomas de Vio, born at Gaeta, hence his Latinized name Cajetanus, Cardinal Bishop of St. Sixtus in Rome. As an opponent of Luther and Hutten, Cajetan—who was made a cardinal at the early age of thirty-nine—has suffered somewhat at the hands of Protestant historians: witness the often quoted remark attributed to Leo X when making Cajetan a cardinal in 1517 that 'another scoundrel more or less makes no difference'. In fact Cajetan was a man of considerable integrity and learning, and in his discussions with Luther several times got the better of his opponent.

11 **weñ sye nun wol beschenckt:** 'when they have been given plenty to drink'.

13 **da er inn auß beuelh des Bapstes relation thůn würt:** 'where he will give them an account of the Pope's orders'.

17 **zů verschaffen / damitt die Teütschē nichts anders / noch fürder-licher / dañ den selbigen kryeg fürnemen:** 'to ensure that the Germans will undertake nothing else before [lit. 'nothing else or earlier than'] this same war.'

20 **Was gewiñes ist er dañ verhoffen?:** 'What does he hope to gain [from it] then?'

27 **ein so streitbar vnd tråtzig volck:** NHG 'trotzig'. The praise of the warlike qualities of the Germans, which was a commonplace amongst

German humanists from Wimpheling onwards, is probably a reminiscence of Tacitus. Hutten had wanted to edit the first six books of the *Annals*, but had been unable to find a printer in view of the papal protection of the Roman printer, who had been given ten years' 'copyright' in respect of the edition published in 1515.

32 **Er gibt sich für einē hyrten auß:** Apart from the various other examples of pastoral imagery in the Bible, especially John 10: 1–16, Hutten is probably thinking particularly of Christ's injunction to 'feed my sheep' (John 21: 15 ff.), which clearly had special significance for St. Peter's successor, the Pope.

36 **über das gebürg:** 'over the mountains', i.e. to Italy.

37 **Bey glaubē:** 'By my faith.'

37 **wo sye anders seine schoff seind:** 'if indeed they are his sheep'.

39 **gôucherey / das sye doch ein weyd sein bedunckt:** 'trickery, which, however, seems to them to be real pasturage'.

62 **das sye sich nun mer betrogen werdē verstehen:** 'that they now understand that they are being cheated.'

70 **Von nôten ist nit edel sein:** The Latin original does not have the slight ambiguity of the German: 'Genere non oportet esse nobilem'.

71 **sond' mag jn helffen:** 'but it may be of service to him, if . . .'

75 **hat vil aplaß bey sich geschürtzet . . . nachfûren:** 'carries many indulgences tucked up in his vestments and is having many authorizations and dispensations sent after him in his bags and baggage'; 'watsâckt' and 'gepâckt' are misprints for 'watsâcke' and 'gepâcke'.

79 **sûn d' erdē:** In his introduction, Hutten records: 'Ein sûn der erden würt im sprichwort genennet / einer der von so gar dunckelem vñ vnbekantē vrsprung ist / dz er auch seinē vatter vñ mûter kaum od' gar nit kennet.'

89 **es der Rômischen brasserey fürsetzen:** 'give it over to the Roman excesses and debauchery.'

92 **voller misßglauben überredt seindt:** 'have been persuaded full of superstition', i.e. they have been convinced (of the validity of Roman claims) on the basis of (assiduously propagated) superstitions. The Latin is clearer: 'Germani, quos nunc infatuatos habet persuasis superstitionibus urbs Roma.'

96 **Also wôllen wir nun wider an den reychs tag:** Hutten has devoted the previous speeches to a discussion of the German 'national vice', drunkenness, which he has castigated as a source of national political and moral weakness. The rather clumsy humour of the following exchanges with Cajetan is intended to illustrate the grotesque presumption of the papacy and its officers. The references to the weather emphasize the fact that Cajetan is a foreigner.

107 **allē wolkē:** misprint for 'alle wolkē'.

109 **Dz ist d' Astrologē vñ sternēgucker schult / wo es and's schult ist:** 'That is the fault of the astrologers and astronomers, if indeed [anders] it is

a fault.' In the sixteenth century the belief in astrology was widespread, even amongst serious scholars and theologians like Melanchthon. The 'Practiken' were the calendars and prophecies which were produced in large numbers. (Cf. Dr. Faust's activities in this respect, p. 219.)

117 **begetē**: misprint for 'begerē'.

121 **vñ dir ist vnbekant / einen Rômischen bischoff . . . was er wôll binden vñ lôßen môgen?**: 'and you don't know that a Roman bishop . . . can bind and loose whatever he will?' Hutten retains the accusative and infinitive construction of his Latin original. The reference to binding and loosing is a travesty of one of the key texts on which the claims of the Roman Church to unique authority are based (Matt. 16: 19).

134 **Dann wil ich dir ein bûsß auffsetzen**: Hutten's protest at the externalization of the sacrament of penance coincides with that of Luther and the humanists. His motive is not so much regret at the prostitution of the sacrament, however, as anger at the authority and power which it confers on the clergy.

150 **niswurtz**: 'hellebore', traditionally regarded as a cure for folly.

152 **Du bist de facto im bañ**: The indiscriminate use of excommunication by the ecclesiastical authorities in order to enforce obedience was a common source of dissatisfaction in the early sixteenth century—another example of the way Hutten's politically motivated satire coincided with strictly religious protest. (Cf. Luther's remarks in para. 17 of *An den christlichen Adel*.)

158 **die durch den Bapst vnd seine Legaten verdampt werden**: Cf. the opinion of Cardinal Medici, who on 7 Oct. 1517 wrote to Cajetan that 'In cases of notorious heresy, no further ceremony or citation (other than the summons to retract) need be observed.'

164 **dastu**: contraction of 'das du'.

176 **dz du yetzo künig Carlen verhinderen wilt . . .**: Holy Roman Emperors were King of the Romans by virtue of their election and Emperor by virtue of their coronation by the Pope. Maximilian I (d. 1519) wished his grandson, Charles, King of Spain, to succeed him. Largely because of its own territorial ambitions in southern Italy, the papacy was anxious to avoid the personal union of Spain and the Holy Roman Empire (the Kingdom of Naples was ruled by Spain) and sought to sway the outcome of the forthcoming imperial election in favour of the candidature of Francis I of France (hence the accommodating attitude to Frederick the Wise—and Luther; cf. p. 265). Hutten misguidedly hoped for great things from Charles.

182 **Lasß sye mich hassen**: 'Oderint dum metuant', a remark quoted by Cicero from the now-forgotten tragedian Attius and commonly used to characterize the attitude of the tyrant.

187 **pestilentz vnnd gehen tott**: 'pestilence and sudden death'. The reference is to the common belief that climatic conditions were responsible for the outbreak of plagues and epidemics.

189 **gelt geyn Rom gefalle**: Hutten uses the word 'pension' in the sense of payments due to Rome. An archbishop was obliged to purchase his pallium

in Rome and all new incumbents had to pay 'annates' (the revenue of the benefice during the first year of office) so that a rapid 'turnover' was very much in the papacy's financial interests. Cf. in this connection Luther's remarks in *Wider Hans Worst*, p. 10.

196 **die newen creaturē:** The reference is to the large number of new cardinals, Cajetan amongst them, created by Leo X in 1517.

205 **du boßhafftiger fůrman:** Phaeton is regarded as the charioteer, but this may be more than a passing rebuke on account of his recent remarks. 'Boßhafftig' can mean 'mischievous', 'wicked' as well as 'malicious', 'evil-minded' (it translates 'scelestus'), and Cajetan may be referring to the legend according to which Phaeton as a boy borrowed his father's sun chariot, but being too weak to control it, burnt up much of the earth.

226 **vff sein abentewer:** 'at his own risk'.

227 **zů tal:** 'downhill', i.e. from the zenith.

229 **Jch habs gewagt:** Hutten's device, used as an equivalent of 'Jacta est alea'.

2. Hans Sachs: *Disputacion zwischen ainem Chorherren vnd Schüchmacher | Darinn Das wort gotes vnd ain recht Christlich weßen verfochten wirtt* (1524)

1 **Bonus dies:** This is spoken by the cobbler. The greeting, not unlike the modern 'servus', was commonly used by vernacular speakers. 'Semper quies' was the standard response.

8 **Was bringt ir mir die pantoffel?:** Punctuation in the present edition is often lacking or misleading. We must read the sentence as though there were a comma after 'Was'. Cf. below: 'Wie hond ir gedroschen' = 'Wie, hond ir gedroschen?'

11 **abgedroschen:** In NHG this means 'trite', 'hackneyed'. An earlier meaning of the verb was 'to pay a debt by threshing'. The canon's use of the word here is intended to indicate that for the Roman clergy communion with God has become a mechanical and distasteful chore.

13 **ich hab mein horas gebeet:** The 'hours' referred to were the prayers appointed to be read at certain times of the day. The emphasis is again on the mechanical nature of the canon's devotions—he can feed his pet bird while praying!

17 **Jch waiß ain schůch macher:** Sachs refers to his own long allegorical poem *Die Wittenbergisch Nachtigall* (1523), where he greets Luther, the nightingale of the title, as the restorer of true faith and doctrine, which the Pope and his clergy have perverted.

21 **die hailigñ vâter:** the cardinals and higher clergy, not the 'Church Fathers'.

21 **außgeholhipt:** 'abused'. The 'Holhipbuben' were bakers' boys who sold 'hohle Hippen'—a sort of cake—in taverns and, like modern fishwives, were renowned for their powers of invective.

23 **fart schon:** 'steady on', 'calm down'.

25 **oben vberhyn:** 'into the bargain', 'to boot'.

25 **ist dañ solches ewer wesen / holhüpel werck:** syntactically a rather unhappy sentence: 'is this then abusing you for your behaviour and what you are?' ('wesen' = 'condition', 'behaviour', 'state', often with negative overtones).

27 **solchs vnser wesen:** The 'solchs' is virtually tautological.

29 **Es steet Exodi am .xxiij:** The arguments rehearsed by Hans here and in the following speeches are commonplaces of Reformation controversy and derive mostly from Luther's treatises of 1520.

34 **die wissen vor wol:** 'they already know', i.e. without his telling them.

44 **weñ sy sein wider euch:** Although the canon here makes no more than a debating-point, there is no denying the underlying charge of selectivity. Luther, however, never argued that each text had equal importance; rather were all texts to be viewed in the light of the over-all message of the Bible, i.e. the message that man was justified by fiduciary faith. Hence, for instance, his 'devaluation' of the Epistle of James, with its emphasis on works.

60 **võ dē steet in gaistlichen rechten. C. Solite. de maioritate et obedientia Sy bedeüten die soñ . . . :** The antithesis of canon law and Scripture is introduced to emphasize the Lutheran claim that the Roman Church holds its own human laws above the word of God. The article quoted is a familiar one in Reformation controversy. Chapters (C. = 'Caput') in the *Corpus iuris canonici*, rather like papal bulls, were known by their first word (here, 'Solite') as well as by their content and a numerical reference. For the imagery of the sun and the moon, cf. Brant's use of it in *Võ abgang des gloubē* (p. 105).

64 **so ist der gewißlich kain Stathalter Christi:** The play on the antithesis of Christ and his Vicar is as old as Protestantism itself. Wyclif had contrasted the poverty, humility, and unpolitical nature of Christ with the wealth, pride, and political ambition of the papacy, and the theme was developed by the Hussites and the German Protestants. Its most celebrated formulation is the *Passional Christi vnd Antichristi* of 1521 with text by Luther and Melanchthon and woodcuts by Cranach.

73 **wa ir anderst auß got seyt:** 'if indeed you are of God'.

80 **Joañ. j. canonica j.:** the First Epistle General of John 1: 8.

84 **wenn der Bapst so bȯß wer:** This article of canon law, to which Sachs gives a fuller reference (*Decreti pars I, distinctio 40, cap. 6, Si Papa*), is another familiar item of Reformation controversy, having been quoted first by Luther in *An den christlichen Adel deutscher Nation* as an example of the diabolical inspiration of the papacy.

114 **Selig ist der man der sich tag vnnd nacht yebett ym̄ gesetz des herren:** The paraphrase of Ps. 1: 1 is rather free.

115 **in der ersten Epistel:** 1 Pet. 3: 15.

117 **der grund fodert die hoffnung . . .:** misprint for 'der grund fodert der hoffnung . . . '

119 **Wie die gens am wetter:** 'Like a duck in a thunderstorm'. Geese, notoriously stupid creatures, were reputed to stare foolishly heavenwards when it thundered in a vain attempt to understand the meaning of the noise. In this reading the canon would thus in fact be conceding Hans's point (cf. the canon's subsequent identification of the 'bibelfester Laie' with Christ and of the clergy with the Pharisees). Kinzel offers a different reading of the line, however, which would also make sense: the geese may not understand the noise they hear, but they survive the storm none the less, i.e. it is sufficient for a Christian to obey the Church to gain salvation—he is not required to understand points of theology.

120 **Jr spot wol dye Juden . . .:** We must read this as though there were a comma after 'wol'.

125 **Jch halt ynn für eynen Christenlichen leerer . . .:** The syntax is somewhat confused: 'I hold him to be a Christian teacher—[more Christian] as I believe, than any since the time of the Apostles.'

134 **Vnd die zway stuck treybtt dye schrifft schyer durch vnnd durch:** 'And right the whole way through the Scriptures are taken up with these two things.'

148 **Spricht doch Jacobus:** The whole of the General Epistle of James and especially the second chapter, which pointed out that 'the devils also believe' and asserted that 'by works a man is justified, and not by faith alone', was a constant source of embarrassment to all Lutherans, so much so that on one famous occasion Luther said he would like 'mit dem Jäckel den Ofen zu heizen'.

160 **Wie das im dann so wenig geleertter . . .?:** 'How is it that so few learned . . .?' The canon is intent on having it both ways and in his next speech seems to contradict the view expressed that it is the ignorant mob which follows Luther. Hans similarly claims popularity for Luther, but then in the light of the text he attributes to Matt. 5 ('Geet ein durch die eng pfort . . .'; actually Matt. 7: 13), accepts the suggestion that the Lutherans are a small minority. The doctrine that only a tiny fraction of the population could ever be true believers was, however, standard Lutheran teaching.

168 **vnd hast sich geoffennbart:** misprint for 'hast sie geoffennbart'.

176 **vnd ir seynd vil die darauff wandlen:** The 'ir' is a genitive plural of the third person governed by 'vil'.

173 **vñ das on alle geschrifft:** 'and that without any scriptural evidence'.

182 **hond mir nichts verübel:** 'no offence', 'don't take what I have said amiss'.

186 **der teuffel sey ynn dem schûster verneet:** 'that the Devil is stitched in the cobbler', i.e. that the Devil speaks out of him.

187 **in harnasch geiagt:** 'made me angry'.

188 **auff den esel gesetzt:** 'made a fool of me'.

197 **ir wurd in mitt dem pantoffel schlahen:** This is more dangerous than it sounds to modern ears; in the sixteenth century 'pantoffel' were wooden shoes with cloth uppers.

208 **von wunnders wegen:** 'out of curiosity'.

214 **ob er gleich hab zů gesagt:** 'whether he quoted correctly'.

218 **schůllerische leer:** 'scholastic teachings'. Again the contrast between human inventions and God-given Scripture!

219 **vnd gar wenig das gaistlich recht:** 'and just a very little bit of canon law'.

236 **vnd allen menschen find:** 'and all human inventions'.

242 **Herr haißtt euch den hanen meer krően / von mir lydts irs nit:** 'Make the cock crow some more to you [i.e. 'Let the fellow go on lecturing you', but intended with heavy irony to produce the opposite effect]. You wouldn't put up with it from me.' The introduction of the Lutheran odd-job-man is a neat touch worthy of the dramatist in Sachs.

248 **das rodt pyrrett:** 'the red biretta', the badge of the canon's ecclesiastical office. Red was, however, normally reserved for cardinals.

251 **es werden euch noch die stain in die oren schreyen:** Luke 19: 40.

252 **ich schaid mit wissen:** 'I know why I am being dismissed.'

259 **ein krammet vogel oder zwelff:** 'about twelve fieldfares' (a sort of thrush regarded as a delicacy).

259 **Es wirt nach eessen meines gnedigen herren Caplon / mit etlichen herren koṁen:** 'My gracious lord's [the bishop's?] chaplain and a few gentlemen will come after dinner.'

261 **Trag die Bibel auß der stuben:** It had been brought in, covered with dust from lack of use, to settle a point in the discussion with Hans.

263 **eyn frischen kartten oder zwů:** 'one or two fresh packs of cards'.

264 **werdt ir vő stundt an nach dem vmbgang heymher gen:** 'will you come straight home after the procession?' The procession referred to is probably a minor one held within the church to mark a special ecclesiastical occasion.

3. Hans Sachs: *Der Pawr inn dem Fegfewer* (1552)

4 **Jch hab es gar als gebrechen:** An 'on' (= 'without') has presumably been omitted after 'gar'. 'I have no lack of anything, i.e. 'I am completely happy.'

8 **ein gefůrster Abt:** an abbot with the rank and privileges of a prince.

41 **nur kůchel zu essen:** literally 'only eating cakes', i.e. 'a bed of roses'.

49 **Solt mir kaum also trawmen than:** 'I would never have dreamed it possible.'

53 **Heintz Düppel**: 'Harry Twerp'. 'Düppel' is a South German form of 'Döbel' (= 'peg', 'nail'), which is often used of persons to mean 'fool'.

62 **ghrecht wie ein spitzmauß**: Normally in the sixteenth century the 'Spitzmaus' (= 'shrew') was synonymous with spite and untrustworthiness on account of its sharp teeth and allegedly poisonous nature. Sachs uses it here as an image for simplicity and gullibility, however.

68 **Hat mich schier in die schwintsucht bracht**: 'He has driven me to the point where I am becoming consumptive.'

70 **Trodt**: NHG 'droht'.

107 **Doch ich euch den nit bringen dar**: 'Dar' is not a separable prefix, but the present of 'turren' = 'to dare'.

115 **So wil ich durch mein kunst thewer**: The object 'in' has been omitted after 'ich'.

Herr Vlrich spricht: He has, of course, not been on the stage during the conversation between Els and the Abbot, and his query enables Sachs to keep the dialogue moving and so fill in the time needed for Düppel to arrive.

122 **Sie ist eben geleich für mich**: 'She is just my size', 'just my meat'.

127 **durch abentheur**: 'for the sake of a joke'.

134 **Auch samb ein Faßnacht spiel thun haltē**: This should not be understood literally, but as meaning 'have a good joke together at his expense'.

139 **ohn gefehr**: 'trustingly', 'without evil intentions'.

153 **Dabt**: contraction of 'Der Abt'.

155 **Mit diesen frischen schlegel birn**: The abbot corrects Düppel's malapropism—which in view of their hardness is not altogether inappropriate ('schlegel' = 'mallet').

163 **So werden zwischen hie vnd Lichtmessen**: The subject 'sie' has been omitted.

164 **als denn mügt jrs wol essen**: The 's' of 'jrs' is an enclitic form of the pronoun 'sie'.

der Abt S.: 'S.' = 'spricht'.

182 **schült**: NHG 'schölte'.

Grölzenbrey: 'Belch-porridge'.

Rubendunst: 'Turnip-fumes'.

211 **int Kirchen**: NHG 'in die Kirche'.

215 **Mit dem Couendt vnd der Proces**: 'Couendt' ('Convent') is used to mean 'an ecclesiastical community living in a monastery', 'Proces' is a 'procession', i.e. they are going to bury him with full ecclesiastical honours.

218 **zum Opffer**: i.e. to the service (mass).

220 **Nun geht jr hin bald / es wirt nacht**: The *virgula* is misleading: 'Go there as soon as it is night.'

231 **Doch das sollichs als heimlich gschech:** 'But take care that this is all done in secret.'

an die vier ort: 'in all four directions'.

247 **Botz:** 'Gottes', a standard euphemism. Cf. 'Ey schendt sie pox leber vnd Lung', below.

249 **an disem endt:** 'in this place'.

254 **nobis Hauß:** Together with 'nobis Krug' a standard euphemism for hell.

268 **Erst wil dem schimpff der bodn außwerden:** 'Now the joke is over.'

275 **dest:** NHG 'tatst'.

316 **Danck habs / hats mein noch nit vergessē:** The 's' at the end of 'hab' and 'hat' is an enclitic form of 'sie'—'I am grateful to her, she . . .'

317 **wenglein:** 'a tiny bit'.

321 **Wie das mir kein Liecht opffern thet:** The subject 'sie' has been run together with 'das'.

329 **von dem tag:** 'by the daylight'.

336 **wenn hab ich bûset gar:** 'when will I have served my penance'.

363 **Wann er hat schmale pfenbart gessen:** 'For he has eaten small pennyworths' ('pfenbart' = 'pfen(ing)wert'), i.e. he has been on short rations.

364 **Jch hab jmbs leichnam gnaw gemessen:** 'I have been very careful about the size of the portions served to him', i.e. 'I have given him very little'. 'Leichnam' is an oath (= 'Gottes Leichnam').

374 **Durch ewr Feistikeit:** 'Through your corpulence'. This is another of Düppel's malapropisms, he probably means to say 'Festigkeit' or perhaps 'Fürbitte'.

beudt jhm thandt / S.: NHG 'bietet ihm die Hand, spricht'.

383 **zum frûambt:** 'to the early-morning service'.

385 **Biß Suntag:** 'Next Sunday'.

389 **Cuntz:** familiar form of 'Conrad'.

395 **Jch kan sein aber glauben nicht:** 'But I can't believe it.' 'Sein' is the genitive of the neuter pronoun governed by 'glauben'.

396 **Las mich triegn denn all mein gesicht:** 'Unless my eyes deceive me in everything I see'.

399 **Als ob er hab ein Kindt erbissen:** A rather strange image: 'As though he had bitten a child to death'.

404 **thut verziehē:** 'wait a minute'.

413 **Was hast im Fegfewer erlieden:** NHG 'erlitten'.

422 **Der stûnck so leichnam hieren vbel:** another oath—one could swear by the brain of God as well as by the other parts of His body.

431 **drumb liebn nachtpawrn mein:** Düppel would probably turn to the audience when delivering this piece of homely advice.

Der Abt von Certal: Boccaccio died at Certaldo. It is unclear whether Sachs thought Boccaccio was writing about a local abbot, or whether he intended this as a tribute to his source.

4. Georg Rollenhagen: *Vom reichen Manne | vnd armen Lazaro* (1590)

1 **Actvs III. Scena III.** Porphyrius, the rich man, is about to give a splendid feast for his guests, who are just arriving. The sick Lazarus is lying at the gate, begging. He will remain visible throughout the act as a living contrast and reproach to the carousing of the guests, the stage being conceived on the 'open plan' principle, so that we can see simultaneously what goes on both inside and outside Porphyrius's house.

2 **Daemones:** Daemones is a friend and sycophant of Porphyrius; Byssinus, etc. are Porphyrius's brothers, Plusia is his wife.

9 **Nach diesm:** 'After this (interlude)'. They have just been entertained by two braggart soldiers who allegedly fought with Varus against Arminius in the battle of the Teutoburger Wald.

10 **die ich bestelt hab heut. Jn meinem Hauß:** As often in ENHG punctuation, Rollenhagen commonly uses the full stop with the force of a modern comma.

28 **kommen wern:** NHG 'kommen werden'.

43 **Wilkom seid jr mir all Gotts sammn:** 'You are all welcome [to me] in God's name.' 'Gotts' is an abbreviation of 'in Gotts namn', 'sammn' = 'zusammen'.

56 **So habt jr jetzt gehört die zeit:** 'You have recently heard how . . .' The following lines point to the association in Rollenhagen's mind between the rabbis and the Roman Catholic clergy.

98 **Ewr Ehrwirdn solln:** 'Your honour is . . .' The third person plural is used as a polite singular form; cf. modern German 'Sie'.

107 **Mit vngewaschen Henden Herr?:** The incident not only contrasts the rabbis' unwillingness to delay over the works of charity with their willingness to delay over empty religious forms, but also in its reference to Matt. 15: 2 contrasts the Jewish (and Catholic!) concern with the 'works of the Law' with Christ's emphasis on the state of mind of the believer.

108 **Bhüt Gott Adonai dafür:** 'May the Lord God keep [us] from such a thing.'

111 **Sag du:** This remark is addressed to a servant, Sosia or Mastyx, even though their presence is not recorded in the stage direction.

157 **Was gilt:** 'What's the betting?'

161 **wer jr denn seid:** 'whoever you are'.

175 **Nein warlich . . . gericht:** 'But no, this is not below [the salt], because it's handy for the food.'

179 **leg für dich:** 'help yourself'.

184 **es darff kein eil:** 'there is no need to hurry'.

194 **O HErr . . .:** Lazarus is appealing to Porphyrius.

207 **Das wir all Menschen . . .:** 'that all we men . . .'

224 **wehr wer er wolt:** 'turn him away, whoever he may [claim to] be'; 'sein' has been omitted.

232 **Oeconomus:** i.e. the major-domo.

246 **das jms Hertze kracht:** 'in such a manner that it will really hurt him'.

254 **Syre:** Syrus was another of Porphyrius's servants.

260 **Galliart:** 'gaillarde', a gay French dance.

263 **Finita chorea:** Mastyx has, of course, to wait for the music and dancing to stop before he can order Lazarus away from the gate.

285 **Actvs IIII. Scena IIII.** The quarrel between the Devil and the angels for the soul of the dying man was a standard item of medieval mythology. The deathbed scene here and the Devil's temptation of the dying man to give up hope in God are strongly reminiscent of late medieval treatments of the same theme in such works as *Ars bene moriendi*. The dialogue, of course, is made to carry the Lutheran teaching on the primacy of faith over works.

290 **Wies hab mit Lazaro ein gstalt:** 'What the situation is with regard to Lazarus.'

304 **Maleach:** another angel.

314 **Der Gnadenstuel:** 'The mercy-seat'; technically, the golden covering of the Ark of the Covenant, in which the Tables of the Law were deposited; Exod. 25: 17.

317 **Der Sam des Weibes:** i.e. Christ. The reference is to Rev. 12.

317 **HErr allein:** 'who alone is Lord'.

331 **Sadiel:** yet another angel.

339 **Was / Habt jr noch nicht außgefecht?:** Death appears as an unconcerned and slightly waggish workman, who clearly enjoys the fight between Satan and Sadiel.

348 **Must besser dran:** 'You'll have to do better than that.'

355 **Emanuel:** i.e. Christ.

366 **ein guten Muth:** 'a good appetite'.

370 **dauon zuuor geschrieben ist vnter den Personen:** The dramatis personae were not listed in order of speaking, but as nine 'Ordnungen' or classes (of mourner) who will accompany the cortège. The action, as Rollenhagen remarks, is anticipated in the 'argument' which precedes each act. The funeral oration, consisting of some ten closely printed pages, was printed at the end of the volume as an 'optional extra'.

373 **Der gelegenheit nach:** 'As and when convenient' i.e. they join their 'Ordnungen'

389 **thu gemach:** 'go easy'.

398 **nim so fůr gut:** 'cheer up'.

414 **Wenn der Sententz nu wird ergehn:** Rollenhagen follows the traditional view that there would be two 'last judgements'. The first took place immediately after death, the soul being sentenced to hell or purgatory, while the body was subjected to the corruption of the grave. This was an individual and private judgement. The second judgement took place at the end of the world, when the dead would arise, and in this general and public judgement, the body as well as the soul would be punished or rewarded for its deeds on earth.

418 **zetr:** 'wailing and gnashing of teeth'.

446 **Drůmb bitt ich Vater:** The following dialogue is a paraphrase of Luke 16: 24 ff.

459 **Vnd vber das / alles fůrwar:** The sentence is more readily intelligible if one ignores the *virgula*.

464 **es wer verlorn:** 'it would be wasted effort'.

489 **nicht drauff gebn:** misprint for 'nichts'.

491 **hett es kein noth:** 'there would be no danger'.

504 **so kan ich Gott darůmb Ansprechen nicht:** By a neat touch, Porphyrius is made to commit the unforgivable sin of despairing in God's mercy, a sin which Lazarus had successfully resisted when tempted by Satan.

IV · NARRATIVE PROSE

1. The 'novel'

(i) *Ein lieplichs lesen vnd ein warhafftige Hystorij wie einer (d' da hieß Hug schäpler vñ wz metzgers gschlecht) ein gewaltiger küng zů Frankrich ward durch sein grose ritterliche mañheit* (1500)

3 **snier:** misprint for 'siner'.

5 **Gernier:** The French form is 'Garnier'.

5 **lanoy:** Orleans.

6 **künig Ludwig:** Louis IV (936–54).

9 **eyns richen mans also mocht in allem Franckrich sin:** 'of as rich a man as there was in the whole of France'.

13 **do selbs:** 'in that place'.

18 **x. oder zwôlff wol gerüster pferd:** Numerals and measurements of quantity usually govern the genitive at this time.

19 **vnd nympt mich frômbd an üch . . .:** 'and I am amazed at you and wonder what this may mean'.

30 **vnd legen ir üch wol an:** 'and if you apply yourself well'.

45 **Do der burger der ritter hort synen vettern also sprechē:** It is not clear why Simon should be held to be simultaneously a knight and a bourgeois, but since he is similarly described in the chapter-heading, it must be intentional. The *chanson* has 'Quant ly bougois oy parler le demoysiel'.

46 **fich selbs:** misprint for 'sich selbs'.

48 **Jch soll anders vor handt nemē:** 'I must do something about it'.

50 **der was sin vast fro:** 'he was very glad at this'; 'sin' is the genitive of the third person singular neuter pronoun dependent on 'fro'.

52 **henegouw:** Hainault.

53 **Berge:** Bergues.

62 **salb vierd:** 'four of them', 'himself and three others'.

71 **er keme sin ī groß lyden:** 'he would suffer greatly on account of this'; 'sin' is a causative genitive of the pronoun.

73 **dinem liebē bůlen:** Although 'bule' is masculine, it can be used for a person of either sex.

82 **ir wol .x.:** 'a good ten of them'.

84 **dz er alles mit gewerter hand enttranne:** 'all of which he escaped by armed force'.

91 **Nyffel:** Nivelle.

92 **vn̄ hat sich darvff bestalt:** 'and had made arrangements for this contingency', i.e. Hug's visit.

93 **harnsch:** misprint for 'harnasch'.

109 **wer mich ouch dar vmb strafft:** This should be read as a subordinate clause belonging to the preceding sentence. Effectively 'ist wol in bůlschaft . . .' starts a new sentence.

113 **hütre:** Utrecht.

114 **genant hugen:** In French the similarity in the names is not so confusing—the King is called Hugon, Hug is called Hugues.

117 **vn̄ was er begert das er ym das sagte:** In response to Hug's request to be allowed to stay in Friesland, he is taken into the King's service. As a result of a scandal involving the King's niece, however, he is forced to flee the country and make his way once more to Paris. Hug's private adventures now merge with political history. The King of France has been poisoned by the rascally Count Savary of Champagne. In order to gain the throne, Savary wishes to marry the late King's daughter, but the widowed Queen, her mother, appeals for protection to the citizens of Paris, amongst whom Hug is now numbered. Naturally, he takes a leading part in the subsequent proceedings.

119 **von der burger wegē:** 'as a spokesman of the citizens'.

131 **Gonnelin:** Ganelon, who betrayed Roland and Oliver to the Moors.

137 **hützûtag:** 'on this very day'.

139 **spielte im syn houbt:** 'spielte' is from 'spalten', not 'spielen'!

139 **mon yoie:** 'Mont-joie' or 'Mont-joie Saint-Denis' was the traditional French war-cry. 'Mont-joie' literally means a 'cairn', in this case the monument erected to commemorate the martyrdom of St. Denis, first Bishop of Paris and patron saint of France.

140 **schlagen vff . . . an gehaben:** 'Smite [them], good citizens,' said Hug. 'I have made a start with the really guilty one.'

148 **der hertzog vō burgundiē. Vñ graff Friderich . . . :** The full stop after 'burgundiē' should be ignored. Friderich, the brother of Savary, is called 'Fedry' in the *chanson de geste*.

154 **Der falsche graue mag üch nit werden:** 'The false count will not fall to your lot', i.e. 'he will not get you'.

161 **Gennosse by burgel:** Gonesse, near Bourget.

165 **wie es da gefaren were:** 'how things had fared there'.

168 **an iren vinde:** Count Frederick and the Duke of Burgundy have risen in revolt against the Queen, and once again she is forced to rely on the good citizens of Paris to defend her.

173 **die vssern:** 'those outside', i.e. the besiegers.

175 **Hugwon:** Hugon, earlier described as 'Hugen'.

175 **von der Felse:** Velsen.

177 **der Constabel:** The Constable of France was the chief officer of the King's household and the Commander-in-Chief of the French forces during the King's absence.

182 **dz er eym tütschē mā wolt haben gesichert:** 'that he needed protection against a German'. The besieging army was a multinational force.

191 **vmb das er in so leid thette:** 'because he was doing them so much harm'. This is not the 'mercy-killing' it would be in modern German!

198 **Estempi:** Étampes.

204 **der ynnern:** 'of those inside', i.e. the defenders. Hug Schapler continues as the champion of the Queen's cause and is rewarded by being made Duke of Orleans. In spite of the intervention of foreign kings and Hug's ten bastards on the royal side, however, the war drags on for a long time. Finally Frederick is defeated and captured, and Hug—inevitably—marries the Queen's daughter and becomes King of France.

212 **alle menglich:** 'a very large number of people'.

233 **vff lyb vnnd gût gebotten:** 'summoned on pain of death and forfeiture of goods'.

245 **vmb begerung gûte fründ zû hoffe sûchen:** 'out of a desire to make good friends at court'.

247 **sich zû entschuldigen wie sie mochten:** 'to excuse themselves as best they might'. Even now, however, peace is not secure. The rascally Count

Frederick again raises the banner of revolt, in spite of the pardon generously extended to him, and is crushed only after many further perils and adventures.

(ii) Jörg Wickram: *Von Gûten vnd bôsen Nachbaurn* (1556)

(*a*)

22 **dann ich nit wissen mag . . . mir bewisen hand:** 'for I cannot know [i.e. I do not think] that the least kindness which you have shown me has befallen me from all my relatives', i.e. he has received more kindness from Robertus than from his own kith and kin.

24 **dann:** here, 'for which'.

63 **er ward gantz kurtz mit jm zů rath:** 'he thought it over quickly to himself'.

72 **so stand ich hie:** present indicative! Cf. 'verstand', p. 299.

78 **dañ mir vâtterliche trew von euch bewisen:** 'for loving care such as a father might show has been shown by you to me'.

79 **Dieweil es dann . . . die meinung hat:** 'Since that is the intention . . .'

81 **Mir aber wil dannocht gebûren:** a characteristic piece of didacticism which in view of the prevalence of arranged marriages was by no means out of place.

96 **souil sie mocht raum vnnd blatz haben / packt sie jrer kleider zů samen:** 'she packed as many of her clothes as she had room for [in her trunks]'.

100 **vbernacht:** 'after a single night'.

106 **Was lieber stund:** 'What sweet hours'; 'lieber' is a genitive dependent on 'Was'.

110 **das die sach einen fürgang haben würd:** 'that the matter would have consequences [would prosper]'.

(*b*)

115 **Auff disen nachtimbis:** Richardus has been to a banquet of the local merchants, when he is attacked.

120 **der sass nit gar weit von herr Roberten haus:** 'he lived not at all far from Master Robert's house'.

121 **eins wegs heim giengen:** 'went the same way home'.

123 **dauor die erbar geselschafft / nit zů schwert kummen kunden:** 'on account of which the honourable company [i.e. the ruffians who were lying in wait] could not attack'.

127 **Bald waren die schâlck alle vier . . . des er gar kein flucht wußt:** 'Soon all four ruffians with weapons at the ready were on top of the good young gentleman, owing to which he saw no way of escape.'

128 **Auff dlest:** 'At last'.

132 **was ansprach habt jr an mich vnschuldigen:** 'what business have you with me who am innocent?'

139 **sind manlich:** 'be brave'.

146 **můst den tod an der pomerantzen fressen:** The pun constitutes one of the few touches of humour in the whole book.

150 **Richarten find:** NHG 'Richards Feinde'.

153 **wohar das kumen môcht:** 'what the reason for it might be'.

159 **der alt herr vñ fraw:** i.e. Old Robertus and his wife, with whom Richardus and Cassandra live.

164 **befalh dem hausgesind fewr vnd liecht / zůuerwarē:** 'ordered the servants to make sure that the fires were damped down and no candles left burning'—a very necessary precaution when houses were constructed largely of wood.

170 **dieweil jm Gott sein leben günnet:** 'for as long as God would give him life'.

(c)

173 **Wie morgens frů zů schiff geblasen ward:** 'How early in the morning a trumpet was sounded as the signal to embark.' Young Lazarus is about to set off on his 'Wanderjahre', accompanied initially by Richardus. The ship has been waiting for a favourable wind for some days, hence the suddenness of the final departure, which prevents Lazarus from taking a private farewell from Amelia, daughter of Richardus and Cassandra, with whom he is in love.

176 **Auroram:** Aurora in Greek mythology was the personification of the dawn.

178 **Phebus:** Phoebus was the Sun-God and drove his chariot daily across the sky.

185 **Er schicket eylends sein trometter in die statt / vmbzůblasen:** 'He sent his trumpeter in haste to sound the signal to embark in all quarters of the town.'

189 **dann jm nit weil werden mocht:** 'for he did not have time and opportunity'.

192 **Lucia:** i.e. Lazarus's mother.

197 **aller ding schon beraidt:** 'all ready and prepared', lit. 'prepared in all things'.

210 **vnd die zeit ertragen mocht:** 'as there was time for'.

224 **wiewol sie nicht d' gleichen thet:** 'although she did not give vent to this anger'. 'Dergleichen' refers back to the action indicated by the verb in the preceding clause.

231 **on gnadet:** 'without taking his leave'. Amelia was, of course, present on the quay when the ship sailed, but as a romantic young lady had expected

a more intimate and private leave-taking. In his interest in Amelia's psychology, Wickram forgets to explain how Lazarus had time to write his letter, but did not have time to seek a private meeting with his beloved.

231 **auff nachuolgende meinung:** 'as follows'.

236 **wie hastu an deinem hertzen haben môgen:** 'how could you have the heart to . . .?'

242 **vnser baider âlteren:** 'of the parents of both of us', i.e. 'of your parents and my parents'.

243 **an disem ort:** i.e. 'to Lazarus'.

243 **dieweil d' handschlag noch nit geschehen ist:** 'since we have not yet shaken hands on it'. Betrothal at this time was an agreement in law, and the handshake would make the agreement binding.

248 **ich kan vnd mags nit wider bringen:** Amelia's decision is not as final as it sounds, however, and Lazarus's letter (and his mother's helpful intervention) soon restores good relations which ultimately lead to their marriage.

(iii) Johann Fischart: *Affentheurliche Naupengeheurliche Geschichtklitterung* (1575/90)

(a)

2 **Elendeiß:** a noun of Fischart's coining on the basis of 'Elen' = 'elk'. Rabelais refers to Gargantua's monstrous steed simply as a mare, but Fischart variously refers to it as 'Elendeiß', 'Vlckthier' (again on the basis of 'Elch'), 'Lastmaul', and 'Chammel'.

7 **drunder vñ drûber:** 'more or less'.

11 **Gurgelstrossa:** a variant of 'Gargantua' = 'large throat'.

16 **den Sturm anlieffen:** 'attacked'.

17 **zog er seinen Schwantz von Leder:** Fischart keeps the image of drawing a sword suggested by Rabelais's 'desguaina sa queue'.

19 **das hoch vnd nider gehôltz / das baw vñ daubholtz:** 'tall trees and underwood, timber for building and for making barrel-staves'.

29 **diß gehôrnecht VrChammel:** 'this horned grandfather of camels'. As well as its other peculiarities, the steed had a horn on its rump.

31 **Wurtzeldelber Land:** 'Land where they dig up roots'.

32 **Tobbrâmen:** 'wild, angry gad-flies'. Having kept more or less to his model thus far, Fischart feels the need to provide a German equivalent for the creation of Beauce, and picks on the Lüneburger Heide. His technique here is characteristic for the way he expands his model: he weaves a fantasy on the basis of a variety of puns and linguistic associations, not all of which are immediately intelligible and which the modern reader interprets at his own risk. It is just possible that Fischart is referring to some now-forgotten contemporary event by introducing so many different European peoples; more probably, he is simply allowing his mind to wander and amusing

himself with his own 'stream of consciousness'. 'Crabro' is Latin for 'hornet', but presumably because of the vaguely Slavonic sound of the word, these hornets are declared to be Sorbs and Wends, two Slavonic peoples who originally inhabited areas in the east of the Empire. By contrast, the Heruli were a Germanic tribe who inhabited northern Europe at the time of the Romans. 'ScharpSchröter' plays on 'sharp' and 'Schröter' = 'beetle' and 'schröten' = 'to cut', 'to hew roughly'. The 'Spanish flood' was natural in an age when Spain was the major sea-power, but the associations of 'Spanish' and 'fly' were sufficiently strong to warrant its inclusion, even if it were not the case that Fischart is clearly thinking in terms of the points of the compass and so needs a 'Western representative'. The mosquitoes are in keeping with the imagery of stinging insects, but probably also constitute a pun on 'Moskowiter'. The 'Zigeiner' could have been introduced for a variety of reasons: Fischart may be thinking of them simply as an odd people with a queer name from the East, or he may be referring to the restlessness of wasps and their reluctance to settle, or perhaps he has in mind the common description of the wasp as 'the gipsy's bee'. His distorted and apparently tautological adjective 'zeunganisch' seems to build on the Italian 'zingano', and may thus be seen as completing the survey of the cardinal points of the compass by anticipating the introduction of the Cantharides (= 'blister fly', 'Spanish fly') from Milan. 'Meylândisch' may itself be suggested by an association with 'Maikäfer'. 'Bommeln' and 'Brâmen' are acceptable puns (Bommeln = 'to buzz'; (Zalt)bommel is in the Netherlands); it is not clear why 'Holm' should have occurred to Fischart here, but as a component in names (e.g. Bornholm) it is, of course, common.

38 **verderbten den Teuffel:** idiomatic for 'to do a lot of damage'.

40 **wie die Scorpion:** The scorpion was traditionally held to constitute an antidote to its own sting.

41 **Brum̄ vnd Hundsbrâmen:** two fresh puns. 'Brum̄' ('brummen' = 'to buzz') is from the same root as 'Brombeer' (= 'blackberry'); 'Hundsbrâme' is not only 'dog-fly', but 'dog-rose', and was commonly used in hedges.

41 **von der Titanischen Himmelstûrmer Blut . . .:** 'Blut' here means 'persons', 'race', and the 'Wolckentrem̄liche Gigfitzen' ('tremmeln' = 'to thrash'; 'Gig' draws on 'Giege' = 'fool'+'Gig(ant)' and adds a personalizing suffix 'fitz') are probably Ephialtes and Otus, the giants who piled Pelion on Ossa to attack Olympus and after their defeat were buried under Etna. Fischart thus seems to be likening the smoke to that produced by a volcanic eruption. The comparison of the Titans to wasps is equally obscure: presumably he is thinking of the metaphorical usage = 'vexatious or dangerous person'.

45 **Wehrebenische vnd Segamenisch Wûrtzwisch von Donnerwurtz:** Bundles of herbs gathered and blessed on the Feast of the Assumption and held to give protection against various disasters. 'Wehrebenische' = 'vervain', 'Segamenisch' derives from Lat. 'sagmen' = 'bundle of sacred herbs', 'Donnerwurtz' = 'birthwort'.

47 **von vilen Jaren:** misprint for 'vor vilen Jaren' (?).

52 **Lazius:** Wolfgang Lazius, author of a twelve-volume survey of contemporary historical, geographical, linguistic, and ethnographical knowledge.

55 **auff desselben Landssprach:** 'desselben' refers to 'Volck'.

(b)

60 **Picrocholi:** The name is derived from the Greek for 'having bitter bile', hence the subsequent references to 'Bittergallier', 'Gallenkoderer' ('koder' = 'mucus', 'slime'), etc.

67 **zeigten da jhr zerrissene Fanen vnd Paner der Plagē:** Rabelais has 'monstrans leurs paniers rompuz' which Fischart mistranslates, perhaps because he actually misunderstands the original, perhaps because the sound of 'paniers' suggests to him the military image of the torn flags, i.e. the havoc wrought by the enemy amongst the cakes on the carts on which they were being transported to market.

71 **Saur im Arß:** the standard-bearer of the cake-bakers' guild who has been wounded in the recent fight. In Rabelais he is simply called Marquet, which was also the maiden name of the wife of Gaucher de Sainte-Marthe. Fischart retains this as a first name (Marcket), but replaces the personal satire with broad humour.

74 **võ Großkâl:** a translation of 'Grandgosier'.

74 **Bangarten / Wingartsknechten vnd Nußschwingern:** 'keepers, vineyard-workers, and nut-gatherers'. Grandgosier's men are agriculturists and herdsmen as opposed to the cake-makers of Lerne. The word 'schwingen' means 'to hit', the nuts being knocked down from the trees with long poles.

75 **Sewiler:** Rabelais calls it 'Seuillé'.

78 **acht vnnd aberacht / Bañ vñ aberbann:** This translates 'ban et arriere ban'. The German equivalent for 'arriere ban' is 'herban' (i.e. the summons to a vassal to give military service), but Fischart understands it as meaning a reiteration of the 'ban'. (Cf. 'mandiren vñ Remandirē', for which there is no equivalent in Rabelais.)

79 **lermen in allen Gassen vmbschlagen:** 'to beat the call to arms in every street'.

81 **so lieb jm die Wcinstraß ist:** 'as dcarly as he values his life'. 'Weinstraß' is a humorous gloss for 'throat'.

82 **Platz di S. Marco:** Rabelais does not give the square a name. Fischart ironically calls it after the principal square in Venice.

83 **Musterplan:** the field used for mustering troops, here the mustering itself.

85 **vñ zwischen der weil dz man dē Jmbiß zubereitet:** Rabelais ends by saying that the wagons were loaded with stores of ammunition for the field and the belly ('et charger force munitions, tant de harnoys d'armes que de gueules'). Fischart lists some forty items of artillery and armour, but neglects the reference to the belly. In view of their highly technical and untranslatable nature, many of the terms have not been listed in the Glossary.

88 **zum vnfriden:** 'in times of war'.

101 **Zwischen dem essen . . . Steckenknecht / Brandmeister:** This sentence translates five words in Rabelais—'En disnant bailla les comissions'.

114 **Trapelum vom Wetterhan:** a humorous rendering of Rabelais's 'Trepelu', but which loses the overtones of the original (= 'ragged'; Urquhart has 'Shagrag').

117 **Truckedillon:** Fischart again loses the sense of the original (Toucquedillon = 'Fanfare').

118 **darunter neun hundert vierzehen grosse Feldstuck:** Fischart expands Rabelais's list of nine different pieces of artillery to twenty-one, adds a whole miscellany of siege and field equipment and transport, and concludes with a recital of the personnel in charge of the equipment.

145 **hinderharrenwertig:** a coining from 'hinter'+'harren'+'warten'.

146 **Rackedennarren:** Rabelais has 'Racquedenare' (= 'Racle-denier'; Urquhart has 'Scrape-good').

152 **Eugulewind von Klatterbuß:** Again Fischart simply supplies a fantastic, but meaningless equivalent. Rabelais's 'Engoulevent' (Urquhart has 'Swill-wind') was the sort of name which in medieval times was given to a horse or messenger (because they ran so swiftly).

170 **machtē inn eim augenblick den Herbst ein:** 'gathered the harvest in a moment'.

171 **auff Moscouitisch für Polotzko:** The idea of Muscovites carrying baskets of earth to strengthen the town's defences is heavily ironical and is intended to suggest ruthlessness. The storming of the Lithuanian fortress of Polack (Polotsk) by the armies of Ivan the Terrible in 1563 was one of the great atrocities of the sixteenth century. After six assaults the town was plundered and razed, the victorious Russians allegedly putting some 20,000 people to the sword.

178 **Der Fucker zu Bredau:** The reference is obscure. Presumably the Fuggers, the Augsburg bankers, must have held Bredau in the Uckermark as surety for loans advanced and cut down and sold the standing timber for their own profit.

180 **vmb den lôffel renten:** a common entertainment during wedding celebrations, the bride giving a prize to the person who retrieved the spoon and brought it to her.

182 **Juncker Frech mut saß im Sattel . . .:** a proverbial expression, 'Sir Boldness sat in the saddle and Lady Familiar-with-Sorrow behind him'.

189 **Botz todenbaum:** 'Gottes Totenbaum', 'God's coffin', an oath.

(iv) *Historia von D. Johañ Fausten* (1587)

1 **D.:** 'Doctor'.

5 **Bestettigung:** Like much of the vocabulary in the first paragraph, this is a legal term (= 'confirmation'). The opening clause might be translated:

NOTES 331

'With my own hand I, Dr. Johannes Faustus, publicly commit myself to and confirm the terms of this document . . .'

6 **Nach dem ich mir fürgenommen:** The auxiliary verb 'habe' is omitted.

7 **vnd aber:** 'but yet . . .'

7 **Gaaben / so mir von oben herab bescheret / vnd gnedig mitgetheilt worden:** This unsolicited—and in the context of the pact highly incongruous—testimonial to the goodness of God is inserted by the devout author to make a theological point and to emphasize the enormity of Faust's action.

11 **Mephostophiles:** The name is variously derived from Heb. 'Mephir' + 'Tophel' = 'Destroyer'+'Liar', or from the Greco-Latin 'Mephites'+ 'Philos' = 'A lover of poisonous miasmata'.

11 **uennet:** misprint for 'nennet'.

12 **in Orient:** As the bringer of light, Lucifer was naturally held to have his dominions in the East.

12 **auch denselbigen:** the object of 'erwehlet', i.e. Mephostophiles.

19 **gut macht haben:** 'have full power'.

23 **Zu festem Vrkundt . . .:** 'As legally binding proof and to give it greater validity . . .'

31 **der Geistlichen Doctor:** possibly an error for 'Doktrin', but the title may be intended as an equivalent for Doctor of Theology.

36 **Jn dem hat er nun sein Thun . . .:** a very confused sentence; the Biblical reference is obscure—it seems to be a reminiscence of texts such as Luke 11: 24—and behind all the verbiage the sentence simply means that Faustus had commerce with the Devil and consequently fell completely into the latter's power. The proverb 'Man soll den Teufel nicht zu Gast laden', which the author quotes again in the final chapter, was the equivalent of the modern 'Man soll den Teufel nicht an die Wand malen'.

57 **wie er sich dann selbst einmal hören lassen:** 'as he himself once said'.

58 **dem Churfürsten:** i.e. of Saxony; Faustus is held to live in or near Wittenberg.

74 **durch Johannem:** John 10: 1.

81 **von Gottseligen Fragen:** Faustus has been asking about various theological problems, the fall of the angels, the nature of hell, etc.

82 **ein gut Werck seyn lassen:** 'accept it with a good grace'.

83 **Fienge demnach an Calender zu machē:** Astrology and matters relating to the calendar fell within the province of the mathematician. The belief in prophecies was widespread and the production of 'Practica'—sixteenth-century equivalents of *Old Moore's Almanac*—was a profitable occupation. As the author suggests here, these 'Practica' were usually kept so innocuously general as to be infallible.

93 **denn er setzte nichts in Calender / es war jhm also . . .:** 'for he put nothing in calendars that was not true, but when . . .'.

110 **welche auch gewiß eine kôstliche vnnd berûhmte Kirchen in der Welt ist:** The adjectives here have superlative force.

124 **aber er muß mich lânger ziehen:** Bobertag suggests 'hold in higher esteem' or 'fatten up longer'. The second alternative seems preferable.

129 **nicht viel Guts:** This has comparative force: 'Subsequently the good Master Faustus did not eat or drink much that was better (than what he had there).'

137 **solche Verblendung:** The writer is, of course, a Protestant. 'Ablaß' here probably means 'remission of sins', rather than 'indulgence'.

151 **ein gut fegen:** The Wolffenbüttel MS. has 'ein guetten Segen'. Our reading is more meaningful and colourful with its coarse play on 'Fegefeuer'.

176 **also kam D. Faustus wider zu Gelt:** In his interest in Faustus as a waggish vagabond and 'Leutbetrüger', the author forgets that, being in receipt of a diabolical pension, Faustus had no need to cheat people in this way.

178 **Am weissen Soñtag:** Lat. 'Dominica in albis', Low Sunday, the Sunday after Easter.

187 **vnd entgegen solche Empôrung entstandē were:** 'and on account of which such a disturbance had arisen'.

190 **Castoris vñ Pollucis Schwester:** or rather half-sister—Zeus was the father of Castor and Pollux.

195 **mit fûrstellung Keysers Alexandri Magni:** Cf. prefatory note, p. 216.

222 **welches sie die Studenten abreissen môchten lassen:** 'which the students could have them draw'; 'sie' refers to the painters mentioned subsequently.

231 **nit leichtlich widerumb herauß zubringen ist:** a characteristic example of the moralizing and puritanical attitude of the author. He not only fails to see any poetry in the Helen episode, but he is inconsistent: a few sentences earlier he explained 'weil sie es aber fûr einen Geist achteten / vergienge jhnen solche Brunst leichtlich'.

271 **Zâen:** 'teeth', not 'toes'!

275 **schlotterten:** 'hung loose', 'wobbled', presumably because every bone in his body had been broken.

2. The *Schwank*

(i) *Ein kurtzweilig lesen von Dyl Vlenspiegel* (1515)

(*a*)

2 **Budensteten:** Buddenstedt, near Magdeburg.

3 **bierthunnē:** 'barrel of beer' rather than 'beer-barrel'.

5 **Als nun d' pfaff bereit wz mit eim krutster:** 'And so the parson was set up with a verger.'

6 **vnd tet sich an:** i.e. put on his priestly vestments. The alb mentioned below is a garment with wide sleeves.

9 **wie dem:** 'what's this?'

11 **der pfaff sprach.:** In our text, as in ENHG generally, punctuation is often erratic and, where it is supplied, is often different from modern usage. The full stop here, and variously below, has the force of a modern colon.

13 **das gelt euch vnd mir ein thuñ bierß:** 'I'll bet you a barrel of beer.'

21 **Da ward die kellerin aber zornig:** The parson's housekeeper had been antagonized by Ulenspiegel, who, because she had only one eye, only did half of whatever she asked him to do.

22 **J:** misprint for 'Jr'.

(b)

28 **thūē:** abbreviation for 'thuren'.

29 **kranckßeit:** misprint for 'kranckheit'.

30 **das hochwirdig heilig sper Cristi:** One of the most treasured possessions of the Nürnberg municipality was a relic alleged to be the lance with which Longinus wounded Christ in the side. Together with other relics and the imperial 'crown jewels', it was preserved in the Heilig-Geist-Kirche, attached to the Heilig-Geist-Spital, where the present anecdote takes place. The 'anderen mercklichē stückē' included a fragment of the wood from Christ's cradle, a nail and a splinter of wood from the Cross, a piece of the table-cloth used at the Last Supper, and a tooth of John the Baptist.

31 **rastē ist:** 'is kept'.

31 **Vñ d' selbē kranckē mēschē d' wer d' spitel meister eins teil gern ledigig gewesen:** literally, 'And of these same sick people, of these the hospital keeper would gladly have got rid of a part', i.e. he would gladly have got rid of some of his patients. 'Ledigig' is a misprint for 'ledig'.

35 **ßelffen:** misprint for 'helffen'.

36 **gelont werdē:** A new sentence now begins.

36 **vlēspiegel d' sprach er wolt in . . .:** misprint for 'im'. 'Ulenspiegel said he would cure [lit. 'make straight'] a lot of his patients for him if he were prepared to put down two hundred gulden and promise them to him.'

41 **Also giēg vlēspiegel in spital . . .:** This long sentence falls into three separate sentences; the first break occurs at 'vō nieman offenbarē' ('vō' is read as a misprint for 'vñ'), the second at 'bei grossem glouben zů'.

46 **bei grossem glouben:** 'with a solemn oath'.

47 **sol ich nū vch krācken zů gesuntheit helffen . . . zů puluer:** 'now if I am to help you sick people and get you on your feet again, this is impossible for me to do unless I burn one of you to powder'; 'ich v'bren dā' is the printer's abbreviation for 'ich verbrenne dann'.

62 **an ein and' end:** 'to another place'.

68 **wie dz er in getrouwt het:** 'how he had threatened them'.

70 **das es Vlenspiegels betrug wase:** misprint for 'was'.

71 **er kund im nüt angewinnen:** 'he could obtain no redress from him'.

(ii) Johannes Pauli: *Schimpf vnd Ernst* (1522)

2 **Wjr leesen von . . .:** Although Pauli does not always acknowledge his source, he makes no attempt to pass himself off as being more than a compiler. Probably under the influence of his unnamed source, Pauli presents us here with a highly compressed anecdote which barely does justice to the content, and surprisingly fails to expound the moral. Cf. Hans Sachs's treatment, p. 118.

6 **sorach:** misprint for 'sprach'.

15 **Nit weit von der Narren kappen:** The cap was, of course, the traditional attribute of the fool and is here used simply as an image for folly: 'There was once a foolish peasant who . . .'

18 **der edelmank am:** misprint for 'der edelman kam'.

21 **vñ ward jm nit:** 'and he did not fall to his (the nobleman's) lot', i.e. he did not catch him.

23 **noch so:** 'but yet'.

26 **greiffen Gott in seinen gewalt:** 'arrogate to themselves powers which belong to God'.

27 **dem da zů gehôrt zů rechen:** Rom. 12: 19.

29 **Aman . . . Mardocheo:** Haman and Mordecai. . . . See Esther, 5: 11–14; 6, 7.

30 **es grebt einer eim ein grůben:** Prov. 26: 27.

35 **Michi vineictam:** misprint for 'vindictam'. 'Vengeance is mine.' The reference is to Rom. 12: 19, where St. Paul quotes Deut. 32: 35. Ps. 94: 1 says much the same thing, but not in the words Pauli quotes here.

38 **was nach Gottes grechtigkeit hiesch:** 'what was required according to God's justice'.

41 **seinen diener einen:** misprint for 'seiner diener einen'.

42 **geschrwē:** 'geschruwen'.

44 **geschimpfft:** a euphemistic use of 'schimpfen' (= 'to jest'). He had raped the girl.

51 **hort jhn beicht:** 'hort jhn beichten'.

54 **ich hab es für kein sünd:** 'I do not hold it to be a sin'.

61 **da lag im das Sacrament:** here 'the wafer'.

63 **der hat sich mir selber geben:** 'he has given himself to me'. As a Catholic, Pauli believed in the real presence.

(iii) Jörg Wickram: *Das Rollwagenbüchlin* (1555)

2 **fůrt:** 'imported'.

2 **Oberlandt:** Upper Germany.

3 **wie er aber seiner schätz nit wol warname:** 'as he did not exploit his opportunity'.

4 **überfůrt wurden:** 'there was a glut'.

24 **des er sich wol versach:** 'and he anticipated that . . .' (lit. 'of which').

30 **so verne er jm auß der sach hulffe:** 'if he could help him to get out of it'. One would expect a *virgula* after 'hulffe'.

32 **God geb was:** 'No matter what'.

34 **vnnd vil auff diesen geklagt ward:** 'and he was severely taxed [with having done something]'.

42 **du wirst mir das nit abblehen:** 'you will not get out of paying me by saying "blee"'.

48 **vñ traff vntrew jren eygen Herrn:** The story Wickram recounts here is a very well-known one. It had been treated in the celebrated medieval French *Farce de Maître Pathelin* and had provided the famous humanist Johannes Reuchlin with the central scene of his Latin comedy, *Henno* (1497), whence Wickram may have borrowed it, possibly via Hans Sachs's version of 1531.

(iv) *Das Lalebuch* (1597)

(a)

1 **das Liecht in jhr Rhathauß zu tragen:** They had forgotten to put any windows in the new town hall and consequently found it rather dark inside.

4 **dann es jhnen allen gegolten:** 'for it was a matter of concern to them all'. The author commonly omits auxiliary verbs.

10 **wessen man sich in fůrgefallenem handel zu verhalten:** 'what course of action was to be pursued in the situation which had arisen'.

11 **widerwertige meinungen:** 'conflicting opinions'.

13 **Vnd als es sich schier ansehen ließ . . .:** 'And when it appeared very much as though the majority wanted . . .'

15 **auff ein newes:** 'anew'.

18 **in wårender seiner Weißheit / eh er sich derselbē verziegen:** 'during the time of his wisdom, before he had renounced the latter'.

21 **Daher dann . . . wöllen:** The auxiliary verb has been omitted from this sentence.

26 **Vtis:** Gk. = 'no one'.

33 **ein Kindbettern gelust:** 'a craving such as pregnant women [lit. "women in their confinement"] experience'.

35 **Vdena:** feminine form of 'Utis'.

37 **als deren was das Butterhåfelin vermôgens were besser als jhme bewust gewesen:** 'who knew better than he did what the capabilities of the butter-dish were'.

39 **Butters / Anckens oder Schmaltzes (wie du wilt):** The author offers his readers a choice of synonyms for butter. 'Ancke' was an Alemannic word which has disappeared from the standard language; 'Schmaltz', an Upper German word, now means 'lard' or, in the metaphorical sense, 'sloppy sentiment'.

44 **seinen Gelust nicht gebûsset:** 'had not satisfied his craving'.

50 **Es thuts nit:** 'It won't work.'

52 **weil ich mich das Wasser nicht hette bedauren lassen:** 'because I would not have regretted [i.e. been mean in the matter of] water'.

63 **zusamen wallen:** 'to bind together'.

70 **Botz kramet:** 'Gottes Sakrament', a common oath.

86 **haben wir allzeit vm̄ so vil zum besten:** 'we have made a permanent gain by so much'.

89 **vnserm vorhaben der Narrey halben:** 'our intention to appear as fools'.

93 **bey dem Eyd gemahnet:** 'having been admonished to comply with their oath [to serve the state]'.

97 **vñ and's:** printer's abbreviation for 'vnd anderes'.

97 **auff ein fûrsorg:** 'as a precautionary measure', i.e. 'in their concern'.

118 **die vngehewren Riesen:** The reference is to the attempt of the Titans to storm the stronghold of Zeus on Olympus by piling Mount Pelion on Mount Ossa.

122 **auffs gmeine Gut hin:** 'at the expense of the community'.

(b)

125 **forchten die Lalen jhrer Haab:** 'the Lalen feared for their goods and chattels'.

137 **lasse dir ... kein graw Har im &c. wachsen:** The expression was 'Lasse dir keine grauen Haare im Arsch wachsen'.

V · THE LYRIC

1. Secular poems

(i) *Von einem Einsidel vnd seinem hônigkrug*

3 **in dem Waldt:** misprint for 'in dem Walde'—the line rhymes with 'manichfalde' and should have eleven syllables and end in a feminine rhyme.

NOTES   337

6 **manichfalde:** The creation of an extra syllable by the addition of an 'e'
in order to meet the needs of the metre was a standard practice amongst
Meistersinger (cf. 'miternachte', 'geren', 'Welte').

9 **das gůlt mir fůnff gůlden geren:** 'it would be well worth five gulden
for me', i.e. he could easily sell it for five gulden.

12 **weren:** a contracted form of 'werden'.

18 **das môcht ich wol geniessen:** 'I should very much like that'.

32 **man . . . kron . . . wan:** In Franconian these would rhyme, 'man' and
'wan' being rounded to 'mon' and 'won'. Such rhymes were, however,
expressly prohibited in the *Tabulatur* and were penalized accordingly.

(ii) *Danheuser*

1,1 **Nun wil jch aber heben an . . .:** The opening lines point strongly to the
fact that the ballad derives from a tradition of poetry intended to be sung
rather than read.

1,4 **Venußinne:** The pleonastic feminine suffix has been added to the proper
name for the sake of the metre.

2,2 **Wann:** 'except that'.

2,4 **Zů andern schônen frawen:** The line *may* be more than a 'fill-in'—
traditionally those who entered the mountain enjoyed relations with Venus'
servants as well as with the Goddess herself (cf. stanza 5, l. 3; stanza 14, l. 4).

3,1 **Herr Danheuser jr seyt mir lieb:** Stanza 3 transports us very much *in
medias res*—Tannhäuser is already wishing to leave the Venusberg. Heine,
who was a great admirer of the ballad and characteristically produced a
scurrilous satirical version of it (see *Die Götter im Exil*), declared the elliptical
suddenness of this opening to be a master-stroke. It was, however, an
'organic' master-stroke, produced by the process of 'Zersingen': R. von
Liliencron records that the Low German version had an additional stanza
between our stanzas 2 and 3 which indicated the growth of remorse in
Tannhäuser after his entry into the mountain. The oath mentioned in l. 3
is actually retained in the Middle English version of the story: 'Here my
trouthe i plyghte to the, etc.'

4,3 **Vnd redt das yemand mer dann jr . . .:** 'And if anyone other than you
were to say that to me, may God help me to be avenged on him for it.'

6,1 **Vnd nem jch nun ein ander weyb Jch hab in meynen sinnen:** From
the sense we must understand 'If I took a woman other than the one I have
in mind', i.e. the Blessed Virgin. In the Swiss version, Tannhäuser actually
meets the Virgin on leaving the Pope, which, taken with the present lines,
probably indicates that in the original legend of redemption the Virgin
was instrumental in his salvation, heavenly love in the shape of a pure
woman overcoming earthly love in the shape of an impure one—a theme
which was to be developed and modified by Richard Wagner. Our version
is a Protestant one, however, and such references to the Virgin as could

be conveniently expurgated have been replaced by references to Christ or to God. Thus stanza 14, l. 3, and stanza 22, l. 3 both read in the version of 1515 'Maria mûter, raine maid'. The present reference clearly did not admit of such treatment—and conceivably was not even understood as a reference to the Virgin—and so was allowed to stand.

10,4 **Von ewrem stoltzen leybe:** 'From your proud (or magnificent) self', i.e. 'to leave your court'. The idiom involving 'leybe' is an archaic survival of a frequent MHG usage where the noun 'lîp' is little more than a reinforcement of the pronoun.

12,1 **Gebrauch jch nun ein frembdes weib:** 'Gebrauchen' here = 'to use sexually'. Syntactically the line does not fit into the rest of the stanza and probably represents a corruption of the original. The version of 1515 has: 'Eur minne ist mir worden laid.'

12,4 **Jr seyt ein Teuffelinne:** Quite apart from the inconsistency—Venus has just been addressed as 'edle Frawe zart'!—this line is, in its abruptness, in striking contrast to the slow pace of the preceding lines. A. F. J. Remy suggests that it is a reminiscence of Frau Venus as a 'loathly woman' and of the hero's original disillusionment: in the English version the lady immediately grows ugly once Thomas of Erceldoune has made love to her.

14,1 **Fraw Venus vnd das wil jch nit:** Syntactically the 'vnd' has no place in this sentence and its presence is an interesting example of the way the text has been corrupted as the language developed: in the version of 1515 the line read 'Frau Venus! das enwill ich nit'. In spite of its retention in stanza 4, l. 1. ('Fraw Venus das enhab jch nit'), the old negative form was probably already felt to be archaic and so in the present case the 'vnd' has been supplied as a meaningless syllable to retain the metre while avoiding the archaic construction.

15,2 **Meyn lob das solt jr preysen:** The—in the circumstances somewhat optimistic—injunction to sing her praises seems to have been part of the original tradition: the English version has 'Whare ever thou fare by frythe or felle I praye the speke none evyll of me'.

15,4 **Nembt vrlaub von dem greysen:** This rather mysterious command has been variously interpreted. Pointing out that the Dutch and Low German versions use a plural form, Remy argues that these 'grey ones' are the dwarfs or trolls often associated with the Otherworld inside the hill. This view is rejected by P. S. Barto, who sees the plural form as a textual corruption and argues that in any case the dwarfs were servants and as such not the people to be able to give permission to leave ('vrlaub nemen' he interprets in its original meaning as 'to obtain permission to go', without explaining why Tannhäuser asks Venus for permission, if another has to grant it!). In his view the 'grey one' is 'Der Alte vom Berg', which was one of Wodan's titles. R. von Liliencron takes a similar view and suggests that the 'grey one' is the Mountain King. Other critics have argued that the 'grey one' is faithful Eckhart, who was reputed to sit before the mountain and warn would-be entrants of the consequences of such an act. It seems unlikely, however, that Venus would show such regard for one who would rob her of potential lovers, and on balance Barto's and Liliencron's view seems the most convincing.

16,4 **Auff eynes Bapstes trawen:** 'Relying on the good faith and offices of the Pope'. The almost jocular note of this and the following lines is in odd contrast to the alleged 'jamer' and 'rewen' of the penitent Tannhäuser.

17,2 **Got můß seyn ymmer walten:** 'God must always protect him.' The 'seyn' would refer to the Pope, and is almost certainly a corruption of 'meyn'. The 1515 version has 'gott well mein immer walten'.

19,4 **Ob jch mŏcht Got anschawen:** i.e. 'so that I might gain heaven'.

20,3 **Als wenig als es grůnen mag:** Our anti-papal author has probably altered the original speech. The staff in the earlier tale of redemption would be used—as in the Low German version—simply as a means of inviting God to make His will manifest: 'If God wishes you to be absolved, He will make this staff blossom.' Our author makes it an image for the impossible, thus pointing to the monstrous presumption of the Pope in withholding absolution from the penitent sinner.

21,1 **Nun solt jch leben nur ein jar:** The order of the stanzas here is suspect: stanza 21 should perhaps precede stanza 20. Certainly it would be more natural to allow Tannhäuser to complete his request for 'beicht vnd bůß' and then have it rejected.

(iii) *Ejn meidlein zu dem brunnen gieng*

1 **Ludo Senfl:** Senfl was born *c.* 1492 and was the pupil of Heinrich Isaac, a Dutchman, whom he succeeded as Master of the Imperial Music. He composed important church music for the newly established Protestant Church. Although Forster here names Senfl as being responsible for the arrangement of our song, he commonly modified the tunes he included in his anthology.

2 **vnd das was seuberlichen:** 'and she was pretty', or 'and that was a pretty sight'.

4 **er kůsts:** The 's' is an enclitic form of the pronoun 'sie'.

5 **jr seid mir nit on mere:** 'I am not averse to you', 'I like you'. It is not clear whether it is the boy or the girl who speaks these words, but since they are followed by the invitation 'tret here', they are probably to be attributed to the girl.

7 **Das meitlein tregt pantoffel an:** Mr. P. A. Thurlow has pointed out to me that it was not uncommon for the bridegroom to give the bride a pair of shoes as a token of proprietorship.

8 **dem schneid sie bald in kappen:** 'she soon boxes his ears'; 'kappe' is a cap, 'in' is a misprint for 'ein'.

9 **kein zucht daran:** misprint for 'tuch', which appears in the scores for the other voices and aptly continues the idiom.

9 **hôfflich zwagen:** 'give him a sound drubbing'. 'Zwagen' (= 'wash') was applied particularly to the washing of the hair or the head, and through euphemistic and ironical usage came to mean 'to cuff, thrash'! (Cf. the expression 'jemandem den Kopf waschen'.)

(iv) *Wol auff gut gsel von hiñen*

1 **Joa. Leonhar. de Langenaw:** Langenau, the arranger of this song, was only a minor figure in his own day and is now almost completely forgotten.

2 **schlag vm̄ vñ weit hindan:** 'turn around and travel far'; 'hindan' (= 'hinten') was replaced in subsequent editions by 'von dan'. In view of the slightly uncomfortable nature of 'hindan', one is almost tempted to suggest the reading 'weithin dan'.

7 **vnd lern eß mit der hand:** The exact meaning is obscure. 'Mit der hand' could mean 'by handwriting', 'by acting as a secretary', i.e. he is working his way through college by selling his literary skills to an unlettered nobleman.

7 **kan wol schreyben vnd lesen / ghôrt einem buler zu:** At first sight it is not clear why a paramour should be able to read and write, and one is tempted to read some obscene meaning into the phrase. The secretary, as a man of some education and polish, however, would have special attractions for any lady married to a boorish country squire, and it may be that the author regards the situation envisaged here as being archetypal.

8 **der herbst ist abgelesen:** 'the harvest is gathered in'.

10 **Jch scheid mich mit dem leybe / laß jr das hertze mein:** A hoary *topos*, cf. *Minnesangs Frühling*, 47, 9.

12 **wer hat dich mich erdacht:** misprint for 'wer hat dich nur erdacht'.

(v) *Jch hôrt ein frewlein klagen*

1 **G. Oth.:** Caspar Othmayr (1515–53), a famous composer and arranger of songs, and a close friend of Forster.

2 **ein weyblich bildt:** 'Bild' often suggests beauty (cf. 'bildschön'), but in the compounds 'Weibsbild', 'Mannsbild' can acquire pejorative overtones. Here the phrase means simply 'a pretty woman'.

3 **jûnglich mildt:** misprint for 'jûngling'.

7 **auff den kasten:** The 'kasten' was presumably some outbuilding or construction on the wall or battlement which housed the watchman.

8 **weckt ewren gsellein:** misprint for 'gsellen'.

(vi) *Dje weiber mit den flôhen*

1 **Niclas Piltz:** Virtually unknown except for his association with Forster.

2 **sie geben gern außlehen:** 'they would gladly give out fiefs [by way of reward], if thereby they could ensure that they were all killed'; 'vñ das mans' is a misprint for 'vm̄ das mans' (= 'man sie').

3 **jr kein:** 'not one of them'.

4 **so hettens frid:** The 's' is an enclitic form of 'sie'.

7 **Der krieg bebt an:** misprint for 'hebt an'.

7 **werd:** NHG 'währt'.

10 **stonen:** The pleonastic 'en' has been added to supply the extra syllable required by the metre.

11 **ston:** presumably originally 'stont', since a rounded form 'hondt' is intended to rhyme with it.

(vii) *Den liebsten Bulen den ich hab*

1 **Bulen:** Although masculine, 'Bule' can designate a person of either sex.

1 **den ich hab:** The old form 'han' has been modernized and the rhyme lost.

1 **leit:** NHG 'liegt'.

4 **Muscateller:** a strong sweet wine made from the muscadine grape.

9 **wil ich dir bald eins bringen:** 'I will shortly drink a toast to you in it'.

(viii) Jacobus Regnart: *Venus du vnd dein kind*

2 **seid alle beide blind:** In mythology neither Venus nor Cupid was blind, although the latter was in more modern times occasionally represented as being blindfold.

2. Hymns

(i) *Ein feste burg ist vnser Gott*

5 **Der alt bôse feind:** In spite of the repetition of 'itzt' and the fact that the hymn was written shortly before the Turkish military successes of 1529, it is probable that Luther is thinking here of the Devil and not the Sultan. As the 'Fûrst dieser welt' (cf. John 14: 30; 16: 11) the Devil would, of course, include all principalities and powers, and along with them the Antichrist in Constantinople and the Antichrist in Rome.

9 **der rechte man:** i.e. Christ. The attribution of the O.T. title of 'der Herr Zebaoth' ('Lord of Hosts') to Christ seems theologically questionable.

14 **wie sawr er sich stelt:** 'however frightful a stance he may adopt'.

14 **thut er vns doch nicht:** = 'nichts'.

15 **ein wôrtlin kan jn fellen:** According to Berger, Luther is on record as describing the 'wôrtlein' as 'Teufel, du lügst', but the name of Jesus or 'Get thee hence, Satan' would fit equally well.

16 **Das wort sie sôllen lassen stan:** i.e. the word of God. The appeal to the Word was, of course, a standard weapon in the Lutheran armoury, and the text of 1 Pet. 1: 25, usually quoted in Latin ('Verbum Dei manet in

aeternum'), for over a century constituted what was virtually a Lutheran battle-cry.

16 **dazu**: 'for doing so'.

17 **auff dem plan**: 'on the [battle]field'.

19 **sie habens kein gewin**: 'they have no profit from it'. The 's' is an enclitic form of the genitive of the third person neuter pronoun.

(ii) *Aus tieffer not schrey ich zu dir*

16 **Vnd ob es werd bis in die nacht**: NHG 'Und ob es währt . . .'

18 **Jsrael rechter art**: 'the true Israel', i.e. the community of Christian believers.

18 **aus dem Geist erzeuget**: John 3: 5 ff.

(iii) *Nu freud euch liebē Christē gmein*

4 **gmein**: 'together'.

5 **all in ein**: 'all together'.

5 **was Gott an vns gewendet hat**: 'what God has done for us'. Much of the point of the poem is to emphasize that justification is a free act of grace on God's part, not something to which even the most virtuous believer has a right.

6 **gar thewr hat ers erworben**: The 'es' which God has obtained for us at the price of His Son's death is that we should be able to sing His praises confident in the knowledge that He has saved us.

13 **Der frey will**: Luther did not believe a man had free will in the theological sense, i.e. he could not choose to work out his salvation. Here the expression means no more than an independent attitude of mind proper to man in his natural state.

13 **zum gut erstorben**: 'dead to goodness, incapable of goodness'.

18 **er lies sein bestes kosten**: Modern German would require 'er ließ es sich sein Bestes kosten'.

20 **zurbarmen**: 'zu erbarmen'.

30 **Denn ich bin dein / vnd du bist mein**: Luther adapts the language of the secular love lyric (cf. *Minnesangs Frühling*, 3, 1: 'dû bist mîn, ich bin dîn').

37 **den geist**: i.e. the Holy Ghost.

42 **der menschen gsatz**: 'that which is instituted of men'. Luther is almost certainly thinking of the papacy.

(iv) *Es ist das heil vns komen her*

5 **er ist der mittler wordē**: A central doctrine of the Reformation was that the believer, as a priest, had direct access to God and that Christ, and not the Church, was the intermediary between God and man.

7 **Was Gott im Gsetz geboten hat:** The following nine stanzas read like a summary of *Von der Freiheit* (cf. p.17).

9 **vom Gsetz erfordert allermeist:** '[which was] the principal demand of the law'.

13 **die sundig art:** 'the sinful nature', i.e. the taint of original sin.

24 **des glaubens recht gestalte / Nicht mehr / denn lieber HERRE mein . . :** The punctuation is confusing here. Other editions have the *virgula* after 'denn' and put the rest of the stanza and the whole of the following one in inverted commas: 'The true form of faith [is] no more than "Dear Lord . . .".'

40 **wolst jn der werck berauben:** 'you would rob it [i.e. faith] of the works'. The argument runs that, good works being a sign by which the faithful might be known, those without faith would not wish to do good works, and that if they did do good works, these would only be the 'gleisners werck' of stanza 4.

43 **der rechten zeit:** presumably the second coming of Christ, as promised in God's word.

44 **zu freud:** 'for our joy'.

47 **Ob sichs anlies:** 'Although things might make it seem . . .'

48 **Deñ wo er ist am besten mit:** 'For when he is nearest to us [with his help]'.

SELECT BIBLIOGRAPHY

A. WORKS OF REFERENCE, GENERAL SURVEYS,
BIBLIOGRAPHIES

Allgemeine Deutsche Biographie, Munich–Leipzig, 1875 ff. (new ed. in progress).
The Catholic Encyclopedia, New York, 1907 ff., (new ed. in progress).
Deutsches Wörterbuch, ed. J. and W. Grimm, Leipzig, 1854 ff.
Realencyclopädie für protestantische Theologie und Kirche, 3rd ed., Leipzig, 1896 ff.
Reallexikon der deutschen Literaturgeschichte, ed. P. Merker and W. Stammler,
Berlin, 1925 (new ed. in progress).
Religion in Geschichte und Gegenwart, 3rd ed., Tübingen, 1957.

Andreas, W. *Deutschland vor der Reformation*, rev. ed., Stuttgart, 1959.
Boeckh, J. G., et al. *Geschichte der deutschen Literatur von 1480 bis 1600*, Berlin,
1960.
Bach, A. *Geschichte der deutschen Sprache*, Heidelberg, 1956.
Bornkamm, H. *Das Jahrhundert der Reformation*, Göttingen, 1961.
Brinkmann, H. *Die Anfänge des modernen Dramas in Deutschland*, Jena, 1933.
Dickens, A. G. *Reformation and Society in Sixteenth-century Europe*, London, 1966.
Goetze, A. *Die hochdeutschen Drucker der Reformationszeit*, Strassburg, 1905;
Frühneuhochdeutsches Glossar, 5th ed., Berlin, 1956.
Léonard, E. G. *Histoire générale du protestantisme*, vol. i, Paris, 1950.
Lockwood, W. B. *An Informal History of the German Language*, Cambridge,
1965.
Lortz, J. *Die Reformation in Deutschland*, 2 vols., Freiburg, 1948.
Moser, V. *Neuhochdeutsche Grammatik* (in progress), vol. i, pts. 1 and 3, Heidel-
berg, 1929–51.
Newald, R. *Probleme und Gestalten des deutschen Humanismus*, Berlin, 1963.
Pascal, R. *German Literature in the Sixteenth and Seventeenth Centuries*, London,
1968.
Peuckert, W. E. *Die Große Wende, das apokalyptische Saeculum und Luther*,
Hamburg, 1948
Priebsch, P. and Collinson, W. E. *The German Language*, London, 1958.
Ranke, L. v. *Deutsche Geschichte im Zeitalter der Reformation*, 6 vols. Berlin,
1839–47.
Stammler, W. *Von der Mystik zum Barock*, 2nd ed., Stuttgart, 1950.
Williams, G. H. *The Radical Reformation*, London, 1962.

Most of the works quoted contain full bibliographies. The standard
bibliography for sixteenth-century history is K. Schottenloher, *Bibliographie
zur deutschen Geschichte im Zeitalter der Glaubensspaltung, 1517–1585*, 7 vols.,
Stuttgart, 1956 ff. The *Luther-Jahrbuch* publishes an annual bibliography of
current sixteenth-century studies. The standard bibliography of sixteenth-
century works is still K. Goedeke, *Grundriß zur Geschichte der deutschen Dichtung*,
vols. i and ii, Dresden, 1884 and 1886. *Index Aureliensis. Catalogus librorum
sedecimo saeculo impressorum*, Baden-Baden, 1962 ff., is still in progress.

B. MODERN EDITIONS OF AUTHORS REPRESENTED;
SECONDARY LITERATURE

Modern editions of sixteenth-century works have appeared in a variety of series, notably *Bibliothek des literarischen Vereins Stuttgart* (BLVS), *Kürschners Deutsche National-Literatur* (DNL), *Neudrucke deutscher Literaturwerke des sechzehnten und siebzehnten Jahrhunderts* (NDL), and *Deutsche Literatur in Entwicklungsreihen* (DLER), (*Reihen: Reformation; Volks und Schwankbücher*, etc.), *Deutsche Volksbücher in Faksimiliedrucken*, ed. L. E. Schmitt and R. Weimann, Hildesheim, 1969 ff.

Authors

BRANT, S. *Das Narrenschiff*, ed. F. Zarncke, Leipzig, 1854, rep. Hildesheim, 1961. Illustrated ed. F. Bobertag, 1889 (DNL 16). U. Gaier, *Studien zu Sebastian Brants Narrenschiff*, Tübingen, 1966. B. Könneker, *Wesen und Wandlung der Narrenidee im Zeitalter des Humanismus*, Wiesbaden, 1966. E. H. Zeydel, *Sebastian Brant*, New York, 1967.

DIALOGUES OF REFORMATION PERIOD: *Satiren und Pasquillen aus der Reformationszeit*, ed. O. Schade, Hannover, 1863. *Die Sturmtruppen der Reformation*, ed. A. Berger, 1931 (DLER *Reformation*, vol. ii).

EULENSPIEGEL, i.e. *Ein kurtzweilig lesen von Dyl Vlenspiegel*, ed. H. Knust, 1885 (NDL 55/56).

FAUST, i.e. *Historia von D. Johann Fausten*, ed. R. Petsch, 1911 (NDL 7/8). G. Milchsack, *Faustbuch und Faustsage* in *Gesammelte Aufsätze*, Wolfenbüttel, 1922.

FISCHART, J. *Sämtliche Dichtungen* ed. H. Kurtz (Deutsche Bibliothek, 8), Leipzig, 1866–7. *Auswahl* ed. K. Goedeke and A. Hauffen, 1895 (DNL 18). *Geschichtklitterung*, ed. with glossary U. Nyssen, Düsseldorf, 1965. A. Hauffen, *Johann Fischart*, 2 vols., Berlin–Leipzig, 1921–2. H. Sommerhalder *Johann Fischarts Werk*, Berlin, 1966.

FOLKSONG: G. Forster, *Frische Teutsche Liedlein*, ed. M. E. Marriage, 1903 (NDL 203/206). *Das Ambraser Liederbuch*, repr. Hildesheim, 1962. R. v. Liliencron, *Deutsches Leben im Volkslied um 1530*, 1884 (DNL 13). A. Goetze, *Vom deutschen Volkslied*, Freiburg, 1921. R. Haller, *Geschichte der deutschen Lyrik vom Ausgang des Mittelalters bis zu Goethes Tod*, Bern, 1967. DLER: *Das deutsche Volkslied*.

FRANCK, S. *Paradoxa*, ed. T. Ziegler, Strassburg, 1909. Selection in H. Fast, *Der Linke Flügel der Reformation*, Bremen, 1963, also DLER, *Reformation*, vol. vii.

HUBMAIER, B. *Schriften*, ed. G. Westin and T. Bergsten, Gütersloh, 1962.

HUTTEN, U. von *Opera*, ed. E. Böcking, Leipzig, 1859–70. H. Holborn, *Ulrich von Hutten and the German Reformation*, New Haven, Conn., 1937.

LALEBUCH, ed. K. v. Bahder, 1914 (NDL 236/39).

LUTHER, M. *D. Martin Luthers Werke. Kritische Gesamtausgabe*, Weimar, 1883 ff. (expected to run to about 100 vols. when completed; revised ed. in progress). *Werke in Auswahl*, ed. O. Clemen, 8 vols. Berlin, 1950–5. P. Althaus *Die Theologie Martin Luthers*, Gütersloh, 1962. R. H. Bainton, *Here I stand—a Life of Martin Luther*, New York, 1950. R. Friedenthal, *Luther*,

SELECT BIBLIOGRAPHY 347

Munich, 1967. H. Grisar, *Luther*, 3 vols., Freiburg, 1911 ff. F. W. Kantzenbach, *Martin Luther und die Anfänge der Reformation*, Gütersloh, 1965, and *Die Reformation in Deutschland und Europa*, Gütersloh, 1965. F. Lau, *Luther*, Berlin, 1959. H. Lilje, *Luther*, rororo Bildmonographien, 1965. J. Mackinnon, *Luther and the Reformation*, 4 vols., London, 1925 ff.

MEMMINGEN (Twelve Articles) *Aus dem sozialen und politischen Kampf*, ed. A. Götze and L. E. Schmitt, Halle, 1953. See also, W. Zimmermann, *Allgemeine Geschichte des großen Bauernkrieges*, 3 vols., Stuttgart, 1841 ff. W. Zöllner, *Zur Geschichte des großen deutschen Bauernkrieges*, Berlin, 1961.

MÜNTZER, T. *Schriften*, ed. G. Franz, Gütersloh, 1968. E. Bloch, *Thomas Müntzer als Theologe der Revolution*, Munich, 1921. M. M. Smirin, *Die Volksreformation des Thomas Müntzer*, Berlin, 1952.

MURNER, T. *Deutsche Schriften*, ed. F. Schultz, 9 vols., Strassburg, 1918 ff. R. Newald, *Elsässische Charakterköpfe aus dem Zeitalter des Humanismus* in *Probleme und Gestalten des deutschen Humanismus*, Berlin, 1963.

PAULI, J. *Schimpf und Ernst*, ed. H. Österley, 1866 (BLVS 85).

ROLLENHAGEN, G. *Froschmeuseler*, ed. K. Goedeke, Leipzig, 1872. *Spiel vom reichen Manne und vom armen Lazaro*, ed. W. Bolte, 1929 (NDL 27/03).

SACHS, H. *Sämtliche Werke*, ed. A. v. Keller and E. Goetze, 26 vols., 1870 ff. (BLVS 102 ff.). *Sämtliche Fastnachtspiele*, ed. E. Goetze, 7 vols., 1880–7 (NDL 26/7, 31/2, 39/40, 42/3, 51/2, 60/1, 63/4). *Sämtliche Fabeln u. Schwänke*, ed. E. Goetze and K. Drescher, 6 vols., 1893 ff. (NDL 110/7, 126/34, 164/9, 207/11, 213/15).

SCHEIDT, C. *Grobianus*, ed. G. Milchsack, 1882 (NDL 34/5).

SCHAPLER, HUG, ed. H. Kindermann (DLER, *Volks- und Schwankbücher*, vol. i).

WICKRAM, J. *Sämtliche Werke*, ed. J. Bolte and W. Scheel, 8 vols., 1901–6, BLVS 222 ff., *Von guten und bösen Nachbarn*, ed. F. Podleiszek, 1933 (DLER, *Volks- und Schwankbücher*, vol. vii), *Sämtliche Werke*, ed H. G. Roloff, Berlin, 1967 ff.

ZWINGLI, U. *Sämtliche Werke*, ed. E. Egli et al., vols., Zürich, 1905 ff., W. Köhler, *Huldrych Zwingli*, Zürich, 1947. F. Schmidt-Clausing, *Zwingli*, Berlin, 1965.

GLOSSARY

(Except in particularly misleading cases, common variants such as 'für' = 'vor' or 'ver', 'zu' = 'zer', 'ay' = 'ei', 'd' = 't', etc. are not listed separately)

A

abbrechen, *vi.* do violence to.
abdringen, *vt.* push aside; extort.
aber, *adv./conj.* again, but.
Abgot, *sm.* idol, false god.
ablan, *vi.* stop, desist.
Ablas(s), *sm.* indulgence.
ablassen, *vt.* remit, forgive.
abreissen, *vt.* draw.
Abscheid(t), *sm.* leave-taking, departure, death.
Absolutz, *sf.* absolution.
abstehen, *vi.* dismount.
abthûn, *vt.* kill; abolish.
achen, *vi.* moan.
Achß, *sf.* axle.
Acht, *sf.* ban, state of outlawry.
Affenspiel, *sn.* 'monkey tricks', practical joke.
alde, *interj.* = 'ade', adieu.
als, *conj.* also, when, therefore; *adj.* all, everything.
alweg(en), *adv.* always.
a(h)n, *prep.* without.
anders(t), *adv.* indeed.
An(n)dt, *sm.* trouble, sorrow.
anfaren, *vi.* run aground, come to grief.
angewinnen, *vt.* overcome; obtain.
anheben, *vi./t.* begin (to sing).
anhin gehen, *vi.* go past.
ankommen, *vt.* get; attack.
Anlaß, *sm.* agreement, undertaking.
anligen, *vi.* concern; pester.
Ans(ch)lag, *sm.* plan, undertaking; intention.
anschreiben, *vt.* put s.t. on the account.
Ansprach, *sm.* claim, business.

anstechen, *vt.* pick at random (as with a pin).
ansuchen, *vt.* visit; attack; ask.
Antrach, *sm.* drake.
antwurten, *vt.* hand over.
anwenden, *vt.* attack.
Anzug, *sm.* tendency, invitation.
arbeit selig, *adj.* industrious.
Arckelleiwagen, *sm.* gun carriage.
argwônig, *adj.* suspicious.
Art, *sf.* nature, breeding.
Aß, *sn.* corpse, carrion.
Auffenthalt, *sm.* sustinence, subsistence; income.
aufflegen, *vt.* impose; show (as evidence).
auffnemen, *vi.* increase.
Auffsatzung, *sf.* imposition, law, tax.
aufsatzen, *vt.* give, devote to, allocate, impose upon.
Aufwickelung, *sf.* wrapping up; unwrapping; incitement.
ausheben, *vt.* lift out; unseat.
ausnehmen, *vt.* rob, plunder.
außrichten, *vt.* carry out, exercise.
aus(s)roden, *vt.* root out; eradicate
austreschen, *vt.* finish threshing.
außziehen, *vt.* plunder, rob.
Aygenschaft, *sf.* bondage, serfdom; quality.

B/P

Bachant, *sm.* young scholar; oaf, lout.
bachen, *vt.* bake.
Pack, *sm.* pact, agreement.
backen, *vref.* clear off.
Balbierer, *sm.* barber-surgeon.

Ban(n)gart, *sm.* keeper, gardener.
Panngett, *sn.* banquet.
Barschafft, *sf.* cash, money.
bas(s), *adv.* better.
Basilisc, *sm.* siege gun.
Patron, *sm.* boss, captain.
Bechring, *sm.* pitch ring (for incendiary purposes).
bedôrffen, *vt.* need.
begaben, *vt.* endow, reward.
behalten, *vt.* redeem, save.
behûten, *vt.* protect.
beissen, *vt.* hunt (birds), hawk.
beiten, *vi.* wait, delay.
bekant, *ppart.* wise, sensible.
bekennen, *vt.* confess, affirm.
bekrôpfen, *vrefl.* feed, guzzle.
beleiten, *vt.* accompany.
beleyben, *vi.* stay.
berichten, *vrefl.* orient o.s., put o.s. right.
Berlin, *sn.* (small) pearl.
beschâchen, *vi.* happen.
Bescheidt, *sm.* account, news; obligation.
beschelten, *vt.* rebuke, blame.
beschei(y)den, *vt.* summon; inform.
beschencken, *vt.* give a present to; give to drink to.
beschicken, *vi.* happen.
beschicken, *vt.* summon.
Beschluß, *sm.* conclusion, thesis, axiom.
Beschneittung, *sf.* circumcision.
beschweren, *vt.* conjure, exorcise.
beschwertzen, *vt.* blacken.
Bestallbrief, *sm.* letter of commission.
bestan, *vi.* continue, endure, survive.
bestellen, *vrefl.* prepare o.s. (for combat).
betôr(e)n, *vt.* make a fool of, deceive.
bet(t)en, *vi.* pray.
Beutel, *sm.* purse.
beuten, *vt.* exchange, change.

bevelhen, *vt.* order; commit.
beweren, *vt.* prove.
beydesander, *adj.* both together.
Pflicht, *sf.* engagement, obligation.
Pfrûnde, *sf.* benefice.
Bickel, *sm.* pick-axe.
bindig, *adj.* binding.
bisß, *imp. sing. of* '*sein*'.
bißweil, *adv.* occasionally.
bitz, *conj.* until.
Blatrock, *sm.* long coat.
blempern, *vt.* blether.
blerren, *vi.* call, moo.
Bletz, *sm.* room.
plewen, *vt.* beat.
Blûst, *sf.* blossom.
Blutfane, *sf.* battle flag.
blutt, *adj.* naked, bare, deprived of.
Bôler, *sm.* mortar.
Pomerantze, *sf.* pomegranate; ornamental missile.
borgen, *vt.* spare; omit.
Bosse, *sm.* joke, prank.
brangen, *vi.* show off.
Breckin, *sf.* bitch.
Brechmeyssel, *sf.* crowbar.
Presaun, *sf.* dungeon.
brinnen, *vi.* burn.
brist, *3rd pers. pres. sing. of* '*bresten*', 'to lack'.
Probstein, *sm.* touchstone.
Profos, *sm.* provost marshal.
Pronnen, *sm.* well.
prossen, *vi.* sprout.
Bruch, *sm.* (everyday) use, usage.
brumlen, *vi.* growl.
Brunst, *sf.* sexual desire.
Bûchs(s)e, *sf.* gun.
Puff, *sm.* blow.
Bund, *sm.* bond, covenant.
bûsen, *vt.* atone for.
Bulerey, *sf.* lewdness, fornication.
Busa(u)n, *sf.* trumpet.

C

Cartaun, *sf.* 25-pounder cannon.
Clamant, *sm.* market-crier, charlatan.

clarificiren, *vt.* glorify.
Cleynot, *sn.* prize; jewel.
Concilium, *sn.* General Church Council.
Contor, *sn.* counting-house.
Creütz, *sn.* cross; suffering.

D/T

tadelen, *vt.* blame, bring into disrepute.
Danckzeychen, *sn.* thanksgiving.
dannocht, *conj.* yet, nevertheless.
Tantmâr, *sf.* silly, idle tale.
daranliegen, *vi.* be important.
darspannen, *vt.* give, offer, sacrifice.
darstellen, *vt.* offer.
darstrecken, *vt.* give, offer.
daruber, *conj.* in spite of this, nonetheless.
Deischselwagen, *sm.* cart with single shaft.
Dekrete, *snpl.* Decretals, Canon Law.
dennacht, dennocht, *conj.* nonetheless.
thienen, *vi.* serve.
Tholm, sm. drug.
thumm, *adj.* stupid.
Thurn, sm. tower.
tichten, *vt.* write, invent.
dick, *adv.* often.
diemuttig, *adj.* humble.
dienen, *vi.* serve, apply to.
Dienstbotte, *sm.* servant.
dieweil, *conj.* since; as long as; while.
dingen, *vt.* hire.
Tochterman(n), *sm.* son-in-law.
toeffen, *vt.* baptise, call.
Tolm, *sm.* drug.
dôlpisch, *adj.* stupid, clumsy.
dorffen, *vi.* need.
Törpel, *sm.* oaf, clown.
toub, *adj.* mad, senseless.
Tracht, *sf.* dish, course.
trachten, *vt.* consider.
trâtzig, *adj.* bold, defiant.
trawen, *vi.* threaten.

treffenlich, *adj.* excellent, *adv.* very much.
Treibmûle, *sf.* mill.
drein greifen, *vi.* intervene, take a hand.
dres(s)chen, *vt.* thresh.
trollen, *vrefl.* go, clear off.
Trometter, *sm.* trumpeter.
Trosser, *sm.* soldier in baggage train.
Trostung, *sf.* grace.
trouwen, *vi.* threaten.
trumpten, *vi.* trumpet.
trüwen, *vi,* trust.
Duck, *sm.* spite, malice.
dückish, *adj.* malicious, mean.
dügen, *vi.* be fit for.
dürfen, *vi/t.* need.
dürre, *adj.* dry, clear, brief.
durâ(e)chten, *vt.* persecute, treat with contempt.
du(ü)rffen, *vi.* need.
tzufallen, *vi,* agree with.
Tzusagunge, *sf.* promise.
Tzweyung, *sf.* quarrel.

E

Eheberedung, *sf.* talk of marriage, unofficial engagement.
Ehegemahel, *sn.* marriage partner.
einbylden, *vt.* imprint, impress upon.
einforieren, *vi.* take up quarters.
eingehen, *vi.* take effect (of wine).
einich(g), *adj.* one single.
Einsehen, *sn.* understanding, forbearance.
Ellend, *sn.* foreign country, wretchedness.
empfliehen, *vi.* escape.
emporen, *vt.* do without, miss.
End(e), *sn.* end, place.
enpfahen, *vt.* receive.
entbor, *adv.* up.
entfrombden, *vt.* alienate, expropriate.
entgelten, *vt.* atone for.
entperen, *vt.* do without.

entpfinden, *vt.* feel.
entschlagen, *vrefl.* cut o.s. off from.
entsetzen, *vt.* dismiss.
Erbärmd, *sf.* mercy.
erbeiten, *vi.* work.
Erbfall, *sm.* Fall of Man.
erdichten, *vt.* invent.
erfinden, *vrefl.* discover, experience; transpire.
erfûr, *adv.* forth.
ergerben, *vt.* tan.
erhaben, *ppart. of 'erheben'.* elevated.
erhoffen, *vt.* hope for.
erkicken, *vi/t.* revive.
erleern, *vt.* learn.
ermûhen, *vt.* tire, trouble.
erschôpffen, *vt.* draw.
erstifften, *vt.* institute, invent.
erstouben, *vt.* thresh; take to task rebuke.
erwacken, *vt.* awaken.
etwan, *adv.* previously; occasionally; perhaps.
eussern, *vrefl.* refrain from, have no part in.
eyffern, *vt.* be jealous, scold.
eygen, *adj.* unfree, living in serfdom.
Eynhålligkeit, *sf.* clarity, simple meaning.

F/V

fa(c)hen, *vt.* catch.
fail haben, *vt.* sell.
Falckenetlin, *sn.* 5-pounder cannon.
Fantast, *sm.* lunatic, madman.
fast, *adv.* very, extremely.
Faustkolbe, *sm.* pistol.
fegen, *vt.* sweep, purge, cleanse.
Fegfewer, *sn.* Purgatory.
Fehle, *sf.* failing, error.
feilen, *vi.* fail, be lacking, absent.
Fendrich, *sm.* subaltern.
Fenlin, *sn.* flag, banner.
verbringen, *vt.* carry out, complete.
verdamnen, *vt.* condemn.
Vergaderung, *sf.* assembly; commotion.

vergeben, *vt.* poison.
vergleichen, *vt.* make equal; repay; *vrefl.* make peace with.
vergult, *ppart. of 'vergülden'.* gilded.
vergunnen, *vt.* begrudge; allow.
verhålen, *vt.* conceal.
verhengen, *vt.* condemn to, impose upon.
veriehen, *vt.* say, tell, confess.
verkeren, *vt.* invert, pervert, make difficult.
verlechen, *vi.* be parched, die of thirst.
ferlich, *adj.* dangerous.
verma(c)hlen, *vt.* marry.
vermanen, *vt.* exhort.
vermeheln, *vt.* marry.
vermeucheln, *vt.* hush up.
vermögen, *vi/t.* be able; own.
Vermûttung, *sf.* presumption, assumption.
vernehmen, *vt.* hear, sense, understand, find.
ferr, *adj.* far.
verschießen, *vrefl.* shoot wide of the mark, make mistake.
verschwätzen, *vt.* tell tales about.
versehen, *vrefl.* expect.
versitzen, *vt.* miss opportunity; occupy.
verstockt, *adj.* obstinate, incorrigible.
verstôren, *vt.* destroy.
versünen, *vt.* reconcile.
vertedingen, *vt.* defend, conduct a law case.
verthon, *vt.* dissipate.
vertragen, *vt.* tolerate.
verursachen, *vt.* tax.
verwaren, *vt.* protect.
verwenden, *vt.* turn, twist; speak in metaphors.
verwenen, *vi.* go mad.
Verwiss, *sm.* reproach.
verworffen, *ppart. of 'verwerffen'* ruined.
verzeihen, *vrefl.* deny o.s.; lose.
verziehen, *vi.* delay.

verzigen, *ppart. of* 'verzeihen'. forgiven.
feyl haben, *vt.* sell.
Virteilbůchs, *sf.* 25-pounder cannon.
visieren, *vt/i.* aim; describe; have a visor(?).
Flachsfladen, *sm.* strip of linen.
flissen, *vrefl.* work hard, strive industriously.
fluchs, flux, *adv.* straight away.
volbrengen, *vi.* complete, carry out.
Fontanium, *sn.* celebration with wine (?).
vorab, *adv.* especially.
vorachten, *vt.* hold in contempt.
vorbringen, *vt.* carry out.
vordern, *vt.* call, summons, demand.
vordrig, *adj.* previous.
vorfůren, *vt.* lead astray.
Vorgeer, *sm.* example, model.
vorhei(y)schen, *vt.* promise.
vorhin, *adv.* previously; *conj.* in any case.
Vorhoff, *sm.* fore-court.
vorschlunden, *ppart. of* 'vorschlinden'. swallowed.
Vorstand, *sm.* understanding.
vorstellen, *vrefl.* change.
vorterben, *vi/t.* perish, ruin, destroy.
Fortrab, *sm.* advance party.
vorwenen, *vt.* deceive, delude.
frisch, *adj.* bold.
Frischt, *sf.* period of time.
frommen, *vi.* help, further.
frum(m), *adj.* pious, docile.
Füllerey, *sf.* gluttony.
Fültz, *sm.* oaf.
Fůndlin, *sn.* trick, device.
füran, *adv.* henceforth.
fürbaß, *adv.* further.
fürhalten, *vt.* show, preach, demonstrate.
Fürnemen, *sn.* purpose, intention.
fürsetzen, *vt.* lend.

Fürsetzzeug, *sn.* harness for additional horse.
Fürsichtigheyt, *sf.* foresight, prescience.
Fůrsorg, *sf.* care, precaution.
Fürsprech, *sm.* advocate.
fürstrecken, *vt.* advance.
Furtz, *sm.* fart.
fůrwitz(ig), *adj.* lascivious, randy, inquisitive, over-clever.
vyhe, *sn.* cattle.

G

gan, *vi.* go.
garten, *vt.* steal, scrounge.
gebrechen, *vi.* be lacking, blemished.
gebrist, *3rd. per. sing. of* 'gebresten'. be lacking.
Gedåchtnuß, *sn.* memorial; memory.
gedencken, *vt.* think of, mention.
Ged(t)icht, *sn.* invention, fiction.
geel, *adj.* yellow.
Gefälle, *snpl.* dues, taxes.
gefallen, *vi.* fall, fall due.
Gefigel, *sn.* fowls.
geheben, *vrefl.* behave.
gehorsamen, *vi.* obey.
geiseln, *vt.* flog, scourge.
geistlich, *adj.* spiritual.
Geit, *sm.* greed, avarice.
g(e)leissen, *vi.* shine, glitter.
Gemach, *sn.* peace, quiet.
gemach, *adj.* gentle, easy.
Gemayn, *sf.* community, parish.
genaden, *vt.* take leave of.
gen(g), *prep.* to, towards.
genůg thon, *vi.* satisfy.
Geplerre, *sn.* noise.
Gepôlder, *sn.* noise, commotion.
Gepreng, *sn.* show, magnificence.
gerawen, *vt.* rue, regret.
geren, *vt.* desire.
geren, *adv.* willingly.
gericht, *adj.* just, proper.
Gesatz, *sn.* law(s).
gescheiden, *vrefl.* depart.

geschickt, *adj.* skilful; 'called' (of God).

Geschreigeschütz, *sn.* heavy cannon.

gesegenen, *vt.* take leave of.

Gespiel(e), *smf.* playmate, companion.

gesprechen, *vt.* say.

gestehen, *vt.* cost.

getarff, *perf. form* (*1st, 3rd, sing. pres. indic.*) *of 'dürffen'*.

Getter, *sn.* grid, grille.

Getzeinge, *sn.* tongue.

Geuckelman, *sm.* conjuror.

gewapnen, *vt.* arm.

Gewelb, *sn.* vault, ware-house.

Geyßfuß, *sm.* crow-bar.

Ghyrn, *sn.* brain.

Gleichsner, *sm.* hypocrite.

gleichwol, *conj.* although, yet.

Glene, *sf.* lance.

Gleyßner, *sm.* hypocrite.

Glimpff, *sm.* honour, decorum, seemliness.

Glinster, *sn.* light, shine.

glosieren, *vt.* write a gloss on.

Gloth, *sf.* fire, heat.

Gmeyn, *sn.* commonality, third estate.

Gnuge, *sf.* sufficiency.

Gouch, *sm.* cuckoo, fool, jackanapes.

Göucherey, *sf.* knavery.

gremen, *vi/t.* worry, grieve.

grindig, *adj.* scabby, scurfy.

Grundtsuppe, *sf.* dregs.

gruntloß, *adj.* bottomless, inexhaustible.

grusamlich, *adj.* cruel, violent.

gruselen, *vi.* run cold (of blood), be afraid.

Gsatz(t), *sn.* law(s).

Guck gauch, *sm.* cuckoo.

Gülden, *sm.* florin.

Gült, *sf.* rent, tithe.

günnen, *vt.* grant.

Gynne, *sm.* official (?).

gynnen, *vi.* begin.

H

Hacke, *sf.* small calibre gun.

Hader leuß, *sfpl.* lice.

Hafen, Haffn, *sm.* pot, dish.

haimsetzen, *vt.* commend to, put responsibility onto s.o. for s.t.

håll, *adj.* bright, clear.

Halskragen, *sm.* collar (also armour).

han, *vt.* have.

Hand, vor der h., *adv.* present.

handeln, *vt.* scold, quarrel with, fight.

handthaben, *vt.* support.

Harnasch, *sm.* armour.

Haß, *sm.* hare; hatred.

Haudt, *sf.* skin.

Hauffe, *sm.* company of soldiers; der verlorene H. rearguard, 'forlorn hope'.

heben, *vt.* lift, lever.

Hebtremel, *sm.* lifting gear.

heimsuchen, *vt.* visit, afflict.

hein(d)t, *adv.* last night; tonight; today.

heischen, *vt.* demand.

Hellebrandt, *sm.* brand of Hell, brand for the burning.

Hemmett, *sn.* shirt, undergarment.

hendeln, *vi.* negotiate.

Hengst, *sm.* type of (stabbing?) weapon.

Herbst, *sm.* harvest; Autumn.

Hert, *sf.* herd.

Heumonat, *sm.* July.

hewer, *adv.* this year.

heymgeben, *vt.* commend to, put in s.o.'s hands.

heysßen, *vt.* demand, order.

hinderdencken, *vrefl.* consider.

Hinderhalt, *sm.* ambush.

hinfürt(er), *adv.* in future.

Hochfart, *sf.* vainglory, false pride.

Hoffarb, *sf.* livery.

hoffeln, *vt.* plane.

hof(f)ieren, *vt/i.* behave in courtly fashion, pay court to; ironically, excrete.

A a

höltzen, *adj.* wooden.
hôn, *adj.* mocking, contemptuous.
hôren, *vi.* belong.
Hôrpauke, *sf.* big drum.
Hort, *sm.* treasure; protection.
hôrt, *adj.* hard, cruel.
hoschen, *vi.* slide, withdraw, disappear.
Houbt, *sn.* head; leader.
Huld(e), *sf.* grace; covenant; oath of loyalty.
Huldung, *sf.* obeisance; oath of loyalty.
Hurnweibel, *sm.* n.c.o. in charge of women camp followers.
Hurst, *sf.* thicket, hedge.
Hütt, *sf.* s.t. entrusted to so.o.'s care; guardianship.

I/J

Janitschar, *sm.* janissary.
jehen, *vt.* say, affirm.
jnlegen, *vt.* contribute.
innbrünstig, *adj.* excited, fervent.
jrren, *vt.* bother, trouble.
jrrsal, *sn.* error(s).
jrrung, *sf.* error.
itzlich, *adj.* each.

K

Kalter, *sm.* cupboard, container.
Kammerbüchse, *sf.* small gun with chambers for quick firing.
Kante, *sf.* tankard.
Karchknecht, *sm.* carter, coachman.
Karst, *sm.* mattock.
Kâßflademer, *sm.* maker and eater of cheese cakes.
Kaßkrapffen, *sm.* cheese cake.
Kasten, *sm.* collecting box.
Kat, *sm.* filth.
Kauff, *sm.* bargain.
Keib(e), *sm.* corpse.
Keiche, *sf.* prison.
Keihel, *sm.* wedge.
Kerb(e), *sf.* notch, cleft; backside.
Kerff, *sf.* notch, cleft; backside.

kiffen, *vt.* nag.
Kipfblock, *sm.* block between front axle and chassis of cart, to which mounting rung is attached.
klapperisch, *adj.* of wagging tongue, scandal-mongering.
Kleinat, *sn.* prize; jewel.
knüffen, *vt.* tie.
Knüw, *sn.* knee.
kônlich, *adj.* bold.
Kouffmanschatz, *sm.* commerce.
Kragen, *sm.* neck, collar.
kranck, *adj.* weak, insipid; valueless; sick.
Krapffen, *sm.* cake.
krâtzig, *adj.* mangy, psoric.
Kraut, *sn.* (pickled) cabbage; gunpowder.
Krebe, *sm.* basket.
Krebs, *sm.* breast-plate.
Krutster, *sm.* verger, sexton.
Kunst, *sf.* skill, cunning.
Kuntschafft, *sf.* information.
kurtzlich, *adv.* briefly, in fine.
Kuster(er), *sm.* verger, sexton.
Kutt(e), *sf.* cowl.
Kûtte, *sf.* quince.
kyesen, *vt.* choose.

L

Ladstecken, *sm.* ramrod.
La(h)n, *sm.* reward.
lan, *vt.* let, leave.
Lanbaum, *sm.* axle-pole.
Lannegel, *sm.* axle-pin.
Lanseyl, *sn.* axle-rope.
Lanstange, *sf.* strut on 'Leiterwagen'.
lappet, *adj.* stupid.
Laub, *sf.* arbour, hall.
lautreisig, *adj.* very noisy.
Lecker, *sm.* fellow, young blood.
Legeisen, *sn.* leg-irons.
leidig, *adj.* sorry, wretched.
Lemeisen, *sn.* leg-irons.
Lerma(e)n, *sm.* alarm, commotion, uproar.
leschen, *vt.* extinguish.

lesen, *vt.* gather.
lestern, *vt.* abuse, revile.
letsch, *adj.* last.
Letz(e), *sf.* parting gift, legacy; farewell.
letzen, *vi.* and *refl.* take one's leave.
Lichtmess, *sf.* candlemass.
Liechtspan, *sm.* taper.
liegen, *vi.* tell lies.
Lochotenent, *sm.* humorous variant of 'lieutenant'.
lon, *vt.* leave, let.
losen, *vt.* buy; help.
Losung, *sf.* pass word; price.
Lot, *sn.* lead, shot.
lûgen, *vi.* look, see to s.t.
lûstig, *adj.* merry; eager.
lut, *prep.* according to.
luter, *adj.* pure.
Lyb, *sf.* love, devotion.

M

madt, *adj.* weak, tired.
Mâl, *sn.* flour.
Malschatz, *sm.* engagement/wedding gift.
Malstatt, *sf.* place of assembly (for councils, armies, etc.).
Malzeychen, *sn.* mark.
Mehr(e), *sf.* story, news.
Meid, *sf.* maid, girl.
meistern, *vt.* criticism, correct.
mengklich, *adj.* many.
menig, *adj.* many.
Merb(m)elstein, *sm.* marble.
Meßner, *sm.* verger.
Metzig, *sf.* butcher's shop.
Metzler, *sm.* butcher.
meynaydig, *adj.* perjured.
Mißhell(igkeit), *sf.* discord.
Mit(ter)nacht, *sf.* midnight; North.
Mog, *sm.* relative.
mögen, *vt/i.* be able.
Monordnung, *sf.* crescent formation.
Monstrantz, *sf.* monstrance.
Mor(e), *sf.* (black) sow.
Môrsel, *sf.* mortar.

Môrtthier, *sn.* pun on 'Mörser' mortar.
mucken, *vi.* complain, revolt.
mugen (mûgen), *vt/i.* be able.
Multer, *sf.* trough.
mumlen, *vt/i.* mumble.
munter, *adj.* awake.
Mûß, *sm.* porridge.
mûssig gon, *vi.* go without, get rid of.
Mûtwille, *sm.* free decision; arbitrariness, wantonness.
mutzen, *vrefl.* deck o.s. out.
myßthon, *vt.* do amiss.

N

nachlassen, *vt.* desist from.
Nachtigall, *sf.* light cannon.
Nâglinstock, *sm.* carnation plant.
Narr, *sm.* fool; heavy cannon.
Narrei, *sf.* foolish thing.
nechten, *adv.* last night.
nemmen, *vt.* name.
Nespel, *sf.* medlar tree and fruit.
Nestel, *sf.* ribbon.
Neue, *sm.* nephew.
nichtzit, *adv.* absolutely nothing.
Nidergangk, *sm.* Occident.
niessen, *vt.* enjoy.
nimm(er), *adv.* never again, no more.
nischen, *vi.* associate closely, cuddle up to.
nort, *adv.* only, just.
Notelbauntze, *sf.* batter-cake.
Notschlange, *sf.* cannon.
Notturfft, *sf.* need, necessity.
nun, *adv.* now; only.
Nußschwinger, *sm.* nut-gatherer.
nüt, *adv.* not.
nützid, *adv.* nothing.

O

ob, *adv./prep.* above.
Oberhand, *sf.* authority
obgemelt, *ppart. of* '*obmelden*'. aforementioned.

obligen, *vi.* be superior to, overcome.
öd, *adj.* foolish, vain, petty.
offen(t)lich, *adj.* open, public; obvious.
Ohnmacht, *sf.* weakness.
ölung, *sf.* unction.
onhåbling, *adj.* unsteady, unstable.
onstehen lassen, *vt.* leave undone.
Opiny, *sf.* opinion, matter for dispute.
Orden, *sm.* group, association of people.
Orgel, *sf.* organ; gun with several barrels.
Oriflant, *sm.* banner, oriflamme.

P *see* B

Q

Questor, *sm.* Questors, official indulgence-seller.
Quickung, *sf.* invigoration, new life.

R

Rantzwagen, *sm.* sutler's van.
Rat(h), *sm.* council; counsel; use.
raufen, *vt.* attack, plunder.
raumben, *vt.* eradicate, remove.
Raumer, *sm.* implement for cleaning cannon.
rechtvertig, *adj.* justified.
rechtvertigen, *vt.* correct, put right, justify.
Regiment, *sn.* government.
Rennfan, *sf.* principal flag.
reumen, *vt.* remove.
Reverentz, *sf.* bow, reverence.
Rew, *sf.* regret.
Reyff, *sm.* frost.
reymen, *vrefl.* rhyme, have meaning, be true.
Reyß, *sf.* journey; campaign.
Reyßbar, *sf.* (travelling) litter.
Rhåtterschafft, *sf.* puzzle, riddle.
rhůmen, *vt.* praise.
Richt(e), *sf/n.* dish, course.
richten, *vt.* judge; execute.
Riffiener, *sm.* bravo, ruffian.

ring, *adj.* light, easy; *adv.* willingly, with an easy mind.
Ringkragen, *sm.* neck and throat armour.
rocken, *vt.* spin.
Roßbar, *sf.* horse litter.
Roßpfal, *sm.* tethering post.
Roßstirn, *sf.* head armour for horse.
Rott, *sm.* council.
Rottmeister, *sm.* platoon commander.
Rotwelsch, *sm.* thieves' cant, unintelligible language.
Rucken, *sm.* back armour.
rüeblich, *adj.* peaceful.
růmmer, *adv.* around.
rumoren, *vi.* make a noise, rage.
růmstern, *vrefl.* belch.
růten, *vt.* root out, clear, prepare (field etc.).

S

Sagra, *sn.* sacristy.
sam, *conj.* as, though.
samb, *adv.* together.
sant, *adv.* together.
Sa(e)ndbrieff, *sm.* (open) letter.
Satzung, *sf.* instituted laws.
schaffen, *vi/t.* create, cause.
Scham(m), *sf.* private parts.
Schantz, *sf.* opportunity.
Scharffentinlin, *sn.* light cannon.
Scharffmetze, *sf.* heavy cannon.
Scharwacht, *sf.* patrol.
Scheid, *sf.* sheath, scabbard.
Scheitt, *sn.* piece of wood. **gen zu scheittern,** perish, come to grief.
schelten, *vt.* scold, call (ironically).
Scherbe(n), *sm/f.* plantpot.
Scherhaus, *sn.* barber-surgeon's shop.
Schiffbruck(e), *sf.* pontoon.
schifften, *vt.* provide with a shaft.
Schimpf, *sm.* jest, joke.
schimpffen, *vi.* jest.
schinden, *vt.* flay; kill; exploit financially.

schlahen, *vt.* strike, smite.

Schlanckenschlange, *sf.* heavy cannon.

Schlapphaub, *sf.* bonnet with wide floppy brim.

Schleb(pp)sack, *sf.* sluttish untidy woman.

schlecht, *adj.* simple, unadorned.

Schlencke, *sf.* catapult.

schleü(y)ffen, *vt.* drag.

Schmacheit, *sf.* shame, opprobrium.

schmacken, *vt/i.* taste, smell.

schmeissen, *vt.* smite.

schmeychen, *vt.* make supple; flatter.

schmucken, *vrefl.* rub up against.

schnappen, *vi.* trip.

Schneller, *sm.* gunner.

Schnůr, *sf.* string; guide-line.

schnůrrichtig, *adj.* straight, direct.

Schragen, *sm.* trestle, table.

Schrifft, *sf.* Scripture, writing, letter, text.

Schrôt, *sm.* shot.

schuchter, *adj.* anxious, afraid.

Schulthe(i)ß, *sm.* chief municipal officer.

Schůrtzer, *sm.* stabbing sword.

schwampelecht, *adj.* dizzy.

Schwå(ee)re, *sf.* sore.

schweben, oben s. *vi.* have precedence, excell.

schwechen, *vt.* violate, rape, deflower.

Schweiß, *sm.* blood, sweat.

schwengern, *vt.* make pregnant.

Schyn, *sm.* brightness; appearance, guise.

Seckel, *sm.* purse.

Seelmes, *sf.* mass for dead.

semlich, *pron.* the same, such a thing.

settigen, *vt.* satisfy.

setzen, *vt.* put, place; postulate; plant.

seyteinmal, *conj.* since.

sidhar, *adv.* subsequently, since.

Sigk, *sm.* victory.

Siechtag(e), *sm.* sickness.

Sigrist, *sm.* verger, sacristan.

Silberkamer, *sf.* treasury; closet for silverware.

Singerin, *sf.* type of cannon.

sitzen, *vi.* sit; reside.

so, *conj.* if, since, though.

Sod, *sm.* stew, broth.

sonder, *conj.* but; *adv.* specially, separately; *prep.* without.

Span, *sm.* quarrel.

Spil, *sn.* band.

Spirole, *sf.* type of cannon.

Spisser, *sm.* pike-man.

Spreüe, *sf.* chaff.

Sprüwer, *sf. & pl.* chaff.

Stadt, *sm.* state, finery, magnificence.

stan, *vi.* stand.

Start, *sf.* watch, guard.

Stat, *sm.* state, condition; dignity; magnificence.

Stat, *sf.* place, town; opportunity.

stat(t)geben, *vi/t.* give way; admit allow, do; establish.

stat haben, *vi.* have effect.

stechen, *vt/i.* stab; joust.

Steckenknecht, *sm.* provost marshal's assistant.

stehn, dran s., *vi.* set about s.t., attempt to cope with s.t.

steiner, *adj.* of stone.

stellen, *vt.* invite (to dance).

Stemmeisenwagen, *sm.* cart with lifting gear.

Stewr, *sf.* help, assistance (also financial); **zu S. kommen,** help, profit.

stickfinster, *adj.* pitch black, so dark one cannot see a 'Stick' (= 'point')

Stock, *sm.* stick; stump (of tree).

Stoltzbaum, *sm.* prop, support.

stôssig, *adj.* quarrelsome; at odds with.

straf(f)en, *vt.* castigate; take to task.

strâlen, *vt.* comb, curry.

strang, *adj.* stern.
Straubholtz, *sm.* prop, support.
Strauß, *sm.* quarrel, skirmish.
Strel, *sm.* comb.
Streublin, *sn.* sort of cake or fritter.
Strimen, *sm.* strip, stripe, ray.
stro(e)n, *adj.* of straw.
Stůr, *sf.* help, provision against.
stůren, *vt.* equip, furnish, provide with trousseau.
Sturmkrug, *sm.* hand-grenade.
Sümniß, *sn.* delay, omission.
sumpen, *vrefl.* delay.
sunder, *adj.* separate, special; *conj.* but.
sust, *adv.* otherwise, in other respects.
sytt, *adv.* since, subsequently.

V = U

vberi(n)g, *adj.* excess, surplus.
vberkommen, *vt.* obtain.
vbernacht, *adv.* after one single night; quickly, soon.
vberschåtzlich, *adj.* of inestimable value.
vberschwengklich, *adj.* superabundant.
vbersehen, *vt.* spare, deal lightly with, overlook.
vbertag, *adv.* day in day out, every day; all day long.
vberwigen, *vt/i.* overcome.
vberwinden, *vt.* vanquish; convict; sentence.
Vfgang, *sm.* ascendant; revival; vogue.
Vmbfrag, *sf.* plebiscite, referendum.
vmbkoren, *vi.* turn round.
Vmhang, *sm.* veil, covering.
vmmen, *adv.* around.
vnaußlaschlich, *adj.* never to be eradicated.
Vnbill, *sm.* injustice.
vnderstehen, *vt.* and *refl.* begin, undertake; prevent.
Vnfahl, *sm.* misfortune.

Vnflat(h), *sm.* filth; wretch.
Vnfug, *sm.* great noise, unseemly behaviour.
vng(e)fehr (vngeferd), *adv.* without evil intention; unsuspectingly; by chance.
vngehewr, *adj.* unseemly, monstrous.
vngepürlich, *adj.* immodest, unfitting.
vngratten, *ppart. of* 'geraten'+*neg. pref.* undutiful, spoilt.
vnkrauttig, *adj.* overgrown with weeds.
vnleidlich, *adj.* free from pain or penalty.
Vnlust, *sf.* quarrel, trouble, conflict.
vnmere, *adj.* worthless, indifferent, distasteful.
Vnmůt, *sm.* sorrow; anger.
Vnra(d)t, *sm.* waste; trouble, unpleasantness.
vnrethlich, *adj.* careless, prodigal.
Vntådlin, *sn.* fault.
vnverstanden, *adj.* foolish, lacking in understanding.
vnuersunnen, *adj.* thoughtless, rash.
Vnvollkommen, *sn.* imperfection.
Vnvormugen, *sn.* incapacity.
vnwißiglich, *adj.* foolish; incomprehensible.
Vnzal, *sf.* large number.
Üppikeit, *sf.* luxury.
Vrlop, *sm.* leave.
Vrste(e)nd(e), *sf.* resurrection.
Ürte, *sf.* bill, cost (of carousal).

V *see* F

W

Wacke, *sf.* boulder.
waenen, *vt/i.* think.
Waich, *sf.* flank, groin.
Walholtz, *sn.* roller.

wallen, *vi.* go on pilgrimage.
wann, *conj.* when; because; but; for.
wannen, *vt.* sift.
warnemen, *vi.* seize (opportunity); take care of.
Warsager, *sm.* soothsayer; one who tells the truth.
warten, *vi.* pay attention to; take care of.
Watsack, *sm.* portmanteau.
Wechsel, *sm.* exchange, commerce.
Weck, *sm.* wedge; biscuit.
weder, *conj.* than.
wege, *adj.* advantageous. **zu w. bringen,** *vt.* obtain.
wehren, *vt.* forbid, prevent.
weichen, *vt.* consecrate, ordain.
weidlich, *adj.* sound, thorough, splendid.
wencken, *vi.* depart from, leave.
wend, *pres. indic. pl. of 'wollen'.* wish, want.
wenen, *vt/i.* think.
weren, *vi.* last.
Weyße, *sf.* way, means, manner.
Widergelt, *sf/n.* reward, recompense.
widerstendig, *adj.* contradictory.
Widerteil, *sn.* opponent.
widerwertig, *adj.* conflicting, contradictory; hostile.
Wiederpahrt, *sm.* opponent.
Wiedertriess, *sm.* annoyance.
Willpret, *sn.* game.
wil(l)fahren, *vt.* comply with, humour.
Wind, *sm.* greyhound.
Windtlicht, *sn.* torch, taper.
wischen, *vt/i,* wipe; move quickly.
Wischer, *sm.* mop (for cleaning cannon).
Witz(i)gung, *sf.* lesson.
wolan, *inter.* well, now then, so be it!
wolschmackend, *adj.* sweet-smelling.
Wôrm, *sf.* warmth.

Wucher, *sm.* profit, interest.
Wûcherey, *sf.* usury, avarice.
wüchten, *vt.* weigh, balance.
Wunderred, *sf.* paradox.
wunsam, *adj.* wonderful.
wüschen, *vt/i.* wipe; move quickly.
Wûst, *sm.* rubbish, dirt; dirty person.
wychen, *vt.* consecrate.
wyder, *adv. conj.* either; than; nor.

Y

yben, *vt.* do practice.
ychtz, *pron.* anything.
yeben, *vt.* practice, exercise.
yergen ein, *pron.* someone or other.
yetget ein, *pron.* someone or other.
yetweder, *pron.* each.
Ysenhût, *sm.* helmet.
ytzlich, *pron.* each.

Z

zâch, *adj.* tough.
Zâher, *sm.* tear.
Zech, *sf.* (drinking) party.
Zehat, *sm.* tithe.
Zeltbaum, *sm.* tent-pole.
Zeltnagel, *sm.* tent-peg.
zemenkummen, *vi.* come together, assemble.
zenckisch, *adj.* shrewish, quarrelsome.
zenichtig, *adj.* worthless, as nought.
zerknitschen, *vt.* crush.
zerstûcken, *vrefl.* be smashed, get broken.
Zerung, *sf.* feast; allowance, gift (of money).
zerzeysen, *vt.* rough up, give drubbring to.
Zeughaus, *sn.* arsenal.
Ziel, *sn.* limit, restriction.
Zielscheit, *sn.* trace bar (on cart).
zubrechen, *vt/i.* splinter, break.
zucken, *vt.* brandish, draw.
zuflambt, *adj.* slashed.
zugehen, *vi.* walk about.

Zugmůle, *sf.* horse-drawn mill (for making gunpowder).

zuhandt, *adv.* at once.

zulumbt, *adj.* ragged.

Zůndrute, *sf.* slowmatch.

Zůndstrick, *sm.* quickmatch, fuse.

zůsagen, *vt.* promise.

zusammen setzen, *vi.* come into conflict, start to fight.

zusammen wallen, *vi.* bind together (of dough).

zu setzen, *vi.* lay about, attack.

zu stan, *vi.* help, rally to.

zůuoran, *adv.* above all.

Zwŏlffbott, *sm.* 'apostle'; heavy cannon.

Zyl, *sn.* limit.

INDEX